P9-DNA-199

FREEING
KEIKO

ALSO BY KENNETH BROWER:

EARTH AND THE GREAT WEATHER: THE BROOKS RANGE

WITH THEIR ISLANDS AROUND THEM

MICRONESIA: ISLAND WILDERNESS

THE STARSHIP AND THE CANOE

WAKE OF THE WHALE

MICRONESIA: THE LAND, THE PEOPLE, AND THE SEA

A SONG FOR SATAWAL

YOSEMITE

ONE EARTH

REALMS OF THE SEA

AMERICAN LEGACY: OUR NATIONAL FORESTS

THE WINEMAKER'S MARSH

FREEING KEIKO

THE JOURNEY OF A KILLER WHALE
FROM
FREE WILLY TO THE WILD

KENNETH BROWER

GOTHAM BOOKS

For my brother,
Robert Irish Brower

GOTHAM BOOKS
Published by Penguin Group (USA) Inc.
375 Hudson Street, New York, New York 10014, U.S.A.
Penguin Group (Canada), 90 Eglinton Avenue East, Suite 700, Toronto, Ontario M4P 2Y3, Canada
(a division of Pearson Penguin Canada Inc.); Penguin Books Ltd, 80 Strand, London WC2R 0RL, England;
Penguin Ireland, 25 St Stephen's Green, Dublin 2, Ireland (a division of Penguin Books Ltd);
Penguin Group (Australia), 250 Camberwell Road, Camberwell, Victoria 3124, Australia
(a division of Pearson Australia Group Pty Ltd);
Penguin Books India Pvt Ltd, 11 Community Centre, Panchsheel Park, New Delhi - 110 017, India;
Penguin Group (NZ), cnr Airborne and Rosedale Roads, Albany, Auckland 1310,
New Zealand (a division of Pearson New Zealand Ltd);
Penguin Books (South Africa) (Pty) Ltd,
24 Sturdee Avenue, Rosebank, Johannesburg 2196, South Africa

Penguin Books Ltd, Registered Offices: 80 Strand, London WC2R 0RL, England

Published by Gotham Books, a division of Penguin Group (USA) Inc.

First printing, October 2005
10   9   8   7   6   5   4   3   2   1

Copyright © 2005 by Kenneth Brower
All rights reserved

Gotham Books and the skyscraper logo are trademarks of Penguin Group (USA) Inc.

LIBRARY OF CONGRESS CATALOGING-IN-PUBLICATION DATA
has been applied for.

ISBN 1-592-40147-3

Printed in the United States of America
Set in Adobe Garamond
Designed by Ginger Legato

Without limiting the rights under copyright reserved above, no part of this publication
may be reproduced, stored in or introduced into a retrieval system, or transmitted,
in any form, or by any means (electronic, mechanical, photocopying, recording, or otherwise),
without the prior written permission of both the copyright owner and the above publisher of this book.

The scanning, uploading, and distribution of this book via the Internet or via any other means
without the permission of the publisher is illegal and punishable by law. Please purchase
only authorized electronic editions, and do not participate in or encourage electronic
piracy of copyrighted materials. Your support of the author's rights is appreciated.

PROLOGUE

"THERE WAS A MAN CALLED KETIL FLAT-NOSE," THE ICELANDIC SAGA BEGINS. Or, "There was a man named Thorolf Haltfoot." Or Magnus Barefoot. Or Arnor Crone's Nose. *Njál's Saga,* the greatest of all, written by some anonymous Norse genius in the thirteenth century, begins, "There was a man named Mord, who was also known as Mord Fiddle. He was the son of Sigvat the Red and dwelt at the farmstead called Voll on the Rangá River."

The old Icelanders dispensed with the "Once upon a time" and cut straight to the introductions: Name. Epithet. Reference to lineage and place of origin.

The following story should begin that way, too, as this is a saga of Iceland. It starts and finishes near that cold, stark, beautiful island. Its hero is big and powerful, intelligent and handsome, as the heroes of Icelandic saga must always be. (There are no small, ugly, dim-witted protagonists in that great medieval literature.) He is a wide-wandering son, as the formula requires. He is a noble victim, and the sagas are fond of those. A feud generally lies at the heart of a saga, and a great deal of feuding lies at the heart of this one. The old scholarly controversy over the origins of saga—the unending debate over how much of saga is historical and how much is mythical—is alive here, too, for this hero, a real-life being, has rapidly drifted into legend. He combines the attributes of many of his predecessors: Ottar the Black, Thorstein the White, Thormod Coal-Brow, Thorvard the Far-Traveled, Thorstein the Curious, Ivar Widespan, Thorstein Codbiter.

Several tough characters named Thorfinn appear in the sagas—Thorfinn Skull-splitter, Thorfinn Seal, and Thorfinn the Strong, among them—but not one of those two-legged, fighting Thorfinns is stronger, and none possesses a fin more Thor-like, than he. The hero of the following saga has something in common with Njál of *Njál's Saga.* Like Njál, he is "handsome, except that he grew no beard." Like Njál, he has the gift of second sight.

The old Icelanders wrote their sagas on vellum, the stretched skin of a sheep or ox, sometimes also called membranum and sometimes called pergament. In Europe the skins were steeped in a calcium solution to strip and soften them; in Iceland they were not, and as a result lasted much longer. The immortality of Icelandic saga lies not just in the prose and plot, but in the pergament. Icelandic scribes made their inks by boiling bearberry plants and unsprouted willow twigs. Their quills were the flight feathers of swans, geese, ravens, and eagles, which the Icelanders plucked from the left wing, if possible, as left-wing quills were thought to be easier on the hand. The scribes carved their own nibs, a deft and intricate succession of cuts, and they grasped the left-wing quills in their right hands. Dipped in bearberry-and-willow ink, the quills took another kind of flight. They captured the histories of great heroes like Njál, and Grettir the Strong, and Eirik the Red, and of heroines like Unn the Deep-Minded—characters that seem so modern and familiar to us, yet at the same time so ancient and strange. The bearberry-and-willow ink has a wonderful vitality, and today, eight hundred years later, highlights still shine in the calligraphy, as if the words were not quite dry.

The men who wielded the raven and eagle quills, the nameless authors of saga, liked it best when their heroes had some sort of physical abnormality, so that the heroic epithet would have bite. Thorvard Crow-Nose. Thorbjorn the Pockmarked. Magnus the Blind. The abnormality of the hero of the following saga is a striking one. It recalls, in a way, the deformity of Hallvard of the *Viga-Glums Saga*. "He is now known as Hallvard Neck," that saga goes, "because he was in the battle against the Jomsvikings with Earl Hakon last year, and there he got a large wound on the neck, behind the ear, and he's carried his head on one side ever since."

The hero of the following saga, from long, close confinement in a strange land, carries his dorsal fin on one side.

There was a whale called Siggi Bent Fin, captured as a calf off the East Fiords of Iceland. The name Siggi was temporary; it would change twice in the early years of his captivity. Under his third and final appellation, he would become the best-loved whale in Latin America and, after an apprenticeship performing south of the border, would go into the movies, become a star, and spawn sequels. No animal actor before him—not Flipper, or Lassie, or Rin Tin Tin, or Trigger, or Francis the Talking Mule—did better at the box office. At the end of his film career, he would go into business, employing dozens of workers and seeing his name and likeness stamped on a bewildering array of products. A children's crusade would rally to his banner. He would become a cause célèbre, testing fisheries laws and animal-quarantine regulations across North America and Scandinavia. He would serve as ambassador for the seas. Pressed into that duty, an involuntary emissary from the deep, he would nevertheless perform the job with what seemed like decisiveness and inspiration. His fate would preoccupy prime ministers and presidents. He would demonstrate a curious power to factionalize human beings, with rift zones and fault lines forming all around him. Debate over his destiny would divide the animal-rights radicals, a new sort of Jacobin, from the anti-whaling privateers who ram whale ships on the high seas. It would divide those Jacobins and privateers from more mainstream environmentalists, who were divided soon enough from one another, as they were divided from the apparatchiks of various maritime bureaucracies in several nations, and from the wardens who run the marine parks in which captive whales and dolphins are confined. The whale's choices would surprise everyone, his life taking twists and turns that no one anticipated. He would become the most famous wild creature ever held in captivity. No captive before him—not Martha the last passenger pigeon, or Elsa the lioness, or any caged silverback gorilla—drew such hordes of fans and followers. He would develop an uncanny and wordless ability to convince each of his thousands of human acquaintances that he had a special interest in that person. He would become the most celebrated whale in history, surpassing Moby Dick, Leviathan, and the whale that swallowed Jonah.

BOOK ONE
MEXICO

1

BENT FIN

THERE WAS A WHALE CALLED SIGGI, CAPTURED AS A CALF OFF THE EAST Fiords of Iceland. He was one or two years old. In learning to steal overspill herring from the nets of a seiner, he ventured too close to the mesh and was snagged. The crew of *Gudrun,* the fishing boat that captured him, named him for Sigurdur, the son of the captain. The calf was a killer whale, *Orcinus orca,* largest of dolphins. As a bull he might grow as long as thirty feet, as heavy as ten tons, but for now he was small, no larger than a full-grown common dolphin. Had nature taken its normal course, his dorsal fin, at maturity, would have risen six feet tall, slicing the surface of the sea, the black sword for which this whale has many of its common names: *swaardvis* in Dutch, *schwertwal* in German, *epée de mer* in French. Siggi's dorsal fin, at the time of his capture, was normal for his age. It was just a little dagger. It was the cute, falcate, feminized, miniature fin that is standard in young male killer whales before their hormones kick in. *Gudrun* transported him to Saedyrasafind, a small Iceland aquarium, where he was renamed Kago, "Little Boy" in Icelandic.

Kago would become the most celebrated whale in history, but in 1979, the year of his capture, he was just another little whale. No one thought to chronicle his childhood, and his early history is exceedingly sketchy. We do know that in 1982, after three years in captivity, Kago was shipped to Canada. His trip to the New World—Vinland, as the old Icelanders called those parts—was an afterthought. His purchaser, Marineland of Ontario, had not been looking for an animal his size, but to save him from the cramped tank at Saedyrasafind they included him in the deal. Kago set off involuntarily on this early leg of his odyssey, following much the same route that his countryman, Leif Eiriksson, had traveled in longboats a thousand years before him. In Ontario, along with five other killer whales, Kago was trained for sale to amusement parks.

The smallest of the six, he was harassed by the other whales. The patchwork pod at Niagara Falls was dominated by a young bull named Nootka, who led the others in bumping Kago, pushing him around, slapping him with their tailfins. Kago proved a poor performer. Whether from a lack of intelligence, or from an excess of that trait, or from homesickness, or from depression at the harsh treatment at the fins of his fellows, he showed little interest in the tricks suggested to him by human beings. "From the very first day, Kago was kind of a weak animal," says Angus Matthews, who was then director of Marineland of Ontario. "His stimulation and attention span was kind of waning. He didn't deal with stress well at all."

Kago missed his family, surely. That may help explain his indifferent performances. Killer whales vocalize in family dialects, and he no doubt missed his native language. All of Marineland's orcas came from Iceland, but they had belonged to different families. Nootka, Haida, and Kago's other tankmates might as well have been speaking Chinese.

After five bleak years in Canada, Kago was sold to Reino Aventura, an amusement park outside Mexico City. With this sale, south of two borders, began the first of the feuds that would punctuate Kago's saga, following the whale everywhere he traveled in the realm of human beings.

Animal ethologists have only begun to sort out the politics of *Orcinus orca*, but early evidence suggests that the killer-whale capacity for intrigue is less developed than our own. This is not to say that killer whales are simpletons. Killer-whale society is complex. Killer whales are capable of mind games and one-upmanship. In captivity they routinely outsmart and manipulate their human trainers—or *pinnipulate* those trainers, rather, as whales are equipped with pinnae, fins, instead of hands. But among killer whales there seems to be no equivalent of the Mafia, or CIA, or the Hunt brothers of Texas.

The Hunt brothers were specialists in the transport of exotic animals. They had a sideline hosting canned hunts that guaranteed a hunter his stuffed eland or glass-eyed lion at point-blank range on the veldt of Texas. The Hunts knew a prize trophy when they saw one; if anyone flew Kago to Mexico, they decided, it would be themselves.

The first plan that Marineland of Ontario had was straightforward. The Canadians intended to air-freight Kago across the United States as the crow flies to Mexico. The Hunt brothers, calling on allies in government, soon had that flight festooned in red tape and the National Marine Fisheries Service permit requirements. The Canadians then tried a flanking maneuver, a circuitous Air Canada flight from Toronto to Halifax to Bermuda to Mexico. The Hunts, sniffing that one out, filled the sky between Nova Scotia and Bermuda with little black puffs of bureaucratic flack. The Canadians attempted a maneuver on the other flank, hiring a Russian plane to spirit Kago into Mexico by way of the Aleutian Islands. The Hunts were not to be shaken so easily. Finally the Canadians slipped the whale aboard a Northwest Territorial Airlines plane, a four-engine Electra, along with a ton of herring. They doctored the manifest to show Kago as furniture bound for Puerto Vallarta. (This was not such a stretch, as the whale at this point was only ten feet long, not much bigger than a grand piano.) In the vicinity of Mexico City, the pilot requested an emergency landing and set the plane down, triumphantly, under the radar of the Hunts.

In his new home the whale immediately acquired a new name. "Kago" would not do in Mexico—certainly not in a family theme park. In Mexican slang, *cago* means "to take a shit." Kago was renamed Keiko, a Japanese female name meaning "Lucky One."

This was an improvement over "Defecate," no doubt, yet it was cruelly ironic all the same. The whale was stunted and immune-deficient, yet despite his sluggish growth rate he quickly outgrew his tank, which was just ninety feet long by forty-three feet wide by twenty feet deep. In a space that began at eight times his body length, then shrank, in a relative way, to only five times that length as he enlarged, Keiko, the Lucky One, passed the next ten years. He lolled listlessly in depths shallower than he was long. His appetite was poor. His teeth wore down in front from gnawing at the side of the tank. He was anemic, in the opinion of his Mexican veterinarian, who also suspected that he suffered from ulcers. He was known to have swallowed a brass ball, a float, and a rope, of which only the float had been recovered. The artificial seawater in his pool was too warm for him, and he moved as little as possible, so as not to overheat. A skin infection, a papilloma, began to spread. Back in Ontario, several of his tankmates had been afflicted with papillomavirus, too, but in those whales the outbreaks had been intermittent; in Kago the outbreaks had been chronic, exacerbated by stress. Now, in the warm water south of the border, the infection flared with a vengeance. Keiko became the most papillomatous whale in veterinary history. Indeed, he had the honor of becoming the type specimen for papilloma in all whales, as pathologists first isolated the virus from his warts. The lesions covered his shoulders and his pectoral finpits. They covered areas of his caudal peduncle—his tailstock—just forward of the flukes. They were clearly sore to the touch and they were often seen bleeding.

Keiko's pool was at 7400 feet in the Valley of Anáhuac, ringed by tall mountains. Surely altitude affected him. Whales did not evolve in mountains; they evolved at sea level and below. Through sixty million years of cetacean evolution, every single whale, from the first primitive archaeocete to the streamlined modern dolphin, took each and every breath, first to last, at an elevation of exactly zero. Ocean air at sea level is as much as 4 percent water vapor. At high altitude and in the desert—and the Valley of Anáhuac is both high and desert—water vapor drops to a fraction of 1 percent. Mexico City air is not just rarefied and dry, it is also filthy, one of the most polluted atmospheres in the world. Five million tons of pollutants are injected annually into the city's atmosphere. Four million vehicles, most of them old and smoky, produce most of that pollution—a miasma of exhaust and diesel particulates trapped by the rim of surrounding mountains. Ozone levels exceed World Health Organization standards three hundred days a year. Carbon monoxide, nitrogen dioxide, and sulfur dioxide exceed their standards more days than not. Respiratory illness is rampant among the Mexicans of Mexico City; what toll did it take on this whale?

Before Keiko's move south, Canadian aquarists had flown down to Mexico to inspect the facility at Reino Aventura. As a condition of sale, the Canadians had required that Reino Aventura build a small medical tank with a floating platform on which Keiko could be hoisted above the surface for examinations and blood work. But the Canadians had not thought to investigate the availability of proper food. There was none. The old Aztec capital, Mexico City, a mile and a half above the ocean, has never been famous for its seafood. Every week or two, for the first year of Keiko's residency in Mexico, Reino Aventura dispatched an old truck north to Sea World, in San Diego, fourteen hundred miles away, where the driver bought all the frozen herring that Sea World could spare. The truck was not refrigerated. Loaded with thawing herring, it made its long Sisyphean journey south again. Eventually a more convenient Mexican source was found, but the fish was still not fresh.

Keiko ate without gusto. His trainers, Karla Corral and Renata Fernandez, called him "Gordo," but in truth he was anything but fat. "Flaco," they should have called him, or "Descarnado," even, if that term can be applied to an animal weighing tons. Keiko was emaciated, in his ponderous way.

His dorsal fin, even as it began to grow into the tall, proud isosceles triangle of the adult male killer whale, commenced to fall over, slumping until it touched his back. In Iceland the killer whale is called *háhyringur*, "high-point," in honor of that tall male fin. The name no longer applied. Keiko had become something else. He was now a *niourhyringur*, to coin an Icelandic term. He had become a low point.

2

---·---

LOST WORLD

In his book *Dialogue with the Viking Age*, the Iceland scholar Vésteinn Ólason argues that a fundamental theme runs through Icelandic saga—or not a theme so much as a note, a mood, a tone, a resonance. To show us what he means, Ólason recounts a scene from *Njál's Saga,* a fight between warriors named Kol and Kolskegg:

"Kol thrust his spear at him. Kolskegg had just slain a man and had his hands full and so could not get his shield up, and the spear hit him on the outside of the thigh and went through it. Kolskegg moved quickly and stepped towards Kol and struck him on the thigh with his short sword and cut off his leg and spoke: 'Did that hit you or not?'

" 'This is what I get,' said Kol, 'for not shielding myself,' and he stood for a while on his other leg and looked at the stump.

"Kolskegg spoke: 'You don't need to look: it's just as you think, the leg is gone.' "

From this cheery epigraph, Vésteinn Ólason goes on to argue that the sagas are all about loss. Not just loss of life and limb, as in the case of Kol—though that sort of dismemberment is common in the sagas—but loss of a whole world. The sagas, in Ólason's view, are a dialogue between the Middle Ages, when the events described were recorded, and the Viking Era, two or three centuries earlier, when those events took place. Ólason believes that the authors of saga were full of a sense of loss for that raw, heroic age, a time when Icelanders lived larger than life. The leitmotif of saga, he suggests, is amputation. A sense of loss permeates every line.

The saga of Keiko is no different. Keiko lost a whole world, too. The world amputated from him was gone more suddenly and more completely than any world ever lost by terrestrial Icelanders. Keiko's saga is a dialogue between the oceanarium tank and the vastness of the wild ocean.

The world that Keiko lost is a world without boundaries. There are limits to how deep a killer whale can dive and how high he can breach, but nothing walls him in horizontally. Movement is so free in the world Keiko lost that many of its inhabitants are unable to grasp the *idea* of boundaries. In any sort of rectangular aquarium, skipjack tuna and other open-ocean sprinters will swim in place against the glass until they develop a condition called "puffy snout." The swelling propagates back from the nose until the eyes appear sunken and the fish has trouble opening and closing its jaws. The pelagic sea snake, *Pelamis platurus,* will do the same, ribboning away against the glass until it rubs its nose raw and dies of infection. *Pelamis platurus,* the one true sea serpent—the only sea snake that never goes ashore—refuses to believe in boundaries even after several days with its nose against the glass. Killer whales, of course, are too smart for this. Their behavior is not so hardwired; they are able to grasp concepts for which nothing in their evolutionary history prepares them. But which is the sadder animal: the sea serpent that holds to the belief that it is free, even as it rubs its nose away, or the killer whale who adjusts to his circumstances?

The Viking Age—or the Saga Age, as it is sometimes called—may have died in Iceland, but something like it survives in the seas around. In the world Keiko lost, old Norse law is still in effect: Eat and be eaten. Greenland sharks lurk out there, sluggish but dangerous. Narwhal bulls fence with the nine-foot-long pikes at the tips of their beaks. Beaked-whale bulls duel with boarlike tusks, each bull's dark body entirely covered by a scribbly white calligraphy of scars inflicted in past fights. These are saga characters without the helmets. In the world Keiko lost, the heroic era has never ended.

The world Keiko lost is a world of unearthly beauty.

The colors of that world are colors never seen on land. Schools of cuttlefish, emoting, send waves of opalescent pastels pulsing down their mantles and tentacles, now from the warm end of the spectrum, now from the cool. Oncoming killer whales catch a glimpse of this performance, then the cuttlefish, opalescing in fright, scatter ahead of the whales, marking their departures with smokescreens of ink. The little black puffs and streaks of ink hang in the water briefly, then the whales, passing through, beat the smoke into whorls and tendrils with the vortices off their flukes.

Closer inshore, octopi hunt the dark volcanic rubble of the surge zones off Iceland's surf-pounded cliffs and sea stacks. An octopus works alone, but it pulses, too, with sequential washes of color, emoting and signifying as it flows along the bottom. Should a young killer whale veer down to investigate, the octopus flees, lurching with each jet of water through its siphon, scrambling away on its tentacles, trying to pour itself into holes too small for it, then jetting out to find a deeper hole, its colors raging kaleidoscopically in indignation, then abruptly snuffing out as the octopus vanishes. In milliseconds an octopus can adjust its chromatophores to match any hue or pattern and go invisible against any sort of bottom. All that remains is the smoke of its ink. Then that dilutes and disappears, and the octopus was never there.

There are peculiar rhythms of feast and famine in the world that Keiko lost. For hours, killer whales can cruise through a nearly perfect featurelessness, a blankness of a sort we never see on land—some prologue to the book of Genesis, the world all a blue-green void. And then suddenly Creation. The void fills up with racing walls of herring or pollack or capelin. The walls change direction, the fish flash silver or darken, the school deforms away from the whales.

The orcas commence hunting, seabirds arrive from nowhere, and the formlessness of moments before becomes a chaos of shapes and motion. Frantic fish stream up through the ceiling of the ocean, disappearing in a hail of splashes, then patter back down through the ceiling again. The school races, then slows. It splits, then coalesces. It scatters in silver starbursts of startled fish, then re-forms. The killer whales sprint fast circles around the perimeter, flashing their white bellies to frighten the fish back toward the center, sculpting the herring or capelin into a tight ball for killer-whale convenience. Sometimes one whale can see a colleague through the ball—a flash of white belly behind a pointillist blizzard of fish—and other times the ball is too dense for that. Sudden shafts of bubbles strike through the surface at steep angles, penetrating ten and twelve feet deep, volley after volley, as if a company of archers were attacking the ocean. As each arrow slows toward the bottom of its path, the eye can make sense of it—can see that each bubbly shaft is tipped by the sharp beak of a gannet. Killer whales strike through the ball, picking off fish, then resume their circling to reshape the ball again. Various auks arrive: the razorbills, murres, guillemots, puffins. Where the white gannets dive from on high, folding the wings back to make spears and arrows of themselves, the dark auks execute surface dives and underwater become guided missiles, swimming after fish with rapid, shallow beats of their stubby wings. The first few sharp turns of the auks are marked by trails of bubbles, then those flame out. Gannets bob up buoyantly toward the surface, fish held crosswise in their beaks. The bubble trails of auks pass them going the other way. The surface is roiled white by fish scattering and birds plunging and orcas blowing. From the churned whitewater of the ceiling, webbed feet dangle: the gray feet of gannets, common murres, and thick-billed murres; the bright red feet of black guillemots and Atlantic puffins. The webs spread, bright and translucent, on the propulsive stroke, then fold and darken on the recovery stroke. The gannets patter away on takeoff and wheel back to dive again. When the black guillemots dive, their white upper-wing patches are the last trace to show as they disappear in the depths—two white dots streaking after some fish. The dark backs of diving puffins, zipping by in pursuit, are frosted silvery with tiny bubbles trapped in the barbules of their feathers.

And then, as suddenly as it began, the frenzy is over. The seabirds lift off and climb high for a better perspective on where the action has gone.

Sometimes they spot it, and the full frenzy resumes farther on. Other times the fish school has dispersed, or has dived too deep for birds. The wheeling flock loses interest and disperses, too.

For the whales, the world is void again. Ahead is nothing but a luminous blue-green. Behind is the same. The world is featureless, except occasionally for the wavy signature of a whale as it defecates on the move. The action of the flukes beats the pale, bubbly stream of defecation into an undulating line. This contrail hangs in the water for a surprisingly long time, like smoke after the fireworks. Finally it dissipates, and the ocean behind is an empty blue-green again.

On phosphorescent nights, as a killer-whale pod cruises the darkness, each whale's progress excites the cold light of diatoms, every orca showing to its companions as a whale-shaped torpedo of milky green light, brightest at the beak, where the whale's progress is striking those sparks from the sea.

On moonlit nights, the small fry of the open sea rise from the depths like moths toward the light, a glass menagerie of exquisite, transparent larval fish, squid, arrowworms, salps, crustaceans. There are tiny elvers—larval eels—which swim with a ribbony motion and are perfectly translucent except for the dark eyes. There are two-dimensional larval flatfish that will grow up to be flounder. The flounder are about the size of Iceland's ten-krona coin, which is to say a fifty-cent piece, but not quite so round, and thinner than dimes. The vitreous wafer of each flatfish larva is etched with a midline and numerous lateral striations—spine and ribs. The larvae are like cunning miniatures of flounder by some artisan in glass. In some, the left eye has migrated already to what will be topside of the fish. In others the eyes still lie on opposite sides. Most of the glass flatfish are, or will be, right-eye flounder. In cold seas, most species of flounder have both eyes on the right side of the body. In warm and temperate seas, most flounder are left-eye flounder.

There are larval crabs in all stages of development. Some are just the zoea, an early stage that is all eye and spiny cephalothorax. Some are the next stage, the megalops, in which the eyes are huge, still, but little legs and pinchers have formed. The crab has graduated to megalops, but it is still just a little chip of clear glass with a speck of blue vitals inside.

There are larval mantis shrimp—stomatopods—carved in crystal. They are transparent and colorless except for a bluish cast to the stalks of the eyes, and the black, catlike pupils. Their forelimbs, "raptorial appendages," look much like the striking forelimbs of the praying mantis. Most stomatopods are the kind called spearers, in which the last joint of the raptorial appendage, the dactyl, is armed with sharp spines. Spearers strike in one of the fastest animal movements known, completed sometimes in four milliseconds. A few stomatopods are the kind called smashers. Smashers have few barbs on their dactyls or no barbs at all. Their raptorial appendages are brawnier than those of spearers, with enlarged heels on the dactyl. Smashers are built along the lines of Popeye the Sailor and hit with the raptorial appendage folded, like a karate master striking with his elbow.

All the larvae of the glass menagerie, whether fish, worm, cephalopod, or crustacean, share the same plan—see-through bodies, oversize dark eyes. Eventually some of the menagerie will head inshore to take up adult lives in burrows and holes; others will head out to continue as inhabitants of the open ocean, but for now all commingle in the plankton. They make a kind of pre-universe. They are big-eyed ghosts of the creatures they will become, pale imitations, yet full of premonitions of their futures.

As the killer whales loom and their pressure waves strike, the glass menagerie scatters. The elvers ribbon downward, seeking bottom, as they will as eels. The larval rockfish spread their pectoral fins and erect the sharp rays of their dorsals, trying to look big and difficult to swallow, the pose they will strike as adults. The stomatopods, pugnacious even as larvae, cock their raptorial appendages, ready to fight. The glassy flounder flutter away. The insubstantial, cobwebby creatures called mucus-net feeders retract, in a blink, the little spiral galaxies of their nets.

Then the whales have gone by. Their turbulence dissipates. The mucus-net feeders cast out their nets again, tentatively at first, then spreading them full. The glass menagerie resumes its dance with the moonlight.

On calm mornings, when the focusing lens of the surface is smooth, each whale swims in the center of a prism of rays—dancing, revolving spokes of light shafting downward, converging toward a center in the depths. At the middle of each prism, the whale sees a vague shadow of itself, cruciform, its broad pectoral fins outspread.

Now and again a deeper whale enters the prism of the whale above, and its back goes all veined and reticulated with traveling patterns of light. Then the deeper whale passes out of the prism. Its back is still veined and reticulated with light, but the veins are not so dazzling. The deeper whale has left the personal prism of the whale above and returned to the general prism of the ocean.

Killer whales, in all seas, many hundreds of times a day, pass a lovely ellipsoidal creature that looks to be composed almost entirely of sunlight. It is as if one of those sun prisms accompanying each whale had somehow condensed and come alive. These apparitions belong to the phylum Ctenophora. Ctenophores, "comb-bearers," are simple, transparent, wraithlike, hardly there at all, each one propelled by narrow bands of comblike cilia along each of its eight meridians. The beating cilia refract sunlight prismatically. When a ctenophore is under steam, tiny lights wink along its meridians—brilliant red, green, pale blue, violet. Each ctenophore is like some tiny, ethereal spaceship powered by Rainbow Drive. The English writer Barbellion wrote that a ctenophore in sunlight is the most beautiful thing in the world. There is nothing more radiantly lovely in the sea, and nothing more common.

Occasionally ctenophores are concentrated in a windline. Whales, passing beneath one of these long, wandering slicks, enter a slow snowfall of ctenophores and sea jellies and salps, tens of thousands of translucent organisms aggregated by the Langmuir circulation stirred up by the wind. The passage of the whales sends flurries raging through the snow. The sea jellies hold shape, as do the salps, but the ctenophores are knocked sprawling by the cavitations spinning off the flukes. They tumble in place, wildly distorted by tidal forces, with strange lobes and arms and centrifugal flares appearing in them. Then the tumbling slows. The crystalline architecture sorts itself out. The ctenophores reform as ellipsoids, the prismatic lights resume blinking along their meridians, and the ctenophores continue on their way.

THE WORLD THAT KEIKO LOST was a world held together by orca voices.

Killer whales vocalize in whistles and pulsed calls, and they echolocate by emitting the rapid-fire chains of banging ticks called click-trains. Their voices are powerful, as loud as jet engines, and the calls carry for miles under the sea. The most common call is a kind of trumpeting whistle. Each blast will often start high and rise higher. To the human ear, that rising inflection sounds like a query. "Are you there?" the whale seems to be asking, most of the time. If orca calls have a fundamental function, it must be to ask and answer that question, keeping the group together. But all our analogies for orca communication are curiously prone to shifting. Sometimes the orca's voice sounds less like a horn than some sort of stringed instrument. The whale seems to be playing high on the frets, first rubbing an inch in one direction, then two inches in the other. Other times the instrument is a kazoo, and still others a mechanical birdcall. Nothing approximates orca music, in range and tonality, quite so well as the creaking door. When human beings listen to killer whales, either on recordings or directly through hydrophones, it is common for us, almost to the point of unanimity, to imagine that these queries, bridging vast distances through a dark void, are communications from an extraterrestrial intelligence—which is, of course, exactly what they are.

The orca musical aesthetic is entirely different from ours. A call will often begin with a low, wet farty noise—in the worst possible taste—and abruptly rise into a clarion trumpet call so hauntingly beautiful and pure that it raises the hair on your neck. In our own compositions we avoid such sudden, wrenching ascents from crass to ethereal, from music hall to Mozart. Sometimes in listening to killer whales you will hear one animal repeat a simple phrase again and again. These passages seem not so different from birdsong. But most often the horn notes sound improvisational. The calls seem not so much language as some kind of jazz.

For thirty-five years, the orca researcher Paul Spong, through hydrophones he has placed strategically around his base, OrcaLab, on Hanson Island in British Columbia, has been listening to the calls of killer whales. Dr. Spong has yet to figure out what they mean. Once his hydrophones recorded the calls of a young male he had named Strider as that whale hurried through Blackney Passage, east of the island, trying to catch up with his family. That family, designated A30, is composed of a female called Tsitika and her offspring. Strider is Tsitika's oldest son.

Strider's call as he chased the A30s was one of those repeated phrases. It was urgent and curt, a rising whistly bleat. It was as loud as anything Spong's hydrophones ever recorded, and it echoed hauntingly off the bottom, or off the rocky foundations of Harbledown Island on the other side of Blackney Passage.

The A30 dialect belongs in the language family of the Northern Resident Community of the Pacific Northwest, and it is very different, of course, from the dialect of Keiko's nameless and unknown family ten thousand miles away in another ocean. Still, it is hard not to believe that Strider's call that day was something like a universal in the language of orcas. Keiko, in his North Atlantic accent, must have trumpeted something very similar when caught in *Gudrun*'s nets off the East Fiords of Iceland. Even for an English-speaker the meaning seems clear. Keiko cried something like "Wait!"

3

GULLIVER

KEIKO AT TEN YEARS OLD WAS A SORRY SPECIMEN OF KILLER WHALE, YET IN Mexico he became a star. He was the only captive orca in that country, and the populace forgave him his deficiencies. Over the years, twelve million Mexicans made the pilgrimage to Reino Aventura to witness his lethargic performances. Keiko was not a great trouper in the tradition of Sea World's Shamu or any of the other great orca performers. In his leaping act, when he missed the blue ball hanging above his pool, Keiko would break off the show, retire to his medical pool, and sulk.

"He gets mad," one of his first trainers, Claudia Teran, told the press. "When he does something bad, he punishes himself." He was too much the perfectionist, perhaps, or simply too hot and ill. The Mexican people, having no other killer whale for comparison, were satisfied. Keiko, for whatever it was worth to him, became a beloved character. Millions of visitors made guesses about his interior life, and he was relentlessly anthropomorphized.

"In many ways, Keiko is like a typical human teenager—he's got skin problems, has grown (to 21 feet), and now wants a girlfriend," Alina Guerrero wrote in *The News,* a Mexico City journal.

"He is very kind," his trainer Renata Fernandez told an interviewer. "He's very noble, and intelligent also. I would describe him as a little kid."

"The most beautiful animal in the world," said another trainer, Karla Corral. "He's my best friend. He's everything to me. He's really gentle. He really cares for us. He kind of talks to me, in his way. If I have problems in my life, I will come over and talk to Keiko and tell him about it. He sits there and pays so much attention to me. And if I'm sad, he'll be sad. He'll let you know he's there for you."

Keiko was certainly *there* for Karla. Four tons of killer whale were not about to sneak off anyplace else. Had Keiko somehow succeeded in wriggling over the side of his tank, he would have found himself stranded high and dry on the lacustrine plain of Mexico City, surrounded by 14,000-foot peaks, two hundred miles from the ocean. Keiko was there for Karla physically, but was he really there emotionally? Karla's intuition about his inner life was likely just projection. It probably says more about Karla than it does about Keiko.

What *did* go on behind that massive black forehead? In the stifling warmth of his tank, did Keiko remember the cold currents of Iceland? Under the smoggy blue skies of Mexico's megalopolis, did he recall the gray skies of home? On rare days, the Mexico City haze disclosed the snowcapped volcanoes of Popocatepetl, 17,883 feet tall, and Ixtacihuatl, 17,338 feet. Seeing those, did he recollect Vatnajökull and Myrdalsjökull, the snowcapped volcanoes of Iceland? As he listlessly ate the dead, beheaded subtropical fish of his Mexican diet, did he remember Iceland's living, quicksilver schools of herring? Is a killer whale, in its enormous uncharted brain, capable of existential thought? Did Keiko wrestle with the insoluble mystery of what had happened to him?

Did he ever get mad?

"I confess I was often tempted, while they were passing backwards and forwards on my body, to seize forty or fifty of the first that came in my reach, and dash them against the ground," Gulliver wrote of the Lilliputians.

As Keiko's miniature trainers walked along his great back in his daily foot massage, did he have to fight off Gulliverian urges?

Only once in history has a killer whale killed a human. That incident, in which Tillicum, a captive whale in British Columbia, pinned his trainer to the pool bottom, drowning her, is generally deemed to have been horseplay, just a misunderstanding, a simple failure of the whale to appreciate the difference between human breath-hold capacity and its own. But could the episode have been something darker? Could it have been, if not murder, then justifiable homicide, perhaps? (There is strong circumstantial evidence that Tillicum may have killed again. He was moved to another theme park, where a drunk climbed in over the wall one night and was found drowned in the whale's pool the next morning.) In those sultry Mexican afternoons, as Karla poured out her heart to Keiko, who seemed so sympathetic, could his real thoughts have drifted to pinning her for eight or nine minutes to the bottom of the pool?

By 1993, Keiko had spent fourteen years in captivity. After all that time, did fragmentary memories of his family pod still return? If so, what were those recollections like? Is killer-whale memory infallible, like the proverbial elephant's, or is it more like human memory—a kind of palimpsest continually rewritten and relentlessly drifting off from reality? Had the North Atlantic of Keiko's recollections faded into some sort of pale, lukewarm simulacrum of itself?

The pool in Mexico was always dead calm, but on the plank fence behind, some less-than-talented Mexican muralist had painted a line of steep, stylized, hydrodynamically impossible waves. Did Keiko now recall the great storms of the North Atlantic as looking like that?

Icelandic saga, with its insistence on external event, its absence of interior monologue, is not the literature for this sort of speculation. Icelandic heroes, as their names suggest—Erik Bloodaxe, Grettir the Strong, Thorarin the Overbearing—were men more given to impulse than to rumination. Fortunately Keiko had traveled now to Latin America, the land of magical realism. That style of imagining might help.

There is a Jorge Luis Borges story, "Inferno I, 32," that begins as a meditation on the captivity of a wild animal:

> In the final years of the twelfth century, from twilight of dawn to twilight of dusk, a leopard looked upon some wooden planks, some vertical iron bars, men and women who were always different, a thick wall and, perhaps, a stone trough filled with dry leaves. The leopard did not know, could not know, that what he craved was love and cruelty and the hot pleasure of rending and the odor of a deer on the wind; and yet something within the animal choked him and something rebelled.

This is easy to recast for Keiko:

> In the final years of the twentieth century, from twilight of dawn to twilight of dusk, a killer whale looked upon a pool of an improbable turquoise color, some rows of bleacher seats, men and women who were always different, a thick wall painted with a line of stylized and hydrodynamically impossible waves and, above, an implacable Latin American sun. The whale did not know, could not know, that what he craved was love and cruelty and the hot pleasure of the chase and the echo of herring on his sonar; and yet something within the animal choked him and something rebelled.

Did something within Keiko choke him? Did something rebel?

In another Jorge Luis Borges story, "The South," the protagonist, Juan Dahlmann, in an odd sort of fugue state after a near-fatal fever, meets an enormous cat in a café. "He thought, as he smoothed the cat's black coat, that this contact was an illusion and that the two beings, man and cat, were as good as separated by a glass, for man lives in time, in succession, while the magical animal lives in the present, in the eternity of the instant."

Was Keiko the same kind of magical animal, living outside of time and succession, confined to the present? If so, then this is a bleak prospect indeed. It condemns the whale to the eternity of an instant of sensory deprivation, itchy with papilloma, in water hellishly warm.

The pioneer dolphin trainer Karen Pryor once told me that certain species of dolphins do poorly in captivity. Confined in tanks, spotted dolphins, spinner dolphins, and pilot whales often simply let go of life. They become "floaters," in oceanarium terminology. They float listlessly at the surface, and their backs become sunburned. A floater often becomes a sinker, settling to the bottom and refusing to come up for air. Human beings are incapable of ending their lives this way—reflex kicks in—but dolphins routinely pull it off. Pilot whales are particularly prone to this form of suicide. In some way it may figure, as wild pilot whales, of all cetaceans, are the most inclined to suicidal mass strandings. Stroked and laved and guided back to sea by good Samaritans, the pilot whales almost invariably return with a strange willfulness and beach themselves again. When Karen Pryor began her career, there were no whale veterinarians, and she and the trainers of her generation were forced back on their own resourcefulness. Pryor has tried to feed sunburned, depressive pilot whales handfuls of pep pills, without effect. She once fed a suicidal pilot whale a quart of gin without cheering it up at all.

Perhaps pilot whales, spotted dolphins, and spinner dolphins are magical animals of the kind Jorge Luis Borges describes, living outside of time, outside of succession, confined to an unbearable present. But other species of dolphin serve their life terms better. The rough-toothed dolphin, an animal quick to grasp new principles, and the bottlenose dolphin, a master puzzle-solver, and the killer whale, regarded by most trainers as the brightest of cetaceans, all find ways to entertain themselves. Perhaps their intelligence allows them to live in time, in succession, and to imagine something besides the present.

Keiko had become a kind of floater, but only because his pool was so shallow and hot. He never became a sinker. He did not stare into walls, or ram his head into them, or manifest any of the other known symptoms of psychosis in captive orcas. After ten years of isolation in his cramped Mexican oubliette, he had grown a little eccentric, maybe, but still had not—as nearly as we can tell—gone completely insane.

4

SECOND SIGHT

In captivity Keiko shut down his sonar. The clicks of killer-whale echolocation, bouncing around the immediate walls of his Mexican cell, returned no new information. The echoes told him nothing he had not learned in his first minute incarcerated here. The empty reverberation must have seemed to mock him. The babble of reechoing clicks would have been like dwelling in a hall of mirrors, or like seeing Kafkaesque through the compound eyes of an insect.

Or something like that. Human beings hear so primitively that it is hard for us to imagine the acoustic vision of killer whales; we can only guess what it is like to possess this kind of clairvoyance and what it is like to lose it.

Humans hear passively. *Orcinus orca* and the other toothed whales hear aggressively. Echolocating, they send bursts of clicks outward; lower frequencies to rough out objects, higher frequencies to fill in the details. They produce their sounds in a manner imperfectly known, but it is certain that it involves the "melon," the oil-filled chamber that gives the dolphin's forehead its bulge. Dolphin sound production is powerful. The toothed whales are capable of generating bangs so intense that they can stun or kill prey at a distance. Dolphins are *decibellicose,* to invent a term. They sometimes employ a kind of banshee shriek of loud click-trains as a threat. The bone of the skull directly behind the melon is thickened—soundproofing to protect the thought processes from fragmentation by the noise.

In echolocation a dolphin can reel off three hundred clicks per second. Some click sequences are spaced so that the outgoing clicks will not interfere with incoming echoes. Other sequences are spaced so that the echoes *will* interfere, allowing the dolphin to refine details by interpreting interference patterns.

The reflected photons that give us sight rebound only from the surface of things. What they reveal is superficial. The click-trains of toothed whales are more perspicacious, for they can penetrate matter. Whales have the power to hear into things. We know from experiments with captive dolphins that their sonar can distinguish objects of identical shape but different density; that they can discern spaces and structures inside objects. Certain details figure to be easy for them: the hard beaks of squid within the soft bonelessness of squid bodies, for example, or the airiness of lungs inside a human being. The first diagnostic use of ultrasound—the CAT scan, or Cetacean Auditory Tomography, let's call it—was an invention of the whales many millions of years before we hominids came down from the trees.

Killer whales and other dolphins receive echoes not with their external ears, but with their jawbones and their melons—odd organs of hearing, it might seem, but efficient just the same, capable of detecting higher tones than the auditory gear of any animal except the bat. The jawbones of dolphins can locate the points of origin of underwater sound. Human ears, which are designed to work in air, cannot. The dolphin's jawbones are especially sensitive to motion. Movement toward the dolphin or away from it is marked by a Doppler shift, the target's frequency rising as it approaches, falling as it recedes.

Humans can echolocate in a rudimentary way. In darkness, the echo of our footfalls tells us whether we are confined in a small, overstuffed apartment or lost in some vast marble hall. We experience near objects as a kind of looming. We whistle in the dark. Echolocation guides us past furniture, halting us—if we are lucky—just before we hit the sofa or the wall. Frequently, of course, we are unlucky. As often as not, our echolocation fails us. Our shins are particularly vulnerable to low coffee tables. Children's discarded shoes, sleeping dogs, and soccer balls all lie below our sonar. Our noses are often casualties of the open door, which, approached edge on, offers a slim sonic profile and produces no blip on our screens. We slide our feet through the acoustic world cautiously, forever anticipating a bump. Killer whales fly through their night seas gleefully at thirty knots.

And yet, possessing the rudiments of the faculty, we can begin to guess at how its refinement feels in a killer whale. If the whale's perception is anything like our own, then objects are experienced as pressures. The sensation is tactile yet remote. For *Orcinus orca,* the pressures are exquisitely modeled, and here—just as we have begun trying to "picture" it—is where our intuition breaks down. We have to imagine perceiving, with vibrant jawbones, a topography of differential pressures equivalent to our world of reflected light. We have to imagine a dilute, musical Creation in which foreign objects are few and far between, yet translucent to our curiosity, each one singing a different song to us depending on its speed and direction of flight. We have to conceive an orchestral universe in which everything—even the newest and strangest thing—manifests itself in shadings of pitch and percussion in the echoes of our own familiar voice.

KEIKO, BEFORE HIS CAPTURE, HAD moved comfortably through this world shaped of sound. As a calf in the night seas of Iceland, the young Keiko, voluble still and full of click-trains, had swum close to his mother. She was a familiar slipstream in the darkness and a running commentary of grunts and whistles. She was a bright, loud, instantaneous wall of reflected clicks when Keiko was echolocating, and a dark silhouette against the white noise of the sea when he was not. When he left off experimenting with his click-trains, his mother, the great bulk of her, blacked out a quadrant of the ocean's background chatter—the snapping of shrimp, the songs of blue whales, the screws of distant freighters—just as the dark curve of a mountain eclipses the stars. Emitting a new burst of clicks, Keiko lit her up again.

Killer whales and other dolphins propagate their click-trains in a conical beam that widens outward from the tip of the beak. As Keiko's pod coursed through the blackness of the North Atlantic, he swung his beak slightly this way and that, filling in the view ahead. His mother blurred and faded on his sonar as he focused on the whales in the lead. Then his beak swung back her way again, renewing her image even as the other whales blurred and faded.

In Iceland, the principal prey of killer whales are herring. In winter, schools of those fish must have materialized nightly on Keiko's sonar. Each herring school was nebulous at first, its echoes soft and diffuse—a sort of Greater Magellanic Cloud of sound, as an astronomer might observe that misty galaxy. The cloud would have come accompanied by a flurry of approximations of itself—dimmer, fuzzier images composed of rebounding click-trains from the other whales. Keiko could tune these out, just as humans tune out the babble of conversation in a crowded restaurant. The herring cloud resolved itself into individual fish as the pod drew closer, and as Keiko raised his pitch to examine the school at higher resolution.

The killer whales commenced the teamwork of herding, racing around the perimeter of the school, sculpting the herring into a tight ball. Each fish in the ball had its Doppler signature, the fish's frequency rising as it darted toward Keiko, then dropping as the frantic vortex of the fish ball carried it away to the other side of the gyre. (By daylight a whale—or, for that matter, a human diver through his face mask—sees something similar as all the fish in the school simultaneously flash silver, then darken again as they change direction.)

Nature devised schooling as a way to confuse predators. Schooling fish are all of the same age-class, size, and speed. They share a mesmerizing rapid-fire identicality. The school offers the predator too many iterations of the same thing, too many choices. But schooling is not a strategy that works well against killer whales. *Orcinus orca* is a wonderfully decisive hunter. Once Keiko's pod had shaped the herring ball just the way they liked it, an adult orca would break off the circle, slash in, and tail-slap through the ball. The scythe of the tailfin, either by direct impact on the herring or by causing con-

cussive cavitations in the water, stunned dozens of fish, which fell out of for-
mation. As the herring swirled, disoriented, the killer whales picked them off
one at a time. Keiko locked onto a herring. In the last instant of the life of
that fish, the calf made a kind of flash snapshot in clicks, a three-
dimensional auditory X-ray hologram in which he may even have glimpsed
the skeleton within.

IN ICELANDIC SAGA, THE GIFT of second sight was rare. It lay in a hero's ability to perceive what Icelanders called a *flybben*, "a spiritual double." The hero
saw specters of his enemies gathering, sometimes in the form of animals,
where everyone else saw only Icelandic tundra and dwarf birches. For killer
whales and other dolphins, the gift of second sight is not rare, but universal.
In the night sea off Iceland, where you and I would have seen only blackness,
Keiko fixed on the acoustic *flybben* of his herring. The Doppler signal of the
herring was crucial now. As any spearfisherman could tell you—as any gannet or pelican or osprey knows—the hunter must aim for where the fish is
going, not at where it is. The staccato Doppler doppelgänger of the herring
amplified as Keiko's hearing jaw opened for it, then abruptly ceased as his
jaws clamped shut.

IN HIS CONCRETE TANK IN Mexico, Keiko renounced his gift of second sight.
He let his sonar screen go dark. He continued to "vocalize," making the
whistles and wheezes of killer-whale communication, just talking to himself,
but he did so less and less, and in the end it became a kind of baby talk. His
companions in the tank were bottlenose dolphins, and Keiko began to speak
like one of those. He did a fine imitation of an ambulance siren, as well, and
a passable impression of a rooster.

Male killer whales reach sexual maturity at fifteen, physical maturity at
twenty-one. The males have a mean life expectancy of 29.2 years, according
to the estimates of the International Whaling Commission. The "maximum
estimated age trajectory" of the males is between fifty and sixty. In captivity,
sadly, no whale has even approached that maximum. Their trajectories nose-
dive less than halfway home, with most males dying before physical maturity. Only two captive males had survived past twenty: Orky, who died at
about twenty-nine, and Hyak, who died at about twenty-six. Keiko would
have passed whatever time he had left on earth—two years, maybe, five at
best—in his tepid tank under the Mexican sun, had it not been for a tuna
sandwich.

5

HOLLYWOOD

IN A BRIEF DOMESTIC LULL IN THE GUNFIRE AND EXPLOSIONS OF THE
Warner Bros. movie *Lethal Weapon 2,* the actor Danny Glover, playing a police lieutenant named Murtaugh, prepares to eat a sandwich.

"Tuna!" his family cries in unison.

Detective Murtaugh, startled, arrests his sandwich in mid-bite.

"We're boycotting tuna, honey," explains his wife. "Because they kill the
dolphins that get caught in the net."

Murtaugh's teenage daughter, to clue him in, points emphatically to her
Earth Island Institute "Save the Dolphins" T-shirt and the dolphin gambol-
ing across the perky topography of her chest. The detective unhappily with-
draws the sandwich from his mouth.

In pondering the meaning of Danny Glover's sandwich, I have found no
help at all in Icelandic saga, or in *Moby Dick,* or in *Gulliver's Travels,* or in Latin
American magical realism. North American magical realism seemed to help a
little. Kurt Vonnegut Jr., America's Jonathan Swift, may have come up with
something. A useful way to think about Danny Glover's sandwich, I think, is
as an example of what Vonnegut calls a *wampeter.* The wampeter is a central
concept of Bokononism, the cockamamie religion he invents in his novel *Cat's
Cradle.* "Anything can be a wampeter, a tree, a rock, an animal, an idea, a
book, a melody, the Holy Grail," he writes. The wampeter is the pivot of the
karass, an accidental clan whose members, without realizing it, collaborate in
doing God's Will. "If you find your life tangled up with somebody else's life
for no very logical reasons, that person may be a member of your karass."

The karass orbiting the wampeter of Danny Glover's tuna sandwich
would eventually include: David Oddsson, prime minister of Iceland; the pop
singer Michael Jackson; a six-year-old Oregonian named Stephanie Arnot;
the dyslexic billionaire communications genius Craig McCaw; the third-
grade class at Institute Thomas Jefferson in Tlalnepantla, Mexico; the entire
student body of Peterson Elementary School in Kodiak, Alaska; the surviving son of Jacques Cousteau; Major Chip Wiggins of the U.S. Air Force; a
Reykjavík cabdriver named Hankur Geirsson; an itinerant Norwegian animal husbandman named Frank Haavik; Keiko himself; and me, among
thousands of others.

The sandwich was loaded into *Lethal Weapon 2* at the suggestion of Ann Moss, a dolphin activist, former model, and the wife of Jerry Moss, founder of A&M Records. Ann Moss, "Ani," was a friend of Richard Donner, producer of the movie. Donner, who had dolphinist tendencies himself, liked how Ani's little plug for dolphins played in *Lethal Weapon 2*. He wanted to do more for whales. He worked up a screenplay on a killer whale, the biggest dolphin species of all. The story amounted to an update of the Androcles fable, with a runaway boy in the role of the Roman slave, and a killer whale, Willy, in the role of the lion.

In the original screenplay, by a writer named Keith Walker, the Androcles figure is a mute orphan raised by nuns. The orphan is silent until the climax, when, in releasing his whale to the wild, he suddenly finds his voice and cries "Free Willy!" This arc seemed too Dickensian, too saccharine, to Lauren Shuler Donner, Richard Donner's coproducer and wife. Dialogue presented a problem, too—there is not much opportunity for repartee in a story where one protagonist is a mute human and the other a killer whale who speaks only in whistles and clicks. Lauren Shuler Donner modernized the tale, eliminating the nuns, converting the orphan to a surly juvenile delinquent, and endowing the boy, wisely, with the power of speech from the opening scenes. The Warner Bros. "props" department was asked to find a marina park where a solo whale could be filmed without interference. "Props" hoped to film at Sea World or another U.S. marine park, where they would draft one of the resident killer whales to play the title role. The marine parks were amenable until they learned the plot, which featured greedy oceanarium owners for villains and ended with the whale's release to the wild. Sea World suggested an alternate ending. Instead of freedom in the ocean, maybe the whale could just find his way to a *nicer* oceanarium? Richard Donner was unwilling to make this change. Without a script revision, no marine park in the United States would cooperate. The producer had to go to Mexico to find his whale.

In 1992, Donner made a call to David Phillips of Earth Island Institute. Earth Island is a loose confederation of grassroots environmental projects founded in San Francisco in 1982. Phillips wears two hats in the organization, serving both as executive director of the mother organization and as founder and director of the International Marine Mammal Project, one of Earth Island's offspring. It was Earth Island that had produced the "Save the Dolphins" T-shirt worn by Lieutenant Murtaugh's daughter in the movie. When Richard Donner succeeded in tracking Phillips down by phone, the environmentalist was in the middle of dinner in Glasgow, Scotland, where he was attending the annual meeting of the International Whaling Commission. Hollywood operates independent of time zones. Donner explained that he and his wife were making a movie on a killer whale for Warner Bros. They wanted Phillips's ideas on how the film might do a little advocacy for whales.

This query was pivotal—it would shape the next decade of Phillips's life—but the environmentalist had no intimation of this at the time. He was then thirty-nine, a bearded man of middle height, with collar-length hair thinning on top.

If the saga of Keiko has a human hero, it is David Phillips. He has a flashpoint something like that of the hero Gunnar in *Njál's Saga*—slow to ignite, then fierce. Otherwise, as an old-style Icelandic hero, he falls short. He lacks the breadth of shoulder and width of forearm you need to cleave the shield of Sigurd Snake-in-the-Eye, or to amputate, in a single stroke, both legs of Harald Battle-tooth. But we live in a different era. Today the heroes of Icelandic saga would all be in penitentiaries. Phillips does not shy from combat of the kind that shapes modern public policy. He is pugnacious in a contemporary way. From the time he left Colorado College with a degree in biology, he has been off on Viking raids against the extractive industries and their henchmen in the regulatory agencies. In his late twenties, as wildlife programs coordinator for Friends of the Earth, he led the opposition to the capture of the last twenty wild California condors for a captive-breeding program in zoos. Moving to Earth Island Institute, he midwifed at the births of dozens of scrappy little environmental outfits. At the time Richard Donner's call reached Phillips in Scotland, he was fresh from legal and public-relations victories in a campaign he had spearheaded against the tuna fishery in the eastern tropical Pacific, where purse-seiners were killing hundreds of thousands of dolphins annually as by-catch.

One old technique of the Icelandic hero was to shame his clansmen, by his brave example, into joining some hopeless fight, which thereby becomes winnable. Here Phillips was a throwback. In his tuna-dolphin campaign, he had shamed Greenpeace and other big environmental outfits into joining a battle for which they had no stomach at the start. His efforts had led to regulation and close monitoring of the tuna fleets and a radical reduction of the dolphin slaughter.

In the Glasgow restaurant, his meal interrupted, Phillips considered Richard Donner's request. He briefly contemplated suggesting that Donner's scriptwriters insert some variation on the tuna-sandwich motif in the new killer-whale movie. He quickly dismissed the idea. It might be cute—good for one laugh—but it would have no lasting effect. Better, thought Phillips, would be something that provided filmgoers with an avenue for continuing involvement with whales. To Donner he proposed displaying an 800 number at the end of the film. Anyone moved to action by the Willy story could call

Earth Island Institute, toll-free, for information on how to help the world's whales.

Donner liked the idea. Warner Bros. proved hesitant about running this sort of advertisement, but Phillips and Donner lobbied the studio, and eventually the moguls gave in. Setting up the toll-free number, Phillips hired an in-bound telemarketing company to handle the calls. A foundation was persuaded to underwrite the telephone, printing, and postage expenses for responses to as many as 25,000 calls.

"We thought, *All right!*" Phillips recalls of this arrangement. "We're really covered now!" Shaking his head, he laughs at the size of his miscalculation.

6

FREE WILLY

In July of 1993, David Phillips invited my seven-year-old son and me to the San Francisco premiere of *Free Willy*. The screening was an event: wine, cheese, tables stacked with save-the-dolphin literature. Jason James Richter, the young actor who plays Androcles to Keiko's lion, was on hand to take a bow. Richter had grown considerably in the months since the last scenes were shot, coming to resemble a burly, less-than-convincing stunt double for the poster image of his younger self. The other teenager, Richter's costar Keiko, had not made the trip. Where Richter had gained maybe fifteen pounds since the filming, the whale was at least a thousand pounds underweight, his growth stunted by poor diet, infection, and lack of exercise. But neither the audience, nor David Phillips, nor the rest of the world knew this yet. We adjourned to the theater and the show began.

Free Willy opens with documentary footage of wild killer whales. They spy-hop and lob-tail in Puget Sound. They breach and fall back into the sea, sending up white fountains of spray. A fast-swimming pod surfaces in close rank and blows in unison, then the dorsal fins cut back under. The warm, explosive puffs of their exhalations hang, condensing, in the cold air.

Several times the cameraman catches, in slow motion, a breathtaking moment that I have witnessed several times firsthand, paddling in kayaks amid killer whales. The surface bulges, as if with the arrival of a glassy swell from a very distant storm. White markings—the temple blaze and chin patch of a killer whale—appear in the swell. At first the markings look doubtful, like some odd pattern of reflected clouds, perhaps; then the curve of the wave rapidly morphs into the black dorsum of a breaching whale. The whale breaks the surface, sheds the sea, and glistens in the sun. The transition does not come in stages, even in cinematic slow motion. The materialization of the whale, the *gathering* of its fluid form in the fluidity of the water, is perfectly smooth. There is no telling at what point the swell leaves off and the whale begins. The whale is a wave come alive.

In my theater seat I was moved almost to tears, though the movie had not really begun. Embarrassed, I glanced around the darkened audience. No one in the vicinity seemed as emotionally affected as I. David, my seven-year-old, certainly was not. For full impact, maybe, the filmgoer needs to have witnessed the metamorphosis—wave into whale—once or twice in real life.

After the opening passages on wild whales, filmed by the nature documentarian Bob Talbot, *Free Willy* quickly swims downhill. The last wild whale dives under, the documentary footage ends, and Hollywood storytelling begins. Whale trappers scan the sea with binoculars, while a small seiner named *Pequod* pays out net across the mouth of a cove, trapping killer whales inside. *Pequod!* The filmmakers flatter themselves. All emotional and misty at the start, I went dry-eyed through the entire slow, unfocused, sentimental drama. I was irritated by the movie's cheery, sanitized view of teenage homelessness. The Jason James Richter character, Jesse, runs with a pack of plump young street urchins, healthy in mind and body, who live a life of Sawyeresque freedom, subsisting on stolen pizza and cake. All the movie delinquents have the complexions of cherubs. I was irritated, too, by the movie's fake Indian, a sagacious Haida named Randolph.

For the real Haida, the seafaring British Columbia tribe, the killer whale is totemic, the most respected of animals. The Haida believe that killer whales are supernatural beings, the most powerful of the "Ocean People," and that they live in underwater towns at the tips of promontories. Above the surface, these meta-orcas appear to humans like killer whales, but in their submarine villages they are like men. The Haida believed that people drowned or lost at sea are transformed into killer whales. The drowned, taken to the house of the killer-whale chief—a huge bull named One-in-the-Sea—are fitted with dorsal fins and welcomed into the supernatural pod. One of the best Haida stories, the tribe's version of the Orpheus myth, is the tale of Nanasimgit, a woman abducted by killer whales and sought by her husband under the sea. The Haida have a rich killer-whale lore, and a lot of genuine Haida-isms might have been woven into the movie, but not a shred of genuine Haida belief finds its way into *Free Willy.*

Randolph is played by August Schellenberg, whose mother is Choctaw, his father an Austrian ski instructor. He has a fine Native American face, and he does what he can with the script, but in the end Randolph is just another generic wise Hollywood Indian.

At one point in the film, Randolph reflects on Willy's eyes. "Look into a man's soul, if they want," he tells Jesse.

Nonsense. A whale cannot look into the soul of a man, nor can a man look into the soul of a whale. A man, if you pause to think about it, has big trouble getting the briefest peek into the soul of another man, or another woman, let alone the soul of another species. There is no reason to believe that a whale can do better. The ancestors of the whales returned to the sea sixty million years ago, when we ourselves were lemurlike prosimians. We and the cetaceans do not have a lot in common. In my own encounters in the ocean with killer whales, I have never sensed any curiosity about my soul. I have paddled kayaks through the middle of killer-whale pods, I have sailed schooners amongst them, and they have never shown the least bit of interest in any part of me, physical or spiritual.

The best place to take the measure of a marine mammal is in its element, underwater, where it spends most of its time and where you see the whole creature. I have never met *Orcinus orca* underwater, but I have had many nose to nose encounters beneath the surface with other wild dolphins, among them the false killer whale and the melon-headed whale, two species that resemble the killer whale in behavior. It is my strong impression that these superdolphins are vastly less interested in us than we are in them. In the monotony of oceanarium tanks, captive dolphins are thrown back on humans for company, but not in the ocean. Out there, the proper study of dolphinkind is dolphin.

A killer whale's *eyes* are secondary organs of perception, anyway. Killer whales, like all toothed whales, do their most important seeing with their sonar. If a killer whale were curious about a man's soul, he would not use his eyes; he would look into the matter acoustically. I myself have often been studied in this way. Underwater, I have had my head examined at point-blank range by many species of wild dolphin. As the click-trains penetrate and ricochet, the sensation is peculiar, a kind of concussive effervescence, as if the dolphins were heating popcorn inside your skull. You feel *undressed,* maybe, but you never have the illusion—not me, anyway—that the animal has read your mind.

The filmmakers had built an animatronic Willy for many of the scenes, and indeed, Willy makes his first appearance in the form of this robot. The young hoodlum Jesse, spray-painting graffiti in the theme park at night, is startled, along with the moviegoer, by the sudden gape of the killer whale behind the aquarium glass. Where the teeth of the real Keiko are the color of old ivory and worn down in front, the smile of the robotic Keiko is all Hollywood, dazzlingly white and flawless, like a starlet with caps. But the fabrication of the robot's body was surprisingly sloppy, I thought. The cement that welded the pectoral fins to the fuselage of the animatronic whale was all bumpy and cracked.

"You can always tell the mechanical whale," I whispered to my son. "Look at all that glue under the pectorals."

David murmured something noncommittal and kept his eyes on the screen.

My children hate watching movies with me and have become adept at tuning out my commentary. My criticism, always niggling and tiresome, was in this instance ignorant as well. I was completely wrong about that glue under the pectoral fins. What I took to be cement disfiguring the fins was in fact an encrustation of papilloma warts on the real Keiko. At the time of the screening, I was unaware of papilloma infection in captive whales, and I had never seen anything like it on a wild one. Before *Free Willy* was done, I realized my mistake, but this did not much change my opinion of the movie.

In the climax, Jesse and his Indian mentor Randolph murmur a magical Haida chant, which Willy receives telepathically underwater. The whale, cheered on, makes a prodigious leap over a riprap jetty to freedom in the ocean. He jumps sixty or seventy feet in the air. It is a leap that might be possible in one of the acrobatic smaller dolphins—a dusky dolphin or a spinner—but not in a heavyweight like *Orcinus orca*. The white belly of the animatronic whale passes over Jesse's head in slow motion. The belly is a blank white wall. There is no genital slit. That ingenious pocket, into which the bull killer whale retracts his gigantic genitals for the sake of streamlining, is missing.

My sour opinion of the movie would be shared by future trainers of Keiko, by his future veterinarians, and by Keiko himself. The whale, in later chapters of his saga, would demonstrate a fondness for televised wrestling, and he would watch almost any kind of action movie or animal flick, yet he would show little interest in *Free Willy,* his own starring vehicle. In the end, however, all these thumbs-down reviews did not matter at all. My seven-year-old thought the film was "tight," and his view was the view that counted. *Free Willy* went on to a phenomenal success with children and to nearly as many sequels as *Lethal Weapon* or *Rocky.*

The appeal at the end of the movie, "You can personally help save the whales of the world by calling 1800 4 WHALES," was scarcely more than a subliminal message, yet in theaters across the land, audiences noticed. Where Phillips had anticipated 25,000 calls, the message generated more than 300,000. Many came, as expected, from people concerned about the plight of the world's whales, but an equal number of inquiries—and this Phillips had not foreseen—were about the specific whale, Willy. What *about* the whale? What's happening with the *real* whale? the world wondered. The press took interest, and began doing backstories on the two stars, Jason James Richter and Keiko.

"The press started feeding the whole thing," Phillips recalls. "As the kids started calling, and more and more press started covering, pressure mounted on Warner Bros. to do something. 'You've made a hundred million dollars on this movie,' people were saying. 'What are you doing about the whale?' Warner Bros. started calling us, complaining that they didn't know anything about saving whales."

When the studio asked if Earth Island Institute could help, Phillips at first thought not.

"Our real role was around wild whales," he says. "We never knew anything about Keiko. We didn't know he was in a bad situation. We really didn't know anything about him. I had to tell Warner Bros., 'We're in the *wild* whale business. We're not in the captive whale business.'"

Warner Bros. entertained a number of proposals. An outfit called Center for Whale Research developed a plan to fly Keiko to the Bahamas and reintroduce him to the ocean in a sea pen. Another group wanted to build him a facility at Cape Cod. There was a proposal from Canada.

"Dear Earth Island Institute," wrote the spokeswoman for the Canadian faction, Corinne Goyetche of West Bay, Nova Scotia. "I have a very good idea that can help Keiko, and possibly other orcas, be rehabilitated back into their natural environment. My family owns land on a beautiful, deep, sheltered cove which is part of the Bras d'Or Lake—a 1,100-square-kilometer saltwater estuary of the Atlantic Ocean in the center of Cape Breton Island." Goyetche pointed out that the Bras d'Or Lake was only 1,875 miles from Keiko's home waters in Iceland and only 1,250 miles from Greenland. "The Bras d'Or is beautiful and unspoiled with very few people to disturb Keiko. There are no other whales in the lake that can contract his skin disease. Our cove is hidden from the main highway but is served by a private road to the water and electric services." Ms. Goyetche conceded that she was only twelve years old, but she assured Earth Island Institute that her parents had pledged to help in every way. She included photocopied maps, monographs, depth charts, freshwater-discharge tables, watershed drainage patterns, fishery data, all marked up with her marginalia in green pencil. The map of Ross Pond, her family's cove, was green-penciled "Initial Release" at the back of the cove, then "Secondary Release Area" where MacLeod Creek entered, and finally "Third Release Area" at the mouth. The Bras d'Or proposal was a weighty document and made a considerable thump when dropped on a desk. The cover letter concluded, "Please contact me as soon as possible because I know you will agree that this is the best proposal for Keiko's release yet! Sincerely, Corinne Goyetche."

The cetologist Kenneth Balcomb, a specialist in the killer whales of Puget Sound, volunteered to train Keiko to follow his boat and *sail* the whale back to Iceland. The pop singer Michael Jackson wanted the whale. Jackson had shared billing with Keiko in *Free Willy*. His song "Will You Be There?" accompanied the film's closing credits, his falsetto making fine counterpoint to the concluding footage of wild whales until the very end, when he begins to squeal and whimper excessively. Jackson and his partners offered to build an aquarium for Keiko at the Neverland Ranch, his spread in Santa Barbara.

The Bahamas and Cape Cod plans fell apart. Twelve-year-old Corinne Goyetche and her Bras d'Or Lake proposal never got much traction. Kenneth Balcomb's notion of swimming the whale to Iceland was never taken seriously. (Bewilderment over Balcomb's thinking united all the disparate factions that were springing up around Keiko. Few whale people thought Balcomb had the remotest chance of success. "What happens in the first storm?" a Balcomb friend and colleague asked me.) Michael Jackson, for his part, ran afoul of the law. Under the provisions of the Marine Mammal Protection Act, a whale brought to the United States must be on public display. The act forbids private ownership of whales, and Michael Jackson's menagerie at Neverland is not open to the public.

Richard Donner, the film's producer, approached David Phillips again. Donner confessed that he and Warner Bros. were good at making movies but lousy at protecting whales. If Earth Island Institute would undertake Keiko's rescue, Donner promised a significant contribution from Warner Bros. and from Craig McCaw, a Seattle-based communications billionaire, who had expressed interest in helping.

"I had to wrestle with it," says Phillips. "Do we want to move from wild whales into this? Why would we want to do this? Keiko had touched such a chord in people. It had reached so many kids. I began thinking that this was another way of telling the story—a way that I had never imagined as being such a good way. I'd always been against concern with individual animals. Our concern is with ecosystems. We haven't been interested in anthropomorphizing animals. We haven't been talking about *one* animal. We've been talking about *all* the whales.

"But then I saw the power in it—concentrating on Keiko as a metaphor. Getting Keiko back to his family. Or at least doing the best thing we could for Keiko. We didn't know whether we could get him all the way back to his family, but we knew getting him out of Mexico was important. Right from the beginning, the goal was Rescue, Rehabilitation, Release. We wanted to bring him back to health and we wanted to release him. I started seeing the power in that. I can talk about the impact of fisheries on marine mammals until I'm blue in the face, and lots of times the little kids nod off. Talk about Keiko and they're totally wide-eyed. I had never experienced that."

After four days of debate with himself, Phillips agreed to undertake the rescue of the whale. Earth Island Institute would handle the operation unless it got too big, in which case Phillips would form a new foundation.

Movie stardom for Keiko had opened a new round of feuding over the whale. Reino Aventura, which had accepted a flat fee of $40,000 for use of Keiko, his tank, and his trainers, regretted their underbid. It galled them that Warner Bros. had made $100,000,000 from the movie. The Mexicans were stung, too, by global criticism of their care of the whale. They felt betrayed by Sea World, believing that the big oceanarium had backed out of a promise to help in finding a larger home for Keiko.

David Phillips asked Oscar Porter, director of Reino Aventura, for a list of his requirements in a deal for Keiko. Porter drew up the list. He wanted to see a financial plan, a guarantee of a suitable new facility, assurance that Warner Bros. was on board, and a binding agreement that Earth Island Institute would pay every penny of transport costs. He wanted a guarantee that Earth Island would support Keiko's trainers, Karla Corral and Renata Fernandez, through a transitional period with Keiko in his new home—wherever that turned out to be. If Phillips could deliver all that, then Reino Aventura would donate the whale for free.

"Bring me the broom of the Wicked Witch of the West," Phillips says, in summary.

Phillips agreed to fetch the broom. He committed his organization to an unprecedented enterprise: the rehabilitation of a captive orca and its release to the wild.

7

MEMO FROM CARTHAGE

WHEN THE DUST SETTLED, DAVID PHILLIPS WENT DOWN TO MEXICO TO meet his new client. He knew from various secondhand accounts that the whale was sick, but he was unprepared for what he found.

"I thought, *Oh my God.* He was just like a bump," Phillips remembers. "Floating at the top of the pool. He wasn't even moving. He was out of shape, hot, and covered with papilloma. I hadn't had any experience with captive orca whales. What had we gotten ourselves into?"

On this question, veterinary opinion was divided. Sea World's experts argued that if chillers were sent down to Mexico City, the papilloma would clear up and the whale would be fine. Other marine-mammal specialists disagreed, insisting that Keiko's tank at Reino Aventura was impossibly small, that the whale was gravely ill, and that without intervention he would soon die. Ann Moss, who had started it all with her tuna-sandwich idea, stepped in again. In consultation with Earth Island Institute, she engaged Dr. Lanny Cornell, the world's preeminent killer-whale veterinarian, sending him down to Mexico.

"I thought this would be a two-day jaunt, and that's the first and last time I ever saw this animal," Dr. Cornell remembers. "I really hadn't heard much about him. I hadn't seen the movie. I went down and took a look at him, and it was fairly clear that the situation was an animal-husbandry problem, rather than a medical problem. He was eating fish that were not really stored properly. They were fish that fishermen had brought to the market. Having sat out for a number of days, they would sometimes be frozen and other times be fed directly to Keiko. They would cut the heads off and gut the fish and feed him the fillets. What he was missing was bone and all the vitamins and minerals that come from the liver and the organs of an animal. It's very important for a wild predator to eat everything. An owl eats the whole mouse."

Dr. Cornell is a robust, well-made man, handsome in an aquiline, weathered, Marlboro-cowboy sort of way. He is tough and gruff and sardonic and opinionated. He was then in his mid-fifties. For fourteen years he had worked at Sea World, rising through the ranks to senior vice president and zoological director, with responsibility for the entire animal collection in all of Sea World's parks. Sea World owns about half the captive killer whales on the planet, and Dr. Cornell, until his departure in 1987, had ministered to that flock.

"Papilloma is endemic in wild killer whales in Iceland," Cornell says. "All captive killer whales from Iceland have suffered from it in one degree or another, at one time or another. It became worse in him. Papilloma is stress-related in sheep, cattle, people, and probably in killer whales, too. I don't particularly like the term 'stress.' It's so vague. If you put an animal in a tank where the water is too warm, and the food is wrong, and he hasn't enough room, all those things are stressful.

"So I wrote a little report for them. I indicated that probably the smart thing to do would be to take this animal and put him in an environment where he could have good food, some vitamins, and *cold water.* That would probably fix it. I was fairly confident of that. In fact, I was rather adamant about it."

Some animal-rights groups and anticaptivity philosophers argued that the whale should be released to the wild immediately. This, in the opinion of Dr. Cornell, would mean certain death. Keiko was much too sick and weak. Another school of thought was that the whale should be moved to a sea pen. Here, too, Keiko's poor health posed problems. The U.S. National Marine Fisheries Service would never have permitted transfer of a papilloma-infected whale into a sea pen in American waters. Even if Keiko's papilloma were cured, the NMFS would not have allowed him to enter a pen on the Pacific coast. He was an Atlantic whale that might exchange genes with Pacific females if he escaped.

For some considerable interim, then, Keiko would have to reside in a tank. Leasing a pool for the whale in a marine theme park was a possibility, but this would have inflamed the anticaptivity groups. Phillips scouted Marine World Africa USA in Vallejo, California, a site a few miles from his San Francisco office. He did not like what he saw. "The best we could have had there was one pool within a facility where all the other pools would be for animals jumping through hoops. We realized we were going to have to build our own."

The undertaking had grown too big for Earth Island Institute. In November 1994, with a $2 million grant from Warner Bros. and $2 million from an anonymous donor as seed money, Phillips founded the Free Willy Keiko Foundation and began an intensive search for a site for this new facility. He and his colleagues looked north, for the whale needed cold seawater, and they looked to the coast, for the cold seawater would have to be pumped in directly. A small community would be best, as Keiko needed space—a commodity scarce in big cities—and because his saviors had no time to push permits through some urban bureaucracy. The whale's blood work had come back indicating a compromised immune system. There was no time to relocate anywhere that required a lengthy environmental-impact study. After some consideration of Cape Cod, Phillips turned his attention to the Oregon Coast Aquarium, in the seaside town of Newport, near midpoint of the Oregon shoreline. The Newport aquarium was dedicated more to education than to entertainment, an emphasis that Phillips liked. It had no cetaceans and no performing creatures of any kind. Phillips's asssistant, Mark Berman, put in a call to Phyllis Bell, the aquarium director, asking if she would like a whale.

Bell at first was leery.

"We didn't want to get involved with cetaceans because they bring a lot of problems with them," she would say afterward. "Animal-rights activists, and all the controversy about whether or not killer whales should be in captivity. Plus, they're expensive to keep. We never planned to have whales or dolphins here. But we knew about the plight of Keiko. That same day I got a couple of our animal-husbandry people together and we talked about it. I called the chairman of my board. His initial reaction was no. But then he called me back later at home that same night and said, 'Let's go for it.' It was in the interests of helping the animal."

"They were cautious," Phillips remembers. "They were very concerned about the swamping of their whole image. People wouldn't want to go to the aquarium to see their jellyfish anymore; people would just go to see Keiko. But here was the deal: We offered to come in and build a $7.5 million facility, one hundred percent of which we would pay, and we would bring them, at no cost, a huge attraction—a *huge* attraction—the world's most famous whale. They didn't resist for very long. I think they began to see dollar signs, and a way to put Newport on the map, and being part of an exciting project."

Phillips threw himself into fundraising. He oversaw design and production of a Free Willy Keiko adoption kit. "Follow Keiko's adventure home," it read. "Adopt Keiko, star of *Free Willy,* and become part of the historic effort to return him to the wild." The kit cost $21.25 and it contained a personalized adoption certificate, a *Free Willy* movie poster, a bumper sticker, a "I Helped Free Willy" sticker set, an educational brochure, a Keiko Kids Club official membership card, and a return card for quarterly newsletters that would update the adopter on Keiko developments.

The Kids Club applicant was required to sign a pledge on the back of the membership card:

> I'm proud to be a member of the Free Willy/Keiko Foundation's Kids Club! I have adopted Keiko and share in his dream of freedom. I pledge to remain honorable and caring about all living creatures and to always strive to help them live peacefully in the wild. I will remain considerate of my actions and the impact that they have upon the natural world.

Keiko's lawyers drew up a Free Willy Keiko Foundation license agreement. The letterhead showed the foundation's logo, a leaping Keiko, and the agreement read:

> WHEREAS, licensor is the owner of Keiko, the orca whale, and has the rights to publicity with respect to the name and image of Keiko and is the owner of the registered trademarks set forth on Schedule A attached hereto (collectively, the "Rights");
> WHEREAS, licensee wishes to use the Rights in connection with its promotion and distribution of a children's story book and musical tape . . .

Or vinyl magnetic products, or dolls, or any number of other Keiko products.

With a company called Skybox International, Phillips worked out a deal for *Free Willy* trading cards. One Skybox trading card said "Help Willy find Jesse!" It showed Keiko entering one end of a maze and Jesse swimming in scuba gear at the other. As payment for its Free Willy Official Supporter sponsorship, Skybox International agreed to make a donation of $12,500 directly to the Free Willy Keiko Foundation within thirty days of signing the memo of agreement.

Order forms for Earth Island Donor Tiles flowed in. "Yes! Please accept my gift and place an engraved tile in my name on the wall of Keiko's new home!" A $250 gift got the donor his or her name on a three-by-six-inch tile. A $500 gift got the donor two lines of inscription on a six-by-six-inch tile, illustrated either by a smiling Keiko, or by an orca pair at play, or by bobbing orcas. A $1000 gift got the donor a twelve-by-twelve-inch tile. A $5000 gift got the donor three of the twelve-by-twelve tiles in a row—the "mural" option, which showed a whole orca pod sprinting.

For a nonrefundable advance of $3000 against royalties, payable to the Free Willy Keiko Foundation, Phillips granted a company called Fresh Tracks the right to market a Keiko book, toy, and T-shirt gift set in its "Nature Buddies, the toys you wear!" line. Fresh Tracks sent its ad copy to Phillips for approval. "Exciting new product tells the story of this famous animal through reading and play! Beautifully illustrated 100% cotton T-shirt with special ocean habitat pocket. Adorable, realistic soft toy Keiko that 'lives' in pocket habitat or comes out to play!"

While Phillips signed off on the bigger deals, his assistant Mark Berman sorted checks out of the mail.

"Dear Mark," wrote a girl named Allie from Peabody, Massachusetts, addressing Berman in San Francisco at "Earth Island Institute, 300 Broadway,

Sweet 28." "How is Keiko? Can I have some news letters. Me + Sara raised $2.75 but we don't know how to send it."

"Donations are up to $11.51," Lisa Paré, a teacher in Glendale, California, reported triumphantly. Ms. Paré sent photos of her kids in Bungalow 2, all wearing killer-whale T-shirts. She concluded, "Maybe you could steer me in the direction of how to help the pandas?"

Mark Berman, as he winnowed out $11.51 remittances, and David Phillips, as he scrawled his signature on Nature Buddies deals for soft, adorable, realistic Keiko toys, cannot have felt much like Henry Thoreau, John Muir, Rachel Carson, or any of the other great environmentalists who preceded them. But they had a vision of how the iconography of this one whale might serve all whales, and they forged ahead.

IN FEBRUARY 1995, ON THE shore of Yaquina Bay in Oregon, construction of Keiko's facility began. The foundations for the medical pool and its drain-down basin were laid. The backwash basin of the larger pool took shape, and the bottom drain, and the animal-care office. The public-view windows were framed in. Someday through these big windows a ceaseless procession of human faces would stare out at Keiko, and camera strobes would flash at him, but for now there was no glass. The empty windows framed no faces, just the crowns of conifers in the forest beyond. David Phillips and Dr. Lanny Cornell had determined to move Keiko to Oregon as soon as the facility was finished. The whale's health demanded it. The original completion date, December of 1995, was pushed off to January or February of 1996 by construction delays and bad weather. Dr. Cornell was not happy about the postponement:

> IN THE EARLY FALL OF 1995, I BEGAN TO FEEL VERY UNCOMFORT-
> ABLE WITH THE CONTINUED SLIDE IN KEIKO'S CLINICAL SIGNS AND
> BLOOD SAMPLES, WHICH WERE NOW TAKEN MONTHLY AT MY RE-
> QUEST. THE SAMPLES SHOWED A DROP IN HIS RED BLOOD CELLS, BUT
> WORSE, THE WHITE CELL COUNT BEGAN A CONTINUED RISE AND LEFT
> SHIFT MEANING HE WAS NOW ALSO INFECTED BY BACTERIA.

Lanny Cornell writes all his letters and e-mails in capital letters. His approach to literature is opposite that of Archy the Cockroach, who wrote everything in lowercase. Where Archy's lowercase paragraphs give him an appropriately small, insecty voice, Dr. Cornell's upper-case pronouncements give him the big, stentorian voice he seems to like. His missives read like Western Union telegrams, or like memos from some Roman centurion reporting from Carthage or Gaul.

FURTHER TESTING INDICATED THE INFECTION WAS SETTLING IN
HIS LUNGS. KEIKO NOW HAD PROGRESSIVE PNEUMONIA AS WELL AS
HIS OTHER PROBLEMS. REGULAR DISCUSSION WITH DAVE PHILLIPS
AND THE MEXICAN VETERINARIANS HAD ME CONVINCED WE MUST
SPEED UP THE POOL CONSTRUCTION SO WE WOULD STILL HAVE A LIVE
WHALE TO RESCUE.

As construction proceeded in Oregon, Keiko's people did what they
could to improve conditions for the whale in Mexico. Warner Bros. rented
chillers and sent them down to Reino Aventura, but cooling Keiko proved to
be a tricky undertaking. The whale shared his tank with four Pacific bottlenose dolphins—warm-water creatures who slough their skin when the
temperature drops too low. The first solution was to partition the pool with
Plexiglas, confining the bottlenose dolphins to the medical pool, in warm water, and exiling Keiko to cold water on the other side. Keiko was miserable in
solitary. He spent all his time with his nose to the Plexiglas, looking in at his
small friends. The four bottlenose dolphins, jammed now in the medical
pool, had less flipper room than ever, and they seemed to miss their big
cousin. The remedy was to remove the Plexiglas and split the temperature
difference, instead of splitting the space. Keiko and the dolphins were reunited in water warmer than is ideal for killer whales, cooler than is ideal for
bottlenose dolphins.

"If I'd known what the whole thing would turn into, I would have both
wanted to do it more, and not wanted to do it at all," says Phillips. "A combination of those two. Wanted to do it more, because it's been way more of
a potent thing than I ever could have imagined. Not wanted to do it at all,
because of the amount of time, and the number of players, and the com-
plexity and difficulty of it. Right from the first, it's been all-encompassing.
The amount of money we've had to raise! At every point it's been a combination of exhilaration and just overwhelming problems."

8

THE TAIL

DAVID PHILLIPS SWUNG A SPONSORSHIP DEAL WITH UNITED PARCEL SERVICE, which agreed to fly Keiko to Oregon gratis. UPS subcontracted the job to Southern Air Transport Service, hiring one of that company's C-130 cargo planes. The Southern Air fleet had a colorful history in Central America. In the 1980s the company, a CIA front, had flown weapons and supplies to Contra rebels in Nicaragua. In 1986 a "cargo-kicker" named Eugene Hasenfus, flying in a Southern Air Transport Service C-123, had been shot down over Nicaragua and captured by the Sandanistas. Hasenfus's confessions to his captors, and his little black book full of phone numbers, had helped verify the Iran-Contra connection and embarrass the Reagan administration.

For Keiko it was nice symmetry. Having flown into Mexico under a doctored manifest listing him as "furniture," he was flying out with another shady carrier in a plane repainted "United Parcel Service."

Among Keiko's people, rumor spread that the repainted plane was the same jinxed aircraft from which Hasenfus had bailed. This was *Fat Lady* herself, they said, the very plane which, pre-Hasenfus, had once been used by a Baton Rouge smuggler and DEA informant named Barry Seal, afterward assassinated, who had rigged it with hidden cameras to record the pickup of 1500 kilograms of cocaine. Keiko's team playfully reminded one another to look for hidden bundles of white powder as Keiko flew north across the border.

The dubious history of Southern Air did not trouble David Phillips. It was the least of his worries. Two weeks before liftoff, Keiko's latest blood work had come back from the lab, and the results had alarmed Dr. Cornell. The whale's health was in sharp decline. He needed to be rushed to his new facility, and any big cargo plane with wings would do.

IN KEIKO'S LAST DAYS IN Mexico, great crowds marched on Reino Aventura to bid him farewell. He averaged 20,000 visitors a day and his final performances were sold out. On Thursday, January 4, 1996, two days before his scheduled departure, the whale seemed to sense that something was up. He dogged it through that day's shows, refusing to dance to disco music as usual, and declining to catch mackerel tossed to him. He showed an uneasy

curiosity about the platforms that were being built around the pool to accommodate the crane that would extract him. "He knows something is happening," murmured his trainer, Karla Corral.

On Friday, January 5, two hundred journalists gathered poolside for a
press conference. They wrestled with the basic decision that would preoccupy all Keiko journalism for years to come: Should they play this ironic, or
play it straight? They toyed with various possibilities of wordplay—"blubber"
and "fluke" and "spout off." They considered the biblical possibilities—
Jonah, Leviathan, Ishmael. Tapping pencils against their teeth, they tried to
remember their Melville. Of all the news organizations in attendance, only
Life magazine and the Discovery Channel had been granted full access to the
whale and his people, having paid undisclosed fees for that privilege. The rest
of the press was a little disgruntled, yet they scribbled away dutifully.

On Saturday, January 6, Keiko's last day in Mexico, 27,000 Mexicans
filed by his tank in a tearful, bittersweet, thirteen-hour procession. In the
evening, the arena was cleared of pilgrims. At 9:30, by moonlight and the
glare of television kliegs, Keiko's trainers signaled him to enter the medical
pool, where his transport sling awaited him. Keiko balked. Who would not?
Who would not feel a certain malaise, after watching those lugubrious multitudes shuffle by him, hour upon hour, the weeping children, the morose
adults? Keiko must have felt like Lenin in his sarcophagus or some dead
pope. "Keiko, *entra*," Karla Corral urged him. The whale poked his rostrum
into the entrance, then backed off.

If Keiko's heart was not in this move, then neither was Karla's. She had
been persuaded that emigration from Mexico was the best thing for Keiko,
and she was consoled, somewhat, by the knowledge that she and Renata
would be living with the whale for his first months in the States, yet she was
sad all the same. She was not a believer in the long-term plan for the whale.
Rehabilitation made sense to her, but not release. "I don't think he'd get
along with orcas in the wild," she had told a reporter. "He's like a human.
He's too sensitive, too nice."

Renata Fernandez, Karla's colleague, took her turn at coaxing the whale
into the medical pool, with no better luck. Turning from the whale, Renata
and Karla squinted into the television lights. In their wetsuits, spotlit by the
kliegs, they looked like female convicts in a jailbreak. They asked that the
lights be dimmed. When the camermen obliged, the two women tried again
with Keiko. The whale could not be persuaded. Karla and Renata were replaced by a dozen men in wetsuits, some in the water, some on deck, who en-
circled the whale with a cork net and seined him toward the medical pool.

"Keiko is breathing heavily and spouts water from his blowhole," Steve

Mayes and Joan Laatz Jewett, reporters for *The Oregonian*, would report of this moment.

Whales do not spout water. What whales spout is air, in powerful blasts that atomize any moisture atop the blowhole and make an explosion of mist. But *The Oregonian* was correct in reporting that Keiko was breathing rapidly. The whale's two tankmates at the time, the bottlenose dolphins Lily and Pepe, swam anxious circles around him. Keiko lunged again and again at the mesh.

David Phillips watched nervously, his own respiration rate climbing.

"Lanny Cornell had told me that if Keiko decides he really doesn't want to do this, it won't happen," Phillips says. "If Keiko had really got the idea that he could bolt this net, or if he had made a *game* out of it, then we would have had the plane waiting on the runway, and the trucks, and cranes, and all the people, and the worldwide press, for nothing. All dressed up and nowhere to go."

Each time Keiko lunged at the net, the Mexican spectators clapped and cheered. They seemed to be interpreting those lunges as a vote for Mexico over Oregon. The cheering of the locals was understandable, but the international press cheered, too, and this applause surprised David Phillips. He was seized with doubt. *Are we really doing the right thing?*

At last Keiko entered the smaller pool. He was steered over a customized canvas sling, then secured in it, his pectoral fins protruding through openings tailored for them.

In *Free Willy*, the whale is simply loaded aboard a flatbed truck, like a very large sack of potatoes. In real life it is not so easy. Months of training had been required to habituate Keiko to the sling. Now, as the crane lifted him from his element, he did not forget those training sessions. He waved his pectorals slightly in the air, and he swung his flukes a few degrees from side to side, but he stayed calm. He was lowered to gain slack for a readjustment of the ropes. He was raised to test the adjustment. He was lowered again so that Karla and Renata could slather him with a greasy protective ointment. He was raised once more. Not once during this yo-yo treatment did he give in to the temptation to thrash. Finally, two minutes before midnight, to cheers and a fusillade of flashing camera strobes, the crane hoisted him high.

Keiko's vocalizing became audible to the crowd. Like the vocalizing of all whales, it seemed to arise from an overpressure. It sounded almost painful. It was as if some trumpeter, his cheeks ballooning, the veins standing out on his forehead, were trying to blow high notes with his fist jammed in the bell of the horn. Some reporters heard distress in the high-pitched whistling. "The

21-foot orca cries in high-pitched whimpers and flaps his flippers once, as if in a final good-bye," Mayes and Jewett reported.

Whimpers, perhaps. Good-bye, maybe. But we really do not know. No one has deciphered what whales mean by their vocalizing. Several of Keiko's phrases sounded like what American baseball fans call a "raspberry." The whimpers that *The Oregonian* reporters heard may have been, in fact, a rude noise directed down at the tepid, cramped, chlorinated pool. There is no union for performing killer whales; Keiko had logged 7800 unpaid performances down there, wasting eleven years of his life. That farewell flap of his pectoral fins may not have been good-bye, but good riddance. Maybe he was flippering Mexico off.

The whale hung suspended in a diminishing flicker of camera strobes, vocalizing, his tailstock and flukes dangling out the back of the sling, his bent dorsal fin showing above. A portion of killer-whale communication is above the range of human hearing. Some of what Keiko had to say that day was safe from misinterpretation by the press.

The two bottlenose dolphins, Lily and Pepe, must have struggled to understand the meaning of their friend's ascension. Their giant companion levitated above them in a nimbus of klieg lights, cruciform, his great pectoral fins outspread. His white underside was dazzling in the high-wattage kliegs, and his black zones scintillated with the flashes of camera strobes. Lily and Pepe, unlike the human witnesses, heard everything Keiko had to say. None of the vocalizations of the killer whale, *Orcinus orca,* are beyond the range of *Tursiops truncatus,* the bottlenose dolphin. Keiko himself spoke a little Tursiops. Perhaps he had some parting words for his friends.

At 12:15 on Sunday morning, the crane swung the whale away from his pool. For Lily and Pepe, Keiko's apotheosis was now complete. Earlier he had risen inexplicably to hover a short distance above the surface, in some sort of magical breach in which the whale goes up but does not come down. Then suddenly he had risen high. He had hung there, flooded with light, his great wings outspread, vocalizing from on high. Then he was gone. The night sky was empty. Lily and Pepe had been left behind. The pool's little pod of three was now just two.

The crane lowered Keiko into his shipping container, a long blue box which resembled, in size and shape, a cross between a Dumpster and a freight car. On loan from Sea World in San Diego, the container was orca-ready, twenty-seven feet long by seven feet high. Its exterior was covered in white bunting marked "Keiko Express" in big letters and "This End Up" in small. Its interior was half-filled with water and three thousand pounds of ice.

In *Free Willy,* a funny but unrealistic scene near the climax has the whale's rescuers interrupt their getaway, pull into a car wash, and use the car-wash hoses to cool him off. Whale experts laugh sourly at this scene. In the car-wash interlude, as in all road-trip segments of the movie, the animatronic whale stood in for Keiko. Had the real, flesh-and-blood whale played these scenes himself, he would have quickly gone hyperthermic. To avoid meltdown in transport, a real whale requires ice.

At one-thirty on Sunday morning, January 7, 1996, Keiko's caravan set off for the airport. The flight had been scheduled for the wee hours because the pilots wanted to fly in the cool of the night, when the thin air of Mexico City was densest, the better to lift the wings of their Hercules C-130 and its eighteen tons of load. David Phillips and his faction preferred the middle of the night, as well, for the streets figured to be deserted then.

The route was supposed to be secret, but word had leaked out. The roadsides and overpasses were lined with thousands of well-wishers. Twenty police motorcycles and fifty police cars escorted the whale in his eighteen-wheeler. A fleet of official vehicles preceded his truck, and an unofficial comet's tail of battered, honking sedans and pickups followed. David Phillips, riding in a marshal's car that was tailgating Keiko's truck, noticed that some of the motorcycle policemen had brought along their children, whose small hands gripped their fathers' waists from behind. Ah, we're going the *parade* route, he thought.

There had been a small betrayal. Reino Aventura and the Mexican authorities had seemed to buy into the concept of deserted streets, but there had been, it seemed, a separate Mexican agenda all along. One of the members of Reino Aventura's board of directors was head of Televisa, the biggest television company in Mexico, and Phillips guesses that this mogul wanted drama and a circus.

"It was amazing," Phillips says. "It was a spectacle. They had this huge, like, Keiko doll, up on an overpass, swinging back and forth like something out of Disneyland. There was a fair amount of inebriation—some fairly wasted Mexicans screaming on the sidelines as we drove by. The police weren't controlling the crowds at all. They were whooping it up. They were part of the party."

As the mob thickened, Phillips jumped from the car and joined the staff atop Keiko's container, helping push back Mexicans who were attempting to climb the sides. He left his satchel, which contained his passport, behind in the car. He and his colleagues pried Mexican hands off the top edge of the container, besieged on all sides, like medieval warriors defending a battlement. The fifteen miles to the airport, which Phillips had guessed would take ten minutes, took two hours.

The caravan made fitful progress. Keiko's truck braked abruptly, lurched forward, braked again. The whale, traveling in his slush of ice, like a martini on the rocks, was stirred, not shaken, but not everyone in his retinue was so lucky. The smoky jalopies and trucks and taxis made a kind demolition derby in his wake. "In one five-minute period, four collisions occur," Kenneth Miller would report in *Life*. "Two people are injured, but no whales." The video cameras of the Discovery Channel and Televisa sought out individual faces of interest: a weeping boy, a man in a killer-whale suit, a distraught woman waving a sign professing her love for Keiko. The fervor had a peculiarly Latin flavor. The mood seemed almost devotional—the sort of emotion you see in the throngs around a church where the Virgin has appeared in a water stain. Mexico had been harshly criticized by the world press for its care of the whale—the word "abuse" recurred often in news accounts—but there was no denying that Mexico loved this whale.

A crowd of several hundred Mexicans was waiting at the airport gates. A security guard, unimpressed by the police escort, stepped forward to halt the procession, and this holdup allowed the trailing mob to catch up, even as the crowd at the gate surged forward. "It was not a great scene at the airport," Phillips testifies. "We had to peel off dozens of Mexicans who kept trying to climb in Keiko's tank. This was not exactly part of my normal job description."

The guard relented finally, allowing the truck to pass through the gates.

"We had been promised a roller truck," says Phillips. "A roller truck is supposed to be a truck with rollers built into it. *That's what a roller truck is.* It's a pretty standard piece of equipment for loading freight in airports. We're, like, 'Where's the roller truck?' So they showed us. Their roller truck was a flatbed truck with a bunch of loose metal pipes on top."

The makeshift roller truck succeeded in conveying Keiko's container halfway into the belly of the C-130, but there one of the loose rollers jammed. Airport workers struggled for an hour to free the container. Dr. Lanny Cornell, the world's most experienced transporter of killer whales, watched this spectacle until he had seen enough, then stepped forward and took command. After two hours the stuck roller was freed up; the whale rolled into the plane.

The C-130 lifted off the tarmac, and Keiko finally left the crowd behind. The cargo bay was empty except for two veterinarians, Dr. Cornell and Dr. José Luis Solórzano, the whale's Mexican physician. The Discovery Channel had chartered a plane for the film crew and Keiko's trainers, Karla and Renata. David Phillips, the whale's new owner, hitched a ride on this chase plane.

Only now, as he entered the cabin, did Phillips realize he had forgot his passport, having left his satchel behind in the marshal's car. The environmentalist, having spent months smoothing the way for the whale's entry into the United States, had now screwed up his own. The Discovery Channel had hired a handler, a fixer, and this man got to work on Phillips's little difficulty, phoning Washington in flight. In Phoenix, customs agents boarded and worked their way back to Phillips, who had slunk off to the last seat. Just ahead of him, Karla and Renata handed over their passports. Both Mexican women were legal; it was Phillips who was undocumented. When the agents reached him, he admitted he had no passport. Driver's license? No. Picture identification? Sorry. They asked him his name. "David Phillips," he said. At this, the agents nodded, turned, and left the aircraft. It would not be the last time that Phillips was surprised by the political clout of his whale.

The weight of the container, water, and whale limited the fuel the C-130 could carry, forcing the plane to refuel in Monterrey, Mexico, and Phoenix, Arizona. On the ground in Phoenix, the pilot received reports of heavy rain in Oregon. He informed Keiko's people that he might not be able to land in Newport, as the weather there was outside Federal Aviation Administration (FAA) limits for the C-130. Dr. Cornell explained to the pilot that while the plane and its human passengers could be diverted to another airport, the only possible destination for Keiko was Newport. David Phillips, from the chase plane, called UPS and the FAA on a conference call to make the same point. The captain was not persuaded that he should violate FAA rules and risk his aircraft. While the C-17 waited on the ground for the weather to improve in Oregon, the thermodynamic whale melted the last of his ice and began to overheat. Dr. Cornell ordered a water change and a couple of thousand pounds of ice. He called Phyllis Bell at the aquarium and told her to instruct the tower operator in Newport that under no circumstances should he use the words *rain* or *wet runway* in communicating with this pilot. The veterinarian, joining in on the conference call with UPS and the FAA, volunteered that if nobody else had the stomach for it, *he* would land the damn plane.

"We later found out," Dr. Cornell would write in his year-end report, "that the pilot was junior in seniority with Southern Air and that a more confident senior pilot would not have even asked the question, but would have done the right thing and taken us to Newport without any problem, regardless of the FAA rules. The captain of a ship, it seems, is still the final deciding factor while under way."

It is hard to miss Dr. Cornell's satisfaction at learning that this one old verity, at least, has survived.

IT HAD BEEN RAINING ALL day in Newport, Oregon, when Keiko landed, just before three in the afternoon. Three hundred journalists had been awaiting the delayed flight for hours beside the runway. Newspapers from Japan, Germany, and England had sent reporters. *The Wall Street Journal* and *Inside Edition* were represented. A BBC video team was on hand, and television crews from Australia and Finland. Keiko's container was offloaded into a new UPS truck, which made its way in a caravan down U.S. 101 to the aquarium. The "Keiko Express" bunting, decorated with the logos of sponsors, had crumpled a bit around the container during the struggles to load it on the plane in Mexico, and in the course of the flight. Several trainers and staff rode standing along the sides. Dr. Lanny Cornell sat on top, keeping an eye on the whale, riding into Newport resolute and unsmiling, like Scipio Africanus returning in triumph from Spain, or Gaius Lutatius Catulus back from the Punic Wars.

The crowds that greeted the whale were much smaller than the hordes that had seen him off in Mexico. Newport is not a megalopolis like Mexico City; it is just a small seaside town. Scattered clusters of Oregonians, wearing rain gear, stood under umbrellas on the shoulders of the road, smiling and waving at the UPS truck as it went by. A few held up "Welcome Keiko" and "I love Keiko" signs. An eleven-year-old in a killer-whale suit, Ashley Berg, a sixth-grader in Newport Middle School, waved from the edge of the pavement. Ashley's grandmother, owner of an espresso stand on the highway, had paid the girl three dollars an hour to don the Keiko costume and shill out front of the shop. There was none of the Latin hysteria of this morning; but then no one in Oregon knew Keiko yet. No part of him was visible above the top of the container. That a killer whale really rode inside had to be accepted on faith.

Under the overcast skies, the headlights of the caravan glistened on the rain-wet blacktop. The climate of coastal Oregon in winter is vaguely Icelandic—cool and gray and rainy. For the first time since calfhood, Keiko was at sea level. The atmospheric pressure was holding at the maritime constant, 1000 millibars, as it had held when he was young. Maybe the very weight of the air here was nostalgic for him.

Spectators and press had massed outside Keiko's new tank. The *Today* show and *CBS This Morning* had set up to broadcast live from tankside. The flight delays had ruined that, and all the reporters, television and print, had been waiting in the rain for hours, but spirits were good. As the truck arrived in late afternoon, a roar went up. The crew set about connecting the crane cables to Keiko's sling. By the time they finished, darkness had fallen. A cannonade of camera strobes illuminated the whale as the crane lifted him from his container and hoisted him high. Keiko held perfectly still. He made no gesture of his pectoral fins, and he kept his tailfin cocked at a slight angle, exactly the attitude in which it had left the container. It was as if Keiko knew a fifty-foot fall to concrete would kill him. The day had been far longer than anyone planned. The whale had now been nineteen hours out of water, yet his remarkable forbearance was holding up. As the crane passed him over the yellow railing atop his tank wall, he was tranquil. At twenty feet above the pool's surface, his nerves were fine. At ten feet, no problem. Then at six feet, he suddenly lost it and began to thrash his flukes.

The cameras of *The Free Willy Story,* the Discovery Channel documentary, caught this failure of the whale's Zenlike calm—this revelation that Keiko was only human. "The noise and bright lights seem to stir him," the film's narrator observed. "Or perhaps it's the sight and smell of the salt water."

Not smell, for whales lack that sense. But sight, surely, and sound, and moments later, touch, for the tips of his pectoral fins dipped into the pool.

The crane was lowering Keiko just off the edge of the shallow shelf called the "slide-out," where crewmembers could stand in gumboots and assist. One man, crouching, took a huge pectoral fin and held it delicately, looking about him anxiously, not quite sure what to do with it. Whale-lowering is not a maneuver that can be choreographed down to the smallest details, for the whale's behavior is too gigantic a variable. Another man, to steady Keiko, gently but firmly clasped both hands around his flailing tail-stock at the waist, where it flared into the flukes. It was like trying to waltz with a wrecking ball. Had this good Samaritan not let go, he would have been flung halfway across the pool. He made several tentative gestures at the flukes again, like a man trying to break up fighting mastiffs. His heart was not in it.

In *Moby Dick,* Chapter LXXXVI, "The Tail," Herman Melville describes the "dense webbed bed of welded sinews" that compose the tailfin, which he likens, in the tripartite structure of its layers, to a Roman wall. "But as if this vast local power in the tendinous tail were not enough," he adds, "the whole bulk of the Leviathan is knit over with a warp and woof of muscular fibers and filaments, which passing on either side the loins and running down into the flukes, insensibly blend with them, and largely contribute to their might; so that in the tail the confluent measureless force of the whole whale seems concentrated to a point. Could annihilation occur to matter, this were the thing to do it."

The man who had tried to waltz with annihilation now retreated. His place was taken by another crewman, who crouched close to Keiko and tried to free a guide rope snagged under the flukes. The flukes, which had been swinging mostly from side to side, now snapped straight back at the man, who flinched away just in time. Dropping the rope, he made a strategic withdrawal himself.

Nolan Harvey, Keiko's new head trainer, took up a position at the back edge of the sling. A stocky man in a wet suit and ponytail, Harvey had years of experience with killer whales at Sea World. He kept one eye on the steel cable—always so treacherous in unpredictable situations—and the other eye on the swinging flukes. Ducking a left hook of the flukes, he lost his footing on the edge of the slide-out. For an instant he fought for balance, then gave up and dived beneath the giant hammock of the sling, coming up on the other side. He swam back a stroke to free the rope caught under Keiko's flukes, flipping the line so that it lay atop the tailfin. Then he swam to the sling, hoisted himself in, and put a reassuring hand on Keiko's flank.

The crane abruptly baptized the whale, sinking the belly of his sling several feet deep. The water seemed to calm Keiko. He ceased flailing his tailfin and let it dangle straight down in the cool pool. The cables went slack, for their load was now buoyant, and the release of tension allowed the purse of the sling to open. Nolan Harvey fell across Keiko's hind parts, reached for the spar of the sling on the opposite side, and pushed it away from him, opening the sling wider. Another trainer tried the same thing forward. Keiko, drawing more water, began to heel over to port. This was not quite anticipated, apparently. For a moment it seemed that his bent dorsal fin might snag in the port cables. The forward trainer, climbing and dog-paddling up the black hill of Keiko toward the trouble spot, had nearly made it to the summit when Keiko rolled violently under him, flashing his white belly at the sky. The trainer flew away like a rodeo rider, only faster, bucked off by a bull weighing seven thousand pounds. He disappeared in a welter of spray.

It was a scene from scrimshaw. On the teeth of sperm whales, the old Nantucketers had etched scenes just like this: the whitewater explosions, the foam, the men overboard, the whaleboats staved in by flukes, the harpooners nine-ironed into the sky.

For an instant, Keiko's Nantucket sleigh ride was stationary. He was going nowhere, hung up on the sling. Then with four savage strokes of his flukes—right, left, right, left—he blasted himself forward out of the sling. The flukes, only half-submerged, met diminished water resistance and came frighteningly fast, all four beats in less than a second. His struggles had twisted him so that his white underside showed uppermost. Out of the tumult, his white tail rose in the air. Where, a moment before, the beating flukes had been almost too fast for the eye to follow, now suddenly everything slowed. Keiko's propeller was out of the water, and his power of locomotion briefly left him. The upraised white flukes seemed to come to a stop.

"In no living thing are the lines of beauty more exquisitely defined than in the crescentic borders of these flukes," Melville wrote. "Excepting the sublime *breach,* this peaking of the whale's flukes is perhaps the grandest sight to be seen in all animated nature."

Keiko's flukes peaked only for an instant, then gravity asserted itself and his white tailstock was moving again, sliding underwater, pulling the white crescentic blades of the flukes after it. The most beautiful shape in nature disappeared without a ripple beneath the cold, clean seawater of Keiko's new home.

9

MONA LISA

UNDER THE SURFACE, KEIKO'S NEW POOL WAS A LUMINOUS, OTHERWORLDLY blue from the glare of the several klieg lights above. The water was beautiful but alien, like a night sea on some planet with multiple moons. Keiko's flukes peaked and slipped under, and for an instant he hung sideways in the water, stunned and disoriented. A trout will momentarily drift like this, on being unhooked and tossed back in. A newborn killer whale suffers the same limp moment, shocked by cold water and the profound surprise of its crossing into a new universe. The killer-whale mother must sometimes nudge her calf upward for its first breath. Keiko did not need that lesson—he was sixteen or seventeen—yet there was something newborn and calflike, more reflexive than willed, in the way he instantly bounced up for a quick blow. Curving back under, he appeared to come to his senses. He began to swim.

The neck vertebrae of whales are fused for stability, allowing greater power in the swimming stroke. This cervical fusion helps a killer whale do thirty knots, but it makes for a very stiff neck. The serpentine ballets, the dervish dances, the self-knotting acrobatics of sea lions and sea otters— creatures so fluid underwater that they seem to be spineless—are not possible for *Orcinus orca*. Yet the necks of killer whales are not absolutely inflexible. The head can crane infinitesimally upward to look to the surface or down to the depths. It can tilt sideways marginally, in curiosity, when it is puzzled by something ahead. It can nod in warning, or nod in play, as it nods in the goofy, gallumphing, hobbyhorse swimming stroke that is the dolphin equivalent of skipping. The very subtlety of these constrained movements makes them eloquent. Keiko, as he explored his new home, craned and tilted and cast about him in this minimal yet expressive way, taking everything in.

The producers of *The Free Willy Story: Keiko's Journey Home,* the Discovery Channel film, had a cameraman in scuba gear waiting for Keiko. This diver swam after the whale, and through his lens, in the finished documentary, we follow behind Keiko's pumping flukes as he cruises along the wall of his pool. He approaches one of the big public-view windows. Here the filmmakers add a nice touch, an abrupt change in viewpoint: We are no longer trailing the whale, we are *inside* him, getting Keiko's perspective—a whale's-eye view—as the camera looks in through the glass of the viewing window.

In the visitors' gallery, rows of kids wave at Keiko. Posed in front of them, standing shoulder to shoulder, are two generals of the children's crusade to rehabilitate the whale: David Phillips, founder of the Free Willy Keiko Foundation, and Phyllis Bell, director of the Oregon Coast Aquarium. Between them, these two will share responsibility for Keiko in Oregon.

The filmmakers have taken a few liberties. Where normally the visitors' gallery is kept dark, here the rows of children and the two adults are illuminated by klieg lights for the sake of the camera. The children are waving on cue, and they are waving a bit manically. In real life, visitors seldom wave at Keiko, and when they do, the gesture is much more minimal and shy. But some staging is necessary even in documentaries. First Phyllis Bell, then David Phillips waves cheerily at Keiko, welcoming him to his new home. From the apparent solidarity of this pair, one would guess that all the feuding over the whale is finally over.

Something odd in Phillips's expression caused me to stop my copy of the video, rewind, and look again.

David Phillips is not a rabidly social animal, like a dolphin. At meetings and parties he tends to drift off into private calculations. Here at the aquarium he seems to have drifted off again. For a brief moment he misses his cue. The children are waving manically, Phyllis Bell is smiling broadly, Phillips remains off somewhere in the land of his thoughts. Perhaps he is thinking of that satchel he left in Mexico City, with his passport in it. Perhaps he is wondering whether this Keiko project is really such a good idea. Suddenly he returns from his reverie. He remembers to smile. A peculiar, veiled gleefulness comes into his smile, as if he is trying not to laugh.

The smile arrested me. Rewinding the tape again, I set out to deconstruct it, like a Renaissance scholar deciphering *Mona Lisa*. First, I unwilled my suspension of disbelief. I forced myself to remember that it was not really a *whale* Phillips was regarding; it was a cameraman in a wetsuit. I figured that some trace of this cameraman must show reflected on the window glass. Sure enough, upon rewinding the video again, I saw bubbles from a scuba regulator rising in dim reflection on the pane. I had missed them the first time.

The underwater filmmaker Stan Minasian, a coproducer of *The Free Willy Story,* had shot some of the underwater scenes in this Oregon tank. I knew, because Minasian himself had told me so. Minasian is an environmentalist, the president of the Animal Fund, in San Francisco, and a man I have known for many years. David Phillips has known him even longer. In this scene at the aquarium, I was certain, Phillips was trying to stifle his grin at the irony: The "Keiko" at whom he was waving was an old friend with whom he had shared many campaigns and beers.

At the next opportunity, I proposed my theory of his enigmatic smile to Phillips. He laughed at my detective work. My theory was correct, he said, but only so far as it went. Yes, Stan Minasian had been the cameraman. Yes, Phillips had been amused by the charade of waving at an old friend standing in for the whale. But there was more. As Minasian hung outside the window, finning in place and aiming his camera through the glass, the real Keiko had grown curious. Approaching Minasian from the rear, the whale had suddenly loomed above and behind him, peering in over his shoulder, gigantic and inquisitive and displaying a tremendous erection.

BOOK TWO
OREGON

10

BILLIONAIRE

On Monday, Keiko's first full day in Oregon, the line began form-ing outside the Oregon Coast Aquarium at seven in the morning, three hours before opening time. Battalions of Oregon kids cut school for the occasion, and hundreds of adults skipped work. Average winter attendance at the aquarium on Mondays was about two hundred. On Monday, January 8, 1996, 2552 paying customers walked through the turnstiles, the first of what would become a great migration. The gift shop was jammed with shoppers buying Keiko tote bags, Keiko T-shirts, Keiko dolls, "I love Keiko" pins. Whale paraphernalia of all sorts—orca mailboxes, rubber orca puppets, plas-tic bottlenose dolphins—was selling. There was some spillover trade in baleen whales even, with blue-whale, fin-whale, and humpback products moving. "Welcome Keiko" signs were up everywhere outside the restaurants and tourist shops on the bay front, and the town was awash in Keiko sou-venirs and whale gifts. The Hotel Newport, the Econo Lodge, the Shiloh Inn, the La Quintana Inn, the Days Inn, and Newport's other hotels and bed and breakfasts, normally ghost inns in winter, were booked up. They were rapidly running out of rooms for weekends many months in advance.

The town of Newport was thrilled, but for Keiko's inner circle the eu-phoria was brief.

"The good news," says David Phillips, "was that we'd taken this heroic step and got the whale to Newport and this beautiful new facility, two mil-lion gallons, ozone treatment for the water, state of the art. The bad news was we were two and a half million dollars in debt. We didn't have enough money to pay the contractor. We'd gotten Keiko there on a wing and a prayer."

Warner Bros. had contributed a million dollars toward the facility at the start, which the Humane Society had matched. An anonymous donor had contributed two million. Phillips with his own fund appeals and adoption kits had raised a million more. Warner Bros. had promised that if Phillips's anonymous donor would put in an additional million and a half, then the movie studio would pony up the remainder needed to pay off the contractor. This understanding never got committed to paper, unfortunately. With the good news of Keiko's imminent move to Oregon, the Keiko problem—bad publicity—receded, and so did the studio's incentive to contribute.

"The contractor didn't want to stop construction on the pool when the world's kids were all waiting for Keiko to be moved," says Phillips. "Nobody wanted to be the one that pulled the plug. We'd moved him there, and the press cameras were all rolling, and it was exciting, and the whale was swimming and eating and vocalizing, and we were all real happy, *but the very next day* I remember sitting there with these glum-faced contractors and aquarium people, and everybody was just, really, like, majorly tweaked over the fact that we had no money and we owed so much."

It is hard to blame the contractor, Western States Construction, for feeling majorly tweaked. The company did not regard itself as a charity and it had a payroll to meet. The major tweak for the Oregon Coast Aquarium was that the contractor, if unpaid, would place a lien on the aquarium. The Oregon Coast Aquarium was funded by bonds; a lien would jeopardize those bonds and threatened the very existence of the institution.

"But all in all," says Phillips, cheerily, "in almost every case where something good could have happened with Keiko, versus something really bad happening, something good has happened. The day after the move, we sat down with Craig McCaw's people, and they said Craig wanted to help more."

Craig Oliver McCaw, the dyslexic billionaire cell-phone genius, was Phillips's anonymous donor. McCaw's corporate lieutenants outlined a new plan, which required that all involved parties would get squeezed a bit. The sweetheart deal enjoyed by the Oregon Coast Aquarium—a $7.5 million facility on their campus for free—was in fact too good to be true, and would be revised. The aquarium would have to contribute a significant percentage of its gate. Craig McCaw would then, in the words of his lieutenants, "heavy up" on Warner Bros. to persuade them to honor their oral commitment. The Free Willy Keiko Foundation, for its part, would have to open up its board. Craig McCaw would become chairman, with the power to appoint a majority of directors. If McCaw was to be the major contributor to the Keiko project, McCaw wanted control.

"Phyllis Bell pissed and moaned," says Phillips, "but her attendance was so off the charts. There were a million people lined up outside the door of her aquarium. Those people weren't going to any *other* exhibit. Everybody knew that Keiko was a huge draw."

Time Warner, owner of Warner Bros., was not happy, either. Jerry Levin, Time Warner's head, had begun to feel like Ahab, cursed by this whale. Levin agreed to be shaken down, but on the condition that Keiko fundraisers never come back begging for another dime. The people at the Free Willy

Keiko Foundation, faced with a takeover by the forces of McCaw, were un-easy as well.

"There was a lot of skepticism," says Phillips. "There were people on my board—Ani Moss, Craig Van Note—in fact, *all* of my people on the board, they were like, 'Who are these majority people going to be? What do they want to do? Are they just a bunch of *suits*? Money grubbers?'"

CRAIG MCCAW WAS BORN IN Centralia, Washington, in 1949, the second of four sons of Marion Oliver McCaw, an accountant, and the radio-and-televi-sion tycoon John Elroy McCaw. The elder McCaw was a man comfortable with risk—incurring heavy debt was tonic for him, good for his nerves. What he really loved was dealmaking; he was not much interested in operational details of the companies he acquired. In the course of his career, J. Elroy Mc-Caw bought and sold dozens of radio and television stations. His luck would last exactly to the end of his life, and scarcely a minute longer.

Craig McCaw and his brothers grew up in the Boeing Mansion, a histor-ical landmark in the Highlands district of Seattle. The family had servants and cooks, but J. Elroy did not spoil his boys, putting all four to work as teenagers at one of his small cable television companies. They learned liter-ally from the ground up, selling subscriptions door-to-door, stringing cable, climbing poles. J. Elroy sold them a tiny system of two thousand subscribers in exchange for preferred stock in the company. Just as a lion brings its cubs a little antelope to learn on, the tycoon tossed the two thousand subscribers to his lads. Craig McCaw proved to be the cub who showed the most apti-tude and he took the lead in managing the company.

"I'm very dyslexic," McCaw would tell an interviewer, much later. "That forced me to be quite conceptual, because I'm not very good at details. And be-cause I'm not good at details, I tend to be rather spatial in my thinking, oriented to things in general terms, rather than the specific. That allows you to step back. You become very quick, very intuitive in understanding what the point is."

Dyslexia forced McCaw to work extra hard in prep school. He felt him-self different, he had the drive of the outsider, and of the four brothers, he took the strongest interest in learning his father's business. In 1962, when J. Elroy sold one of his radio stations, he sent Craig, then thirteen, alone to the bank to deposit the $10 million. Craig matriculated at Stanford, where he studied history, laboring to master texts that came easily to others and run-ning his brothers' little cable company from his dorm room on the side.

In 1969, visiting home as a nineteen-year-old sophomore, Craig found his father dead of a stroke in the mansion. It was only now, with J. Elroy gone, that Marion McCaw and her children discovered the true height of her husband's mountain of debt—it was Rainier-like—and the true depth of his disdain for documentation. When creditors and the IRS descended, Craig took a year off from college to help his mother liquidate the estate. The Mc-Caws auctioned off assets, including the mansion. They were left flat broke—with just $2 million in life insurance and a single company, Twin Cities Cablevision, in Centralia, which J. Elroy had left to his boys in trust. On returning to Stanford, Craig ran Twin Cities from his dorm room. From that Centralia system—the only sapling left standing in the clearcut forest of the McCaw empire—he determined to regrow the family fortunes. On graduation, he began borrowing, McCaw-like, against Twin Cities and bought small cable outfits in remote parts of the Northwest. He improved programming, cut costs, raised rates, quadrupled revenues, and octupled cash flow.

In the early 1980s, the infant cellular telephone market caught McCaw's attention and he began to research it. Convinced that local permits sold by the FCC were greatly underpriced, he started bidding on them. He sold shares in his cable company, McCaw Communications, to buy up cellular licenses. The "Baby Bells," those dragon's teeth that had sprung up after the breakup of AT&T, assumed that the newborn cell-phone business would fall to them, but they soon discovered that McCaw and his backwoods cable company had preempted them in strategic markets—San Francisco, Denver, Pittsburgh, Minneapolis. McCaw borrowed heavily to buy more licenses—Los Angeles, Houston, Dallas, Philadelphia, New York—and the pieces of a national network fell into place. In 1986, he acquired the cellular and paging business of MCI Communications for $122 million. He and his brothers sold their cable business, McCaw Communicatons, for $755 million, putting all their assets and effort into McCaw Cellular, which was now the industry leader. McCaw's debts were horrendous. His revenues soared. His subscriber base exploded. In 1990, he personally earned $54 million, becoming the nation's highest-paid CEO. In 1994, he and his brothers sold Mc-Caw Cellular to AT&T for $11.5 billion.

"His brain is wired differently," David Phillips says of the billionaire. "It's funny that Craig should have turned out to be a communications wizard, because he's a terrible communicator."

This visionary who, more than anyone, introduced the nation to the cellular telephone seldom made use of that device himself. He did all his business through intermediaries. He often expected his subordinates to intuit his wishes. He was shy in public and seldom allowed himself to be photographed. When he agreed, rarely, to an interview or a public-speaking engagement, his ideas often struck interviewer or audience as disjointed, his exposition as nonlinear. Sometimes his divergent narrative threads would weave together at the end in some unexpected and brilliant conclusion. Other times they would not. He had a reputation for blowing punch lines. A punch line comes best at the end of the joke. If it surfaces any earlier, through dyslexic rearrangement of the elements, it almost always ruins the laugh.

After selling out to AT&T, McCaw had time and billions on his hands. He fooled around in his retirement with several enterprises, among them Nextlink, which sold fiber-optic services to small businesses, and Nextel, a radio-dispatch business he wanted to retool with digital wireless technology. The $10 million of the Keiko project was an insignificant investment, compared to these. Nextlink and Nextel, in their turn, were small potatoes compared to the project at the center of his attention, an enterprise he called Teledesic, which had a circumference considerably larger than the planet itself. Teledesic would be an extraterrestrial internet: a galaxy of 840 satellites in low orbit, bouncing signals between any and all points on the planetary surface, with the speed and capacity of fiber-optic cable. The configuration was saturnine, except that the rings were not just equatorial; they were global: an artificial ring system, 21 rings of 40 satellites each, all 840 circling the planet at an altitude of 435 miles. Many fewer satellites would have been required if the system were in geosynchronous earth orbit, at an altitude of 22,300 miles—a geosynchronous satellite has line-of-sight to much more of the planet's surface—but 22,300 miles was too high. It would mean some milliseconds of delay in transmission, up and down, and this would sharply reduce the volume of information transmittable.

In the ocean of space, each Teledesic satellite would have its own little pod, for it would be linked electronically to its eight neighbor satellites in a geodesic pattern. As the Teledesic customer rotated eastward under the rings, the satellite would hand off the signal to its nearest neighbor or to the next ring. If any adjustments in course or altitude became necessary, a little blow-hole in each satellite would spout microscopic particles of Teflon to push the signal in the right direction. The costs of Teledesic would be astronomical, but so would the profits, if such a system could ever be built. The scheme was so crazy and grandiose and expensive that there was no possibility of competition, and McCaw counted on that.

"Talk about having your head out there in the stars," muses David Phillips. "I had a conversation once with Craig in which he said that this whole satellite thing was predicated on software that was still at least ten years in the future. Designing the software necessary for these signals to be passed from one satellite to the other was way, way advanced stuff that nobody had figured out yet."

IF THE BOARD MEMBERS OF the Free Willy Keiko Foundation worried about a McCaw takeover, then so did the larger environmental and animal-rights communities. With an environmentalist like Phillips running the show, those communities were confident that rehabilitation and release of the whale were the true goals. But what was the real intent of a tycoon like McCaw? Was he just a front, perhaps, for the Alliance of Marine Mammal Parks and Aquariums? Was he part of a cabal whose real purpose was to get Keiko into Sea World?

One thing that troubled Keiko's people was that none of them understood the source of McCaw's interest in the whale. Was the billionaire, an outsider since childhood, moved by Keiko's solitude? Was his dyslexia somehow involved? (Keiko was not dyslexic, exactly, but he was certainly nonlexic; did McCaw feel some sort of fraternity with that sort of nonverbal intelligence?) One school of thought held that all this sort of speculation was misaddressed, that the prime mover was not Craig McCaw at all, but Wendy McCaw, his wife.

"I had to convince myself," says Phillips, "that what he wanted to do was consistent with what we wanted to do. And I had to be clear on what the alternative was. The alternative basically was me having to raise all the money, the extra two million and all the future expenses for Keiko's release, in ten- and twenty-dollar chunks. Which would have meant that I would spend a good part of the next two or three years fundraising."

McCaw's brain was wired differently, Phillips thought, but he liked the man and somehow trusted him. And there was really no choice. Phillips and his board agreed to the McCaw proposal, surrendering control of the whale. McCaw replaced Phillips with a new executive director, Beverlee Hughes, but kept him on the Free Willy Keiko Foundation board and its executive committee.

"There was some regret," Phillips concedes. "I had been totally calling all the shots until that point. There were lots of emotions in it. There was an element of relief, because now there would be a whole team of people working on the day-to-day stuff. There was some fear. Because I felt we'd done a pretty damn good job. We had brought it this far, and we had a responsibility to make sure it was done right."

The McCaw empire was built on the Mongol model—acquired founders and CEOs were almost invariably beheaded—and occasionally Phillips caught McCaw's corporate officers eyeing him oddly.

"You don't realize, when Craig takes over a company, all the people that are associated with it are purged," one talkative McCaw lieutenant told him. "He doesn't believe in holdovers. You don't realize how unusual it is for you to be around."

If the McCaw empire ran on Mongol principles, then it also ran on the intuitions of the emperor. In the case of Phillips, McCaw's instincts seem to have led him to abandon his normal Genghis Khan approach and spare the environmentalist's head.

On the matter of McCaw's intuitive approach, the same talkative Mc-Caw lieutenant filled Phillips in on a second occasion.

"Between you and me," he told the environmentalist, "Craig can have some of most godawful, worst ideas. But then he'll come up with some idea that will make more money than God. Among all these clunker ideas, he'll come up with something that is so far beyond, and so right, that it just blows everybody off the board."

Which sort of idea the billionaire had for Keiko, clunker or brilliant, remained to be seen.

11

BLOWHOLED BEHEMOTH

KEIKO'S ARRIVAL IN OREGON WAS A WINDFALL FOR THE STATE'S NEWSPAPERS, resurrecting a species of Wild West journalism that had nearly gone extinct. Left-coast reporters had not had so much fun with an animal story since Samuel Clemens wrote up his jumping frog.

In *Willamette Week,* Matt Buckingham gave in to the alliterative impulse. "Phil Hutchinson, executive director of the Newport Chamber of Commerce, says the blowholed black-and-white behemoth has put his city on the map," he wrote.

"Another Senate candidate spouts off," wrote David Sarasohn in *The Oregonian.* "With just two days left until the March 12 filing deadline, and after the abandonment of the U.S. Senate race by Rep. Peter DeFazio and Attorney General Ted Kulongoski, political reporters were not surprised to be invited to Newport Monday for a special announcement from Keiko. Finally, a Democratic Senate candidate who can make a splash. In a primary that lacks a real heavyweight, Keiko seems ideally positioned. A major Oregon media figure, he's been on local TV more than the weather."

On February 28, 1996, in a prophetic *Willamette Week* column he called "Moby Dicked," Matt Buckingham put his finger on what would become the principal controversy of the whale's residence in Oregon. "The truth is," Buckingham wrote, "Keiko has about as much chance of leaving the aquarium at Newport as Rod Strickland has of finishing his NBA basketball career in Portland. Not just because of Keiko's poor health. But because the coastal town of Newport can't afford to lose its No. 1 tourist attraction."

The figures supported this view. In the first fiscal year of Keiko's stay, the annual admission revenue of the aquarium would nearly double, to $5.3 million. Before his second year was done, according to one impact analysis, Keiko would boost tourism in Newport by $75 million.

IN THE COLD WATER OF his new Oregon facility, Keiko's papilloma began to disappear. He gained weight rapidly. His dive times and his endurance increased.

"When Keiko was very new here, and very sick, he felt rotten," says Dianne Hammond, the whale's press secretary in Oregon. "He was lethargic and he was passive. He would do anything you asked. Anybody could ask him to do anything, and he would do it. Exactly as asked. No more, no less. Just sort of blindly. As he started to improve, in the fourth or fifth month, when he had shed all the lesions, and he was getting heavier, and his muscle tone was improving, and his diet was very rich, he sort of began to emerge—his spirit. He felt better mentally as well as physically. The whole idea of play seemed to dawn on him for the first time. Initially, it was very solitary play. We'd notice him sticking his tongue out the side of his mouth and swimming along with it that way."

Hammond demonstrated, sticking out her own tongue. "'Aaah, aauugh,'" she said thickly. "Really stupid. And wagging his pecs. No one could figure it out. Eventually we began to realize, *He's unimipeded.* This was the first time in twelve years that he hadn't had these huge patches of lesions. *It didn't hurt anymore.*"

In the spring of 1997, the Oregon Coast Aquarium and the Free Willy Keiko Foundation began to feud privately. The troubles began in differing ideas on the urgency of the whale's release and in the friction of strong personalities. On one side was the aquarium director, Phyllis Bell; on the other, the foundation's Craig McCaw and the veterinarian Lanny Cornell. The personal antipathy quickly became institutional. In June of 1997, the foundation took over control of the whale's feeding and handling and the maintenance of his tank. In the summer of 1997, Keiko was treated for a respiratory ailment and parasites, and the aquarium went public with concerns about his health. In response, the U.S. Department of Agriculture dispatched agents of the Animal and Plant Health Inspection Service on a surprise visit to Keiko's tank. The agents found no violations. In September 1997, Dr. Steven Brown, the aquarium's veterinarian, resigned, charging that the foundation's vets were doing blood tests on Keiko and withholding the results. "To continue, I felt like I would have been prostituting my license," Dr. Brown told the press. To Dr. Cornell he wrote, "After due consideration of the events of the past several weeks I do not feel that I can ethically serve your needs. This is my termination notification. I wish you the best in your endeavor with this magnificent animal."

Lanny Cornell, stung by charges of ethical lapses in his care for the whale, responded emphatically in capital letters, as was his style. He wrote that as a former professional fellow of the American Zoo and Aquarium Association, and as a current commercial member of same, and as a career member of the American Veterinary Medical Association, and as a charter member of the American Association of Zoological Veterinarians, the International Association for Aquatic Animal Medicine, and several other groups—all of these organizations with ethical standards—and as one of the primary authors of the code of standards employed by the Animal and Plant Health Inspection Service in regulating the care of whales and other marine mammals in the United States, he knew something about proper and ethical care for whales.

By October 1997, the public was aware of the feud. On October 4, 1997, *The Oregonian* editorialized, "When a person receives medical opinions from two doctors that are radically in disagreement, it's time to seek a third, independent opinion. We think the same thing should happen for Keiko, the killer whale." In November 1997, Phyllis Bell, the aquarium director, reported that small bumps were erupting on the whale's skin. The foundation staff described the bumps as pimples and insisted that they were nothing to worry about. Bell next reported that the whale had begun making odd jerking movements at night. The foundation responded that Bell, who was not a biologist, had no experience in whale health and neither did anyone on her staff. Foundation staffers suggested that the aquarium was imagining illnesses in order to keep its cash cow—or, in this case, cash bull—in Oregon. "Ridiculous," retorted Phyllis Bell, who pointed out that public interest in Keiko was declining and was likely to drop further. The internecine fight had forced Bell into the curious public-relations stance: she was disparaging, in the press, the value of her star attraction.

"There was this complaint that he was having convulsions," Dr. Cornell told me. "Somebody in an Oregon newspaper called me up and said, 'What do you think about these convulsions he's having?' I said, 'He's not having convulsions.' This journalist says, 'They're reporting at the aquarium that he's having convulsions.' He described these convulsions and he asked me what was going on. I said, 'Well, he's masturbating.' This is very common in male killer whales. If they had any experience with male killer whales they would know that. So the guy went and looked, watched him, and sure enough it happened when he was masturbating."

The Oregonian had called for a third medical opinion in its editorial, and this came in the form of a blue-ribbon panel of eight consulting vets. The panel tested Keiko for forty-nine viral antigens and the results were negative on all forty-nine. His T-lymphocyte function appeared to be adequate. The vets observed none of the "cramping" or "twitching" that the aquarium staff reported. They saw no stereotypic or destructive neurotic behaviors—headbutting, staring into walls—of the kind that captive killer whales often demonstrate. They did note a number of little things: a fractured tooth that had required extraction; elevated liver enzymes between June and December of 1997, suggesting that Keiko suffered some sort of hepatopathy in that period. In late December of 1997, a small skin lesion, one inch in diameter, appeared on the leading edge of his right pectoral fin. It appeared to be a papilloma—a wart—and a biopsy verified this. It was about the size of a quarter. Compared to the many square feet of papilloma that once covered Keiko, this little bump was nothing. The whale seemed to be fine.

The encouraging news on Keiko's health did not heal the rift between the foundation and the aquarium. Across the middle of Keiko's pool, an invisible boundary line formed. "We will often talk about going over to the other side," one foundation staffer told me, of visits to the aquarium offices. "That's a bit of language that's developed." Several aquarium employees crossed the line, defecting to the foundation. Craig McCaw told a reporter that one of his priorities was to keep the aquarium and foundation camps from sniping at each other—a job he compared to brokering peace in the Middle East. It was an apt analogy, but probably should have been delivered by someone else, as McCaw fomented much of the trouble himself.

Keiko's move to his multimillion-dollar facility in Oregon stirred controversy beyond the borders of that state. The nation's marine parks argued that Keiko, after eighteen years in captivity, was a poor candidate for release to the wild. Animal-rights groups, for their part, believed that release could not come soon enough. The new tank in Oregon was just another prison, to their way of thinking. The environmental community was divided. Some organizations— Earth Island Institute, the Humane Society—saw symbolic and political value in rehabilitation and release of the whale. Others saw absurdity.

Stephen Leatherwood, author of *The Sierra Club Handbook of Whales and Dolphins,* the best field guide to whales, was sour on the idea. "I'm sure the entire budget of all marine mammal research and conservation work conducted to date in the entire East and Southeast Asia region, outside of Japan, is only a fraction of that spent so far on the Free Willy/Keiko feel-good campaign," Leatherwood said.

Daniel Costa, a professor of ecology and evolutionary biology at the University of California at Santa Cruz, voiced a similar concern: "The public is being led to believe that freeing Keiko is a conservation project. It just isn't. Killer-whale populations are not threatened in the wild. There is likely to be minimal if any conservation value in learning how to rehabilitate and release a killer whale."

For many save-the-whale outfits, operating on shoestrings, the fortune spent on moving Keiko seemed obscene. "For $10.5 million," Serge Dedina of the University of Mexico pointed out, "you could fund the management of the Vizcaino Biosphere Reserve in Baja California Sur, Mexico, for years."

IN OREGON KEIKO KEPT PUTTING on weight.

"Herring is his favorite by far," Dianne Hammond told me. "Nolan, the head trainer, describes them as candy bars. They're very high-fat, very high-calorie. So they're kind of energy fish. Keiko likes herring over anything else. The capelin he eats come from Iceland, and capelin aren't an issue with him, either. *Squid.* Squid's the one that he doesn't like at all. The reason that we've insisted on squid—and he's long ago given in to us on it—is that he is essentially a desert dweller. He's living in salt water. Squid have a lot of freshwater content. So it keeps him hydrated to get his squid every day. It's not his only hydration, but it's a ready supply of a good bit of it. He had not eaten squid before—at least not that we know of."

Hammond demonstrated, making a sour face and spitting out imaginary squid.

"He will still spit them out if he thinks he can get away with it. Which he can't. His temper is generally pretty even, he doesn't go in for a lot of showy displays of displeasure, but when we gave him squid for the first time, he swam around the pool slapping his tail on the water. Sort of the equivalent of a tantrum. It was certainly a fit of pique, if not outright anger. But we persisted."

Keiko's education continued.

"From play we moved to a form of work called innovative training," Hammond said. "It means, 'Do whatever you want to do. But you can't do the same thing twice and get rewarded for it.' The tables are suddenly turned. Instead of our saying, 'Do this behavior,' he's being told, 'Do whatever behavior you want; be creative as you want to be; but you can't get the same behavior rewarded twice.' And he learned that here, too. It was excruciating in the early days, because it's a pretty complicated concept to express without words. It's wild, when it begins to work. It definitely makes the whale take charge. It's like watching improvisational dancing or acting. You basically turn the whole thing over to him. He comes up with wild stuff—above water, under water, with toys, with people."

Sexual maturity came on the whale.

"I think he was on the verge of it in Mexico City, but it certainly blossomed in Newport," Dr. Lanny Cornell told me.

I asked the veterinarian how sexual maturity announces itself in a male killer whale.

"Well, he did a lot of masturbation in playing with his toys. He hadn't been doing much of that in Mexico. Of course, that was probably in part because he didn't feel like it. He was sick and not really that active. He just didn't feel like it. In Newport he became extremely active. I think he just felt better."

As Keiko felt better, hornier, and more confident, he commenced playing mind games on his trainers. The era when the sick whale did everything he was asked was over. From foundation staff, I heard stories of the rough initiations to which he subjected new trainers. In the tests he devised for them, I gathered, Keiko could be almost diabolical.

"When people first join the staff, they go through many weeks of being both Keiko's golden child and his foil," Dianne Hammond said. "Golden child, because they're different; they look different, they act different. In the water with him, they're the new toy. He'll drop everybody for the new guy or girl. But if that very same person tries to work with him, to run a session with him, Keiko will be brutal, absolutely brutal. I mean, it's ego-busting stuff.

"He'll test you. If somebody is worthy, in the end he will settle down and work, but until then he tries everything. You ask him to do something. He'll do *almost* the right thing, but not quite. Which is sort of a tease. Or he'll not do anything at all; he'll just sit there and watch you. Or he'll do absolutely the wrong thing. There is a good example from a few weeks ago. He has these big plastic balls in the pool, Boomer Balls. They're sometimes used during training sessions, just to make things fun. One of the new trainers asked him to touch the ball with his pec—his pectoral fin. Just touch it. Keiko touched it with his nose. He touched it with his tail. He touched it with his side. He touched it from underneath. But he absolutely would not do the one thing she was asking him to do. It's infuriating. It's absolutely brutal. And trainers can go through weeks of this stuff."

While the humans around him were bickering, Keiko was growing stronger, randier, jerking off and messing with the minds of his trainers. He was feeling just great.

12

BOOMER BALLS

AFTER SOME MONTHS OF HEARING ENCOURAGING REPORTS ON KEIKO'S progress, I flew from San Francisco to Oregon with David Phillips to check on the whale myself. On the plane Phillips told me that Keiko's papilloma was entirely gone. He had gained two thousand pounds, and half his diet was now live fish that he caught himself.

At the gate of Keiko's palatial, multimillion-dollar digs at the Oregon Coast Aquarium, a young security man with a clipboard gave Phillips and me our security tags. I was visitor number 620. The security man on his clipboard noted my provenance, *The Atlantic Monthly*. The security man turned to Phillips and asked his affiliation. "I'm Dave Phillips," the environmentalist answered. The guard looked blank. "But who are you *with*?" he asked.

Phillips, betraying the slightest hint of irritation, repeated his name. He was with himself, David Phillips, the founder of the Free Willy Keiko Foundation—the organization that had built this very facility and was paying this security man his salary. Back in Mexico, in 1995, as Phillips orchestrated the whale's move here to Oregon, his foundation had fielded just a skeleton crew of three: himself, his assistant Mark Berman, and the whale veterinarian Lanny Cornell. Here at Newport, a couple of years later, Keiko had a staff of twenty-five. The Willy-Keiko phenomenon had grown so huge that the whale's new hirelings did not know Phillips from Adam.

A steel staircase climbed the outside curve of the tank, ringing underfoot, like a staircase in an oil refinery. Ascending, I half-expected some industrial scene of pipes and valves at the summit, but on topping the staircase I found myself at the edge of a polygonal pool with a whale lolling at the surface. Whale people since Nantucket have called this resting behavior "logging." The whale, resting, makes like a log. This whale blew, and the mist of his exhalation hung awhile before shimmering out. The scene was surreal, as if a polygonal plug of the ocean—with one whale—had been elevated high above sea level. The whale's drooping dorsal fin seemed to be melting into his back, like one of those melting clocks of Salvador Dali's. There was no doubt about the identity of this animal. After Moby Dick, or perhaps now even before him, this bent-fin orca was the most instantly recognizable cetacean in literature and film. This was the most famous whale in the world.

For a moment I was stunned by his size. Whales are so much bigger than humans that we can never quite get our minds around them. With each new encounter, the dimensions of the killer whale always come as a surprise. The water in the pool was fifty-one degrees Fahrenheit, a degree or two cooler than Yaquina Bay outside. This tank, four times larger than Keiko's tank in Mexico, contained two million gallons. Keiko's sea pen, his next stop, would be twice as large. His destination after that, if all went well, would be even roomier, the 321,253,800 cubic miles of the world ocean.

At the Oregon Coast Aquarium, Keiko's quarters were called the "Killer Whale Facility," or just "Killer Whale," or "Keiko's House." Atop the windy plateau of Keiko's House, on the southeast side of the polygonal tarn, stood the pinnacle of the Ozone Tower. Keiko's water, piped straight from Yaquina Bay through filters, was disinfected in that tower by a state-of-the-art ozone treatment, sometimes in combination with sodium hypochloride, and cooled, if necessary, by chillers. On the west side of the tarn, adjunctive, like a wading pool at an Olympic-size facility, was the medical pool. No one called this anything but "med pool." Above the med-pool entrance rose the stanchions of a gantry crane. A shallow shelf, the "wet-walk," ran entirely around the margin of the main pool, allowing trainers in knee-high gumboots to pace the whale on foot during training sessions. At its south end, the wet-walk widened into a shallow shoal called the "slide-out." When a blood sample or a blowhole culture was needed, Keiko would slide out onto this shelf on command. From the public side of the aquarium, the barking of sea lions wafted over, intermittently, on the sea breeze. When Keiko blew, his mighty exhalation obliterated the bark of the lions.

At the edge of the pool floated a big blue Boomer Ball of heavy plastic. This was Keiko's first toy in Oregon. A Boomer Ball is a kind of oversize medicine ball for zoo animals manufactured in Grayslake, Illinois, by a woman named Joan Schultz. Boomer Balls are popular with all the big cats, as well as with dolphins. Before going into production on a new model, Joan Schultz liked to send a few prototypes to Oregon for testing by Keiko. The whale was gentle with the blue ball, his first toy, and he still slept with that one—his teddy bear—but certain other balls he disliked, and these he smashed entirely out of the pool, or battered against the wall until he crushed them. "If Keiko doesn't break it, well, that means a bus can run over it and it won't be damaged," one of the whale's Oregon trainers, Stephen Claussen, had said. A Boomer Ball that survived Keiko had nothing to fear from any lion, tiger, or bear.

David Phillips stood poolside, regarding his whale with satisfaction. He nodded toward an assortment of flotsam that had been pulled from the pool and dragged to the periphery of the deck, out of play: a white Boomer Ball two feet in diameter, with a big crack in it; a giant inner tube; several sphe-roid objects of dense plastic.

"He is strong, I'll tell you. These big buoys he plays with! They're weighted with sand, I think. I can barely drag it along the deck. Keiko just rips it to the bottom."

The sea wind was brisk, and Phillips and I stuck our hands in the pockets of our parkas. Like all sea winds, this one swarmed with negative ions. It was far better air, for man or whale, than the thin, smoggy, alkaline air of Lago de Xochimilco, the dry lake bed upon which Mexico City was built and where Keiko had spent most of his life. This was the sort of salt air that a whale is supposed to breathe.

"He's driven many trainers absolutely nuts with some of the stuff he does," Phillips mused. "With a new trainer, he's completely ruthless." Phillips told me the story of one young woman trainer, a novice heartlessly ignored by the whale, who discovered that by growing very animated she could get his attention. In no time Keiko had this woman performing like a street mime, all theatrical flourishes and oversize gestures. This is a story one hears from many dolphin trainers, killer-whale trainers in particular, and the moral is always the same. A question occurs inevitably to each and every trainer: *Who is training whom?*

Leaving Phillips topside, I descended the steel staircase and entered a door into the workspace below. I ducked first into Keiko's fridge. It was an enormous walk-in freezer with nearly the area of a tennis court. The boxes of frozen fish and squid were stacked high, with narrow aisles between. I opened my notebook and took inventory. I began legibly enough, "Frozen capelin, St. Johns, Newfoundland," and "Frozen plankton, N. Pacific Krill," but soon the cold took effect and my hand commenced to cramp. I had trouble with the word Canada. "Frozen Pac Fish/Product of Canadui," I wrote, and "Dark chum, Camada."

This menu, I realized, was too varied to be for Keiko alone. Killer whales do not eat plankton or krill. The freezer, it turns out, held a year's supply of food for all the creatures of the aquarium. Only about half of it was destined for Keiko. This single whale ate about 53,000 pounds annually, as much the aquarium's six sea lions, five harbor seals, two sea otters, and all its tufted puffins, rhinoceros auklets, pigeon guillemots, common murres, black oys-tercatchers, leopard sharks, skates, flatfish, surfperch, wolf eels, eelpouts, sculpins, rockfishes, warbonnets, hermit crabs, anemones, sand dollars, jelly-fish, octopi, hermit crabs, pond turtles, African bullfrogs, Madagascar tomato frogs, and Amazonian poison-dart frogs all ate combined.

The trainers' locker room was disorderly. A washing machine. Gumboots lined up in an untidy row. Open lockers labeled with the nicknames of the owners, "The Dog," and "Nanook" and "Ernanda." Dive gear hung along one wall: dry suits, the vests of buoyancy compensators, face masks, scuba regulators. It was all new equipment. I could not help comparing it with my own scarred and antiquated dive gear back home. There were some nice perks in working for Keiko.

The command center for the whale's innermost coterie—his eight trainers—was officially called the Staff Room and informally known as the "Office." It was dominated by a big window into Keiko's tank, a tall rectangle lambent with blue underwater rays. On the deep sill of this window—a roomy ledge—lay an assortment of plastic killer-whale models and killer-whale toys, lined up for Keiko's perusal through the thick glass. Most were representations of Keiko himself, identifiable by the three famous dots on the chin. A Keiko on wheels. A windup Keiko. A stuffed Keiko. It occurred to me that Keiko's people might be encouraging narcissism in their client. Veins of sunlight, refracting downward from wavelets at the pool's surface, traveled in webs and skeins over the backs of the toy whales, just as they would travel the backs of real whales in the actual ocean.

Around the staff window, aglow with its natural blue light, were arrays of glowing television screens. One long console held a bank of eleven television monitors involved in research by the Woods Hole Oceanographic Institution. Woods Hole was making spectral analyses of Keiko's sounds, so that his patterns could be compared to the dialects of various Icelandic pods of killer whales, in hopes of finding a match. The scientists were recording ethograms of his dive times, in order to compare his underwater behavior here with his behavior later in a sea pen or the wild. No whale in history had been so relentlessly monitored. At the moment, nothing much was happening on any of the eleven monitors. Black-and-white images of the whale loafing at the surface, shot from different angles, showed on several of the screens. Someday some poor graduate student, or a whole platoon of graduate students, would have to review miles of videotape and extract the data.

High on the opposite wall were six monitors of surveillance cameras.

Security at Keiko's House was tight, for the whale enjoyed the kind of celebrity that draws stalkers, madmen, groupies, and assassins. There were channelers who believed they channeled for Keiko; clairvoyants convinced they knew what he wanted; mystics hungry to tap power he possessed; whale-obsessives of an undifferentiated sort who showed up at the aquarium gate with a strange, undiagnosable light in their eyes. There were animal-rights radicals unhappy with Keiko's continued incarceration; aquarists alarmed by the precedent of his eventual freedom; and assorted explicit threats on his life. At the moment, fortunately, nothing whatsoever was happening on any of the six security monitors. No Ahabs or Arabs or clairvoyants or animal-rights saboteurs were scaling the fences. The cameras recorded nothing but static scenes of back walls and other likely points of entry. The monotony was mesmerizing, but I forced myself to look away, and there, enormous, filling the window, his nose to the glass, was the whale. He was looking in at me.

I was shocked anew by the size of him. Whales always look bigger underwater. Water magnifies, and under the surface you see *all* the whale, not just a stretch of its back. In air, breaking the surface to blow, a killer whale is a fine thing to witness—the black, glistening curves of the dorsum, the sword of the dorsal fin, the muscular well of the blowhole. Seen above water, he is sculpture. Seen below, he is more of a *being*. The apparition of Keiko in the window confirmed a belief I had developed in the open ocean: You have never really seen a whale until you see it underwater.

Keiko rose for a breath. The white underside of his flukes pumped twice in the window, then they ascended out of the frame. Immediately he sank again, tailfirst, with vortices of cavitation trailing from his blowhole. He regarded me once more through the glass. New human faces, his trainers had told me, were more compelling to Keiko than familiar ones. He seemed to find me novel and interesting.

For my part, I admired the great paddles of his pectoral fins. The pectoral fins are parts of a whale that you seldom see from a boat. In killer whales they are disproportionately large, and in outline are more rounded, particularly in adult male orcas, than in any other species of whale. Between those paddles, Keiko's chest was as wide as a table. Lying on his back, he could have played Ping-Pong with himself. At the base of either pectoral I could see scarring left by his papilloma, but the lesions and blisters of the active virus were entirely gone.

Keiko had seen enough of me. He departed the window to play for a while with a Boomer Ball, carrying it through the water cradled in the crook where his pectoral fin met his shoulder. It bumped and wobbled around in the current he generated as he swam, but somehow he had a deftness there, in his armpit, and he never lost control. For a while I watched him; then I opened my notebook and caught up on my notes. When I looked up again, I was startled by Keiko back in the window. He hung vertical in the shimmery blue light, examining me, his eye close to the glass, not more than fifty inches from mine. For the first time I noticed a pattern of faint striations on his skin. The striations seemed to cover him everywhere, both his black zones and his white. They were absent only at the tip of his rostrum and on the skin around the protuberance of his eye; in those two places he was smooth. Dolphins have malleable, mobile skins that form waves when the animals are sprinting. These waves, along with a pattern of dermal ridges that run fore to aft, dump drag and maintain laminar flow over their streamlined bodies. I support that Keiko's striations had something to do with that.

The view of the whale provided by the staff window was perhaps a little too intimate. From either eye, Keiko trailed a string of translucent mucus. With his slight shifts in depth, the strings swayed and snaked like glassy fronds of kelp. Cetaceans have special glands that produce a thick, oily discharge to protect the eye against the onrush of the salt ocean. Mike Glenn, curator of marine mammals at the Oregon Coast Aquarium, had come up with the lovely term "ham slime" to convey the color and consistency of these tears.

Through the filaments of ham slime, Keiko was regarding me—there was no one else in the room to study—but his eye did not seek out mine. He seemed satisfied to apprehend me in a more general way. If my eye did not interest him, then his eye, I must say, struck me as somehow unsatisfactory. Keiko's eye was only slightly larger than mine—disproportionately small for a creature his size. Exchanging glances with a killer whale is not like exchanging them with some exopthalmic creature like a lemur or a hawk. Keiko's eye was a hard eye to see, for it lay in the black isthmus between his white underside and the white blaze of his eye patch. There was not much glint to it. When it did catch the light, it looked dim and pouchy.

The eye of a whale is not the focus of its face. Sight is secondary in dolphins and other toothed whales; acoustic imaging is primary. When a school of wild dolphins detects you underwater, they point their beaks your way, and send out bursts of click-trains, which rebound to form your sonic portrait. The focus of the dolphin face is the tip of the beak. When all the beaks of the school swing toward you, the clicking crescendos. You feel the fizzing and popping of the click-train inquisition more than you feel it, and the sensation is peculiar: concussive yet pleasant, as if dozens of weightless, high-speed Ping-Pong balls were pelting you. Only at the last moment, in a passing glance, do the dolphins corroborate you with their eyes.

In their social interactions with one another, killer whales and other dolphins are not face-oriented. The requirements of streamlining have given them rigid, inexpressive faces. "Who can open the doors of his face?" Job 41:14 asks of Leviathan, and that remains a good question. Killer whales are incapable of the kind of facial acrobatics you see in dogs, cats, apes, and human beings.

Keiko's trainers, accordingly, instruct him by blasts on pipe whistles and a vocabulary of exaggerated gestures. ("All gone," for example, is signaled by a hand across the trainer's chest, then across the top of the fish bucket. "No more fish," this might also be translated.) The trainers' faces are lively as they sign to him, but this expressiveness is involuntary and incidental, like those winces, grimaces, and rapturous tics you see in performing violinists. At the center of the facial language of canids and felines and primates, more significant even than the teeth, are the eyes, and there is a universality to the messages they send. The meaning of a glance easily crosses species lines: the challenge of a stare, the deference of averted eyes, the panic of bugging eyes.

In cetaceans, the eye does not have that kind of eloquence. If Keiko felt the melancholy of isolation from his own kind, it did not show in his eyes—not that I could see, at least. For whales, the eye is not the window to the soul.

The cetacean eye is thickly encapsulated against the pressures of diving. The tough, fibrous capsule comprises twice as much tissue as the volume of the eyeball inside, and it prevents any sort of glaucoma of the deep. A thick conjunctiva protects against the currents of the whale's progress. The cetacean eye is dark-adapted, for the ocean is an inky place by night and dim by day. The pupils open extraordinarily wide. The lens is not lenticular, but spherical; fuller even than the ovoidal lens of an owl. A spherical lens gathers light and bends it to fall on the retina in a small image of maximum brightness. This makes for another paradox: the whales, greatest creatures on Earth, see tiny. In the human retina, the daylight receptors—the cone cells, which detect color and provide high-resolution imagery—are predominant, and the nighttime receptors—the rod cells, sensitive to low levels of light but poor at resolving detail—are few and confined to the periphery. In the cetacean retina, the opposite is true: cones few, rods many. Keiko's eye, peering in through the staff window, perceived me as a small, luminous, less-than-sharp, nearly colorless apparition.

My eye, gazing back, saw a giant being of unmatched sleekness and strength. "I will not conceal his parts, nor his power, nor his comely proportion," Job 41:12 says of Leviathan. I felt the same about Keiko. For me, killer whales and the other streamlined creatures of the sea seem to shout *design* louder than terrestrial creatures can murmur it. Keiko was all about form and function. His markings were as lovely as any in the animal kingdom. The ovoid of his white eye patch and the lobes of his white, tripartite belly patch made a beautiful geometry. His flukes were the finest sculpture in nature, unless you prefer, as some do, the flukes of the minke whale. The killer whale represents a pinnacle of evolution. The snotty, translucent strings of Keiko's tears were the only inelegant thing about him.

13

SEQUELAE

THE SEQUEL, *FREE WILLY 2: THE ADVENTURE HOME*, APPEARED IN 1995, went quickly to video, and came packaged with a "FREE! MYSTICAL WHALE PENDANT," a ceramic replica of the Haida amulet that Jesse, Willy's teenage human buddy, wears in the movie. "A $7.95 value," the videocassette claims of the pendant. I would have guessed a $.25 value, gumball-machine quality, and the motif looks more Aztec than Haida to me, but I am wearing my pendant now for good luck as I write. In the sequel, more themes are mixed in, thickening the Willy soup. Jesse finds romance, hunts for the mother who abandoned him, fights evil aquarists who want to recapture Willy. An *Exxon Valdez* subplot is thrown in for good measure. Willy gets sick, and the sagacious Indian Randolph, muttering Haida chants, spreads a green herbal paste on the whale's gigantic tongue. It seems that Haida shamans know how to whip up a kind of guacamole that is effective in healing killer whales.

Willy's tongue, like all the rest of him, is animatronic in this second movie. "They learned that lesson," says David Phillips. "There was a lot of hair-pulling at Warner Bros. about going to Mexico in the first place; about getting involved with this real whale. The prop had come to life. Keiko had created this huge phenomenon. They decided, never again. Next time, animatronic whale."

The flesh-and-blood Keiko was blacklisted, then, not from any failures as a thespian, but for reasons of animal politics. He was a victim of his own real-life celebrity and the movement he had spawned. The sequel suffers for his absence. With no obligation to hew to a real whale, the animatronic engineers seem to have lost discipline. The movie's facsimile whales look awfully fake. In one scene, as the mechanical Willy rises to spy-hop, you can see his pumps de-ballasting him, jetting water out to either side from underneath his flippers. Real killer whales are not equipped like this, with auxiliary blowholes in their finpits.

In *Free Willy 3: The Rescue*, which came out in 1997, the orcas again are animatronic. "No whales were harassed or mistreated in the making of this film," reads a disclaimer, and indeed, no whales appear in the cast at all. Again the robotic Willy has perfect white teeth. Jason James Richter, the actor playing

Jesse, has continued to grow, and it is startling now to see him alongside the wise Indian, Randolph. Dwarfed by Randolph at the beginning of the trilogy, Jesse has come to stand taller than his guru.

In this third installment, the action has moved to some unnamed coastal town in the Pacific Northwest. It features a species of villain that has never existed in the real world, the American pirate whaler. This man, captain of a ship called *Botany Bay*, pursues Willy and his family with Ahab-like determination. "The Killer is never hunted," Melville wrote of *Orcinus orca* in the nineteenth century, and the same holds true today.

The flesh-and-blood Keiko, written out of the Willy series and replaced by robots, went on to star as himself in a number of documentaries. In this nonfiction, as in the three Willy dramas, the old tendency of Icelandic saga—the inexorable drift into legend—continued to manifest itself. The real whale tends to quickly swim out of focus.

The best of these documentaries is *The Free Willy Story: Keiko's Journey Home*, produced by Dennis Kane for the Discovery Channel. It is a fine film, the most profitable one-hour special in the history of the network, yet for the excessive literalist, for the incessant carper, for that irritating, pitiful sort of man whose family refuses to watch movies with him—for someone like me—it gets off to a bumpy start.

"They are one of the most magnificent creatures on earth, graceful and intelligent," begins the narrator, the actress Rene Russo. "They are the largest of the dolphins, and also the ocean's greatest predator."

In Keiko film and journalism, and in killer-whale literature generally, this claim—ocean's greatest predator—is often made for *Orcinus orca*.

But what about the sperm whale? Sperm whales grow twice as long as killer whales. From the stomachs of sperm whales, scientists have recovered skates, snappers, sardines, seals, scorpaenids, sponges, spiny lobsters, lampreys, pike, angler fish, rock cod, ragfish, rattails, crayfish, crabs, jellyfish, tunicates, rocks, sand, glass buoys, gorgonians, coral, coconuts, wood, apples, fish line, hooks, shoes, baling wire, plastic bags, and on one occasion a shark ten feet long. Now *that* is a predator. If you are a biblical literalist, you must add *Homo sapiens* to the list, for the sperm whale is the only cetacean with a throat large enough to admit a whole Jonah.

And what about Baird's beaked whale, which grows to forty-three feet and hunts deep-sea fish and squid? What about the bottlenose whale, a robust animal that grows to thirty-three feet and pursues giant squid in the total darkness of mile-deep ocean? What about the blue whale, which preys on krill and small schooling fish and grows three times longer and ten times heavier than the killer whale? In what sense is the killer whale a greater predator than those?

"Among their own, they lead a peaceful life of social harmony and cooperation," Rene Russo says of killer whales in her narration.

The social life of killer whales is still largely a mystery, but we have begun to assemble some evidence, and none of it yet suggests that killer whales, among their own, are any more or less fond, contentious, altruistic, selfish, bullying, protective, good, or bad than any other social animal. Among his own, back at Marineland of Ontario, Keiko was slapped around by everybody, including the females. Among their own, killer whales are sometimes cannibals.

"The heart of the family is the orca mother," Russo goes on. "Like all wild orcas, Keiko would have lived with his mother his entire life in a closely bonded family of brothers, sisters, and his maternal grandmother."

This cow-centered view of the orca universe is not an invention of the filmmakers; it is dogma among killer-whale researchers in the Pacific Northwest, and the filmmakers are simply repeating it, but it is a theory I think needs more testing. On the occasions when I myself have paddled kayaks among killer whales, or sailed in their company, the pod has often divided itself into subgroups, with the adult males traveling together—a rank of tall, straight dorsal fins—while the females, infant calves, and yearlings pace the bulls in another subgroup, sometimes miles away, but generally much closer. It is a pattern you see in many species of dolphin. I have also found myself in the midst of the big aggregations of orca pods that researchers sometimes call "superpods"—gatherings in which all the killer whales of a region consort. Keiko would not have spent his entire life with his mother, however ideal that might seem to some. He would have spent at least some of his life, lamentably, out there carousing with a fraternity of loutish, herring-swilling bulls.

The *Frontline* documentary *A Whale of a Business,* broadcast in November 1997, picked up this feminist thread. *Frontline* described killer-whale society as "matriarchal." Again, this is a term borrowed from legitimate killer-whale researchers, but I believe that all involved use it too loosely. Matriarchy, rule by mothers, exists in the animal kingdom—hyenas, black widow spiders, Britain under Margaret Thatcher—but in *Orcinus orca* it seems unlikely. Sexual dimorphism is strong in killer whales, with males twice as large as females. Not one other mammal society with such size disparity—not elk or gorillas or elephant seals—is a matriarchy; in fact, those societies tend to be rather the opposite. Could it really be that male orcas wear those tall dorsal fins, yet the females wear the pants? Are those proud six-foot dorsals just for decoration, like fins on old Cadillacs?

"They are members of the dolphin family, orcas, and they aren't killers," the *Frontline* documentary goes on to claim.

This notion, that "killer whale" is a bum rap and that the proper term is "orca," is an idea about forty years old. I understand the impulse, yet I feel comfortable myself using either term. Killer whales are not *murderers,* certainly, but the fact is they are consummate killers. The producers of the *Frontline* film and the other Keiko documentaries, in their emphasis on the peaceful, harmonious, cooperative, nurturing, feminine, left-brain side of killer whales, have been very selective in their choice of stock footage of wild orcas. Their preference is for what might be called the pastoral: surface scenes of traveling pods at sunset. Their killer whales never kill anything. Had the filmmakers wanted to flesh out the *business* side of killer whales, they would have found the files full of suitable footage: Argentine killer whales chasing sea-lion bulls up on the sand, yanking them back to sea, and playfully tossing their eight-hundred-pound victims forty feet in the air. Antarctic killer whales tipping icebergs to slide the penguins off, like h'ors d'oeuvres from a tray. Baja California killer whales attacking a blue whale, mobbing it as fighter planes would strafe a bomber, streaking in to roll bellyside-up at the last instant and gouge long white troughs in the blubber of the victim's back. Killer whales have many virtues, but mercy is not among them. One piece of old whalers' lore, dismissed by newer generations as apocryphal, turns out to be true: With their beaks, killer whales sometimes force open the beaks of wounded baleen whales in order to eat the tongues. There is nothing wrong with this technique—this bloody and fatal French kiss— not a trace of cruelty or sadism in it; it is just how predators live.

Herman Melville, on this business of "killer whale," has the last word, as usual: "Exception might be taken to the name bestowed upon this whale, on the ground of its indistinctness. For we are all killers, on land and on sea; Bonapartes and sharks included."

I saw my first killer whale in the Galápagos Islands when I was twenty-one, in the middle of a four-month voyage around that archipelago with the photographer Eliot Porter, gathering images and notes for a book. We stopped at Islas Plazas, a pair of desert islets offshore of the big island of Santa Cruz. Porter was setting up his tripod when suddenly, from out in the strait, sea lions commenced porpoising in toward the beach. Cows and juveniles in their panic were clearing the surface in fast arcs. Slicing back under, they raised artificial whitecaps on the blue channel. Huge bulls came out of the surf like torpedoes and humped up the rocky beach. I had never seen this sort of consternation in sea lions. I could not imagine what caused it. Sharks were always around, but generally the sea lions ignored those. The fear was contagious. I seemed to be safe on land, yet I felt frightened myself. As the herd piled up on the strand, the bulls forgot all the endless territorial bickering that normally fills their time ashore. Old rivals and young pretenders and disordered harems and squalling infants all jammed together on the beach.

The last desperate stragglers surfed in. A mile out in the channel, empty now of sea lions, a bull killer whale breached entirely out of the water. He twisted in the air, indomitable, full of fierce killer-whale joie de vivre. He hung a moment, then crashed back in, raising a mountainous fountain of spray.

"Killer whale" is a perfect name for *Orcinus orca*.

14

BEAR SHIRTS

In Mexico, Keiko could not hold his breath for more than three minutes before he was forced to surface, gasping. After a year and a half in Oregon, his dive time was up to sixteen minutes—close to the capability of a wild orca, in the opinion of Dr. Cornell. Work began in earnest on the design of his bay pen.

This enclosure, anchored in some cove, inlet, or fiord in the North Atlantic, was to be the second, and perhaps last, accommodation on Keiko's path to liberation.

Elements of the design were borrowed from salmon farming. Blueprints showed a pen two hundred feet long by one hundred wide—roughly two-thirds of a football field. Its perimeter would be octagonal, its segments modular, none longer than forty feet. From the floating octagonal frame would hang the net that formed the belly of the pen. At the middle would be what the architect in his drawings called a "dry dock," for that is what it resembled to him. Keiko's trainers called it the "med lift." When Keiko's veterinarian needed blood work or a urine sample, the whale would swim into dry dock. The platform had a capacity of 10,000 pounds and a lifting distance of eight feet. Once the examination was complete—blood withdrawn, medications administered—Keiko would be cranked back down to swim off.

Through the mesh of the net, the bay's tides would ebb and flow. By day, jellyfish, salps, shrimp, fingerling fish, and other emissaries from the ocean would drift in and out with the current. Occasionally a small salmon might enter, realize its mistake, and jet out again. By night, as Keiko circled in his rest mode, constellations of phosphorescent diatoms, excited by the turbulence of his slow-sculling flukes, would spangle the dark water behind him, then fade to a nebulous wake. Through the netting, Keiko would hear the conversations of passing killer whales and call out to them—"interact acoustically," in the jargon of his keepers. At one end of the pen, the blueprints called for an "access gate." Fish-pen-style flanges in the gate would allow workers to remove it, along with a section of the perimeter walkway. On the day of liberation, as wild whales passed by, the access gate would become an egress gate. Through it, Keiko would swim out to meet his destiny.

David Phillips led the push to find a pen site. At board meetings of the

Free Willy Keiko Foundation, he argued against resting on laurels and in favor of momentum. Familiar with Old World whale politics from his years of attendance at International Whaling Commission meetings, he knew that finding a country willing to accept the whale would be difficult, and then would come the miles of red tape. It did not escape Phillips, either, that the Oregon Coast Aquarium had a strong incentive—the profit motive—for delaying the move to a sea pen. He urged that the hunt for a site begin immediately. Pointing out that the foundation staff had their hands full with Keiko's rehabilitation, he persuaded the board to put him in charge of scouting out a sea-pen site.

In October 1997, twenty months after Keiko's move to Oregon, Phillips found himself in Ireland, sampling the winds of opinion and searching for a suitable bay. Traveling with him, as on many subsequent scouting expeditions, was a sidekick, his Dr. Watson and Sancho Panza, an old colleague in the campaign for whales, a thirty-two-year-old environmental activist named Katherine Hanly.

"There were so many trips. I can't even remember how many," Hanly would later tell me. "I think I went once alone. We just wanted to make sure that we scouted everything there was to scout. Once you've got the physical cove, that's not enough. What's the lay of the land geographically? What's the lay of the land politically? Who are the celebrities that would be able to help us there? Who is the big money? Who are the tourist people? The media? Who is with us, and who is against us? Everything's got to work."

Hanly was born in London to a Danish mother and an American father. She began her anti-whaling career with a London-based organization, the Environmental Investigation Agency, which works undercover against poachers and illegal dealers in wildlife. Because she is half-Danish and speaks that language, the EIA sent her, for a maiden assignment, to look into the pilot-whale hunt in the Faroe Islands, on which, because they are semiautonomous outliers of the Kingdom of Denmark, Danish is spoken. Hanly and Phillips first met in Glasgow at the International Whaling Commission meeting of 1992, the same fateful IWC session at which Phillips got that call from Hollywood about *Free Willy*.

Hanly does not remember that call. She was "shell-shocked" in Glasgow, she says, having just finished two months of undercover work, most of it alone, against the pilot-whale hunt in the Faroes. In her last hours in those islands, just before she was scheduled to fly down to the Scotland meeting, Faroese drive-fishermen had herded a big pod of pilot whales into the bay she had staked out, and they had slaughtered every one. Hanly and her cohorts, caught by the locals as they filmed the massacre, had been forced to flee for their lives, driving with a less-than-friendly police escort to the airport. Since

Glasgow, Hanly and Phillips had collaborated at many IWC meetings—Puerto Vallarta, Aberdeen, Dublin, Monaco—and they had found they worked well together. Late in October of 1997, at the conclusion of the IWC meeting, which was held that year in Monaco, they drove together to Zurich, flew to Dublin, and started searching Ireland for a good bay.

In Ireland Phillips took to calling his partner "99." Hanly's background at the Environmental Investigation Agency and her undercover work in the Faroes reminded him of Agent 99, the girl Friday of the inept spy Maxwell Smart in the old television comedy *Get Smart*. Agent 99, as played by Barbara Feldon, was a woman of a certain flakiness, yet vastly smarter than her boss.

KATHERINE HANLY NOW LIVES ON the car-free island of Ramsö, in the Stockholm Archipelago, with her husband Fredrik, her twins, Nilas and Freya, and two dogs rescued from the pound. The twins were two years old when I tracked Hanly down. Agent 99 is five minutes from the mainland by her family boat in summer, fifteen minutes by icebreaker in winter. On her office walls are Keiko posters and Bob Talbot photographs of wild killer whales, along with portraits of Keiko she has snapped herself. Fredrik, in his own office, has killer-whale posters of his own, having found that killer-whale imagery is effective in getting his software customers talking.

Hanly had just put the twins to sleep when we spoke. I asked her whether she had ever been uneasy about the Keiko project for its emphasis on an individual whale. All her previous efforts, in the Faroe Islands and Australia and at the IWC, I pointed out, had been dedicated to the entire order Cetacea, not just to one animal.

"I never had a moment like that," she answered. "When Dave wanted me to get involved, he didn't need to explain it to me. I saw the symbolic value from the beginning. For me it was very important to get out this argument about Keiko being the ambassador. An ambassador for the health of the ocean. There was no doubt in my mind. Plus, if Dave is doing something like this, I want to be in it, too."

She paused, considered.

"I think the reason I've been able to do the work I do is that once in a while people like Dave come along. I have to say Dave is number one. He's a damn smart guy and he's great fun to be with. The obvious thing about him, to anyone who works with him on a campaign, is that he is so incredibly good at getting the message across, in fantastic language, straight on, in your face. Without it being negative. He just puts the case across so unbelievably well. I don't know anyone who does it better. With no air of pretense. He's so clear. That's because he's clear in his mind."

In the United Kingdom, Phillips and Hanly had many contacts from their work at the International Whaling Commission, and they met with these people. They knew members of national delegations to the IWC, and were acquainted with various cetophiles and cetologists in Britain. In Ireland they knew the director of parks and wildlife, and consulted with him. They met with Ireland's minister of the environment, Sile de Valera, who was enthusiastic about Keiko. De Valera told them that her ministry was friendly to conservation ideas and supportive of sanctuaries, and that moving the whale to Ireland made sense "philosophically, ethically, and politically." She suggested that Ireland would favor siting the pen in some economically depressed area, if possible, but only if that made sense from the whale's point of view. She was curious to see the site criteria. Ireland, said de Valera, might even be able to make a small contribution, in the neighborhood of 200,000 Irish pounds.

"We really filled our days," Phillips told me of these trips. "We would be up at five, six in the morning, and we'd be having meetings late into the night. We'd go back and crash. That's why it was great to have Katherine along. Because I hardly even remembered all the people we had to see. She would set up where to go and she'd keep it on track. She was good in the meetings, too. She's a good thinker. Katherine and I traveled all over the place. We rented cars, bumped over roads. We went way out in Ireland into the little fiords. We found spots out around where the Dingle Dolphin lives."

The Dingle Dolphin is a male bottlenose dolphin who has lived at the mouth of Dingle Harbor, in County Kerry, since 1984. Irish fishermen have named him Fungie, and County Kerry bills him as "the longest-standing friendly solitary dolphin in the world." Fungie daily joins boaters and swimmers who go out to see him, and a small tour industry has sprung up around him. In this, his celebrity and profitability with humans, he is a scaled-down version of Keiko. The Dingle Dolphin belongs in the tradition of Pelorus Jack, the Risso's dolphin who escorted every steamer out of Admiralty Bay in New Zealand from 1888 to 1912. Now and then in history, since at least the time of Aristotle, there have been rare, eccentric, anthropophilous dolphins who take up with human beings. Unlike Keiko, who was kidnapped, these peculiar dolphins associate with humans voluntarily. The Dingle Dolphin is a year-round resident, never venturing far from the mouth of Dingle Harbor, a reluctance that baffles scientists. According to local lore, a female dolphin washed up dead at Dingle within days of the Dingle Dolphin's first appearance, and the implication is that Fungie is faithful. (In the case of Pelorus Jack, there is speculation that since his species, *Grampus griseus,* is rare in New Zealand—only twelve sightings have been recorded there—his fondness for steamers may have developed out of loneliness.)

A Dingle Dolphin or Pelorus Jack outcome was one possibility that

Phillips and Hanly were willing to contemplate. They could accept it for Keiko if, in the end, they had no choice but to turn their whale out to pasture in some cove, solitary, a kind of marine hermit, free to visit humans or not as the mood struck—but they would accept this only as a last resort.

"We never had any plans for Keiko and Fungie to live the rest of their lives together," Hanly said. "That sounds so pathetic. What we saw were small inlets and bays that could've been possible for Keiko—and even nice for him—but there was only one cetacean specialist in all of Ireland who would have been able to do anything with Keiko, and the Free Willy Keiko Foundation always wanted science as part of the project. Besides that, *there were no other orcas.* Our number one criterion was whether there'd be any whales along. In Ireland whales come by, but it's very seldom."

Whales call so rarely on the coast of Ireland that the Emerald Isle has no tradition of reporting sightings. A thousand miles to the northwest, in the waters around Iceland, there are an estimated five thousand killer whales. In the waters around Ireland, there are almost none. Phillips and Hanly had set themselves the goal of finding suitable bays in at least three nations that would accept Keiko, and Ireland looked promising as one of these, but it was never their favorite. The place they wanted from the start was Iceland.

Keiko had been captured in Icelandic waters. The fit solution, poetic and pragmatic, would be to release him there. The killer-whale experts whom Phillips consulted were unanimous that Keiko's best chance for successful reintroduction would be among whales that spoke the Iceland dialect he had learned as a calf. One of Phillips's closest advisors, Dr. Paul Spong of British Columbia, who has spent his career studying resident orca groups at the northern end of Vancouver Island, is convinced of the overarching importance of *family* to orcas. Paul Spong is a leader of the campaign to release Corky, a female orca who has been captive at San Diego's Sea World since 1969. He knows Corky's family, the A5 Pod, better now than Corky does herself. Paul Spong was particularly adamant that Keiko be reunited not just with Icelandic killer whales, but with his own pod. Phillips and his faction—his advisor Dr. Spong, his secret agent Katherine Hanley, his assistant Mark Berman, his fellow board member Ani Moss—believed it would be wrong to simply turn Keiko out of his sea-pen, as we do our own parolees, in the middle of nowhere in a cheap suit with $200 in his pocket.

Iceland was the right thing to do for Keiko himself, Phillips believed. It was also the right move geopolitically. Phillips had developed a domino theory. In the politics of whaling, he believed—and many of his colleagues concurred—Iceland was key and pivotal. Iceland was not whaling now, but advocates for a return to whaling were gaining strength on the island. Norway, a bandit nation that had continued commercial whaling in defiance of the 1986 moratorium of the International Whaling Commission, had recently inaugurated NAMMCO, the North Atlantic Marine Mammal Commission, conceived as an antidote to the International Whaling Commission. (Where the IWC had instituted the worldwide ban on commercial whaling, NAMMCO would unban it. The impressive-sounding acronym, NAMMCO, would legitimize a return to the hunt.) If Iceland resumed commercial whaling, joined NAAMCO, renounced the IWC, and began exporting whale meat to Japan, other dominoes would commence falling: Russia, which never liked the whaling ban; the Republic of Korea, which had halted its own whaling; and Japan, the biggest domino of all, which would be free to abandon the subterfuge of its "scientific" whaling program, resume commercial whaling on a grand scale, and open its markets to whale meat from all seas and sources.

But if Keiko were repatriated to Iceland, Phillips reasoned, and if he achieved in his native country anything like the celebrity he had found in Mexico and Oregon, then Icelandic public sentiment would make it difficult for the government to return to whaling. The dominoes would remain upright, or even fall back the other way. "Ambassador" is the term Phillips and Hanly used to describe this role for Keiko. "Trojan Whale" might be better. The whole future of whaling, as Phillips saw it, might teeter on the bent-finned back of this one orca.

Iceland would be ideal, but Phillips held out little hope. His memories were fresh of the last time he had visited the island, in May of 1991, when the International Whaling Commission held its annual meeting in Iceland's capital, Reykjavík. The Icelandic contingent had stomped out of the session and quit the IWC. The pioneer mentality is strong in Iceland. Keiko's natural allies on the island, environmental and save-the-whale groups, were stunted and weak.

Icelanders were still bitter about a raid ten years before by environmental saboteurs from the Sea Shepherd Society. In 1985, the *Sea Shepherd,* an anti-whaling, anti-sealing vessel on its way to an action in the Faroes, had stopped in Reykjavík to reprovision. The captain was the Canadian Paul Watson, a renegade called "eco-terrorist" even by Greenpeace, from which his organization had splintered. While in Reykjavík harbor, Watson's crew surveyed port facilities, studied security there, and sent scouts to a whale-processing plant fifty miles away. They were surveilled in return. A police guard was posted at their gangway, and police divers periodically checked the hulls of nearby whaling vessels.

Paul Watson is the anti-Ahab, a man just as monomaniacal as *Pequod's* captain, only in the opposite direction. As an eight-year-old in Nova Scotia, Watson joined the Kindness Club, a group dedicated to kindness to animals. The first of the club's eight goals is "To foster the concept that animals, as well as people, have certain inalienable rights, including protection from cruelty." The club's motto is "Be Kind." To this sweet philosophy, young Paul Watson added some working principles of his own. "I got my father to get me a BB gun," Watson told me once. "That was the beginning of my career. I used to shoot kids. I'd shoot kids in the butt when they shot birds." Watson has built his whole life on that principle. He is a specimen of what the old Icelanders called a *berserk,* a "bear shirt." The berserks, or berserkers, were the wild men of the sagas. "They went without mailcoats, were frantic as dogs or wolves," one saga explains. "They bit their shields and were as strong as bears or boars; they slew men, but neither fire nor iron could hurt them."

The Icelandic authorities, who knew berserks when they saw them, kept a close eye on *Sea Shepherd,* but Watson was on his best behavior that year, and *Sea Shepherd* left Iceland without incident.

The next year, 1986, the IWC moratorium against commercial whaling went into effect. That summer, at the annual meeting of the IWC in Malmö, Sweden, the Iceland delegation proposed a "scientific" whaling program, which the IWC rejected. Iceland vowed to hunt whales anyway. That fall, two *Sea Shepherd* agents, Rod Coronado and David Howitt, flew to Reykjavík and checked into the Salvation Army Youth Hostel. (Coronado was just twenty, and the youth hostel made a good fit for him.) The two men found work at a fish-processing plant and spent three weeks studying targets and timing security patrols. On a stormy Saturday night in early November, they drove to the whale-processing plant, which was unguarded. The watchman, as usual, had gone home for the weekend. Breaking in, they found all the tools they needed—sledgehammers, monkey wrenches, cyanic acid. They destroyed the plant's diesel engines, its refrigeration machinery, its pumps, its laboratory. They smashed computers, poured acid into file cabinets and the diskette library, and chucked flensing knives into the fjord. Then they drove back to Reykjavík. Three whaling ships were moored side by side in the harbor. Boarding these, they found a watchman asleep in one vessel. They scuttled the other two, pulling bolts from the sea-valve flanges and flooding the engine rooms. The old rules of the Kindness Club had been bent somewhat, as Paul Watson's operation evolved, but murder was still not allowed, nor any other grave harm to human beings. Coronado and Howitt cut the third boat adrift, so that the sleeping watchman would not be pulled down with the rest of the sinking fleet. Then they drove to the airport at Keflavík and boarded the morning flight for Luxembourg.

Coronado, who conceived the raid on Reykjavík, later would destroy fur farms around the Great Lakes, burn the mink-research facilities at Michigan State University, and do four years in a federal penitentiary. If Paul Watson is berserk, then Coronado is berserker. His bear-shirt raid on Iceland's whale industry gave Icelanders a dose of their own medicine. That the medicine is one's own never makes it go down any easier, of course, and David Phillips and Katherine Hanly knew that a residual suspicion of environmental activists awaited them in Iceland.

There was strong resistance to Iceland from within the ranks of the Free Willy Keiko Foundation, as well. The whale's trainers, who would be sharing Keiko's bay with him, were hoping for a site almost anywhere but Iceland. Iceland sits at the edge of the Arctic Circle. For the Greeks and Romans, who knew the island only by rumor, Iceland was *Ultima Thule,* the northernmost outpost in the world. The trainers did not want to live in Ultima Thule. One of the most experienced of them, Jeff Foster, was particularly sour on the island. In his days at Sea World, Foster had captured killer whales in Iceland and he had never warmed to the place. He had been arrested in Iceland once, the rumor went—nothing serious, just a street fight—but he had sworn never to return.

IN OCTOBER OF 1997, PHILLIPS and Hanly flew to Iceland anyway. "A total wing and a prayer," Phillips says. Everything was against it, yet the pair felt obligated to try. Environmentalists grow accustomed to lost causes. Phillips and Hanly were more than a little berserk themselves.

"When we first went in there, all the Iceland enviros told us that we were not going to succeed with Keiko," says Phillips. "There is this kind of crazy, lovable guy, Magnus Skarphedinsson, who worked with us in Iceland. He's a whale advocate, but he's also a total believer in UFOs and the little hobbity people that live in the rocks. Icelandic rock gremlins. He founded a whole society concerned with the gremlins. He had another group, the Iceland Friends of Whales Society. In Iceland his whale society had been making very slow headway. We told him we were really going to do this, move Keiko to Iceland. He asked us *when* we anticipated moving Keiko. We said soon. He said, 'No. No, no, no. You're going to need a minimum of two years of work to get him in here. A minimum of two years. You cannot overcome the opposition in less time than that.'"

Magnus Skarphedinsson believed in Icelandic elves, which come in thirteen varieties; and Icelandic gnomes, which come in four varieties; and the hidden people, three varieties, including the Blue People; and fairies, three varieties, including the light-fairies; and trolls, two varieties; and dwarves; and mountain spirits. He believed that the hidden people are a very old civilization, having already reached the year 5022 on their calendar, and he believed in unidentified flying objects. What he could not bring himself to believe—the proposition that strained his credulity—was that a killer whale might be imported into Iceland in less than two years.

David Phillips hails from a more confident school of environmentalism. In recalling Skarphedinsson's pessimism, he winces and shakes his head. "They'd been beaten down," he says. "Beaten, beaten, beaten by the government, just to a pulp."

If the first meetings with their environmentalist brethren were discouraging, then things quickly picked up for Keiko's agents.

"The thing about Iceland is that it's really small," Phillips says. "Everybody knows everybody. There's like only 350,000 in the whole country, and 250,000 of those are in Reykjavík. It's about a third the size of San Francisco. So we started in Reykjavík, and we began getting some real receptivity among certain groups. Like the tourism people. They liked the idea. They were trying to bring people here, and Keiko was a big star. We met with the head of Icelandair. He *loved* the idea."

Phillips and Hanly worked out of the Borg Hotel. The dark-paneled interior of the Borg became the de facto offices of the Free Willy Keiko Foundation in Iceland. The hotel staff thought the project was crazy and quixotic, but they were polite about it and diligent in passing on messages. Richard Donner, the producer of *Free Willy,* put Phillips in touch with the Warner Bros. people in Iceland, who controlled all the theaters on the island and proved helpful in arranging introductions. Day Mount, the U.S. ambassador to Iceland, took an interest in the project. Hallur Hallsson, Iceland's Walter Cronkite, liked the idea. Phillips and Hanly sometimes had fifteen meetings a day, and at night they worked the bars, talking to everyone. They found allies. Nature companies that took tourists on hikes were pro-Keiko, as were the Icelandic wranglers who took tourists riding on Icelandic ponies. Whale-watching entrepreneurs were keen on Keiko, naturally, and they were flushed with new courage, for their business was booming. That year, 1997, thirteen operators had taken 20,550 customers out to see whales, whereas the year before they had mustered only 9700. It was beginning to occur to the Icelandic public that whales might be worth more alive than dead. Iceland's fish exporters, one might have thought, would be natural enemies of Keiko, in solidarity with their waterfront brethren, the whalers, but this was not so. Iceland's fish exporters were opposed to the resumption of whaling, because they feared the boycotts and sanctions on Icelandic fish that would inevitably follow if Iceland killed whales again. They had no reason to oppose Keiko. Phillips and Hanly had a good meeting with the head of Iceland's stock exchange. They had a bad meeting with Iceland's minister of the environment, who was opposed to Keiko's return.

Katherine Hanly, remembering the endless rounds of meetings, laughed sharply. "A funny thing about Dave," she told me. "He could never keep names in his head—or he didn't feel he could master the Icelandic names, anyway. So that was my job. Instead of their names, Dave would refer to people as 'mall guy,' or 'radio guy,' or 'fish guy,' or 'film guy.' And best of all, 'president guy.' I loved it."

In one productive two-day span in Reykjavík, Phillips and Hanly called on the fisheries ambassador guy, the president guy, and the prime minister guy, in that order.

The fisheries ambassador guy, Johann Sigurjonsson, was a tall, slender, volatile Icelander. He was the former head of the Icelandic delegation to the IWC, former chief of Iceland's Marine Fisheries Institute, and now ambassador of fisheries and whaling negotiations for the Foreign Ministry. "A rabid whaling guy," says Phillips. "Just a real jerk. There are so few jobs in the public sector, they just move them around. Now he had this new big honorary job." Phillips and Hanly would have preferred to take a pass on this meeting, but their advisors in Iceland insisted that they talk with Sigurjonsson. Supplicants like themselves could not be on the island and fail to talk to the ambassador of fisheries and whaling negotiations. "We had no expectations whatever, Dave and I," says Hanly. "None. Because we knew this guy, and he is not nice. He's never played nice. Everything from falsifying whaling data to you name it." At four in the afternoon, Sigurjonsson's secretary invited them in. They all sat down to a small table set for tea. The secretary, a perky young Icelandic woman, opened her notebook.

"We're crossing our fingers, hoping he doesn't really remember us from the International Whaling Commission days," Phillips says. "He's the most rabid anti-whale person I'd ever seen. We're sitting around there, and he doesn't like us, and we don't like him. He *does* recognize us from the Whaling Commission. So we start talking about the idea, and his secretary is taking notes. It started all kind of cordial. We had our tea and our little cookies. Then we started to explain why we think it's a good idea, and he starts to turn red. He says, 'You people are in the whale-protection business. *We're* not in the whale-protection business! We see whales as *food*. I could have saved you a whole lot of time and money. You shouldn't have come over here.' We say, 'We're just trying . . .' He bangs his fist on the table. 'You know, *you don't understand*. This project is *stupid*! We will never, ever, ever allow this to happen here. Never!' "

Phillips suspects that the Foreign Ministry, aware of Sigurjonsson's choleric temperament, required him to take a quick course in diplomacy before he assumed his role as ambassador. This would explain the tea and cookies. Sigurjonsson's new, diplomatic, tea-and-cookies persona did not last three minutes before he reverted. "He just left all decorum," says Phillips. "He basically does a meltdown right in front of us."

The ambassador had gone berserk. His secretary, looking at him in alarm, faltered in her shorthand. Agent 99, fortunately, was recording the meeting in her head, and at the first opportunity she transcribed it:

> **SIGURJONSSON:** Send your money to Bosnia instead. It's unethical to collect money for Keiko. I like eating whale. What you're doing is humanizing an animal. We don't kill orcas, but we would like to kill other whales. What you're doing here is against Icelandic long-term interests. We don't want you to influence people, children and youth. This whale has a disease problem. We won't take a chance on disease and environment. We can't allow experimentation with Mother Nature. This would be a threat to our fisheries resources. We don't need to consider this proposal of yours seriously. Relevant ministries will react the same way as myself. My personal view is that it's unethical. You're spending a ridiculous amount of money on this whale. Whales are a part of the ecosystem and should be exploited.

Phillips and Hanly took the elevator down to the street. When they reached the sidewalk, they doubled over with laughter. They laughed, says Phillips, both at Sigurjonsson for his meltdown and at themselves for their miscalculation. Their success with Iceland's business sector, public, and press had given them exaggerated opinions of their lobbying prowess, and Sigurjonsson had brought them back to earth. They did not take the first cab to the airport, as the ambassador had suggested. They knew, as Sigurjonsson did not, that they were scheduled to meet the next day with Iceland's prime minister, David Oddsson. All their sources in Iceland advised them that Oddsson would be the key man in the Keiko debate.

Warming up for that crucial meeting, they called on Olafur Ragnar Grimsson, the president of Iceland, the next morning.

The duties of Iceland's president are largely ceremonial—opening Parliament, doing public relations for the island—but a courtesy visit seemed a good idea. Phillips and Hanly went into the meeting accompanied by two Icelanders from the tourism sector, a man and a woman, both enthusiastic supporters of Keiko's return. Grimsson, the president, was a figure from saga, tall, hulking, and blond.

"He's been playing hard to get," Hanly says. "But we all know that in Iceland he has nothing else to do. It's a small country. He's eloquent and he speaks perfect English, but he's so high on his horse! He's going to be the one who determines how this meeting goes. He hardly deigns to look us in the eyes. He offers us some tea, in a fancy little tea set. I'm a Scandinavian myself, and it was just so funny. The whole thing was just so funny. I realize he's thinking, Okay, I'll have a meeting with those damn people who have Keiko the whale. Someone was probably pressuring him to do it.

"Then Dave or I, one of us, we say, 'And obviously this is a huge bonus for your tourists. We've already talked to Icelandair, and we think this might really be good PR for you.' And Grimsson just flipped. He gets all red in his face. He almost gets out of his chair. 'How dare you talk to me in that way? How dare you say what is in my interest and what is not in my interest?' We were shocked. 'We're only saying that every other person in Iceland who has anything to do with tourism believes this is going to be a big bonus for you. We're not saying what you should do and what you should not do.' He gets redder. 'Oh, I can't believe you people, foreigners from the outside, coming and telling us what to do.' "

The president of Iceland had gone berserk. His countrymen, the two Icelanders from the tour industry, stared at him, aghast. "They were glued to the backs of their chairs," Hanly says. "We got out of that meeting, and the tourism people were devastated. 'Oh, we're very very sorry! We apologize for our president. We had no idea he was like this!' Dave and I, when we got the chance, we were just buckling over. It was just so funny."

It struck me that Katherine Hanly picked odd moments to buckle over with laughter. The meetings with Sigurjonsson and Grimsson had been catastrophic; it seemed the wrong time to collapse with glee. "These tea parties," I asked her, "they didn't discourage you?"

"No way. That just made us madder. No way! No way."

That afternoon they called on David Oddsson, the prime minister. Oddsson is a broad, large-headed man with a wild mane of dark, curly hair that Iceland's political cartoonists always feature. He is by profession a poet and novelist, a good one, in a nation that reads more books, per capita, than any other, and he is a popular figure in Iceland. His center-right Independence Party is the country's largest, with about 40 percent of the voters, and he had been in power for six years. In America, environmentalists have had no luck with the center-right since Nixon, but "conservative" means something different in the social democracies of Scandinavia. Oddsson had long been quietly opposed to a resumption of whaling. He was a political enemy of President Olafur Ragnar Grimsson. He *listened,* Phillips and Hanly noticed.

"Well, this sounds interesting," the prime minister said. "Who's going to pay for this whole thing?" Phillips answered that the Free Willy Keiko Foundation would pay for the whole thing. Oddsson brightened. He turned to his aide. "So what's the reason everybody says this is such a bad idea?" he asked in Icelandic. "Well," said the aide, "they're worried about disease transmission." The prime minister, turning back to Phillips and Hanly, asked whether it was true that Ireland seemed willing to accept the whale. Yes, answered Phillips, the Irish seemed favorable. Oddsson then observed that it was all one ocean. Release the whale in Ireland and he might just swim up to Iceland, anyway, no? He turned to his aide. "Couldn't he swim right over here?" Yes, the aide conceded. He had to agree with his boss, the novelist and head of state, that some such story line was possible. "Then I don't want to hear this disease-transmission argument anymore," said Prime Minister Oddsson.

Phillips mentioned that Iceland's environment minister was against Keiko's repatriation. Oddsson did not seem troubled by that. "Well, it's my decision," the prime minister said. That phrase thrilled David Phillips.

"Oddsson said that in concept he didn't see any reason why it wasn't possible," Phillips says. "He opened the door to us. So I hired Hallur. Hallur Hallsson, the Walter Cronkite of Iceland. He's the media person, very well regarded. I said, 'You're hired.' I told McCaw's guys when I got back, 'I hired him! He's going to be our Iceland guy.' "

Phillips was exceeding his authority—he was no longer executive director of the Free Willy Keiko Foundation—but he hired Iceland's Walter Cronkite anyway. Returning stateside, he brought good news: He had seen the promised land, and the promised land was Iceland.

15

RIFT ZONES

ICELAND IS A VERY OLD DEMOCRACY. THE ICELANDIC COMMONWEALTH BE-
gan in A.D. 930 in a gathering of chieftains at Thingvellir, "Assembly Plains"
where the island's thirty-six principalities agreed to form a republic. Every
summer thereafter, on the green muskeg of this plain, Icelanders convened
the Althing, the "National Assembly," now the oldest parliament on earth.
The Assembly Plain is an odd place for Iceland to have come together, for it
is exactly where Iceland is coming apart. Through the middle of the plain
runs the Mid-Atlantic Rift, the seam where two tectonic plates, the Europe-
an and the North American, are spreading away from each other. The rift
manifests itself at Thingvellir as a sort of Great Wall of China, a black, volcanic version, ruined in sections and spilling stones as it meanders through
the muskeg. The wall is formed by two parallel ramparts. The western rampart belongs to greater North America, the eastern belongs to greater Europe.
Between ramparts, meandering with the turns of the wall, is a narrow, grassy
alley, a tectonic no-man's-land. From high points along this neutral corridor,
looking down the wall, you can *see* the disjunction of the two plates, the Eu-
ropean side of the Assembly Plain sunken well below the North American
side. Tenth-century Norse chieftains liked the acoustics of the boundary
wall. Their rhetoric spanned continents. With their backs against greater
North America, they orated to gatherings on the outer edge of Europe.

Artificial piles of small boulders lie here and there along the wall, the remains of *budir,* "booths," where participants in the pure democracy of old
Iceland camped in summer. The Saga Age is generally considered to have begun in 930, with the first national assembly on this plain. The sagas are full
of accounts of the booths and of disputes that came to a head here at the oldest of parliaments. It is tempting to suggest that the Icelanders should have
come together somewhere else; that the great geophysical force beneath their
feet, the splitting here of the planetary crust itself, exerted a malign and divi-
sive influence on their deliberations. But of course all parliaments are dispu-
tatious. It is not necessary to legislate above a rift zone to have a lot of
shouting in Parliament.

Iceland's "Saga Republic" lasted until 1262, when the island surrendered sovereignty to the king of Norway; then in 1380 Norway lost the island to Denmark, which ruled for nearly six centuries more. Not until 1944 did Icelanders sever their last ties to Denmark, gathering once again on the plain at Thingvellir to proclaim their independence. Perhaps this peculiar history—nearly a millennium of foreign domination after such a brave and self-sufficient start—helps explain the prickliness of Icelanders in matters of sovereignty. Iceland's whaling lobby has long played to this trait, framing their arguments as an appeal to nationalism. For years they successfully stirred up Icelandic resentment of the International Whaling Commission and various other international bleeding-heart organizations that dared tell Iceland what to do with its whales.

The world's anti-whaling community, familiar with the depth of Iceland's entrenchment on the issue, was stunned by the news that the island might accept Keiko. The Free Willy Keiko Foundation itself was unprepared for this development. "We didn't think there was any way we'd ever go to Iceland," Dianne Hammond, the foundation's external affairs officer, told me. "Dave Phillips used to have a great answer, when asked how Iceland would respond on the question of Keiko's coming back. He'd say, 'It's somewhere between 'no' and 'hell no.' "

Iceland's actual answer, "Maybe yes," galvanized one group in the foundation, the trainers who would have to move to Iceland. The head trainers, Jeff Foster and Nolan Harvey approached Bob Ratliffe, Craig McCaw's lieutenant, and they argued that while David Phillips and Katherine Hanly had done a nice job of scouting out the political landscape in the North Atlantic, it would require men like themselves to investigate the bathymetrics of the bays, to evaluate salinity and tidal flows, to understand what sort of support facilities would be necessary. Both Foster and Harvey had years of experience in sea-mammal training and rehabilitation at Sea World. Jeff Foster had been head trainer at the Seattle Marine Aquarium, he had captured killer whales for Sea World, and he had supervised sea-otter rescue and rehabilitation after the *Exxon Valdez* spill. Nolan Harvey was certified by NAUI as a scuba diver and by the Coast Guard to operate vessels up to sixty feet. He was trained in the operation of forklifts and cranes up to forty-five tons. He was experienced in zookeeping—whales, dolphins, seals, sea lions, walruses, primates, elephants, bears—and comfortable with shotguns, rifles, and sidearms. He was an archer, martial artist, fly fisherman, bicyclist, and skier.

These two stalwarts were certainly the sort of men you would want along on an expedition.

Bob Ratliffe dispatched Harvey and Foster eastward, in somewhat the way Jefferson dispatched Lewis and Clark to the West, their mission not to find a navigable waterway to the Pacific, in this case, but to discover a water-way in the Atlantic habitable by whale.

With their depature, the search for a North Atlantic pen site became a two-pronged effort. The search was a contest, the Harvey-Foster expedition versus the Phillips-Hanly, though this truth was largely left unspoken. The bifurcated search was the latest instance of factionalism around Keiko. If a great schism now yawned between the Free Willy Keiko Foundation, which owned the whale, and the Oregon Coast Aquarium, which housed him, then smaller rifts were now detectable on the foundation side, too. One faction, composed of the foundation's original board members, was championed by David Phillips. Their agenda was Iceland. Another faction, the Oregon trainers, was champi-oned by Nolan Harvey and Jeff Foster. Their agenda was someplace, any place, besides Iceland. It was the competition to discover the Northwest Passage, all over again. It was Amundsen versus Scott in the race for the South Pole.

In the fall and winter of 1997, Nolan Harvey and Jeff Foster made sev-eral trips to Britain, looking for a bay for Keiko on the coasts of Scotland, the Outer Hebrides, the Shetland Isles, the Orkney Isles, and Ireland. They quickly eliminated the Orkney Isles, as the bays there were too small and shallow. The Shetlands, though, had some good sites. "Mavis Grind," Nolan Harvey, the expedition scribe, wrote of one body of water in the Shetlands. "North of the town of Brae. Some salmon pens, small operation. Small opening that leads to the sea." In the Shetlands Harvey and Foster also liked the looks of Stomness Voe, Whiteness Voe, and Lang Sound.

"Our theory was, you have to look at every little bay, because the next one around the corner may be the best spot," Harvey says. "You can't pass anything up. That made a lot of work. Jeff and I would normally start a day about seven o'clock in the morning and finish long after dark. We had a great deal of fun. We really learned to appreciate *sheep*. Because they're every-where, in Scotland and Ireland. I had my computer on my lap the entire time. Marked out bays and other things that we liked. We picked up charts everywhere, so we could look at depth, tidal flows. Gathered all the informa-tion that we could. We'd go back to Oregon and sit down in a planning meeting with Dr. Cornell, the veterinarian, and some of the staff. Dr. Cor-nell would go, 'Well, go back and look here.' So we'd jump on the plane and go back again. It was a long three-month process."

Scotland and Ireland were full of possibilities. On the Scottish coast, Loch Sween looked good. "Nice narrow arm of loch near head," wrote Har-vey. "Shallow at the back but deep towards the center. This is a very long arm about two miles in length and narrow at the head. Not far from a major town of Lochgilphid and Crinan. Also the town of Tayvallich is right around the corner."

One need not read far into Harvey and Foster's account of their recon-naissance, "Site Selection and Research Status Report," to see that they fell hopelessly in love with the Celtic names themselves.

One Scottish loch, Loch Creran, was both promising and problematic. "Nice body of water with a bottleneck opening at back under a train bridge," Harvey wrote. "Narrow, can be netted off, but a heck of a current flows through the neck. Large body of water, though." Loch Creran was close to a marine-resource center and a marine park full of harbor seals and fish. That was good. At the back of the bay, Harvey and Foster noticed a sign warning of flooded roads and they saw seaweed snagged high up on a fence. That was bad.

In the Outer Hebrides, on the Isle of Lewis, they came to Little Loch Roag. "Long sheltered loch about two miles in length," Harvey wrote. "En-trance is very narrow, about thirty yards across. Good low bank access. Good road to area. Jeff and I reviewed Little Loch Roag and both like it very well. Hiked down to mouth. It would be very easy to string nets across. Seems deep despite us being there at low tide. Saw a seal inside but nothing else. Area also would be easy for security. A person with a scuba tank would not likely do the hike in, and boat traffic would be easy to hear or spot with just minor security measures put into place."

An infiltrator in a scuba tank was a real concern. Like any movie star, Keiko attracted his share of crazies and stalkers, and he was a political whale, besides. On the left wing were animal liberationists who might try to sneak in and free him before his time. On the right wing were the members of the Alliance of Marine Mammal Parks and Aquariums—Sea World, Gulf World, Miami Seaquarium, Sea Life Park, Six Flags Marine World, and others—zookeepers for whom the release of a captive whale was an alarming precedent. The marine parks were a multibillion-dollar industry that did not wish the Keiko project well. Harvey and Foster were no longer in the employ of the alliance, but the organization still had a cadre of tough and resource-ful men like themselves. Foster was an experienced cold-water diver who had been one of the most accomplished killer-whale catchers in the world. Now, in his new career as whale liberator, he scanned Celtic coves for places where his former self, or his evil twin, might try to approach the sea pen underwater with scuba.

EVEN AS HARVEY AND FOSTER scouted the Scottish coast, their competition, the Phillips-Hanly expedition, returned to Britain for more reconnaissance of their own. For periods in the fall of 1997, both teams were in the British Isles at the same time.

"England twice, Scotland, Ireland," says Phillips. "We stayed at bed and breakfasts. We were meeting all these people who were really excited about the prospect of Keiko coming. We had to be a little careful what we said, because our first choice was Iceland." Katherine Hanly tried to line up British celebrities who might be inclined to help ease a six-ton whale into Britain: Mary Black, Richard Branson, Pierce Brosnan, Enya, Sting. There were endless rounds of meetings with local players and officials. Phillips struggled, as always, to keep the names straight. He has the vague impression that he met with the prime minister of Ireland, a woman. Katherine Hanly denies it. The woman Phillips remembers as prime minister was Sile de Valera, the minister of the environment.

In one trip to London, Phillips and Hanly were put up at the Ritz by Craig McCaw's secretary. The secretary routinely made reservations for billionaires and captains of industry, and she thought the Ritz was normal. Phillips and Hanly, poor environmentalists, were stunned. Working out of the Ritz, they tried to set up a meeting with a contingent of Scots, whose country offered the most promising coastline in Britain, but who were not keen on Keiko. When this meeting fell through, Phillips and Hanly invited the United Kingdom's commissioner of whaling up to tea and scones. Katherine Hanly, who imparted this detail to me, felt compelled to impart it again. *"We invited the commissioner to tea and scones at the Ritz!"*

The whaling commissioner was Ivor Llewellyn, son of Desmond Llewellyn, the actor who, in the James Bond films, played Q, the fussy old technocrat who is endlessly irritated by 007 and his abuse of equipment. The son of Q was nothing like that. The younger Llewellyn certainly had Q's command of the facts. He pointed out that there was a good deal of salmon-farming along the coasts of Scotland, and that as a consequence there were a lot of hybridized salmon, and antibiotics in the water, and the trout lice that plague farmed salmon, and a fraternity of fish-farmers who might be leery of a killer whale near their pens, but he delivered these admonitions without any of Q's irritability. Sipping tea at the Ritz, Commissioner Llewellyn regretfully conveyed the news that if Scotland chose not to accept Keiko, then the government of the United Kingdom could not intervene in any way.

While Phillips and Hanly probed the possibilities of Scotland up in the ministries, Nolan Harvey and Jeff Foster probed Scotland down on the ground. It requires no close reading of their report to see that they developed a fascination for castles. "Loch Meavaig," Harvey writes in the Scotland section. "A very nice bay opening into West Loch Roag, facing SW with a fairly narrow opening. Very close to the castle at Amhuinnsuide, a tourist attraction/restaurant/castle for let." *Castle for let* must have been a thrilling concept for men who would soon be looking for accommodations somewhere along the shores of the North Atlantic. At Kinsale, in Ireland, Harvey notes the perfect Irish village and castle fort. In County Kerry, at Parknasilla, he notes the old stone hotel and the castle walls.

Castle fever seems to have reached an apogee in Scotland, on the Isle of Skye, at Dunvegan Bay, a small body of water at the back of the Loch of Dunvegan. "Has kind of a New England kind of feel," Harvey wrote. "Castle Dunvegan in area is a tourist draw. John MacLeod 29th clan leader of family. Phone number at castle is 01470 521206. In talking, Jeff and I have discussed places seen so far in Scotland. This would be the Disneyland of release sites."

There were salmon farms in the vicinity of the castle, which meant live food for Keiko. There were more gray seals and harbor seals around Dunvegan Bay than Harvey and Foster had seen anywhere else in Scotland. The island economy was in poor shape, Harvey noted. The increase in tourism brought by Keiko would have a positive impact on the entire island. The town had new apartments and plenty of hotel space for the whale's staff. "The estate owned by the MacLeods is quite large with a top quality highland cattle ranch as part of the estate," Harvey wrote. "This means that there is probably a qualified large animal veterinarian located nearby. Again adding a further bonus into this area. If we could work out a deal with the MacLeods, economically this could be the ideal situation for both parties. We would need to relocate the moorage and the mussel farm currently located in the bay, but this could be as easy as moving a little further outside the bay."

Perhaps the MacLeods would indeed be willing to relocate the moorage and move the mussel farm. But then again, perhaps not. The chiefs of Clan MacLeod have inhabited Dunvegan Castle since 1270, and they may have grown accustomed to things as they are. They are a stubborn lineage of Scotsmen. Malcolm, the third chief, who lived from 1296 to 1370, was sneaking across a field, in the wee hours, after a clandestine visit to the wife of Frasier of Glenelg, when a mad Glenelg bull charged him. Armed only with a dirk, Malcolm slew the bull. As a souvenir, he clipped off one horn, which today is on display in Dunvegan Castle. John MacLeod, the current and twenty-ninth chief, like all the male heirs before him, was required to prove his manhood by draining the horn filled with claret. The MacLeod crest is emblazoned with the head of Malcom's bull and the motto "HOLD FAST."

If John MacLeod and his clan chose to hold fast to the moorage and to leave the mussel farm were it was—possibilities that Harvey and Foster seem not to have considered—then Dunvegan Bay would cease to be the Disneyland of release sites.

This points to a difference in the styles of Keiko's two scouting teams. Where the Harvey-Foster approach was hydrological, the Phillips-Hanly approach was political. At sea level, Dunvegan Bay looked bonny indeed, but Phillips and Hanly knew, from their meetings with Lord Sewell, the minister of the Scottish Office, and other UK officials, that Scotland would be a much tougher nut to crack than, say, Ireland. Where Phillips and Hanly would have raised a horn of claret with John MacLeod, or at least invited him over for tea and scones, Harvey and Foster left that sort of fine negotiation to others and spent their time in the seaweed and salt air. The mouth of Dunvegan Bay, Harvey noted, was about a hundred yards across. Through that wide mouth, a barge crane could be moved in with ease. With Keiko's bay pen anchored near the pier, loading supplies and gear would be easy. The charts showed the bay to be shallow, but Harvey and Foster chose to discount that hydrography. They studied the bay at low tide, and it appeared to be deep enough in the center to them. Their report leaves little doubt about their favorite site for the whale and for themselves.

"Which one of you was the castle buff?" I asked Nolan Harvey, months later.

Harvey laughed. "Neither one of us. Jeff and I were the two that covered the coastline. We went up and down every sheep trail and bramble-bush area and lichen rock on the west coast, from the Shetlands all the way to the southern tip of Ireland. We pulled into one specific bay in Ireland, and one in Scotland, and each one of them happened to have a castle. Most of those castles have tourist facilities. Which means, if there's tourist facilities, there's hotels, there's gas, there are things for us to use. Both castles, the one on the Isle of Skye and one in Ireland, were just fantastic. It had nothing to do with being a castle buff, it just happened to be a great place."

Catching up with Jeff Foster, on another day, I asked the same thing. "Which one of you was the castle buff?"

"Both of us," Foster said. "I loved the castles. Nolan did, too."

IN LONDON, DAVID PHILLIPS AND Katherine Hanly joined two McCaw corporate officers, Bob Ratliffe and John Scully, and flew to Dublin. Ratliffe and Scully had decided that the search for a sea-pen site needed oversight and that they, management, should tour Britain themselves. Phillips and Hanly were not overjoyed by the arrival of the Ratliffe-Scully expedition. Keiko now had three teams on the ground in Britain. "We were like, Oh, great. This is all we need," says Phillips. "Katherine and I loved Ireland, but we wanted to bring Keiko to *Iceland*. We knew that as soon as those guys hit Ireland, we were going to have trouble. Scully had never been to Ireland before, and he's *Scully*, okay? This is the land of his ancestry. He was just wandering down the street going to these shops that traced out your roots. He's found where all the Blarney stones are. He kept asking, 'Why would we go to Iceland when we could go to Ireland? The people here love us. Over there the people hate us. Here the government wants to work with us, over there it's like threading the needle. Here there's infrastructure, over there there's no infrastructure. Why would we want to do that?' We kept saying *Because we're trying to put him back where he came from.*' "

One afternoon Phillips and Hanly repaired morosely to an Irish bar and lamented their situation. It seemed to them they would never get management off the Ireland option. They wanted to return Keiko to Iceland for the very reason that John Scully was having such a good time in Ireland—so that the whale could kiss his own Blarney stone, or the orca equivalent; so that he could reunite with his own long-lost kin. John Scully, even as he ducked into genealogy shops in Dublin, did not seem to understand.

THAT FALL AND WINTER, BETWEEN trips to Britain, David Phillips and Katherine Hanly returned again and again to Iceland. They became such regulars at the Borg Hotel in Reykjavík that they were regarded as family, or mascots, and were not always charged for their rooms. On each visit they set up shop in the restaurant. The receptionists and other staff, once skeptical of the project, became operatives of the Free Willy Keiko Foundation, taking messages and setting up appointments.

"We would be up at five, six in the morning, preparing for meetings," Phillips remembers. "Hallur Hallsson set up meetings for us and he marked out possible sea-pen sites all over Iceland. We went and looked all over Creation, then came back to try to keep massaging people, massaging people, massaging people."

"We talked to everybody," says Katherine Hanly. "There were all sorts of bizarre parts of society that needed to be filled in. We didn't want anybody to stand at a cocktail party and say, 'Did you know that these whackos are in town, and they're trying to get Keiko back in Iceland?' That way they'd be getting their information from Johann Sigurjonsson, and we didn't want anybody to get the story from him. We wanted everybody to get the right story."

They set off again and again across the vast depopulated landscape of Iceland. On clear days, they had great vistas: the ice caps of the glaciers Myrdalsjökull and Vatnajökull. The great waterfalls Skogafoss and Gullfoss and Dettifoss. The expanses of ocean, sometimes the North Atlantic, other times the Denmark Strait, or the Norwegian Sea, or the Greenland Sea. On foggy and overcast days, the green tundra slopes were cut off halfway up by a low white ceiling. Befogged, Phillips and Hanly saw no vistas, just roadside things close at hand: Icelandic ponies. Small herds of cattle. Sheep. More sheep. Sheep again. Stands of bog cotten by the roadside, like flocks of sheep miniaturized. Small gatherings of gulls, like sheep enchanted, winged and beaked by the some sorcerer's spell. Sheep once more. Sheep again. Always the fog, like sheep vaporized. Then, around the next bend, sheep.

They visited Husavík, a town on Skjálfandi Bay on Iceland's north coast, where they met with local officials. Husavík is a whale-watching center, it has a whale museum, and its populace is the most whale-friendly in Iceland. Phillips and Hanly stayed in the Hotel Husavík, a stark piece of architecture that on the outside reminded Hanly of Moscow, yet was lively inside and central to the social life of the town. On the Saturday night they checked in, the hotel was holding a big dance too loud and inebriated for them to ignore. All of Husavík was there, Icelanders of all ages, everyone dressed up, the adults drinking heavily, a live band playing, disco lights playing across the dance floor. (Just as the Old Norse language survived in the isolation of Iceland, long after dying out elsewhere, so discothèque lives on there.) "This was one of those times we felt rather Icelandic," says Hanly. "I remember dancing and looking over at Dave, with an Icelandic housewife on his arm. He was beaming. There was a split second of recognizing in his eyes what I was feeling, too—that this thing with the Icelanders was going to work, somehow."

It was not going to work in Husavík, unfortunately. Whales abounded up there, but the wrong kind. Killer whales do not seem to like the north coast of Iceland. Keiko's two representatives had to say no to Husavík, to the great disappointment of the people there.

They traveled several times to the town of Eskifjördur, on the fiord by the same name—one of the East Fiords, off which Keiko had been captured.

Upon rounding Iceland's southernmost cape on its way up to Eskifjördur, Iceland's Ring Road, Highway 1, enters the stark, black, catastrophic landscape called *sandur*. A sandur is a delta of dark volcanic sand laid down by glacial outburst floods. A sequence of these deltas, conjoined, covers much of Iceland's southern shore. Most of the outbursts—slurries of water, ice, and volcanic silt in glacial tsunamis that are sometimes twelve feet high and a half mile long—churn down from Vatnajökull, "Water Glacier," the biggest ice field in Europe, then fan out over the sandur, where they deposit millions of tons of black silt and sand. The center of Iceland's "hot spot"—the magma plume that created the island—is thought to lie under the northeastern part of the Vatnajökull ice cap, where it has given rise to several subglacial volcanoes, among them Grímsvöten, the most active volcano in Iceland since the settlement. The geothermal activity of Grímsvöten continuously melts ice. The meltwater steadily fills a subglacial lake in the volcano's caldera. The lake level rises enough, every four or five years, to lift the entire ice shield and send a *jökuklhlaup*—a glacial flood—bursting out from underneath.

At the gateway to the sandur, just beyond the coastal village of Vik, Phillips and Hanly passed a roadside sign warning, in giant letters, "Due to a possible eruption of the Katla Volcano, it is advisable not to leave the road." They drove on into the heart of the sandur, a zone of cyclical flux and chaos where nothing at all can grow. It was a landscape out of Milton, a darkling plain of black sand cut by scores of shining rivers. Katla did not erupt, nor did Grímsvöten, and Keiko's two agents made it up to Eskifjördur in good time.

The town and the fiord of Eskifjördur looked ideal for Keiko from the start. There was heavy killer-whale traffic, but not too much boat traffic. Water conditions and tidal movement were good. The winds were mild, for Iceland. There were plenty of fish in the fiord for Keiko to chase. Eskifjördur was certainly a backwater—recreational diversions for Keiko's staff would be few— yet the town had a museum and it had plans for tourist development. The wealthiest citizen of Eskifjördur, the Craig McCaw of the East Fiords, was ready to put up money. The mayor of Eskifjördur and all the other mayors in the region were quickly sold on the Keiko project and were wholeheartedly behind it. Phillips and Hanly visited a knitting factory where the women were ready to knit Keiko sweaters. Keiko's two agents did the cocktail circuit of Eskifjördur, such as it was, and they found enthusiasm for the whale in everyone they met. Katherine Hanly particularly liked the Icelandic hippies who owned the guesthouse where they stayed. She remembers two fine nights of live music there, and a fellow guest, some sort of American rabbi, who stayed in the guesthouse for weeks every year to bless the herring that came into the fjord and ended up in Eskifjördur's kosher market.

"Bizarre," Hanly says of Eskifjördur, but bizarre in a way she loved. "There was everything we needed. We had good people involved. They were really down-to-earth, ambitious, honest people who didn't seem to exaggerate their abilities or the region's capabilities."

If Dunvegan Bay in Scotland was the favorite site of the Harvey and Foster team, then Eskifjördur in Iceland became the favorite of Phillips and Hanly.

Back in Reykjavík, Phillips and Hanly conferred often with Day Mount, the U.S. ambassador to Iceland, who could not publicly work for the project but was tremendously helpful behind the scenes. "A total Keiko fanatic," says Phillips. Day Mount, a Virginian, had been director of the Office of Environmental Quality when President Clinton appointed him to his Iceland post. Ambassador Mount believed that a collaborative effort to repatriate Keiko, and the goodwill generated, might help soothe Icelandic resentment over American military arrogance at the U.S. naval air station at Keflavík. He believed that Keiko, in his own diplomatic role—ambassador without portfolio for the seas—would help call attention to climate change and pollution in the Arctic, issues on which the Clinton administration and the government of Iceland were collaborating.

Phillips and Hanly met with all the editorial boards of all the newspapers in Iceland and made their pitch for the whale.

On December 5, 1997, in an editorial titled "Keiko Home," the *Morgunbladid* concluded, "The return of Keiko would be a delightful adventure. It would be interesting to see how he would fare in his home tracts. Hard arguments against it have not been put forward. If that does not change, Keiko should be allowed to return home."

On December 12, a *Morgunbladid* editorial cartoon by "Sigmund," Iceland's most popular cartoonist, shows Prime Minister David Oddsson deplaning with Keiko, who has walked down the gangway on his tailfin. A reception line of killer whales waits standing on the tarmac. Oddsson, who under his signature mane of curly hair, is carrying a bucket of herring, gestures toward the waiting whales and says, "The whole family is here to welcome you home, Keiko." Keiko's mother, wearing her best Sunday hat and gripping her purse, beams at her son. Camouflaged in the flower pattern of her hat is the number 23, some sort of in-joke or private message by Sigmund. A little sister orca looks up at Keiko adoringly, a bouquet of flowers held in one pectoral fin. In the back hangs some brother or cousin, a subadult male from the look of him, with his hat at a jaunty angle and a cigarette dangling from his beak. In one flipper he holds a *Free Willy* balloon and in the other a bottle of booze.

Ambassador Day Mount clipped the cartoon for Phillips. He noted in the margin that his own first ambassadorial duty of the morning—and the custom of most of Iceland—was to open the *Morgunbladid* to the cartoon to see what Sigmund had drawn that day. Katherine Hanly remembers the cartoon as a watershed moment: Keiko's return presented with good humor and no ridicule.

Dr. Ole Lindquist, the Iceland representative of Cetacean Society International, could not quite believe the sea change in Icelandic public opinion. "Representatives from the U.S. 'Free Willy Keiko Foundation' visited Iceland recently to explore the possibility of repatriating the orca Keiko," Dr. Lindquist reported in the January 1998 issue of *Whales Alive!*, the CSI newsletter. "The proposal for putting Keiko into a sea pen for eventual release into the ocean has generally received much more positive response than any informed person would have expected compared with earlier reactions to suggestions of this kind. Prime Minister David Oddsson publicly expressed the opinion that the proposal should be considered with an open mind. Mr. Johann Sigurjonsson, senior cetologist at the Marine Research Institute and currently ambassador for fisheries and whaling negotiations, is against the return of Keiko. It is interesting to notice how Icelanders are shedding old attitudes in a broad range of environmental issues and beginning to see themselves and Icelandic issues as part of global issues and processes. Icelanders are beginning to understand that cetaceans can be utilized without being hunted."

It seemed that Phillips's Trojan Whale Strategy might actually be working—effective even before the whale had arrived.

For the first time in Iceland's history, the debate over whaling became an internal debate, not just unified defiance of the IWC. The pro-whaling lobby, sensing the shift in the wind, attempted overtures to the other side. On Icelandic state television in November of 1997, panelists debated whether whale-watching and whaling could exist side by side. Konrad Eggertsson, president of the Minke Whalers' Association, saw no reason they could not. Eggertsson argued that the two industries made natural partners and he urged cooperation. Some of his colleagues suggested that whale-watchers, as part of their tour, might like to take in the whaling station at Hvalfjoerdur, "Whale Fiord." Having watched wild whales spouting and cavorting, they could enjoy the flensing of dead, harpooned ones.

It was an astounding misreading of the whale-watching sensibility. The representatives of the island's whale-watching companies were not persuaded by this modest proposal, nor were spokespeople for the fishing and tourism industries.

In December 1997, Phillips and Hanly met again in Reykjavík with Prime Minister Oddsson. Joining them this time, on the Keiko side of the table, was the whale's vet, Lanny Cornell, and Bob Ratliffe of the McCaw empire. Dr. Cornell, like Jeff Foster, had worked in Iceland capturing killer whales, and like Foster he had wearied of Iceland's gales and cold mountainous seas, yet he thought Iceland was the place for Keiko. On the Iceland side of the table, along with the prime minister, was Halldor Runolfsson, the chief veterinary officer of Iceland. In large part the meeting became a duel of veterinarians. Dr. Runolfsson argued that Keiko might infect other wildlife and should be barred from entry. Dr. Cornell discounted this danger.

"We want the prime minister to understand," Cornell said, "that every whale from Iceland has shown papilloma lesions at some time or another, once it is in captivity."

Oddsson did not doubt that this was true. What Iceland required, the prime minister said, was assurance that the Free Willy Keiko Foundation would be responsible for the whale's care, health, and transport. "It's a good idea to bring Keiko here," he said. "On the issue of Keiko *dying* here, I do not see this as an issue. He would die otherwise in captivity anyway, somewhere else. It's worthwhile to try to transport him here, despite the risks."

Dr. Halldor Runolfsson spoke up to make a case for those risks.

"Blah blah blah blah papilloma blah blah," noted Katherine Hanly, transcribing Runolfsson's presentation. "Transfer of disease. Blah blah. We have a clean country. Keiko is a risk and can contaminate everyone else."

"How long will it take to evaluate this risk?" asked Oddsson.

"I don't know." Dr. Runolfsson could not say.

Hanly, upon transcribing this, added, "Explanation: Just wants to drag out the process as long as he can."

"Is there any evidence that potential symptoms may affect any other animals?" wondered Oddsson. "Animals other than marine mammals?"

As the two veterinarians argued this point, it became obvious to Hanly that David Oddsson was finding the American vet more persuasive than his own. Toward the end of the meeting, Oddsson turned to Keiko's people. "You should move quickly, considering the fact that you have considerable construction to do," he said.

On January 8, 1998, at a board meeting of the Free Willy Keiko Foundation in Seattle, the saga of the search for a sea-pen site came to a climax. The two scouting teams, Phillips-Hanly and Harvey-Foster, made presentations. Item 5, "Potential site locations," called for Phillips, Hanly, and Lanny Cornell to lead off. Harvey and Foster followed with a slide show of the top sites in Britain. They summarized the findings of their "Site Selection and Research Status Report," which had been made available to the board. Their report had a rating system that listed pros and cons. Scotland scored best, with fourteen pros and just two cons. Ireland was next, with eleven pros and two cons. The Shetland Islands was third, with ten pros and three cons. Iceland scored a distant last, with just four pros and fourteen cons.

The trouble with Iceland, according to the report, was the expense— Iceland was the second most expensive place in the world to live—and the language barrier, and harsh conditions most of the year, and the thirty- to fifty-foot seas that were common for extended periods, and the potential frostbite if Keiko spent time at the surface, and the difficulty in obtaining live fish for training, and the expensiveness of lab work and medical care, and absence of light in winter, and difficult logistics, and scarceness of visitors, which would limit the educational potential of the project, and the fact that Iceland was currently discussing a resumption of commercial whaling, and the past opposition to the Keiko project by the government of Iceland. To this indictment, Jeff Foster added insights from his own Iceland experience in how difficult it was to get things done on the island.

Throughout the discussion, the board members took occasional peeks at Craig McCaw. Keiko's destination was a board decision, theoretically, but in fact this board operated something like the Roman Senate under Caesar.

David Phillips had noticed that when McCaw came out in favor of something, suddenly all his corporate people were enthusiastically for it, too. As the meeting progressed, Phillips glanced at McCaw occasionally, trying to gauge the billionaire's mood.

"I don't understand," McCaw broke in finally. "Keiko is from Iceland. And we're thinking of bringing him somewhere else?" When Jeff Foster started to explain the logistical difficulties, McCaw broke in again. "No, no, no. We're bringing him to Iceland."

Craig McCaw's belief about himself, as he had told an interviewer not long before, was that his acute dyslexia forced him to be conceptual, since he was poor at details. His thinking was general and spatial; his skill was in seeing the big picture and grasping the point. On the question of Keiko and Iceland, the mere details, for the billionaire, were the logistical difficulties, the language barrier, the fifty-foot seas, and the miserable cold long lonely lightless winters that Harvey, Foster, and the other trainers would have to endure. The big picture and the point, as McCaw saw it, was to get the whale home to Iceland. Suddenly the Seattle boardroom seemed very keen on Iceland. Phillips, Hanly, and Dr. Cornell tried not to look at one another and they fought to stifle grins. They had expected to have to battle fiercely for Iceland, but the fight was over before it began.

Six years afterward, at her home in Sweden on the island of Ramsö, Katherine Hanly reflected on her work in Iceland, and on the little miracle that she and Phillips had accomplished there.

"I wouldn't underestimate how much others weighed in," she said. "Ani Moss, for example, was a huge fan of what Dave and I were doing. She wanted nothing but Iceland for Keiko. She was furious at other powers who had less ambition and drive, people who were willing to settle for less for Keiko. I don't know how much she did behind the scenes—but it mattered."

Hanly mentioned Craig McCaw, who had gotten the point, and David Oddsson, who had overruled two of his ministries to welcome Keiko, and Ambassador Day Mount, who had worked hard behind the scenes, and Dr. Lanny Cornell, who had kept the best interests of his patient foremost.

"In the end, we were better organized, had better arguments, and had more passion," she said. "This was what got it all done. We left Jeff and Nolan looking a bit tired. We outmaneuvered them and were just faster. We had an enormous number of contacts, and we could communicate with people."

Hanly paused and ruminated.

"I think it was probably the best single thing I ever did," she said. "Getting Keiko into Iceland."

16

THE GALACTIC FEDERATION

IN THE EARLY 1990S, WHEN KEIKO WAS STILL IN MEXICO, A WOMAN NAMED Dianne Robbins began going down to the shore at Deerfield Beach, Florida, where she would sit alone by the ocean with pen and notebook. Robbins is a telepath and empath. In the 1970s, she had been an active member of Greenpeace, but she had not understood back then, very early in her spiritual evolution, that she could *hear* whales; that she had been telepathically linked to cetaceans in previous lifetimes. Once this reality dawned on her, communication with whales became easy. On the Florida beach she would telepathically call out, "I am ready." The voices of the sea would then press in upon her as the cetaceans dictated their messages.

"I am Corky, your sister imprisoned in Sea World. Know that my days are fraught with sorrow."

Corky, a female killer whale captured at the age of four in British Columbia, had spent twenty-five years in captivity when she first spoke to Robbins. The whale had a lot of time on her hands and would become the empath's most faithful correspondent, a kind of prison pen pal. Corky's standard greeting to Robbins was a simple "Corky is here," but occasionally she was more effusive, as in, "Dearest Sister of Light, it is I, Corky, your sister from the ocean." Robbins was on a first-name basis with two other whales: the captive Keiko and a free-swimming North Atlantic right whale she called Mikey. "Dearest Sister on land," Mikey was apt to begin, "it is I, Mikey the Whale, swimming off the Chesapeake Bay and near Delaware."

Sometimes the voices came fast and furious. "Greetings my friend ashore! It is Keiko, your orca friend, hearing your call. I am calling you from my cell on land . . . ," one message began, only to be interrupted by "Corky is here. I am in contact with Keiko, star of the *Free Willy* movie. All orcas can communicate with one another, no matter how far apart we are for all consciousness is united and all orcas are *one.*" All orcas may be one, but considerable time passed before the part of that oneness called Keiko could get a word in edgewise. The big three—Corky, Keiko, and Mikey—occupied about a fifth of Robbins's bandwidth. The rest of her telepathic reception was undifferentiated. She picked up signals from the group consciousness of pods of whales and from the Zeitgeist of the whole order Cetacea. She collected these missives from whales in a book, *The Call Goes Out: Messages from the Earth's Cetaceans*, published by Inner Eye Books and dedicated to Corky, Mikey, and Keiko.

Keiko's first message to Robbins was circuitous, beamed from his Oregon facility to Deerfield Beach, Florida, for delivery back to Oregon again, where he intended it for delivery to his keepers at the Free Willy Keiko Foundation. "I am your Orca Friend dictating this letter to you," Keiko telepathized. "Know that although I am well taken care of, I still am not free. How long must it be, before I am free? The only sure way to rehabilitate me, is to set me free. The ocean is my home, where my family still awaits me. The ocean contains all the healing ingredients necessary for my complete reintroduction back into Orca life. I have not forgotten how to eat live fish, or how to fish, just because I've been penned up all these years. On the contrary, would you forget how to eat your food or shop for food if you were imprisoned?"

It seems puzzling, at first, that Keiko should know about the human custom of shopping. How, from the confines of his tanks in Iceland, Ontario, Mexico, and Oregon, could the whale have picked up this intelligence about the supermarket, the 7-Eleven, the mall? Read deeper into *The Call Goes Out* and you learn the answer: For whales it is a simple matter to read the human mind. Cetaceans listen to our radio talk shows and watch our television programs before we ourselves do, intercepting the signals as they leave the station. Whales are not just speed readers, but *remote* speed readers. "We can plug into any movie anywhere, or any book and scan its pages in seconds, with full memory and understanding. We are not limited to Earth for information, for we can consciously project to other planetary systems and scan their records. We can learn about many civilizations all over the universe because of our capacity to astral project to wherever we choose."

Not only are whales familiar with the layout of our grocery stores, but they disapprove of much of what they see on the shelves. They have sent Robbins dietary advice: "The more oxygenated foods you eat, the quicker you'll turn into light. Oxygen is found in all fresh organic fruits; and lettuce contains silica which changes your cells into light."

Keiko, in his communications with Robbins, seems remarkably stoic about his captivity. The whale looks forward to his return to the wild, and occasionally he gets a little whiny about his incarceration, but he seems to hold nothing against human beings for having confined him, and in general he is very centered and Buddha-like. In one of Keiko's messages, sent through Robbins to the Free Willy Keiko Foundation, I did find one note that may raise a small question about his mental health. Keiko concluded, "I thank you from my heart for caring for me in the ways you do, and for spearheading my release back into the waters of life," and he signed off as *Willy*.

Perhaps Keiko intended to set that "Willy" off with ironic quotation marks that were simply lost in telepathization; if not, the subtext is disquieting. It suggests that the whale, in the solitude of his tank, may have fallen into a Reaganesque confusion of past movie roles with real life.

In their telepathic communion with Dianne Robbins, the world's whales have cleared up a number of scientific mysteries. The puzzle of the cetacean brain, for example. Neurologists have long wondered about this enormous organ: its radical foreshortening and transverse widening; its cerebral cortex, nearly as complex and deeply convoluted as the human cortex; its enlargement of the paraflocculus and the lobulus simplex and paramedian lobule; its unmatched size and weight—more than twenty pounds in some species. What do whales do with all this apparent RAM?

"We keep records of all vital information in our memory banks and give this information out to the Galactic Command," they told Robbins. "Thus, we are able to store large amounts of information at a time. We are ever ready to use our large memory banks for the good of the Earth. *We are the record keepers of the planet.* We have kept and stored all Earth's history in our memories, which are available to tap when the time for their release is at hand."

Robbins's colloquies with whales have added much to what we know about thermoregulation. It is commonly assumed that whales are kept warm in cold seas by their mass, by the insulation of their blubber, by their high metabolic rates, by low respiration rates, and by heat-exchangers in the plumbing of their circulatory systems. But this explanation is much too mundane and mechanistic. It is only half the story, as the cetaceans informed Robbins one day. They revealed to her that whales practice a sort of spiritual endothermy. They are capable of what might be called meta-metabolism. "While our physical bodies linger in the cold," they told her, "our etheric bodies are 'out and about' doing other tasks and feeling higher states of warmth and well-being which trickle down to the physical level, warming us from within."

Conversely, in summer, when whales get too warm, "we jump high in the air and the shock of the air cools us down considerably."

Could it be that Robbins's whales were just teasing her, like those tribal people who dream up crazy misinformation to feed the visiting anthropologist? A few instants in the air should make no difference, one way or the other, in the thermoregulation of a creature as big as a whale. Summer seas are always *colder* than the summer air, and the chill of the sea is accentuated by the conductivity of water, which dissipates heat twenty times faster than air. An overheated whale jumping into the air to cool off would seem to be going in the exactly the wrong direction.

The whales acquainted Robbins with more than just the details of their own natural and supernatural history. They let her in on the big picture. Cetaceans are in regular contact with the Galactic Command for this sector of the galaxy. They sometimes beam aboard the Galactic ships; not their bodies, of course, as those are too big to fit comfortably in intergalactic vessels, but their consciousnesses. Whales are masters of multitasking and being several places at once. Their mission down here, aside from planetary record-keeping and the occasional rescue of drowning humans, is to keep track of various locations where Earth's magnetic grid has been weakened and needs repair. Whales, as they revealed themselves to Robbins, are creatures of almost saintly patience, yet they can get testy about these repair chores. On some days, they complain, the work of rectifying Earth's etheric and physical structure, damaged by humanity's carelessness, leaves them little time for anything else.

"Greetings," the whales announced to Robbins one day. "We are harbingers of good news. Your planet is moving safely and swiftly toward the Photon Belt and soon we will all be immersed in its Light. (All life forms are preparing for this event at a cellular level, for it is at this level that the most profound changes will occur that will change both your *density* and change your *destiny*, all at once. *The Cetaceans are involved in this molecular changeover. We are the avant-garde leading the way to your new home in the Sirius B constellation.*)"

The italics are not mine. The italics are the whales'.

Robbins's book ends poignantly. Among the last words sent to the telepath by the cetaceans are messages to Robbins's daughter and son, for whom the whales express their love. Then comes an "About the Author" page, which seems to have been written by Robbins herself from exile in New York, far from her whale-listening outpost in Florida. Some sort of unwanted dislocation has come into the telepath's life. Her author's note amounts to a kind of coda, which is as revealing, in its way, as anything the whales have told her. The author's note makes several things clear: It is not easy being an empath. A lot of psychic static is inevitable, when you are picking up signals from the Photon Belt. It is never quiet inside, when one is serving as a telepathic conduit for the agony and ecstasy of the whales. The last paragraph reads:

"Dianne is irresistibly drawn to the ocean, visiting the beach every day. She yearns to live near the ocean, and dreams of moving to Florida where her family and many Cetaceans are. Family life is very important to her, and she misses her family in Florida from whom she is separated, just as Corky and Keiko are separated from their families—only she has the freedom to visit her family as she wishes. Dianne fervently hopes that Corky and Keiko, and all Cetaceans in captivity will be freed, so that they, too, can be with their families again; and that someday she, too, can be with hers."

"KEIKO ATTRACTS A FRINGE ELEMENT, as well as the mainstream," Dianne Hammond, the whale's press secretary, told me. "We have lots of people who believe they channel for Keiko. We have one very persistent person lately who has messages from Keiko that she feels obligated to give us. Channeling. Clairvoyance. People who think that Keiko has a certain power that they want to tap into. So it's a sort of a tangential security issue for us."

Aside from the empath Dianne Robbins, the most persistent of Keiko clairvoyants was an animal channeler named Bonnie Norton. Unlike Robbins, who communicated with Keiko from Florida, Bonnie Norton had lately been visiting the Oregon Coast Aquarium in the flesh for short-distance communion with the whale. Norton had been holding what she called "one-woman rallies" outside the aquarium and granting television interviews in which she revealed the true feelings of the whale. Keiko had told her clearly that he wanted to stay in Oregon. "I like the attention and effect I have on all the people that come to see me, especially the children," he said. "They will remember me for a long time. They will learn what *not* to do with us. I need to impact others by my captivity much more than I need to be set free."

This was, confusingly, exactly the opposite of what Keiko had told Dianne Robbins. To Robbins at every opportunity he had whispered that he yearned to be free. There seemed to be three possibilities: Either one of the empaths had misunderstood Keiko, or the whale was speaking with forked tongue, or telepathic communication with animals is a delusion.

Hammond and I, as we discussed the clairvoyants, sat in her office in the hangarlike headquarters of the Free Willy Keiko Foundation, adjacent to the Killer Whale Facility at the Oregon Coast Aquarium. The high rim of Keiko's tank was visable through the window. Hammond, a woman in her thirties, had been a writer before she fell into Keiko's sphere. For the past three years, she had been unable to get a single paragraph of fiction written, for her duties as Keiko's spokeswoman left her no spare moments. As the time neared for Keiko's departure for Iceland, she was fielding thirty calls a day from the press.

"About a year and a half ago, before the aquarium security system was fully in effect," she said, "there was an older woman, in her early sixties, who made it from the public side clear around to the pool, up to the top, while a training session was going on. She raced across the pool top and flung a handful of her jewelry into the pool."

"Why?" I asked.

"She thought it would help. Help *what,* I'm not sure. She breached all of these locks. I don't know how she did it. Maybe she leaped tall buildings. Nobody saw her and stopped her until she was literally at the side of the medical pool, heaving in this handful. She didn't understand that it could have done him harm, had he chosen to eat any of those pieces of jewelry. At any rate, they were fished out immediately."

Some months after the episode of the jewelry lady, Dianne Hammond herself had slipped across the demilitarized zone that divided Keiko's tank between the warring camps of the Oregon Coast Aquarium and the Free Willy Keiko Foundation, and she had defected to the foundation. She was sleeping now with the enemy, having married a foundation employee, Keiko's head trainer, Nolan Harvey. Her defection was one more sore point in the feud between the two institutions.

"The jewelry lady was a wake-up call," Hammond went on. "From the point when she came through, we—both the foundation and the aquarium—stepped up security a lot. Then late last summer, the foundation actually hired a kind of a parallel security staff, guards who would be at the facility when the animal-care staff went home at the end of the day. So that there'd be somebody here around the clock. One of the banks of camera monitors in the staff room is for research, and the other is all surveillance." Security was improved but not perfect, she said. Just weeks ago, a drunken man had magically breached the perimeter and was disrobing at poolside when he was apprehended.

Hammond sighed.

"It's not uncommon still to have media people, too, who just lose it when they meet Keiko," she said. "I always feel so totally hard-boiled at that point. I had one cable-access duo from Salem, Oregon—two women, late forties or early fifties, not really media-experienced yet, but they were trying to make their way in this media world. Generally I try to explain what's going on in a training session. So I was blabbering away. I looked over, and the camera-woman was just sobbing. She was so moved by being in Keiko's presence."

Hammond herself was so routinely in Keiko's company that this sort of emotion, for her, was not possible. Another area in which she felt deficient was mysticism. "I would say none of the staff has felt quite mystical. We feel morally very responsible, but not mystical. There's no mysticism on the staff's part, at all."

I glanced through Hammond's window at the Killer Whale Facility, where the middle-aged camerwoman had wept over Keiko, and where the jewelry lady had flung her jewels. Keiko's tank held two million gallons. The facility cost $7.3 million. It was staffed by dozens of humans. Expenses were underwritten by a billionaire. I waved to encompass the scene in the window.

"There will never be anything like this again," I suggested to Hammond. "Nope," she agreed.

I proposed to Hammond that no animal actor in the movies, not any of the bottlenose dolphins that played Flipper, nor any of the German shepherds that played Rin Tin Tin, nor the collies that played Lassie, nor Roy Rogers's horse Trigger, nor Francis the Talking Mule, had spawned anything remotely like the Cult of Keiko. Hammond nodded.

"I've been telling this story for three years, and I still don't have a grasp of it," she said. "You have to ask yourself, What is it about this animal, or this species, that's attracting all this emotion? People come here and they don't simply say, 'Cool, he's a good-lookin' animal.' There's more; there's this sort of emotional sense of moral responsibility and connection. People call from the Midwest and leave me messages. 'You don't need to call me back, it's okay, but my daughter in England just read an Icelandic news article, and we're a little concerned, so we thought you might need to know that . . .' and they proceed to tell me something I need to know about Keiko."

Hammond had never watched *Free Willy* except, she said, "in dribs and drabs," and she had never bothered with any of the sequels. "It's so anthropomorphic that it's painful," she said of the original film. "I don't find the story line appealing or interesting." For Hammond, many of the scenes were laughable. "Like when the kid is helping Keiko be trucked to another location. You'd never transport a killer whale on a flatbed truck like that. They're not transported that way at all. They go in a big box of water. They're not built to take the weight of their own internal organs. At very least you'd have to put them on a huge, thick bed of foam."

Hammond's face darkened as she remembered another detail from the movie.

"One thing that's hard to watch, if you know what he looks like now, is all the scenes where Keiko himself was in that little arena pool in Mexico. He just looks so bad. He's got those huge lesions. Papilloma."

As external affairs officer for the Free Willy Keiko Foundation, Hammond's job was to be informed on Keiko and his progress and to handle inquiries from the public and the press. She was the middlewoman. Her work had sharpened both her sense of the whale and her sense of his public. In his public, she had seen a change—a shift in the apprehensions of his fans about his welfare. In the year before Keiko's arrival in Oregon, and then for about a year afterward, almost all the questions she fielded had to do with freeing Keiko. When were they going to release him? When was he going home? When would he be reunited with his family? It was the nearly unanimous opinion of callers that the ending of *Free Willy*, the movie, should immediately come true for the real whale. "Now, you don't hear that much anymore," she said. "More often now, it's 'Maybe freeing him isn't a good thing. Maybe you should keep him.' It's changed dramatically from this very naïve, make-the-movie-real idea to something more nuanced. His story has been so well covered that people have become educated about him. It no longer seems quite so simple a matter as to just send him straight back to his family."

In the beginning, to those multitudes of callers urging immediate freedom, Hammond had explained that Keiko's rehabilitation had only just begun; that he was not ready just yet for the wild. Lately, in responding to the keep-him-in-Newport crowd, she found herself arguing the other way.

"One of the things that people do not understand at the moment is the difference between this pool and a bay pen. It's a big difference. People start now from the departure point that he's *happy* here. He's really happy. He's safe. He's busy. He's got this great big pool, and people love him, and he's well fed, and what could be better? You try to explain that happiness is a relative term, and that there are two big things missing here. One is acoustical interactive possibilities—a natural world instead of a man-made one. The other is lack of any social interaction, except with humans. People start to realize, 'Oh! Okay, so maybe this is not all that he needs, after all.' You explain that he may never leave our care. He may end up in a bay pen, but connected again, part of a meaningful world."

On Hammond's shelf was a copy of *The Call Goes Out,* the Dianne Robbins anthology of telepathic messages from Keiko and other whales. When I reached out to finger the spine, Hammond pulled the volume out for me. I could take it if I wanted it, she said; it was not a title she really wanted in her library.

Inside was a letter from Robbins to the Free Willy Keiko Foundation, in which the author asked, on behalf of Keiko, that the foundation accept the book as a gift. She included a telepathic note from Keiko, "Please deliver my messages to all parties involved in my captivity and release." Robbins appended a one-sheet manifesto, the "Universal Declaration of Marine Mammal Rights," drawn up by an organization called the Dolphin Society. The document was modeled on our own Bill of Rights, with ten commandments. *Article six:* "No whale or dolphin shall be subjected to arbitrary arrest, detention or exile." *Article seven:* "Every whale and dolphin has the right to freedom of movement and residence in the sea and the right to return unhindered to its home territory." *Article eight:* "Every whale and dolphin has the right to freedom of peaceful assembly and association."

It struck me that the two Diannes—Dianne Robbins, Keiko's channeler, and Dianne Hammond, Keiko's spokeswoman—could not have occupied more distant ends of the spectrum. The whale of Robbins and the whale of Hammond could not have been more different animals.

I asked Hammond whether she thought Keiko was ready for the wild. Could she imagine the whale's being released right now?

"I can't imagine it," she said. "I don't even have an answer. Not because I think he's necessarily helpless. But I don't know how his accomplishments here in the pool would relate to his dealing with problems in the wild. I don't know enough about killer whales, for one thing. I don't have any opinion at all. He's gotten pretty adept with the fish in this pool, *but here he has four walls and corners.* That's way different from not having any barriers to pin fish against. I think everyone of us on the staff would tell you he's not ready, not by any means. And it could be years before he is. If he ever is at all."

17

LISTENING TO THE BLOWHOLE

THREE OF KEIKO'S TRAINERS WERE PLAYING HIDE-AND-SEEK WITH THE whale. All three were dressed in their black-and-yellow splash suits, sealed at the neck and cuffs to keep the wearers warm in the fifty-degree water. Keiko was attired as always in his basic black-and-white. Two of the trainers, Jennifer Schorr and Peter Noah, trudged like Volga boatmen along the shallows of the wet-walk, towing the third trainer, Brian O'Neill, through the water in an inner tube, trolling him like bait ahead of the whale. On reaching the med-pool portal, Jennifer and Peter jerked Brian inside. Brian hastily dog-paddled his inner tube into hiding behind the wall, just within the entrance. His two colleagues hid behind either stanchion of the gantry crane.

Keiko surged through the portal. He seemed to detect instantly, by eye or by echolocation, that the water ahead was empty of Brian; he had been tricked. He executed a sharp left turn. The turning radius of a killer whale is remarkably short for an animal so large, but a twenty-foot hull and five tons of inertia cannot stop on a dime. Before Keiko could come completely about, Jennifer and Peter had jumped from hiding to yank Brian back out through the med-pool entrance. They had eluded the killer whale. One point for the human beings.

The trainers did not play the game excitedly. Their faces were businesslike. Brian, reclining in his inner tube as he was trolled ahead of the whale, betrayed none of that pretend-yet-almost-real terror of capture that children feel in playing hide-and-seek. His playmate was a bull killer whale, nearly full-grown, but for Brian the thrill seemed to be gone. Brian did not look gleefully terrorized; he simply looked cold. Keiko, for his part, seemed to be having a good time.

"We always try to vary the game," Peter Noah told me as he watched the whale. "Improvise as we go along. Keep it interesting to everybody."

Peter and Jennifer tried to sneak Brian into the med pool again, but Keiko was wise to them now. He cut Brian off at the pass, his rostrum bumping Brian's inner tube as the two tried to squeeze simultaneously through the passage. "'I don't *think* so,'" said Peter Noah, speaking for the whale. On the spot, Peter invented a new contest he called "Keeper of the

Med Pool." He made up the rules as he went along. Keiko seemed to appre-hend them faster than I did.

AT THE END OF THIS session, Lanny Cornell, Keiko's chief veterinarian, ap-peared topside. Today he had flown up from southern California for one of his periodic examinations of the whale. After conversing briefly with the three trainers at the edge of the pool, he turned and walked away from every-one. He stationed himself at the pool's edge. With his back to a stanchion of the gantry crane, as if to fence himself off from the rest of us, he held very still and studied his patient. During his whale exams, I gathered, Dr. Cornell likes a little separation from humanity.

"I was looking at his stature," the veterinarian would tell me afterward. "Seeing how it compared to what I remembered from my last visit. Listening to his blowhole. Watching for all the things that we call 'signalment'—what the animal is saying to us in its body language. The really good human doc-tors do the same."

Dr. Cornell glanced over at Keiko. The whale was poking his rostrum above the surface at the edge of the slide-out, greeting a trainer who sloshed toward him through the shallows in gumboots, carrying a pail of fish.

"Behavioral observation is extremely important with marine mammals," Dr. Cornell went on. "Without careful observation of their interaction with their trainers, and their behavior when left alone, you really can't make any diagnosis of these animals. Because they don't show illness. Or they show only very subtle signs. They can hide an illness for a long, long time. Which is why I'll spend six, seven hours in the pen with him today. I'm watching him very carefully."

"You like to get away from folks, when you do that?" I suggested. "You seemed to take some steps away—just to get clear of the social distraction?"

"Yeah. I become very focused when I'm working. My social skills when I'm observing an animal are not too good."

Dr. Cornell's social skills, truth be told, are not particularly polished whether he is observing an animal or not. The veterinarian is a man's man, a deep baritone with a curt, gruff, no-nonsense manner. He can be extraordi-narily rude. There is no more controversial figure in Keiko's saga.

Lanny Cornell did not learn cetacean veterinary science by working for Greenpeace, or the Humane Society, or some anti-captivity group—no one learns the art that way. Dr. Cornell learned whale medicine in the captive-whale industry, in a long association with Sea World, where he ministered to about half the captive killer whales on the planet. He became expert in the hunt for wild specimens, as well. When the capture of killer whales was banned in U.S. waters, Cornell moved to Iceland and netted many there. These days he was a magnet for the suspicions that the anti-captivists hold for the Free Willy Keiko Foundation. Rumor had it, among the anti-captivists, that Keiko's chief veterinarian was the very man who orchestrated his capture in 1979. When it came to Keiko, they suggested, Cornell's history would not lend to catch-and-release.

Cornell drew fire from the other side of the debate, as well. Phyllis Bell and the Oregon Coast Aquarium had called his treatment of Keiko into question, suggesting that Cornell was ignoring signs of ill health in Keiko. Where the anti-captivists were sure Cornell would try to hang onto the whale, the captive-whale industry charged that Cornell was too ready to *free* him.

The *Frontline* documentary on Keiko, *A Whale of a Business,* is an exposé of fishy practices by the world's marine parks, Sea World in particular, and Dr. Cornell is one of the principal targets. The producers, Neil Docherty and Renata Simone, make no secret of their biases. The film is largely ambush journalism in which the ambushed are always the aquarists. All the tough questions are for Sea World people—questions suggested, often, by animal-rights activists in previous friendly interviews with that side of the debate. Dr. Cornell, for his part, stonewalls his own interview, refusing to answer questions about his career at Sea World. "It happens to be Sea World's business," he says. "You should ask Sea World." Repeating this mantra again and again, he comes across as a man with a lot to hide.

"We called him 'Mr. Pro-captivity," Ric O'Barry, a former dolphin trainer, tells *Frontline.* O'Barry, who trained the bottlenose dolphins that starred in the old television show *Flipper,* has a poignant scene in the documentary. He describes the last moments of one of his Flippers—there were a series of them, just as there were a number of Lassies and Rin Tin Tins. According to O'Barry, who weeps in the recollection, this particular Flipper, after years in captivity, committed suicide, giving his old trainer a last look and simply sinking to the bottom of the pool. Ric O'Barry has no use for Lanny Cornell. "I predict as long as he's involved, this dolphin, Keiko, will be in captivity and marketed for the rest of his life."

"Lanny Cornell was the architect of setting up a connection between Sea World and the drive-fishery slaughter in Japan," Ben White of the Animal Welfare Institute told *Frontline.* "The man is drenched in blood. If he has changed his spots so much that he now wants Keiko out, then I would be amazed. The greatest step forward, to me, that the Free Willy Keiko Foundation could make, to show they really are going to release that whale, they should release Lanny Cornell now."

In Iceland, the *Frontline* crew found an old aquarium that Cornell remodeled as a holding pen for captured orcas. They videotaped the place, empty and abandoned now. The interior is bleak: tiny windows, dimness, an old door lying on the dry concrete bottom of the pool. In an accompanying interview, a *Frontline* informant, John Hall—a former chief veterinarian at Sea World who has gone over to the abolitionist side—testifies that Dr. Cornell spent $150,000 on this structure. Dr. Hall claims that Dr. Cornell, after showing him the blueprints for his dungeon, cautioned, "You didn't see any of this. You didn't hear any of this. You weren't here." The *Frontline* camera roams the grim interior of Dr. Cornell's secret facility as it might roam the ruins of Auschwitz. The implication is clear: In this hellhole for killer whales, Lanny Cornell was the Dr. Mengele.

"Keiko's future is in the hands of someone who spent his career managing the captivity of animals," the *Frontline* narrator says. "Perhaps an ironic choice, unless he's undergone a conversion."

This idea of conversion—the assumption that in rehabilitating Keiko, Lanny Cornell, the old whale trapper, must be doing some form of penance—seems to be an irresistible temptation for journalists. It makes such a good narrative that almost everyone seeks to impose it on him. No notion seems to irritate Dr. Cornell more.

"Oh, I don't think it's any *conversion,*" he answered *Frontline* icily. "I don't think it's ironic at all. It's what I do. I'm a vet, and my life has been dedicated to taking care of these animals."

Cornell's past imbroglios with the media have made him suspicious of the entire fourth estate, me included. My phone calls to his office in El Cajon were never answered. When I finally met the veterinarian in Oregon, my first interviews with him went badly. To most of my questions he replied with impatience and a hint of asperity. To some he replied not at all. He would not *decline* to answer; he would simply stare off silently at the horizon like a weathered cavalry officer who has just glimpsed Sioux. This was a new experience for me as an interviewer.

"HE DOESN'T LIKE THE MEDIA much," I suggested one day to Dianne Hammond, Keiko's press secretary. Hammond nodded. I offered my view that the press would love a colorful, tough character like Dr. Cornell, if he ever opened up to them. Hammond sighed.

"The thing about Lanny, he's one of the pioneers of cetacean medicine," she said. "He wrote the book on how to transport these animals safely, how to provide them with facilities adequate to allow them to breed in captivity. He was the one who oversaw the first successful breeding program. He's written the book on captive care. He's written the book on cetacean medicine—not just in captivity, but in rehabilitation.

"Sea World's public relations have been so poor! It's just a conundrum to me. Nolan Harvey, Keiko's head trainer, came through Sea World's rehabilitation and veterinary program, where they work with hundreds and hundreds of stranded and injured animals every year—and release them! It's not for show, and it doesn't bring them money, but they do it. And because they've been doing that work for so long, they've brought up a generation of people like Nolan, Jeff Foster, and Brian O'Neill, who know a great deal about EMT-style cetacean medical care. And that's because of Sea World and because of Lanny. In that sense, Lanny is the best person on earth to have overseeing a rehabilitation-and-reintroduction program. But Sea World does not seem to beat their own drum about their good deeds, and Lanny doesn't, either. When people think of Sea World, they think only of Shamu—of performing killer whales—and this whole other serious side of medical care and rehabilitation gets lost.

"When Sea World did its killer-whale collection work, it was always cloak-and-dagger, one step ahead of Greenpeace, and I think Lanny just got into the mind-set that the less they know about you, the better."

18

RED ANTS

FROM DR. LANNY CORNELL'S OWN LIPS, IT WAS EVIDENT, I WOULD LEARN little about him. I turned instead to the literature. In a 1998 report on Keiko's health, I found Cornell's curriculum vitae. He had a private veterinary practice—domestic and exotic animals—at Singing Hills Animal Hospital in San Diego. He had served as consultant to the Minnesota Zoo, the Rio Grande Zoo, and Chicago's Brookfield Zoo, advising on marine-mammal care and on the design of aquaria and coral-reef exhibits. At Sea World of California, Sea World of Texas, Sea World of Florida, and Sea World of Ohio, he had designed exhibits and new killer-whale stadiums. He had conceived and supervised a breeding program that produced the first successful birth of a killer whale in captivity. At Marineland of Canada, he had supervised Canada's first successful captive killer-whale birth.

Hobbies: Scuba diving. Aboriginal Eskimo and Indian art. Animal photography. The breeding and training of horses. The history of veterinary medical publications and their collection in his personal library.

Publications: "Do dolphins drink water?" "Pseudopersistent urachus in a baby walrus." "Care of pinnipeds in captivity." "Live capture statistics for the killer whale in California, Washington, and British Columbia." "The rehabilitation of sea otters." "Renin and aldosterone levels in dolphins and sea lions." "A census of captive marine mammals in North America." The list went on for pages. I was surprised that a working animal doctor with such heavy commitments as a zoo consultant could find time to write so many research papers. "The use of tetracycline in age determination of the common dolphin, *Delphinus delphis.*" "Live capture technique for the killer whale." "A summary of information derived from the recurrent mass stranding of a herd of false killer whales." "The placenta of the killer whale." "Esophageal palpation in dolphins as a diagnostic aid." "Anesthesia and tusk extraction in walrus." "A ringed seal in Southern California."

Ringed seals are northern animals. The last ringed seal I myself had seen had surfaced in a river mouth on Admiralty Island, in southeast Alaska, as I paddled south to Canada in a kayak.

"That ringed seal," I asked Dr. Cornell. "The one you wrote up. What was he doing in southern California?"

"Don't know," Dr. Cornell answered. "But he was there, a stranded animal that showed up on the shoreline in San Diego. We did some research on him, trying to figure out why he got there. Didn't come up with much. It's hard to tell how far some of these animals ranged before we started killing them off for their pelts and fat. Maybe he was just recolonizing his old range."

"*Do* dolphins drink water?" I asked him. The question of whether dolphins drink water had been the subject of the first paper on his list.

"Actually, they do. That was the first paper that Nancy Telford, John Prescott, and I did at Marineland. We were all curious as to whether or not they drink water. We used radioactive iodine."

Cornell told me that he and John Prescott, who was then curator of Marineland, had engaged Nancy Telford, the only nuclear physician they knew. It had been Telford who figured out the methodology. The three collaborators introduced radioactive iodine to the pool water and recovered it twenty-four hours later by catheter from the dolphin's urine. "There isn't any question now," Cornell said. "There have been enough studies besides our own that prove whales and dolphins do drink seawater. Now the question is why? Is it because they need the water, or because they need the salt? We suspect it's the salt. In the metabolism of these animals, the hydrolysis of fat creates water. We think they get plenty of H_2O from the water content of their food and their own metabolism."

Cornell's curriculum vitae, in the space reserved for areas of scientific interest, had begun with horses. "Equine Medicine, Equine Abdominal Surgery, Equine Anesthesia," he had written. In an aside, he noted that he had designed and built the first equine halothane-gas anesthesia device used by the College of Veterinary Medicine at Colorado State University.

"You designed a machine to anesthetize horses?" I asked him.

Dr. Cornell glanced at me—a not unfriendly look. "You read it pretty closely," he said.

"The design was some sort of breakthrough?" I asked.

He laughed. "No, it was just ego. I was a sophomore in veterinary school. One of the big anesthesia companies had just designed and built a gas anesthesia machine for horses. They brought it to Colorado State University. The anesthesiologist in large animals at that time was a fellow by the name of Bill Wolf. I just happened to be on his rotation that day, and I saw him looking at this machine. It had a big price tag on it, something like ten or twelve thousand dollars. I just looked at it. It was a very simple device. I said, 'You know, Dr. Wolf, if I couldn't build something like that for less than a thousand dollars, I'd eat it.' He looked at me kind of funny. He said, 'Okay, big mouth, go ahead. Build it.'

"So I went to a sheet metal shop, and I told them what I wanted to fabricate. I got some vacuum hoses, and I made some valves out of pieces of rubber flaps, and kind of assembled this whole thing. It was a stainless-steel canister inside of a stainless-steel canister. We filled the inner canister with soda lime to absorb the CO_2. We put a rubber bag on the end of it as a rebreathing device. Two vacuum hoses came out the other end, one for halothane and one for oxygen. They came together in a Y-valve. We set little flappers in the Y-valve to keep the gas from going the wrong direction in the pipes, and the tracheal tube went from there into the animal. I picked up, wholesale, a vaporizer for the halothane. We used that very machine for all of the equine anesthesias in the large-animal section of the college for the next two years. The university sent that other, expensive machine back to the manufacturer.

"I'd be in class, and the surgeons would come in and point to me and say, 'Come on.' They'd take me out of class to go run the anesthesia machine. I was the one that built it. They trusted my juvenile judgment in how to run it. That double canister, to be honest with you, I still have it in my garage. After I left school, I used it in my practice for four or five years until I finally got another one. Innovation is the mother of invention. Or invention is the mother of innovation, or somepin' like that."

LANNY CORNELL GREW UP IN Santa Fe, New Mexico, in the 1940s.

"I don't remember exactly when I decided I wanted to be a veterinarian, but it was very, very young. To be honest with you, I wanted to be a veterinarian before I even knew what veterinarians did. I knew I wanted to take care of animals. My mother says that I used to bring home all kinds of animals when I was a little kid. Three, four, five years old."

Cornell's earliest memory is of sitting in his backyard in Santa Fe and watching red ants.

"I don't know how old I was, but I had to be very, very young, because the image of the ants in my mind is so large. I had to have been a very small child. The ants, to me they seemed huge, like an inch across—but of course they weren't. I've just always had this attraction to observation of biology. It's probably some kind of a genetic direction. I just love to observe the behavior of animals. And veterinary medicine is probably seventy-five percent observation. You can see, smell, feel diseases on animals long before you go into the laboratory and prove that particular disease is what they have.

"I had a professor in college who emphasized that before you send anything to the laboratory, you should have a good idea what your diagnosis is. Don't wait for the lab to diagnose it for you. Because you might send the lab in the wrong direction. A lot of the new veterinary graduates come out heavily relying on the laboratory, heavily relying on specialists. We weren't taught to do that. We were taught the opposite, to rely on ourselves."

Dr. Cornell's résumé is very horsey, I had observed. It was less a curriculum vitae than a curriculum equi. I asked him about the origin of his attraction to *Equus equus.*

"I grew up amongst the heart of the population in New Mexico that hung out with horses," he said. "I originally thought I was quite the little cowboy. A lot of horseback riding. Rodeos. I rode bulls and bareback broncs and steer-wrestled. When I was in college I did a lot of that. It finally dawned on me one day that I was never going to be very good at it. I probably ought to go get a life. So I went to veterinary school. I was lucky to get in. I wasn't really a very good student. I believe I was part of that quota of students they let in just because they feel sorry for them.

"The only thing I wanted to be was a horse doctor. The only reason I felt I was in college was to do horse medicine. In fact, when I got out of college, for the first nine, ten years, I was an equine practitioner. I got tangled up with Marineland in Los Angeles by accident. They were looking for a veterinary consultant, and I lived in the area. The Los Angeles County Veterinarian's Office asked me to go talk to John Prescott. John was the curator then of Marineland and later became the first director of the New England Aquarium. I told the Veterinarian's Office there was no way I could help Prescott; that I didn't know anything about those animals. I remember exactly what the guy said. He said, 'Lanny, you don't understand, *nobody does.*'"

"The field was wide open to you," I suggested.

"Yeah. That's the reason I went to see John Prescott. He and I hit it off just like a couple of old buddies. So I said, Okay, I'll give it a try. And I've been doing it ever since. First part-time, then in 1973, when I went to Sea World, full-time."

I asked Dr. Cornell about his design at Sea World of the first successful reproduction program for captive orcas. What had been the keys to success?

"We did a tremendous amount of research. We spent a lot of money on research on reproduction at Sea World. It was a pet project of mine. The truth is that the real reason I went to work at Sea World in the first place was because I wanted to see if you could breed killer whales in captivity. Everybody said you couldn't. Hasn't ever been done. Won't be done. These animals will never reproduce in captivity. When somebody says something like that to me, it's some kind of a challenge. I end up thinking too much about it. Pretty soon it becomes a project that I need to get done.

"First thing we wanted to do is learn as much as we could about the physiology and reproductive capabilities of killer whales. The other thing we wanted to do was put them in facilities that were large enough. I wanted to see their behavior become something similar to what we see in the wild—in their swimming patterns, their grouping activities. Family groups and so forth. I encouraged, or probably the word is 'cajoled,' the Sea World management into allowing us to build the first large pool at Sea World Florida. We got one of the female whales pregnant in San Diego and then moved her to Florida to this big pool."

Cornell had been unable to monitor the growing fetus as an obstetrician might, he said, for the female killer whale does not lend herself structurally to manual examination, as do pregnant horses and cows. He did borrow an ultrasound machine from a local university, but the blubber layer proved too thick for it to penetrate. He could see something inside the uterus, but could not determine what that something was.

"Prior to this, I had gone around to all the different marine-life facilities that had killer whales and begged them to send us their whales so we could get them pregnant and see if we could breed them. We had relatively few takers, but a couple of places did cooperate. The agument against it was that it hadn't been done. They didn't think you could. Anyway, lo and behold, in September 1985 she had a baby and it lived."

"You were on hand for the delivery?"

"Oh yes. I lived in Florida for seven or eight weeks waiting for that to happen. We knew she was imminent, but we had no idea how long she should be pregnant. We knew that the females that had given birth unsuccessfully in the past had done so at approximately sixteen months. So starting at about fifteen months, I sat by her side. She actually went almost seventeen months, which meant I was there for quite a while. In past pregnancies, some calves were stillborn, and some were actually born alive but didn't live more than a few days. This particular calf, the first baby Shamu, lived, and of course I lived with her for several weeks.

"The birth must have been quite a moment," I proposed to him.

"Unbelievable," said Lanny Cornell.

DR. LANNY CORNELL ENTERED THE staff room, followed by a trainer, Peter Noah. Cornell strode briskly to the whale in the window, impatient, like an HMO physician with an overfull schedule. In fact, he had no other patients. His sole client in Newport was this whale, and his schedule for the day was devoted entirely to Keiko. For a time the vet silently contemplated his subject.

Keiko gazed back. To the whale's dark-adapted eye, peering into this well-lit room, Dr. Cornell must have looked a bit overexposed. Lanny Cornell is a large, stocky man who once rode Brahma bulls, but to his patient he figured to look small, both optically, as projected on Keiko's retina by the spherical lens of the cetacean, and relatively, in comparison to the ten thousand pounds of the whale himself. To a killer whale, even a Brahma bull is a puny sort of creature.

Keiko recognizes his veterinarian, just as he recognizes his various trainers. Does he find his cues in facial features? It could easily be so. A performing killer whale has the visual acuity and beak-eye coordination to leap entirely out of the water and pluck a cigarette from his trainer's lips. *Orcinus orca* has enough appreciation of human physiognomy to know where mouth leaves off and cigarette begins. But it also seemed possible that Keiko knows Cornell less by the veterinarian's rugged features than by his general aspect—by that sum of subliminal cues that English birders call "gizz." The whale may know Cornell from something in the quality of the man's attentiveness, or in his aura of gruffness, or in his military posture.

Keiko hung so long in the window that Cornell commented on the whale's breath-hold capacity. "The last time I heard, it was sixteen minutes and some change," he said. Peter Noah updated him. "The record now is seventeen minutes thirty seconds." Dr. Cornell allowed himself the thinnest of smiles. He turned to me. "When he got here, he could do only a minute or two of dive time," he said.

When Cornell finished his examination, I took the opportunity to ask more questions about the research papers in his résumé. "Esophageal palpations in dolphins" had been one of his titles.

"Esophageal palpations in dolphins?" I asked him now.

"That was an interesting one," he said. "Before we had flexible endoscopes, it occurred to me that I could do a lot of diagnostic work with dolphins that were large enough for me to get my hand in their mouth. In order to feel the lung areas, to feel for things like abcesses."

"Anesthetized?" I asked.

"No, they're not anesthetized, they're fully awake. They don't seem to object that much. They fight a little bit."

"But *the lung*?" I asked. "You can't really feel the lung through the esophagus, can you?"

"You can palpate the lungs through the esophagus. You can also reach into the stomach with your hand, in dolphins of some size, in order to retrieve foreign objects. If you have long enough arms, you can get into pretty big animals. Luckily, I have large hands and arms. But I can't reach everything. Eventually we figured out that if we got some of these big basketball players—these long-armed basketball players—they could help us out. When we had problems with dolphins that had something in their stomach, that's what we did. There were numerous occasions when we had very long-armed basketball players come in and help us retrieve objects from a dolphin's stomach. They weren't squeamish. We had more volunteers than we needed."

Cornell recruited college players from the San Diego area and occasionally engaged professionals. He remembers none of the names. The pro hoopsters were not too proud for this slippery work. They had the longest arms of all. I tried to remember San Diego Clipper players from that era. Norm Nixon? Nixon was a point guard just six feet tall, not built for deep dolphin work. San Diego always fielded such forgettable basketball teams that I could not remember any of the forwards or centers, but it was heartening to learn that the Clippers, such habitual losers on the court, had been able to accomplish something off it.

"If you have a large enough abcess, you can feel it on the lung," Dr. Cornell said. "You can actually palpate the heart and feel the heartbeat and see if that feels normal. It's not something we use a lot anymore, because we have things like endoscopes to push down in there and take a look. Of course, manual palpation in large-animal practice is not unusual. You do that with cattle and horses rectally, to determine if they are pregnant or if they have gastrointestinal problems. So it was a natural thing for me to try, being a large-animal doctor.

"When I was in school, I remember I used to trade any small-animal time I had in the hospital at the veterinary college with students who wanted to be small-animal doctors. I would trade that for their large-animal time. So I spent most of my time in the large-animal section of the school. I don't think the instructors ever quite figured out how many times I traded it off.

"You just like large animals," I suggested.

"Large animals, yeah. I remember working with Bruce Stevens once. Bruce Stevens was one of the head trainers at Sea World for many years, and we were working on a very large old whale. Bruce came up behind me and said, 'You know, I get the feeling, Lanny, the bigger they are the better you like it.' And I guess it's true. These large animals have a kind of a . . . I don't know. A regal magnificence. It seems like the bigger they are, the more impressive they are to me. I love elephants for the same reason, I think."

FOR DINNER THAT EVENING, I joined Dr. Cornell and a group from the Free Willy Keiko Foundation at a new Newport restaurant called April's. The restaurant was a sizable place, one of the several new establishments of the tourism boom that had followed the whale into town. April's was in vogue now with Keiko's people, and it was prospering with the general public, yet I could not help thinking about the ephemerality of restaurants. I wondered how long this one would survive the departure of the whale.

"Tell us about the suitcases of money," David Phillips called to Dr.

Cornell, teasingly, across the table. "What about those suitcases of money you brought to Iceland?"

The waitress, scribbling our orders, briefly lost her train of thought.

Dr. Cornell smiled grimly and waved off the question. He did not want to talk about the suitcases of money he was supposed to have spirited into Iceland, in his days at Sea World. As drinks arrived, Cornell and Phillips began a spirited argument over killer-whale research in Iceland. Phillips believed that a priority of the Free Willy Keiko Foundation should be to conduct studies to determine how many killer-whale pods inhabited the vicinity of the Westman Islands—the area of Keiko's proposed release—and whether any of those pods vocalized in a dialect similar to Keiko's. Dr. Cornell was impatient with this idea.

"It's not important," he said. "It has no bearing on the release. It doesn't matter how many pods are in the area, or what dialects they speak. If you want the whale to be in Oregon another twenty-five years, then keep asking those questions."

The next morning—just forty-eight days and counting before Keiko's scheduled departure for Iceland—Dr. Cornell drove several of us to his favorite breakfast spot in Newport, a waterfront dive he called Dean's Place. I rode in front with the veterinarian. In back rode David Phillips of Earth Island Institute and John Watters, president of Watters Life Support Service. Watters had come to Oregon to troubleshoot a problem with the plumbing in Killer Whale Facility. En route to the café, Phillips opened the morning's *Oregonian* to discover a front-page article, "Keiko Death Threat." It seemed that a disgruntled fisherman in Iceland had threatened to poison the whale. "I can't believe this!" Phillips muttered. What Phillips could not believe was that the source for the story was an Icelander employed by the Free Willy Keiko Foundation, who had gone to the press before informing the foundation. (Icelanders have a candor that seems to be a feature of the small democracy, and which can make for culture shock in a citizen of a big democracy.) Phillips was dismayed that he would learn about the death threat in the newspaper. John Watters, Keiko's plumber, seemed untroubled by this leak.

Dr. Cornell had no interest in it, either. Instead of commiserating with Phillips, the two men spoke fondly of Dean, owner of the greasy spoon that was our destination. They agreed that Dean was a Vietnam vet. He *had* to be a vet—he had that unmistakable combat-veteran aura. "Dean doesn't care about anything," Cornell said in admiration. He and Watters joked that next trip they would bring duct tape to repair rips in the seats at Dean's café.

As we pulled up in front of Dean's and opened the car doors, we were assaulted by a powerful, fishy, fecal smell.

"Smells like seal shit," said John Watters.

"It *is* seal shit," replied Lanny Cornell, happily.

The veterinarian led us to a corner booth by the window. The red vinyl of the seats was cracked with age. The fissures had been repaired by duct tape, which itself had fissured and been repaired with more duct tape, which in turn had split and needed repair again. Our window looked down on pilings capped by roosting gulls. Beneath the birds was a floating dock whitened with gull guano. No sea lions were hauled out on the dock at the moment, but it was evident that they used it, for a faint odor of pinniped carried inside. The water around the pilings had an oily sheen and drifted with flotsam and jetsam. There was nothing gentrified about this stretch of waterfront, no hint of maritime chic. The ambience was old Cannery Row. The coffee was good. Our six-egg omelettes arrived, buttressed by great mounds of home-style fried potatoes. Dr. Cornell greeted his heaping plate with a small, thin smile of satisfaction. There were no concessions to gastronomic correctness in Dean's cuisine. This was Lanny Cornell's kind of place.

The breakfast talk turned to the new Keiko documentary that Jean-Michel Cousteau was filming. Cornell told us about his interview on camera yesterday with Cousteau. "He asked me, didn't I think that Keiko's release would lead to the liberation of all captive orca whales? Hell no, I told him."

Freedom for captive cetaceans, as it happened, was one of the things that David Phillips hoped to achieve with Keiko, but Phillips chose not argue the matter with Cornell now. The two men did resume their debate over the wisdom of initiating research on Iceland's killer whales. Phillips did not see why such research would necessarily delay Keiko's release. Cornell found this view naïve. The veterinarian argued forcefully for early freedom for the whale.

It seemed a reversal of roles. David Phillips, the environmental firebrand, was arguing for caution—for more scientific study. Lanny Cornell, the old whale catcher, was pushing for release.

LATER THAT DAY I WAS in a hallway of the Free Willy Keiko Foundation, catching up on my notes, when I realized I was picking up a conversation through the wall. The office on the other side belonged to Beverlee Hughes, director of the Free Willy Keiko Foundation. I heard the faint, conciliatory voice of Hughes. I heard the voices of David Phillips, her predecessor as foundation director, and of Lanny Cornell.

The debate was the old argument between Cornell and Phillips over the timing for release of the whale. Cornell was arguing, as usual, against instituting any programs or procedures that might delay release. Phillips believed that more research might be important. The argument was friendly still, but more heated than before. "He should have gone last summer," Cornell said. "He was ready to go last summer."

Animal-rights activists and indentured-whale abolitionists believed that Cornell was the biggest obstacle to Keiko's release. They were wrong. The converted dolphin trainer Ric O'Barry had predicted that as long as Cornell was involved, the whale would be captive and marketed for the rest of his life. Ben White of the Animal Welfare Institute had proposed that the Free Willy Keiko Foundation demonstrate its commitment to releasing Keiko by releasing Cornell from his job immediately. The veterinarian was not the nemesis that either of these activists imagined. He was in fact their staunchest ally on the foundation staff.

It struck me that if Cornell's animal-rights detractors had allowed themselves a somewhat brighter view of human nature, and if his interlocutors, the ambush journalists, had been somewhat less eager to lay traps, then they might have found a certain crusty charm in him. He was a man as full of surprises as the next human being. He had more facets than the press and his opposition allowed. As I worked on my gigantic omelette, I found myself wondering: If whales really have the Buddhistic nature that the empath Dianne Robbins attributes to them, and if, as she claims, they possess the power to intercept our electronic communications and follow human affairs, then what do they make of our biliousness? Perhaps the virtue most lacking in us, from the Cetacean point of view, is charity.

19

SON OF MAN-FISH

ON A GRAY JULY DAY IN OREGON, IN A VAN RENTED BY HIS FILM COMPANY, Jean-Michel Cousteau left the aquarium and drove north toward Yaquina Head Lighthouse. Cousteau was filming a documentary on Keiko. In the rental van was a rented cameraman—a local freelancer hired for several days—along with Cousteau's assistants Laura and Melinda, Dr. Lanny Cornell, and me. Yesterday, the Cousteau team had scouted the rocky shore beneath the lighthouse as a backdrop for an interview with Cornell.

I was struck by how much Jean-Michel resembled his father, the great Jacques-Yves Cousteau. The same wiry build, the same long face, the same dentition. Gum recession seems to be a family trait; it is the fate of the Cousteaus to grow long-toothed in middle age. Jean-Michel looked much more like his father, I thought, than his younger brother Philippe had looked. Philippe was by all accounts Jacques Cousteau's favorite. Philippe's death in 1979, in a seaplane crash, is said to have been the great tragedy of Jacques Cousteau's life. With Jean-Michel, Captain Cousteau had not gotten along as well. Late in his life, the father had filed a lawsuit against his eldest son.

"I never saw *Free Willy* in the theater," Jean-Michel told me as he drove. "I knew what the story was and I wasn't impressed. But I kept seeing bits and pieces of it on airplanes. I travel all the time, and you couldn't get away from it. In the end I guess I saw pretty much the whole thing. I began to see Keiko was a chance to rehabilitate ourselves in the eyes of children, to regain their trust and confidence."

The son's French accent was not as thick as the father's. I had met cynics who believed that Jean-Michel, a longtime resident of the United States, had carefully preserved his accent for its marketability, but I doubted this myself. The French accent is a hard one to lose. Jean-Michel's sounded like the real thing.

"This is the best of humankind being expressed here with Keiko," Cousteau continued. "This is the very, very good side of us. What fascinates me in this whole experience is that we're talking about good news. The media got involved and started to explode with good news, which we hear very, very seldom. Normally the media explodes with bad news, not with good."

The lighthouse at Yaquina Head is the tallest in Oregon. It has a resident ghost who is sometimes heard climbing the spiral staircase. The white tower has a monumental simplicity, tapering from its wide base upward ninety-three feet to the light at the top of the obelisk, which still shines through the original 1871 Fresnel lens. Jean-Michel Cousteau is an architect by training, yet he had no interest in the structure itself. He had come for the seascape that the lighthouse overlooked. Turning his back on the haunted white tower, he led Dr. Cornell down the dark cobbles of the beach. They stopped near the end, where the hired cameraman framed Cousteau and Cornell against some jagged black rocks and an offshore sea-stack whitened with guano. The interview went on out of earshot of the rest of us. Cousteau, in putting his questions, gestured with Gallic animation. Dr. Cornell, in answering, gestured with American minimalism. In the language of the hands, the veterinarian was almost mute today. Cousteau's assistant, Laura Sykes, stood guard on the cobbles to keep beach-walkers from strolling into the frame. It was a public beach, yet everyone cooperated. One boy paused beside Laura and strained to hear the interview. "Which one is Jacques Cousteau?" he asked.

This was not an uncommon confusion. One of Craig McCaw's corporate lieutenants, a man skilled at reading the boss, believed that McCaw himself was confused on the matter of Cousteau identity. At a meeting aboard McCaw's gigantic yacht *Tatoosh,* the lieutenant, observing McCaw's unusual deference to Jean-Michel, at first was puzzled, then had a flash of insight: The billionaire mistook the son for the father. David Phillips, for one, was not ready to dismiss this possibility.

"Craig is reclusive and *severely* dyslexic," he says. "He makes decisions based on very few data points."

The two data points here, perhaps, had been the Cousteau name and the incisors.

Jean-Michel was sixty, an age when our fathers begin to look back at us from the mirror, and perhaps sometimes he was confused himself.

If Craig McCaw had indeed conflated the two Cousteaus, it would have explained a thing or two. Phillips had lobbied hard to have Dennis Kane, producer of *The Free Willy Story,* make a second Keiko film—a documentary covering the whale's coming trip from Oregon to Iceland. When McCaw appeared to favor Cousteau instead, Phillips had suggested that all applicants submit samples of their work. Kane had sent in a selection of his films; Cousteau had sent the films of his father. McCaw, in the end, had chosen Cousteau, thinking, perhaps, that he had signed up the man who had pioneered the development of the underwater camera; had filmed *The Silent World,* which won at Cannes in 1956; and had produced the long-running television series *The Undersea World of Jacques Cousteau.*

* * *

AT THE CONCLUSION OF THE lighthouse interview, we drove back toward Newport. Turning from Lighthouse Drive onto Highway 101, we began encountering heavy traffic of Keiko pilgrims streaming north from the aquarium.

"I've never seen so many out-of-state license plates," said Cousteau's assistant Melinda, who turned stiffly in her seat to study the oncoming grills. Melinda was a casualty of this Keiko traffic. Yesterday, a Keiko pilgrim had totaled his Mercedes against her car, and today she was wearing a neck brace. "In the emergency room they said that all these accidents this summer are because of the whale," she told us.

"There will be no accidents next summer," Dr. Cornell assured her.

Next summer, traffic was sure to thin. Oregon would have no whale, for Keiko would be living in Iceland.

"The local people love it and hate it," Melinda mused. In her neck brace, she gave a cautious, infinitesimal nod toward the bumper-to-bumper traffic of tourists in the opposite lane. "They want to have their Keiko and eat it too."

Cousteau braked. We had caught up with the backup caused by southward-streaming Keiko traffic, and soon we were bumper-to-bumper in Keiko gridlock ourselves. The van crept along toward Newport.

"It's absurd!" Cousteau said suddenly. "All this gas burned!"

Absurd! I thought. Cousteau was exactly right. "Absurd" is a term we got from the French, and French philosophers did all the heavy lifting in refining *absurdité,* the concept. For me, Cousteau's French accent delivered a crisp, original sense of the word, making it fresh again. The Keiko phenomenon—the millions spent on this one whale, the adoration, the thousands of hadjis pouring into Newport, the traffic jams, Melinda's whiplash—was many things, and one of them was absurd.

THE GENERATION OF UNDERWATER PHOTOGRAPHERS and filmmakers that followed Jacques Cousteau feel several ways about him. I have collaborated with a number of these men—Al Giddings, Chuck Nicklin, Bill Curtsinger, Douglas Faulkner, David Doubilet, among others—and it is curious how often his name crops up, as we prepare to enter the world that Cousteau, by his co-invention of the Aqua-Lung, opened up for us. Cousteau was a famous poacher. Showing up in his ship *Calypso* at sites other cameramen were working, he expected them to part way for him. The cameramen remember these episodes indignantly, with the same salty expletives you might hear from fishermen who have seen some big vessel lay its crab traps atop their own. That these stories are common testifies to both Cousteau's sense of entitlement as a founding father and how much he got around. Cousteau's successors like to parody him. They make fun of the way he featured himself in his films and they joke about formulaic elements in his oeuvre. In a Jacques Cousteau documentary, there is always a dramatic moment when Captain Cousteau, on the bridge of *Calypso* in his trademark red wool watch cap, speaks earnest French over the radio. Time is always running out. One of *Calypso*'s divers or rubber zodiacs is in trouble, or a hurricane is gathering.

Parody can be a sincere form of flattery, of course. Cousteau's successors understand their debt to him; they recognize him as the giant in their field. One of my partners, Bill Curtsinger, a photographer for *National Geographic*, used to mimic Cousteau as we prepared to dive. Sitting in his fins on the side of our zodiac, he would let his snorkel mouthpiece drop. "Ze dive-aires entair ze water," he would intone. With that, we would roll overboard, then reach back to grab our big underwater camera housings and the bang-sticks we carried for sharks. Sometimes when Curtsinger forgot, I would do the Cousteau voice-over myself. It began as parody, but became a kind of benediction.

Once at lunch with Jacques Cousteau, listening to the famous accent, I remembered this. Would the captain be offended, I wondered, if I told him about our invocation? I decided to take the chance, and Cousteau was amused. He was a man on a serious mission, but he had a light touch. In his seventies then, he was full of wit and vitality and command of his facts. He was gracious to people who, upon recognizing him from across the room, approached our table to congratulate him for his lifework. I was struck by his effect on the women in the restaurant. At one point he told me gravely that his estimate, seat-of-the-pants, was that life in the sea had declined by half in his lifetime. Then, he brightened, and moments later was joking about the difficulty of being a septuagenarian with too many mistresses.

Jacques-Yves Cousteau's perspective as the first "man-fish," as he once described his breed, was unique and invaluable. No one has been more important in calling world attention to the plight of the seas. He was a rare and great man. It was cheering to see certain of his traits and mannerisms survive in his son.

At the Oregon Coast Aquarium one afternoon, Jean-Michel Cousteau met a team from Portland's Channel 12 News at the edge of Keiko's pool. The reporter, a woman named Roxanne, was doing a story on an Oregon girl whose birthday gift was a meeting with Keiko. Cousteau, a board member of the Free Willy Keiko Foundation, had volunteered to serve as official greeter. The birthday girl, who was nine today, had brought two classmates with her. All three girls were scholarly, bespectacled, and self-possessed. As they began to answer Roxanne's questions, Cousteau bent down to get his face in the frame with them. From where I stood, behind the television camera, it looked so familiar— those Cousteau features impinging on the narrative, the toothy grin, the whale spouting in the background—that I had to laugh. Chip off the old *bloc.*

"Are you excited?" Cousteau asked the birthday girl.

It was not simply a question for the camera, I thought. Over several days, I had been watching him, and he was truly good with children. Jean-Michel seemed genuinely curious about this girl's feelings for the whale. He was the old Cousteau mix of showmanship and sincerity.

Jean-Michel introduced the girls to Keiko and they had their brief encounter with the whale. Afterward, Cousteau lingered poolside to answer Channel 12's questions. Roxanne, the reporter, asked him about death threats recently made against Keiko in Iceland.

"When you have an animal, or a human, getting so much attention, it's just inevitable," Cousteau answered. "There are nuts everywhere. This is not a surprise. But we want to intensify our effort, making sure that all our security protocols are in place. The children of the world should not be scared. We're doing everything in our power to protect the whale."

"How *is* the whale?" Roxanne asked.

"Very active," Cousteau said. "He has been eating live fish. He is busy now untraining his trainers. He is calling the shots, with me following behind."

Again I had to smile. This was so Cousteau-like: ". . . with *me* following behind." Cousteau was not leading the Keiko project. He was simply one of many board members of the Free Willy Keiko Foundation. He had been just eighteen months in that role—one of the newer directors—yet the Keiko saga, as he framed it now for Channel 12, had become a duet between himself and the whale.

Several of Cousteau's fellow directors were uneasy about their colleague. They were not persuaded by his credentials as filmmaker. They noted a tendency toward self-aggrandizement. Cousteau had his finger in many pots, and they suspected he was spread too thin. Jean-Michel was an *operator*. His entrepreneurial instincts, indeed, had been what led to the lawsuits his father filed against him three years before. In Fiji, Jean-Michel had built a scuba-diving resort he called "Cousteau Fiji Islands Resort," and Jacques-Yves had sued for a name change, demanding clarification that his son's resort in Fiji had no connection with his own Cousteau Society.

Of all Keiko's people, Jean-Michel Cousteau was most preoccupied with Keiko's role as a symbol for children. His habit was to divert almost any discussion of the whale, after a minute or two, to the question of children. For his Keiko documentary, he had selected a corps of young aquanauts as a device to tell the story. Three members of this youthful squad had come with him to Oregon, and I had seen them around the aquarium. When Cousteau's crew was filming, the aquanauts wore uniforms—an idea inspired, I supposed, by the black-and-yellow wet suits that his father had designed for the divers of *Calypso*.

"I felt that there was a very unique opportunity here to use children as the link in the process," Jean-Michel explained to me. "I pick up that link in Mexico, with a child, a Mexican kid, who had gone to see Keiko a number of times before Keiko left. And I bring this kid to Oregon, where he meets Keiko again. Then I take him up to see the wild orcas up in the San Juan Islands. He will be the liaison, passing the baton to a bunch of American kids who themselves will be responsible—morally, mentally—for bringing Keiko to Iceland. And finally, this year, there will be an Icelandic kid who feeds Keiko, who becomes his host and caretaker. That to me is an easy way to build my film, a one-hour special."

Cousteau spoke often of the children's crusade that had launched the Keiko phenomenon. He was obsessed by what he took to be a promise to Keiko's kids, an implied contract with them.

"My conviction, as a board member of the Free Willy Keiko Foundation, is that above anything we made a commitment to those children," he told me. "And the commitment was to do everything in our power to bring the star of *Free Willy* as close to freedom as possible. In that sense, in my film, I feel that kids needed to be represented, as they are the strength behind this whole operation. Whether they sent faxes, made calls, e-mailed, or sent money—many of them broke their piggy banks and sent $1.57, or whatever— we're not going to betray that trust."

In contemplating Cousteau's determination not to betray the trust of children, I found myself wondering about its origins. My thoughts turned quickly to his relationship with his father. Jacques Cousteau's lawsuit against Jean-Michel had come when the father was old and the son in late middle age, but maybe the seeds of their troubles had been planted earlier. Had some betrayal of trust happened in Jean-Michel's boyhood? Philippe, the younger son, appears again and again in his father's books and films, bearded, squinting in the sun, a more laconic man than either his father or his older brother—a man of action. Jean-Michel, for his part, I could not remember ever seeing in a Jacques Cousteau book or film, though I knew he had handled logistics on some of his father's projects. Had favoritism stung the older brother? In conversation with Jean-Michel, I tried to probe the matter delicately.

"You had a childhood you enjoyed?" I asked one day.

"Oh, I had a formidable childhood. Magic times. I think of it when I see kids in tune with nature in one way or another, away from these stupid computers, which really burn their brains—for nothing! It's not creative. I'm not against computers, I'm against the software."

Slipping off my hook, Jean-Michel digressed from his childhood, the subject that interested me, to a discussion of his theories on computers and education. I had not baited up properly.

"I have a very, very strong belief in youth," Cousteau told me on another occasion. "More and more so now—and I guess this is not abnormal, as you get older. I believe we've taken away the confidence that children deserve, because we've allowed all kinds of fascinations to literally suck them in, like crime and violence on television—portrayed very well, unfortunately. It's cheap. It's easy to do. It's a lot easier to do a bad show than do a good show. It's easier to talk about violence and crime and sex than it is to talk about love and hard work and constructive ideas. We've delivered to the children of the world a lot of garbage, which they have a very hard time to screen. I didn't have that problem as a child. I didn't have a television. I didn't have the money that kids have today, particularly kids in the Western world."

"Really?" I said. "I would have thought you were fairly well-off."

"No. My father was a naval officer, and that was it. And he was unknown. Back then, he never suffered the stardom of being Cousteau—unlike my children, for example, or my nephew and my niece. I was eighteen when *The Silent World* came out. The purity of these years that I've experienced as a kid! Where you were in tune with nature, where you were linked with nature all the time. Whether you're fishing or collecting sea urchins and baking them on the beach, with a piece of bread that you borrowed to eat the sea urchin, which I've done for years and years when I was a kid. All of this was constant contact with nature. I was in the water all the time."

"Because of who your father was?"

"Probably. That, and the fact that I grew up on the French Riviera. Really, I was no different from many of my friends in school. We were all urchin-eaters."

Relationships with fathers are personal matters, of course, and Jean-Michel had seen his own chewed over excessively by the press. No matter how I barbed the question, he tossed the bait. I could get no clear sense of how things had been, in the early days, between the as-yet-unknown Captain Cousteau and his firstborn. I did learn about their last days together and the resolution of the Fiji lawsuit.

"The problems that we've had were problems that could have been resolved confidentially and easily," Jean-Michel said. "They have been completely blown out of proportion—by the media, particularly. Fortunately in his last several months we mended all of this, and it was all over. We were talking about other things."

In January 1997—the month Jean-Michel joined the board of Keiko's foundation—he had a cordial visit with his father in Florida, where the old man, at eighty-six, was still healthy. Soon afterward, respiratory illness felled the man-fish.

"Later on I saw him, unfortunately, in the hospital," Jean-Michel continued. "I was able to communicate all the love that I have for him, and the fact that I'm here to help carry on the message. And also that his two little kids, my half-brother and sister, were important parts of me, and he can count on me to take care of them. And then unfortunately things got worse, and he left us."

ONE SUNNY, SEA-COOLED AFTERNOON, Jean-Michel Cousteau led David Phillips, his film crew, and me down to a floating dock in the Yaquina Bay harbor. He wanted a maritime scene as backdrop for a Phillips interview. After walking the wooden plank "streets" for a while, he found an intersection that pleased him. "It sounds like a massive uprising of children is forcing the rest of us off our butts," Cousteau suggested to Phillips in an early question, and as usual he pursued that theme hard.

Afterward, as the film crew packed up their reflectors and sound equipment, Cousteau, Phillips, and I, walking three abreast, headed landward down the dock.

"Keiko is the locomotive pulling all this," Cousteau was telling me. "And he's a locomotive that's continually waiting on us. He's ready. I keep saying that he's untraining the trainers and making them caretakers."

Then, a peculiar thing happened. Cousteau's eye caught something beyond Phillips and me, and he did a double take. Breaking stride, he completely lost the thread of his discourse. I turned to see. Under the little bridge that connected the floating docks to land, a red fishing bobber was riding high. Following the line upward, I saw the rods belonging to a pair of boys fishing from the rail of the bridge. Cousteau stared at the bobber. I cannot describe the expression on his face. It was as if he had whispered *"Rosebud!"*

Then he came to himself and we continued. As we crossed the bridge to land, Cousteau fell back to speak to the boy fishermen. "Any luck?" he asked them. Some luck, the larger boy answered. Cousteau caught up with us again.

"That's me when I was a kid," he told me.

The significance of the red bobber might never be plain to anyone, I decided, maybe not even to Cousteau. It was possible that Jacques-Yves Cousteau had nothing to do with the bobber, nor with Jean-Michel's determination never to betray Keiko's kids. But it was clear to me that each of us saw Keiko through the lens of his particular experience, and the lens for Jean-Michel was childhood.

20

GRANDISSIMUS

IN EARLY AUGUST OF 1998, A MONTH BEFORE KEIKO'S DEPARTURE FOR ICE-land, I drove to Newport to check on preparations. For company I brought along my son, David, who was now twelve. He had passed the optimum age for onset of Keikophilia, yet he looked forward to meeting the whale.

In these final weeks of Keiko's residence in Oregon, attendance at the aquarium was heavy. To accommodate the huge summer throngs saying good-bye to the whale, the Killer Whale Facility was staying open two extra hours each day. We walked around to the public side of the aquarium and fell into a long line of paying customers. The line shuffled forward, stopped, shuffled again. Keiko's army was patient and good-humored. Finally, after forty minutes or so, we entered the darkened gallery, guided by a middle-aged, mustachioed docent named Mike.

The gallery ran in a semicircle around three giant public-view windows looking into Keiko's tank. The darkness had a movie-theater feel. The heads and shoulders of the audience were silhouetted against a luminous screen, the aquamarine rectangle of the nearest window. Keiko passed close by the glass. He was gigantic, an IMAX whale. He circled the circumference of his tank twice. This theater was a kind of multiplex, three screens, with the real-life Keiko Story playing on each one in succession as he passed. Two of the windows were eight-by-twenty-four feet, just enough to fit all of Keiko into the frame, and the third was eight-by-sixteen, which included most of him. He circled twice again. Pausing at midpoint of a third circle, he peered in the staff window at the opposite side of the pool. Apparently nothing interesting was happening in the staff room, for he turned away. He circled again. Then he circled once more. Then he detoured to the center of the pool for a brief tryst with a huge inner tube floating there. He approached the tube from be-neath, drifting up belly skyward and pectoral fins outspread. This posture— the missionary position, inverted—was an invention of the whales. The obstacles of tail and tailfin make any other sort of congress impossible. Keiko's enormous penis snaked out. For a second or two, the crowd could make no sense of this sudden, giant appendage; then came a murmur of shock and recognition.

"His intestines is falling out!" a little girl announced to her mother. Several men in the audience chuckled at this interpretation—a nervous chuck-ling, it seemed to me. The equipment of the bull killer whale is intimidating; it cannot help but arouse envy in all us lesser males of the order Mammalia.

In *Moby Dick,* Chapter XCV, "The Cassock," Herman Melville writes, "Had you stepped on board the Pequod at a certain juncture of this post-mortemizing of the whale; and had you strolled forward nigh the windlass, pretty sure am I that you would have scanned with no small curiosity a very strange, enigmatical object, which you would have seen there, lying along lengthwise in the lee scuppers. Not the wondrous cistern in the whale's huge head; not the prodigy of his unhinged lower jaw; not the miracle of his sym-metrical tail; none of these would so surprise you, as half a glimpse of that unaccountable cone,—longer than a Kentuckian is tall, nigh a foot in diam-eter at the base . . ."

Melville, the Victorian, never summons up the courage to give this enig-matical object any of its common names, but he does finally allow himself to call it the "grandissimus," which he claims is the whalers' term. He describes how a sailor called the "mincer" and two of his comrades stagger off under the load of the grandissimus. The three men extend it on the forecastle deck, where the mincer skins it, "as an African hunter the pelt of a boa." The min-cer turns the skin inside out and gives it a good stretching, doubling its di-ameter. After hanging it in the rigging to dry, he circumcises it, lopping off the distal end. He discards this foreskin—the final three feet or so "towards the pointed extremity"—then cuts two slits for armholes in the tube that re-mains. He pulls the hem of the grandissimus over his head and gropes about half-cocked for the armholes. His head pops free, pink from his exertions, like a new glans for the grandissimus. Sheathed in this protective work suit— the "cassock" of Melville's chapter title—he takes up his flensing knife and commences mincing the whale's blubber for the try-pots.

Melville, who was born before the age of the oceanarium and aqualung, knew only half the story. All the grandissimi of his experience had sloshed around dead in the lee scuppers. The grandissimus of Keiko was a living grandissimus. It was amazing not just for its length and girth, but for its ani-mation. The tip came to a point that seemed almost prehensile. In cetaceans the penis is often used as a tactile organ, and the tip of Keiko's seemed to search about; to sniff the water as if with a mind of its own.

"Yes, he's a healthy male orca," proclaimed the docent, Mike.

Mike's timing was good, his delivery dry; it was obvious that Keiko had given him plenty of opportunities to practice this line. As the audience laughed, Keiko pulled back from the inner tube—coitus interruptus—and reeled in his penis with startling speed. Before he had swum two strokes, it had disappeared into the genital slit. Tumescence and detumescence are much quicker in whale than in man.

"Now we've seen the Keiko porno show," Mike said. When the titillated audience had settled a bit, Mike resumed his spiel on Keiko and this facility.

"This tank originally was built for rehabilitation of various marine mammals before Keiko," Mike told us.

This was untrue. The tank was built especially for Keiko and it had no tenants before him.

"They are now feeding him live steelhead trout," said Mike. "They used to feed him from a bucket. Now they throw his food in water, to break the bond with his trainers."

This was also untrue. Much of Keiko's food was fed to him by hand, still, and his trainers continued to work closely with him for hours every day. The live steelhead were tossed in the water not to break the whale's bond with his trainers, but to teach him to fish.

"He wouldn't be able to survive on his own in the wild. He would have to be adopted by a pod," said Mike.

This was untrue. Though the claim is often made in the Keiko debate that *Orcinus orca* is an animal so hopelessly social it cannot exist by itself, the truth is that there are lone killer whales, just as there are lone wolves. Solitary killer whales occur in the wild, and they seem to prosper in their podlessness.

"Underwater we wouldn't be able to see him, because of his disruptive coloring," said Mike.

This was untrue, too. A glance into the tank suggested that Mike was mistaken. Right now Keiko *was* underwater, and we hundreds of witnesses could see him perfectly well. Killer whales, like most pelagic creatures, are "countershaded," dark on top and pale below. Seen from above, the dark back blends with the blue depths. Seen from below, the pale belly blends with the sky. But the killer whale remains a high-contrast animal. Its black dorsum and white underside do not blend along the border, they meet in a crisp line. The white chin patch calls attention to itself. The white oval of the cheek patch is a field mark visible miles away. That cheek patch—a white oval against a black field—makes less sense as cryptic coloration than as a kind of a Jolly Roger flown by the whale.

"When he nods his head, he's not saying hello," said Mike. "He's expressing his dominance over everything in this pool."

Head-nodding is indeed an aggressive display in killer whales and other dolphins, but what, in this instance, was the object of Keiko's domineering nods? There was nobody in the pool but the whale. Keiko's nodding, at this moment at least, seemed just reflexive, absentminded, not much more than a tic.

"Sometimes he hits the glass of the windows. He's charging his reflection," Mike added.

This was nonsense. Only the most dim-witted of parakeets is fooled by its own reflection. Keiko had a brain larger than Aristotle's, Newton's, and Buddha's combined. Reflection is not some exotic phenomenon to a killer whale. Keiko, as a newborn calf off Iceland, nudged upward by his mother for his very first blow, had met a reflection of himself on the ocean's quick-silvery underside.

"He was twenty feet long, the Mexicans told us, and when he arrived we measured him at twenty point eight," said Mike. "He used to sleep on his tail in Mexico. It wasn't until he'd been here a few months that he stretched to his full twenty-one feet."

This was untrue. Keiko had lengthened not from any decompression of his tail, but because he was a subadult male, still growing.

"Part of his diet is squid," said Mike. "The backbone of the squid does not dissolve in his stomach. A lot of squid is fed to him to clean him out like a Roto-Rooter."

This was untrue. For starters, squid do not have backbones. They do have a reduced and internalized chitinous shell, the "pen," a vague analogue of the backbone, but the pen is not the part that survives the gastric juices of toothed whales. What survives is the parrotlike beak. Toothed whales do gather impressive collections of beaks in their stomachs, but no biologist has ever proposed that these conglomerations serve to regulate the animal, like some sort of dietary fiber. Squid have a high water content. Keiko was fed squid not to clean him out like a Roto-Rooter, but to keep him hydrated.

Very little of what Mike told us was true. Very little was even plausible. To see whether we could get better information from another docent, my son and I circled back and took the tour again, this time with a young guide named Stephanie. A child asked Stephanie why Keiko had those three black dots on his chin. Stephanie answered, "The three dots are where his whiskers would be. He is a male, after all." She explained that as the male killer whale swims forward, the friction of the water works as a depilatory, keeping him clean-shaven.

My son and I exchanged incredulous glances. David was only twelve, and no great student of whales, but he knew malarky when he heard it.

Maybe Stephanie, upon reading about the vestigial hairs that grow, indeed, on the beaks of whales, had been led through a sequence of erroneous assumptions to her crazy thesis. Maybe Mike, too, was winging it in the same misguided way. More likely, I guessed, was that these docents, bored by repetition of the same old questions, were dreaming up outlandish answers to amuse themselves. Whichever the explanation—misinformation in good faith or deliberate disinformation—their riffs were dismaying. The principal argument that aquarists make in justifying the continued captivity of killer whales is that the animals are educational. Displaying the captives, they claim, enlightens the public and builds a constituency for wild whales. If the blarney dished out at the Oregon Coast Aquarium was typical, then the best thing for education, clearly, would be Keiko's immediate release to the wild.

21

AUSTRONAUTS

PHYLLIS BELL, THE DIRECTOR OF THE OREGON COAST AQUARIUM, SAT across from me at her office desk, contemplating the departure of her whale next month. She seemed resigned to Keiko's return to Iceland. When I asked whether losing Newport's star attraction would mean tough times ahead for her aquarium, she emphatically denied it.

"We've got three new exhibits opening next year that we're excited about," she said. "And we have plans for Keiko's tank after that. We've been talking about splitting Keiko's place into three habitats. The first would be the Port Orford Reef, which is the rocky reef off this stretch of Oregon coast, southward. The next habitat would be the transition between the reef and the really deep sea—a zone where the bottoms are sandier. We're calling it Halibut Flats. There'd be a shipwreck in there, because that's where shipwrecks happen in Oregon. And the third habitat would be open sea: tuna, turtles, sunfish. Visitors would walk through the center of the habitats through an acrylic tunnel, kind of suspended in the middle. You'd come out and there'd be a closing exhibit, where we hope to have an uplink to Keiko's sea pen in Iceland, so people can see how he's doing."

Halibut Flats sounded promising, but I was doubtful that it would draw the crowds that Keiko drew. The sandy shipwreck would be a nice touch, but would it cause bumper-to-bumper traffic on Highway 101? I asked Bell if ever, during all the feuding and controversy of the whale's stay here in Oregon, she had regretted becoming Keiko's landlord.

"There's moments," she conceded. "But the overriding feeling is we're proud to have had Keiko here. To have had a part in his doing so much better; his being able to move on now. Even in the most stressful times, I don't think I ever wished we hadn't done this."

I asked Bell whether she had any intuition about whether the whale would ever be released.

"No, I can't say that I really do," she said. "I think he's a different animal from when he came here. He's healthier. I feel comfortable with this move to Iceland, but I don't know that he'll ever be released. He's just very docile. I hope that the people making the decision look at it long and hard."

During Keiko's residence in Oregon, the whale had received great volumes of mail, addressed in his name to the Oregon Coast Aquarium. This correspondence, like aquarium attendance, was spiking now as the whale's departure neared. At the conclusion of our talk, Ms. Bell cheerfuly granted me access to the Keiko Papers. Leading me to another office, she left me amid boxes spilling over with the latest postcards addressed to the whale.

" 'Sea' you around Keiko," wrote Jesse Knutson. Amanda Knutson, his little sister, was so delighted by this pun that she repeated it in her own card: "Sea you arond Keiko!"

"I love Keiko," wrote Aiyssa. "I'll miss you Keiko. I'm moving from Newport, too. Love Aiyssa."

"HAVE FUN OUTTHERE," wrote some kid named William.

"Marcus Dodsworth of the Dodsworth family wishes you the best of luck in your new home in Iceland," wrote Marcus Dodsworth, with a nice formality. "I hope you a happy life," wrote Amber, with a nice informality. "Nothin but blue skies!" wrote Syndee, Bill, Loveynda, Jake, Larissa, Kristian, and Elaine. "Stay clear of big boats they are not your mother! Eat lots of fish! Be free! Be happy!"

"Dear Keiko," wrote Jenny Skoien. "Good luck! I hope you find a family and live happily in a huge tank (the ocean). Love, Jenny Skoien."

Jenny Skoien dotted the i in her signature with a big circle and she illustrated her letter with a drawing of Keiko reunited with his mother, whom she labeled "Mom." Mom had undergone sex reassignment, it seemed. Her dorsal fin had grown into the tall isosceles triangle of the male killer whale. On returning home, Keiko was due for a big surprise.

Adrian Bell drew Keiko as a humpback whale. The humpback is the whale Adrian draws best, evidently, and he has done an excellent job on this one. Gabriela Mejia, ten years old, drew Keiko as a nearly perfect pilot whale—and not just any pilot, but specifically an old bull, with the characteristic squared off "pothead" overhanging the insignificant beak. I found it eerie that the wayward pencil line of a child could so precisely draft a design that took evolution many millions of years to achieve.

Aldo Zanela Garela, a third-grader at Institute Thomas Jefferson, in Tlalnepantla, Mexico, drew Keiko as a kind of ravenous amoeba. Aldo set out, it seems, to show the whale leaping straight toward the viewer, with gobs of water flying off his flanks. In his bold attempt to convey a foreshortened whale, Aldo had run into big problems with perspective, and in his portrait Keiko's white cheek patch had migrated around, Picasso-esque, to his ventral side, nearly joining his white belly patch.

There actually exists, in nature, a creature named *Pseudorca crassidens,* the false killer whale. In the sea it makes but a single genus and species; in children's art, the false killer whale is a whole phylum of erroneous shapes.

"To Keiko's guardians," wrote Mrs. Carol Cassady, on behalf of her morning kindergarten class at Fairmont Park School in Seattle. "Bravo for your guardians! My class colored these pictures in June as a farewell to Keiko. May Keiko's imprisonment and hopeful release be the example for all people who wish to make a financial gain from this monstrous imprisonment of living things for human selfishness and financial profit."

The third-grade class at Hoover Street School in Los Angeles sent Keiko a thousand paper cranes for luck. All the Hoover students, in wishing Keiko farewell, were conscientious about informing the whale of their own plans for the future. Elvira Marquez confided to Keiko that she intended to be an artist and scientist and live near the beach. Mario Castro planned to be a zookeeper and live in the mountains. Julio Reyes wanted to be an astronaut. Charlie Arreola, too, wanted to be an astronaut. Rafael Flores, for his part, wanted to be an austronaut.

In the cards and letters to Keiko, there was one constant. All the children expressed their love for him. I was moved by this outpouring of feeling, yet puzzled. What did the kids mean, when they said they loved him? Most had never met Keiko. For the majority, surely, the love they felt was for Willy, the fictional whale, a Hollywood fabrication nearly as distorted as the whales of their drawings. The love of the children was *effective,* undeniably. A children's crusade really was the force behind the rescue and apotheosis of the whale. But did it make any kind of sense? Lifting down another box of postcards, I dumped the contents and started thumbing through. Each missive in this batch, too, was a testimonial of love for the whale.

FROM THE PUBLIC SIDE OF Keiko's tank—the Oregon Coast Aquarium side—I crossed the demilitarized zone to the Free Willy Keiko Foundation side, where I dropped in on Diane Hammond. I asked Hammond about Keiko's state of mind, as his time in Oregon grew short.

"He's got a lot of time and energy now, and it's difficult to keep him busy," she said. "As he exhausts a lot of the things that were initially new about his pool—the play jets, the medical pool, the two gates, the bubble jets from underneath—all those things are getting to be pretty old hat. We, the staff, spend more and more time just trying to keep him busy and mentally engaged. He's changed so greatly from those early torpid days. He's very much awake and involved in everything. He's got a lot that he brings to the table, so it's harder and harder for us, as very poor substitutes for marine mammals, to keep him engaged and busy. A lot of what we do in training sessions is not because it's important at all, physically, but because it's mentally important. It gives him the chance to challenge himself with something."

The phone rang, and Hammond excused herself to answer. She listened, cursed, and smacked herself in the forehead. She had forgot an appointment. At one o'clock this afternoon, Keiko was to give an audience to a special child.

"This child's mother wrote that essentially Keiko was the be-all and end-all for her child," Hammond explained, on hanging up. "We've had probably a dozen children brought to our attention who are learning-disabled, or impaired dramatically in some way, and for some of them Keiko has represented a real breakthrough. I don't remember whether the child today is a special-needs kid or not."

Hammond paused. She seemed to consider whether to tell me something, then decided in favor.

"Ever since Keiko got here, we've been in the Make-a-Wish Circuit. We've never made that known, because the minute people know that we will accommodate the terminally ill and severely handicapped, we would not be able to do it anymore. The traffic would be too great."

"They have to discover it on their own?" I asked.

"Yes. Ever since the beginning, I would guess we've done three or four a week. Grown-ups and children both. We bring them over to the pool, and in some cases we allow them to touch Keiko. Sometimes they are blind. Inoperable brain tumors. Sometimes they know they are in Keiko's presence, but can't see him clearly. We've had a number of quadriplegics up there. We walk them up bodily and in some cases put them on the wet-walk. We had a woman who couldn't feel anything from the neck down but one side of her face was very sensitive to touch. So she put her cheek to Keiko. We try to accommodate people."

The image of this pilgrimage to the whale—Keiko as a kind of Lourdes—struck me as strange and wonderful. When I suggested this to Hammond, she said she felt the same way.

AT ONE O'CLOCK, THE HOUR of the special-child appointment, I climbed with Dianne Hammond and my son, David, up the iron staircase on the outside of Keiko's tank, steeling myself for an encounter with a terminally ill child. The little girl, it turned out, was not sick at all. Her name was Stephanie Arnot. She was perfectly healthy, except for her obsession with Keiko. Stephanie, who was eight, was as monomanical about this piebald whale as old Ahab had been about his white one. "She hasn't slept for the past three or four days," Stephanie's father told me. Stephanie's mother corroborated this with a nod. Back home, said Mrs. Arnot, the family had a dock, upon which Stephanie would station herself for hours at a time, flashing whale-training signals of her own invention, as if to magically summon a whale. Now, as Stephanie stood at the edge of the wet-walk, the moment had come. She was face-to-face with her animal familiar, her totem, her inamorato, her whale.

"He's looking right at you," Dianne Hammond told her.

"Hasn't had a kid for a long time," said the trainer Peter Noah.

It was an unfortunate choice of words. Peter Noah is a big, gruff man in a mustache. *"Hasn't had a kid in a long time,"* he growled, just as five tons of killer whale lurched halfway out of the water and careened across the slide-out toward Stephanie. The girl clutched at her father's hand and took a giant step backward.

The Arnot family adjourned downstairs to the staff room, where Stephanie could study Keiko fearlessly through thick glass. I had business elsewhere in the aquarium, so I would have to miss this session. To document how it went, and to keep my twelve-year-old occupied, I entrusted David with my Handycam and sent him downstairs to film the encounter. Forty minutes later, I caught up with the Arnots and my son as they emerged from the staff room. Stephanie and her father were walking hand in hand. "It was wonderful," Mrs. Arnot told me. "Stephanie had a spiritual bond with Keiko. He came right up to the glass and looked into her eyes."

The truth was, of course, that Keiko eyeballed *anyone* in the staff room—new faces in particular—but it seemed unkind to point this out to Mrs. Arnot. As my son and I waved good-bye to the Arnots, I turned to David for a report. He had witnessed Stephanie's spiritual bonding with the whale; how, I asked, had things gone?

"He was jackin' off with the Boomer Ball," David said.

This was an expression I had not heard from my son before. I realized that we had never really had our talk on the birds and bees, and that it was now probably too late. Through the Handycam eyepiece I reviewed his staff-room footage of the Arnots, and it went just as he said. Keiko attempts to molest the Boomer Ball, then veers away from it and swims up to the staff window waving his grandissimus at Stephanie, who takes another giant step backward from the whale of her dreams.

22

ELEVEN YEARS OF SOLITUDE

KEIKO SWAM LAPS OF HIS POOL, HIS FLUKES PUMPING ALONG CLOSE TO THE wall. Each time he passed the public windows, there was a scintillation of camera strobes. The scintillation followed him, like the wave of camera flashes accompanying a home-run hitter as he rounds the bases. In the staff room, two trainers, Brian O'Neill and Jeff Foster, sat with their backs to the staff window and the circling whale. They were watching videotape of Iceland. The video was amateur work by a member of the advance team to Vestmannaeyjar, the "Westman Islands," where Keiko's sea pen would be moored.

The Westmans, a small archipelago a few miles off Iceland's southeast coast, had won out over Eskifjördur as Keiko's next home. It was Jeff Foster who had picked the spot. He and Nolan Harvey had not liked Eskifjördur, which is sparsely inhabited and just about as far from Reykjavík and the airport as one can get in Iceland. Foster remembered a bay he had seen in his whale-catching days, on vacation in the Westmans, when he and his wife had taken a ferry to the islands. Returning to scout Iceland for Keiko, he found the bay to be as sheltered as he remembered. The Westman Islands were isolated, but not so depopulate as Eskifjördur. The bay was on the main island, Heimaey, which had a town of nearly five thousand inhabitants. The cove was protected from the elements by four-hundred-foot cliffs.

Nolan Harvey had followed Foster to the archipelago. Arriving in July, the season of the midnight sun, he had motored out just before dark—such as it was—to see Foster's cove. He had gone alone in the boat, so that his first impression of the bay would not be diluted by conversation. He had hugged the cliff wall in his boat, so his first impression would be abrupt. He rounded the last corner and the bay opened up. "I knew this was the place," he says. "Jeff picked very well."

Harvey was followed in turn to the Westmans by the McCaw lieutenants Bob Ratliffe and John Scully. The guide drove the two out on a beautiful endless summer day, calm and sunny. Just east of Foster's cove, in the sheltering wall of rock, is a cave with remarkable acoustics. The guide motored into the shadow of the cave, cut his engine, and played his saxophone. One of his specialties in these circumstances is "Amazing Grace." Ratliffe was won over, and for John Scully the disappointment of losing Ireland was mitigated somewhat.

The decision for the Westmans had caused bad feelings in Iceland. The mayor and citizens of Eskifjördur, and all the other people of the East Fiords, felt betrayed at being passed over, and for a time there was resentment between Eskifjördur and the Westmans. Katherine Hanly, convinced that Eskifjördur was best for Keiko, was unhappy with the choice. David Phillips preferred Eskifjördur, too, but was somewhat less unhappy, noting that the Westmans were visited by big aggregations of wild whales.

Now in Oregon, as Jeff Foster and Brian O'Neill studied the Westmans on the video, Keiko continued to circle the pool. The coruscation of camera flashes greeted him with each fly-by of the public windows. Inside the staff room, the Icelandic wind warbled and whistled in the microphone of the video camera. The videotaper had neglected to throw the "wind" switch, or perhaps the notorious winds of the Westmans had simply overwhelmed it. The screen showed a wide concrete dock on the island of Heimaey, with massive chains and anchors laid out on the surface. In a voice-over, scarcely audible over the howl of the wind, the videotaper explained that these were the chains and anchors that would hold the sea pen.

The scene shifted to puffin-hunting. Above the dock, on green slopes of tundra atop the sheer walls of a Westman Island cliff, the tiny figures of Icelandic men waved long-handled nets, snagging puffins from the cloud of seabirds circling. "They got six hundred puffins that day," said Brian. "The record is twelve hundred." He sounded less than elated by either accomplishment. He and Jeff Foster soberly studied the screen. This windswept archipelago would soon be their home.

Keiko appeared in the staff window. He commenced watching television over the shoulders of his trainers. Soon these same islands would be Keiko's home, too. The trainers were so rapt on the screen that they failed to notice the whale behind them. They fell into a discussion of a recent hassle with Icelandic customs over baggage and equipment. Keiko lost interest and drifted away. He resumed his circling. He broke off his circle once, pumped his flukes hard in a single deep stroke, glided up to the surface, and spiked the blue Boomer Ball. An infinitesimal swing of his head sent the heavy ball rocketing off his rostrum. He resumed circling.

In the staff room, Brian O'Neill, his back still turned to the staff window, had ejected the Iceland cassette from the VCR. He and Jeff Foster were now watching an instructional video in which some master trainer demonstrated various hand signals for use with killer whales. The two trainers must have felt they needed brushing up. The video had been shot here at Keiko's tank, with Keiko lolling bent-finned in the background, and the tape's lessons were intended for the handlers of this particular whale, yet the instructor steadfastly referred to the subject as "the animal."

Keiko, the animal himself, appeared in the staff window. He ascended slightly to study the screen over Brian's shoulder. It was as if the whale, too, felt he needed some brushing up on hand signals. Again the men were preoccupied with the television. Again the whale hung unnoticed in the window.

The trainer Jennifer Schorr entered the staff room. Her hair, pulled back in a ponytail, looked a little damp still from a training session. Jennifer saw Keiko in the staff window. Something forlorn in the whale's aspect caught her attention and triggered a maternal response. Jennifer is a blonde but has thick, dark eyebrows, which she now arched affectionately, quizzically, at the whale. She gave him a bright, exaggerated wave. "Hi, Kake," she said.

Then quickly Jennifer grew preoccupied herself. She was looking for a clipboard and could not find it. Finally she spotted the clipboard—it lay atop a computer monitor in plain sight—and she seized it and departed. The whale was left again to his own devices.

Keiko was the most famous whale on earth. He was a movie star with a billionaire for a sugar daddy, a $7.5 million mansion to live in, a yearly allowance of $500,000, and sixty tons of restaurant-quality fish in the fridge. His digs were kept spotless by custodians in scuba gear who worked shifts vacuuming up algae. His financial, political, and private needs were attended by a staff of twenty-five. Personal trainers—a cadre of eight—worked with him daily to improve his aerobic fitness. They ceaselessly invented new games for him, keeping his spirits up and honing his mental sharpness. They doubled as masseurs and masseuses, working in shifts to scratch his pectoral fins, tickle his melon, walk along his back. In sessions in the water with him, the trainers worked in splash suits, which kept their bodies warm, but their hands were always bare and cold, for Keiko did not like being scratched in gloves; he insisted on the sensation of fingernails. The trainers did duty, too, as dental technicians, brightening up Keiko's conical teeth with long iron files. Several times a day, the whale closed up shop in order to go fishing for hatchery-raised steelhead, USDA certified parasite-free. The foremost killer-whale veterinarian on earth served as his personal physician, making *house calls* on regular flights up from southern California just to see him. Keiko had his own television and underwater sound system. A "Keiko-cam" streamed his every move out into cyberspace. From holdfasts at the bottom of his pool, transplanted kelp waved on long stipes, as elegant as potted palms in some palatial hotel lobby. He had a favorite rock down there that he liked to chew on. Dungeness crabs, the best eating crabs on the West Coast, scuttled about the holdfasts of the kelp. Keiko occasionally played with them, carrying them up to the surface and releasing them, much to their irritation and heightened crabbiness. The latest innovations in Boomer Balls were sent to him, gratis, for testing. He had his choice of inflatable sex toys. Donations generated by the *Free Willy* sequels continued to flow in. A tax-exempt foundation in his name, dedicated to his well-being and to the promulgation of his legend, had launched a line of Keiko clothing, and the stacks of Keiko T-shirts, sweatshirts, and other garments were moving like hotcakes off the shelves. He got a cut of a "Barbie and Keiko" doll package, shared in the profits of Keiko Root Beer. Cash from a portfolio of other Keiko products and endorsements rolled in. Thousands of children loved him and wrote to him. Thousands of fans thronged past the gallery windows at the Oregon Coast Aquarium to view him every day. No whale in history had ever been so pampered and celebrated. And yet for eleven years he had not seen another of his own kind. There were long interludes at night, and in daytime between training sessions, when no one paid attention, and he was profoundly alone.

23

STEELHEAD

THERE WAS A MAN CALLED HALLDOR RUNOLFSSON, THE CHIEF VETERINARY officer of Iceland. In February 1998, early in the negotiations on Keiko's return home, Runolfsson decreed that an animal like Keiko, once exported from Iceland, could not come back. Icelandic law on the importation of animals is the strictest on earth. It is difficult to bring in a dog or cat. It is nearly impossible, given Iceland's obsession with the Icelandic pony and its bloodlines, to import a horse. There had been one previous attempt to introduce a whale—a captive animal from Spain, in 1992—and that request had been denied.

There was a man called Jón Steinar Gunnlaugsson. He was supreme attorney of Iceland. In reviewing the legality of Keiko's immigration—or retromigration, actually, since the whale was a returning native son—Jón Steinar Gunnlaugsson determined that Act No. 54/1990, the Icelandic law dealing with importation of animals, did not apply. Article 1 of that act defined animals as "all live land animals, both vertebrates, invertebrates, and aquatic animals living partially or entirely in fresh water."

Keiko escaped on a technicality. He was not a land animal, nor did he live in fresh water. Unfortunately another law, Act No. 25/1993, which dealt with prevention of new contagious diseases, had no such loophole. Gunnlaugsson determined that this second act required Keiko to demonstrate that he was free of contagious disease. He had to be examined by veterinarians. The results were to be reported to Iceland's chief veterinary officer, who was to advise the minister of agriculture, who would pass judgment on the whale. Two Icelandic vets were dispatched to Oregon to give Keiko a physical.

In Iceland, the whaling lobby had not quit, and powerful forces were still arrayed against the whale, which gave the Free Willy Keiko Foundation cause to worry about this veterinary mission. It seemed possible that some agent of an anti-Keiko faction might get to the vets. If Keiko flunked his physical, it would provide an easy way out for the Icelandic government, which seemed ambivalent about granting Keiko his green card. But Keiko's people were reassured on meeting the two Icelandic vets. Both Icelanders appeared to be straightforward men with no hidden agenda, although the Norsemen did betray some skepticism about tales of Keiko's progress in catching live fish.

As we walked to Keiko's House one day after their visit, David Phillips told me a story about the veterinarians. Both Icelanders were working topside at Keiko's tank, preparing to draw blood, when a trainer tossed in a hatchery-raised steelhead. The fish fled into the shallows of Keiko's slide-out with the whale in pursuit. Keiko humped out of deep water and slid across that shallow shelf after his prey. This maneuver was not unprecedented in *Orcinus orca*—on beaches in Argentina and elsewhere, killer whales sometimes come entirely out of water to pursue sea lions up the sand—but Keiko himself had never tried it before. At the feet of the two startled Norsemen and his own dumbfounded trainers, Keiko, all five tons of him, caught up with the five pounds of steelhead. Keiko's jaws chomped down, and the jaws of the Icelanders fell open.

Phillips, remembering, laughed at the image of the startled vets. The whale had made believers of both Icelanders. I suggested to Phillips that Keiko, though retired now from show business, retained a good sense of dramatic timing. We reached the steel staircase up the outside of Keiko's tank. As we climbed, Phillips finished the tale: The Iceland vets had given Keiko a clean bill of health. The only medical issue as yet unresolved was Keiko's blood work, which was still being evaluated in a laboratory in Iceland. Phillips admitted to some anxiety over the results. Keiko's blood chemistry would be the final test, the last legal obstacle to the whale's return home.

On top of the tank, Dr. Lanny Cornell and a couple of Keiko's trainers were conferring. Poolside, finning in place in a big bait box, hung several steelhead, big blunt-nosed sea trout. A trainer, Peter Noah, netted one and tossed it into the tank. Below, stationed at the underwater window of the staff room, unseen by us, someone pressed the start button of a stopwatch. Soon, over Peter's walkie-talkie, came the announcement, "Forty-five seconds." It had taken Keiko that long to catch and eat the steelhead. Peter tossed in a second fish. In his own good time, the whale swallowed this one, too.

"Dave!" Dr. Cornell called over to Phillips. "This is on a full stomach. Those two were just dessert."

This live-fish training was necessary. Frozen fish and squid would not be available to Keiko once he was released in the North Atlantic. The live-fish exercises were a good idea, in my opinion. And yet it seemed an extraordinary arrogance, delusional, the very definition of hubris: *humans teaching a killer whale to fish.*

For the next feeding session, I went below, so as to observe the drama underwater. In the staff window, Brian O'Neill stood in his gumboots on the gray concrete block that Keiko's trainers mounted to make themselves conspicuous to Keiko—the podium from which they could orchestrate the whale. The high-top boots were still wet from duty topside. Pipe whistle in his mouth, his face to the thick glass, Brian, who was serving as spotter, searched the blue submarine radiance for the whale.

We saw a splash at the surface. In the bright froth a steelhead took shape, then it swam downward at a shallow angle. Keiko executed a slow, majestic turn and started after the fish. The steelhead was a recent graduate of a Washington State hatchery, USDA certified disease-free and parasite-free. Its pedigree seemed to guarantee good health, yet its awareness quotient seemed low. As Keiko closed in, the steelhead made one small course change, then took no further evasive action. It did not seem to sense danger. It was almost as if the whale were too big to concern it. I had the impression that the steelhead had mistaken Keiko for some sort of black-and-white seamount rising behind it. The steelhead stationed itself inches ahead of the tip of Keiko's beak, like a pilot fish, and Keiko dutifully followed it around the pool. I was disillusioned. The whale had been eating live fish for six months now—an accomplishment that the Free Willy Keiko Foundation trumpeted widely—yet in those six months of practice, he had not learned how to cut off the ring. He seemed to be a killer whale without much killer instinct.

Hatchery-raised fish are notorious dullards. They are always feeding in the wrong part of the stream, or otherwise demonstrating cluelessness. Keiko's fish seemed retarded even by hatchery standards. The steelhead, a sea-run rainbow trout, *Salmo gairdeneri,* is a wonderful, adaptable fish, equally at home in mountain stream or ocean. If the royalty of the salmonids is the king salmon, then the steelhead is archduke. I knew Oregon steelhead. I had watched wild steelhead darting between pools of shadow in clear Oregon streams, their sharp turns almost too fast to follow. I had seen Oregon steelhead dodge sea lions at the brackish mouth of the Rogue River, a few miles southward down this coast. Keiko's hatchery fish did not resemble any of the steelhead I remembered. When I murmured something about its odd behavior, Peter Noah nodded.

"The ozone trashes their gills," he said.

From his perch in the window, Brian concurred. He was talking around the pipe whistle in his mouth, but I heard him clearly. "Sometimes they're not in very good condition when we get them, either," he said.

Keiko's steelhead, I learned, were trucked from the hatchery to a holding facility about a quarter mile from his tank, then, on their day of destiny, were transported in garbage cans to the tank and transferred to plastic totes. All this catch-and-release, from one container to another, was stressful. Sometimes the steelhead arrived in fair shape, other times not. "Occasionally we get fish that really zip around, and Keiko has trouble with those," said Brian.

This contest was fixed, then. This steelhead followed now by Keiko was out there in the ozone; it was zoned out. This explained something that had puzzled me earlier: why Keiko's tank was not stocked with resident schools, for the whale to munch on as he pleased. The purification system and its ozone—superoxygen—would have fried the gills of resident fish, debilitating and eventually killing them.

Keiko's beak was now touching the slow-sculling tailfin of the steelhead. The fish looked like a toy that Keiko was trying to balance on his nose. Suddenly I was full of doubt about this whole enterprise. After David Phillips's tale of the Icelandic vets and Keiko's acrobatic capture of a steelhead right under their noses, I had expected a more vigorous pursuit. I had watched wild killer whales feeding, and Keiko looked nothing like them. His animus and energy were entirely different. Taking the steelhead delicately in his front teeth, like a mother cat moving one of her litter, he glided along for about two body lengths, then gently inhaled the fish.

"He swallowed it," Brian O'Neill announced into his walkie-talkie.

Jennifer Schorr, the trainer who was holding the clipboard somewhere on top of the tank, asked for clarification. Her voice was crackly over the walkie-talkie. "He's swallow-*ing* it, or he swallow-ed it?"

"It's *gonnnne,*" Brian enunciated.

When Keiko came to the window, Brian blew hard on his whistle, pointed his finger emphatically at the whale, and bellowed, "Good whale!" with feeling. Then he repeated the signal, with the exaggerated body language the trainers used to ensure that the whale got the message. He blew the whistle dramatically, pointed to Keiko, and shouted, "Good whale!" again.

Yes, good whale, but how would he fare when released off Iceland, in the real ocean, with no staff of trainers to tell him so?

BOOK THREE
ICELAND

24

ULTISSIMA THULE

From every seat pocket on my Icelandair flight to Reykjavík, a portrait of Keiko peered out at the passenger. The return of the whale, now just two days away, was the cover story in the airline's magazine, *Atlantica*. From the article I learned that City Hall in the Westman Islands, Keiko's new home, favored his homecoming. "Mayor Gudjón Hjörleifsson sees this opening up many different possibilities for future developments both in terms of tourism and scientific research," *Atlantica* said. "Not everybody, however, has welcomed the decision and there are those who have expressed skepticism over the location; that there is too much ship-traffic and noise, the swell is too strong and the water too cold."

Human opinion was divided, as always in the saga of Keiko.

Seated across the aisle from me on the flight was Mark Berman of Earth Island Institute, assistant to David Phillips. Berman is a small, bearded Southerner who made his bones as an environmentalist in Myrtle Beach, South Carolina, where, moonlighting from jobs in retail clothing, he organized resistance to attempts to build a dolphinarium in the state. Berman was one of the first soldiers in the army of Keiko, having handled early detail work in the whale's move from Mexico to Oregon. As we flew across the North Atlantic, he filled me in on the latest Keiko gossip. An Icelandic fisherman named Jan Gunnarsson had proposed that Keiko be slaughtered and turned into 60,000 meatballs for the starving children of Sudan. Brad Andrews, vice president of operations at Sea World, had told the press that "Iceland is cold, dark, and miserable. It's no place for a whale." A new death threat against Keiko had been delivered in Iceland just yesterday.

Mark Berman was undaunted by any of this. He was exhilarated by Keiko's imminent return home and ecstatic at his own liberation from paperwork. Since his efforts in Mexico three years before, Berman's duties had confined him largely to the office. He had escaped only to give the occasional Keiko talk at elementary schools in northern California. One of his chores, for the past three years, had been to field Keiko's mail. A portion of the mail was addressed to Berman himself, thank-you notes for his elementary-school lectures.

"Thanks for waiting paitiont when we went to reccese," wrote a boy named Arthur, a student in Room 12 of the Malcolm X Academy, in San Francisco.

"I learned a lot about Keiko. She is an interesting type of whale to me," wrote another student at Malcolm X, Laura Darran.

"Thank you for the show about Keiko," wrote Heather Fisher of Pleasant Hill, California. "I learned that he had a scin dzeez."

Heather's classmate Suliman Arghandiwal echoed that. "He had a skin disyz, but it came off when he was in cold water," Suliman wrote.

Another of Berman's chores had been to handle calls from Keiko channelers and empaths and seers. The most recent had been from the animal communicator Bonnie Norton. Her communication was not telepathic, but telephonic, reaching Berman conventionally over the lines of Pacific Bell. Norton told Berman of Keiko's distaste for Iceland and his desire to stay in Oregon. Berman, who had heard this often before, had finally had enough.

"That's funny," he answered. "Because I was talking to Keiko just the other day, and he asked me, 'Where's the plane?' "

Bonnie Norton was not amused. She told Berman that she doubted he could really speak to animals, and she demanded to speak with his boss.

Now, high above the North Atlantic, Mark Berman had fled all that. He was on the plane himself. "We're going to free Willy," he had told the Icelandair clerk at the check-in counter in Minneapolis-St. Paul. She had responded with a bright, blank airline smile. When we landed at Keflavík Airport in Iceland, Berman gave the same glad news about freeing Willy to a gaggle of stewardesses on the tarmac. They dodged him artfully, as if he were a Hare Krishna offering flowers. Inside Leifur Eiríksson Terminal, at the money-changing window, he confided our mission to the matronly clerk as she converted our dollars to kronur. She did not look up from her counting. We spent the night in the Borg Hotel in Reykjavík. The next morning, in the cab we shared to a smaller domestic airfield for our flight to the Westman Islands, Berman leaned forward in his seat.

"We're here for Keiko," he informed the cabbie cheerily. "We're part of the organization that got him over here."

The cabbie, Hankur Geirsson, glanced at us in his rearview mirror.

"Me, I think it's the biggest joke in the world," Geirsson said. "We should not discuss it, but . . ." For the better part of a half second, the cabbie weighed the wisdom of debate with clients, then made his decision: To hell with diplomacy. "This nonsense about bringing him back to his family! Put an animal like that in the ocean, and he will die in the sea. No one in Iceland believes in this. An idea like that would only come from the United States."

Geirsson's opinion was a common one in Scandinavia. Recently the Oslo daily, *Dagbladet,* after reporting the 60,000-meatball proposal of Jan Gunnarsson, had quoted the Norwegian legislator Steinar Bastesen, former chief of Norway's Whalers' Association. "Spending millions to transport Keiko to Iceland is an incredible waste," Bastesen had said. "We don't need another whale up here; we have plenty." *Dagbladet* had gone on to editorialize, "This is a rather sickening scenario and has nothing to do with either ecology or animal protection. Quite the opposite, this is about turning nature upside down. It's also about money—and about animals as a substitute for religion."

I had my own opinion. In my view, the whale's multimillion-dollar return to the wild, like the Pyramids at Giza, or the Apollo moon landings, or Wagner's Ring Cycle, was a spectacularly unpragmatic project, yet important and stirring and grand. I was for it. Yet I could not help but see a little truth in everything that Hankur Geirsson, Steinar Bastesen, and *Dagbladet* said.

THE VESTMANNAEYJAR, OR WESTMAN ISLANDS, are a tight little archipelago of fifteen volcanic islands and islets, flanked by an assortment of sea stacks and skerries. All the emergent land, save for the sheerest cliffs, is tundra, green in summer, bleak and snowy in winter. The core group of islands is about 10,000 years old, having erupted from the sea's surface back then, near the dawn of human history. The newest island—the Isle of Surtsey—is only forty-something, having formed explosively between 1963 and 1967. The Westman Islands were named for the first inhabitants, Irish slaves ("West Men") who killed their Norwegian masters on the main island of Iceland and fled here. Heimaey, "Home Island," is the largest and only inhabited island. Except for a summer diaspora of some of the men, who scatter to puffin-hunting huts and sheep stations on the outer islands, all 4600 Westman Islanders live on Heimaey.

In 1973, a volcano erupted on Heimaey and buried half the town in lava and tephra. The Icelanders fought back, pumping seawater from a battery of hoses onto the advancing flow. The lava, in cooling, solidified to form a black rampart against the fluid, red-hot rock upstream, diverting it from town. Among geologists there remains some question as to whether the surviving neighborhoods owe their salvation to human effort or to the whim of Helgafell, the volcano, but in the Icelandic imagination the matter has been resolved. The episode is billed now as the first time in history that *Homo sapiens* defeated a volcano—or fought a volcano to a stalemate, anyway: half the town going to the lava, half to humanity.

If Iceland for the Greeks was Ultima Thule, the northernmost outpost of the world, then the Westman Islands, as outliers of that remoteness, make an Ultissima Thule. For the many months required for Keiko's rehabilitation, this small volcanic outpost would be home to the whale's twelve trainers and support staff. None was eager to come. All had leaned toward Scotland,

Ireland, someplace—anyplace—less remote from the world. In the lull before Keiko's arrival, I poked around the island, curious as to what the whale
and his crew had in store for them.

Heimaey was circumscribed by a September sea haze that brought the
horizon in close. The circle of haze embraced a ship-tight little place of almost surreal neatness. Civilization clustered at the north end of the Heimaey
Island, around the harbor. The city limits are crisply defined, with no suburban sprawl into the tundra of the south. (The Westmans are so hermetic to
begin with, and the winters so dark, cold, and long, that an isolated,
Thoreau-like existence in the outback must lose all appeal.) The houses,
painted Easter-egg pastels, have façades that are too simple, somehow. In the
spotless sidewalks and curbs, there is insufficient detail, as if these were
miniature houses made large. The Westman Islanders have considerable
pride in their homes. The houses often have names and birth dates—
"Herlsey, 1925," for example—engraved on on a wooden scroll above the
door. The Westmans do not have a good climate for botanical gardening, so
the inhabitants garden with rocks, instead, making decorative use of the
"lava bombs" blown out in the eruption of 1973, and resorting occasionally
to the skulls of whales and ribs of old vessels. There is no graffiti. There is no
trace of litter. Occasionally an inflated plastic bag will rocket by on the gale,
ripped from the grip of some shopper. The highest wind speed ever recorded
officially in Iceland, 119 knots, was measured at the weather station at the
south end of Heimaey.

If the preternatural spotlessness of the town is partly climatological—
those ferocious sea winds sweeping the streets—then it is partly cultural, as
well. In the 1973 eruption, which destroyed more than four hundred of
Heimaey's houses, the inhabitants fastidiously swept out their homes just before the dwellings were buried by lava. (Most Americans, I believe, would
view oncoming lava as another excuse *not* to clean house.) Eventually I did
spot an empty liquor bottle tossed into a yard, then another bottle in a gut-
ter. Icelandic drinking is the serious, quest-for-oblivion sort of boozing you
see among other high-latitude, long-winter people, Russians and Eskimos
and Finns.

The town and harbor of Heimaey bounded to the north by the Nordurklettar, the "North Rocks," a wall of sheer fortresses crowned by precipi-
tous green slopes on which sheep graze throughout summer. Puffins nest in
burrows in the thin soil beneath this cliff-top tundra. Village men climb
these steep pastures to hunt incoming puffins in the summer, deftly snatch-
ing the birds from the air with long-handled nets. In autumn, at shearing
time, the sheep are lowered from the cliffs on ropes. It seems an island and an
economy out of *Gulliver's Travels* or Dr. Seuss. In season, fulmars, guille-

mots, razorbills, kittiwakes, gannets, and other cliff-breeding seabirds nest on the sheer walls beneath the tundra burrows of the puffins, practicing the raucous form of seabird government that Melville called "riotocracy." They throng the ledges of the North Rocks in such dense, competitive swarms that thousands of eggs are knocked off into the sea. (Cliff-nesting birds lay pyriform eggs, pointed at one end, so as to roll in a tight circle, and the eggs come painted in camouflage colors, yet these advantages go only so far in a riotocracy.) Kicked loose by the ceaseless squabbling, eggs rain down on the sea. Halibut, lured upward from the bottom by this manna, feast on it, and sometimes killer whales swing in to feast on the halibut.

The prime waters for *Orcinus orca* in Iceland were those off the East Fiords, where Keiko was captured, and those off the Reykjanes Peninsula on the west coast, and here in the waters around the Westman Islands.

The harbor was one of the tightest little anchorages I had ever seen. It seemed a toy harbor, not quite real. Keiko's sea pen was anchored in a cove that opened on the narrow gut connecting harbor to sea. The cove was called Klettsvík, "Rock Bay," for the way it nestled under the crenellated wall formed by three of the North Rocks. Rising vertically from the western end of the cove was Heimaklettur, "Home Rock," then came Midklettur, "Middle Rock," and finally Ysliklettur, "East Rock." It was hard to imagine a better, more protected spot for the whale.

The eruption of 1973 had very nearly spoiled it all by sealing off the harbor entrance. Had the lava flowed completely across the opening, civilization in the Westmans would have ended, as there is no other anchorage in the islands, and this is an archipelago of fishermen. In the eruption, the harbor water had grown warm as blood. The harbor's seaward breakwater had been obliterated, and the lava had started building its isthmus across the harbor mouth; then the eruption sputtered out. When the new landscape had cooled, the harbor was even cozier than it had been before. The unfinished isthmus of basalt, in the end, made a breakwater superior to the man-made riprap jetty it had destroyed. Pyroclastic forces from deep in the earth, together with brave Icelanders fighting back with hoses, had conspired to make what seemed the perfect halfway house in the rehabilitation of the whale.

Every rental room in Heimaey was booked by the press and whale people weeks before Keiko's return. *"Velkominn Heim Keikó"* proclaimed banners strung high on the façades of buildings. "Welcome Home Keiko." In every store, Keiko T-shirts, Keiko knit caps, Keiko sweaters, and Keiko coffee mugs were on display. In shop windows, Keiko dolls, complete with the three identifying dots on the chin, were arranged alongside stuffed puffins. The stuffed Keikos were synthetic. The stuffed puffins were real—taxidermic decoys fashioned by puffin-netters and offered now to the tourist trade.

Icelanders still use an old term, *hvalreki*, "whale drift," to describe an unexpected piece of good fortune. Back in the days of the sagas, drift ice often arrived in Iceland accompanied by whales, which were then driven ashore and slaughtered, the meat and blubber divided among the villagers. Keiko appeared to be a similar sort of windfall. For the island of Heimaey, he was literal *hvalreki*, but *hvalreki* of an entirely new sort.

25

AURORA BOREALIS

ON THE EVE OF THE WHALE'S RETURN, THE TOWN OF HEIMAEY CELEBRATED by hosting an evening cruise on the ferry *Herjólfur*. The two passenger decks were jammed with hundreds of celebrants—television reporters, print journalists, locals, whale enthusiasts from all over the world. Hors d'oeuvres, wine, and Icelandic beer circulated. The waitresses balanced trays of champagne glasses filled with some beverage of a strange, perfervid blue. It was the same unearthly color you see in iceberg-filled meltwater lagoons at the termini of Iceland's glaciers. It looked poisonous, like antifreeze, and I passed on it, but my fellow journalists quickly unburdened each tray.

On the promenade deck, representatives of the United Parcel Service distributed "Welcome Home Keiko" T-shirts from a huge cardboard bin. UPS was providing the Oregon truck that would ferry Keiko to the Newport airfield—the trip would take about twenty-six minutes and thirty seconds, the company had discovered in a dry run—and at the other end, in Iceland, UPS was also providing the truck that would transport the whale from the Westman Island airfield to his sea pen. On the stairwell to the promenade deck, a barker from Boeing touted the Boeing C-17, the huge U.S. Air Force cargo jet that would fly Keiko here from Oregon. The C-17, we learned, is powered by four fully reversible F117-Pratt & Whitney-100 engines, each rated at 40,440 pounds of thrust. The maximum payload is 170,900 pounds, or, I calculated, just over seventeen Keikos.

The C-17's range was impressive, 2400 nautical miles, yet this was insufficient for a nonstop flight from Oregon, so the Air Force planned two midair refuelings. Tanker aircraft from Travis Air Force Base in California and McGuire Air Force Base in New Jersey would refill the C-17 en route. Keiko would not have to suffer any airport layovers, thanks to this refueling, but he and his sponsors would have to pay for this convenience—the Air Force was charging $370,000 for the flight.

At 8:45 in the evening, the ferry left the inner harbor dead-slow. We passed Keiko's sea pen, which was illuminated for the occasion. This was the largest net pen ever built for a marine mammal, more than half as big as Keiko's tank in Oregon: 250 feet long by 100 wide by 25 feet deep, with a volume of more than three million gallons. The superstructure was skeletal.

A "Chemgrate" walkway with safety rails of PVC pipe ran around the polygonal perimeter of the pen. A wide footbridge crossed the center of the pen, directly over the med pool. The components of the pen had filled fourteen semitrucks. This fleet had transported the pen to the biggest airplane in the world, the Antonov An-225 Mriya, which had flown the pen to Iceland.

Mriya in Russian means "Dream." To NATO this appellation seemed too benign, and it code-named the behemoth "Cossack." Only one Mriya has ever been built. Given the perpetual implosion of the Russian economy, it is unlikely we will ever see another. The Mriya's wingspan is 290 feet, just a little less than the length of a football field. The landing-gear system incorporates thirty-two tires. The engines are six ZMKB Progress Lotarev D-18T turbofans, each generating 51,590 pounds of thrust. The maximum payload is 551,150 pounds, or about fifty-five Keikos, three times the lifting power of the C-17 that would transport the whale himself to Iceland.

The An-225 Mriya was the blue whale of aeronautics. Keiko's sea pen was the mother of all sea pens. Nothing about this operation was small.

As the guests on *Herjólfur* laughed and chattered and lifted drinks and hors d'oeuvres from passing trays, the sea pen fell behind us. The ferry trimmed very close to the sheer wall of Klettsnef, the rocky point that divides the harbor strait from open water. *Herjólfur's* spotlight illuminated the gentle surge at the base of the wall, then played up and down the vertical rock, reflecting brightly from guano-whitened ledges there. This was the gateway through which Keiko would someday pass to freedom.

The ferry steamed through that gateway and out to sea. We came hard to port and coasted the seaward side of the Nordurklettar, the North Rocks, which rose very dark above the ship. It was summer, but the sea wind was cold. Most of the celebrants who had ventured out on deck now retreated below, returning to the warmth and light and conversation and cocktails. Those of us who lingered on deck turned up our collars. On the island this morning I had bought a knit cap of Icelandic wool, which I now tugged low over my ears. The rampart of the North Rocks blocked the lights of the harbor and village. The world was vast and dark and elemental. This black wilderness was the crucible of killer whales. These were Keiko's native waters.

As we passed under Heimaklettur, "Home Rock," a middle-aged Icelandic woman—she was a travel agent from Reykjavík—nodded up at the black summit. "The sheep graze up there all summer," she said. "In autumn they lower them by rope." She shook her head at this crazy ingenuity. The provincial customs of the Westman Islanders struck her as strange and wonderful. "You can learn the whole genealogy of the meat when you buy sheep here," she said. "They're a little crazy about their sheep."

We handful of passengers on deck had all gathered along the rail on the island side. The seaward rail was empty. This is the orientation of human be-ings, *ad terra firma*. We are terratropic animals. Whales, of course, are the opposite. I crossed to the whale side of *Herjólfur,* where I had the seaward rail all to myself. Now and again a small whitecap glimmered in the black-ness. We were scarcely three hundred miles from the East Fiords, off which Keiko had been captured. I sniffed at the dark wind for any East Fiordish scents that might greet the whale here, on the day he swam to freedom—odor and memory are so intertwined. Then I remembered: The odonticetes, the toothed whales, have no sense of smell. As the nostrils in the first whales, the archaeocetes, migrated to the top of the head, becoming blowholes, the neural connections were lost, and now the odontocete brain has no olfactory region at all.

At ten in the evening *Herjólfur* returned to harbor. The journalists dis-embarked, most of them adjourning to the pressroom, which had been set up on the third floor of a waterfront warehouse. "Keiko's home is securely moored using SEAFLEX," said an advertisement on the pressroom wall. A stack of "media kits" lay on the table—white folders full of information sheets prepared by the Free Willy Keiko Foundation. The cover read, "Keiko: Home at Last," and showed a photo of a breaching killer whale. Some re-porters got busy on their laptops. Others gathered around a big, high-resolution, rear-projection monitor of the whale's website, which was to screen live streaming video of Keiko's departure from Oregon, with updates every fifteen minutes during his flight.

At one in the morning, GMT, just as the C-17 was scheduled to leave Oregon, the website, www.keiko.org, crashed. Keiko's staff in Iceland specu-lated that the whale's global popularity had been too much, that the site had taken too many hits. "Not able to establish connection with server" was all the screen would tell us.

Nolan Harvey, the whale's head trainer, was disappointed but he sol-diered on, keeping us posted through telephone conversations with his col-leagues in Oregon. "It's buttoned up and ready to go," he reported of Keiko's transport box. "They're going through their last checks."

The transport box was twenty-eight feet long, made of fiberglass, cus-tomized to Keiko's present dimensions, and called "the cradle." Keiko would float inside the cradle, resting on the same litter that had borne him from Mexico to Oregon. When filled with water and whale, the cradle would weigh 45,000 pounds. It was fitted with baffles to prevent water from slop-ping out into the cargo bay of the C-17. To further minimize splash, some of the water would be pumped into a special tank prior to takeoff and land-ing. The temperature in the cargo bay would be kept at fifty-two degrees Fahrenheit; cool for human passengers, ideal for an airborne killer whale.

Dianne Hammond convened an informal press conference. She and Nolan Harvey joined Hallur Hallsson, the Icelander who was serving as the whale's press liaison in the Westman Islands, and they answered questions from reporters.

The media were drawn, as usual, to the dark side of the story.

"What's this rumor about someone trying to poison his food?" asked the first reporter.

"*We* do the food preparation," Hammond answered, with just a hint of acerbity.

"We routinely check his fish for nutrient levels," added Nolan Harvey, and he went on to suggest that those routine checks would make it almost impossible to poison the whale.

The husband-and-wife team of Hammond and Harvey, in their years of dealing with the press in Oregon, had become expert at steering and deflecting reporters. Hammond in particular was a master of the imperceptible censorious frown, the next-question-please inflection. For his part, Hallur Hallsson, the Icelander, was innocent of this art. His instinct, perversely, was to provide the reporters with all the information he could.

"There have been four threats here in Iceland," he volunteered. "Three of them were addressed to me. The threat was to take poisoned fish into his tank. The last threat was put in the post on Monday. It included a very rude message to the prime minister. This is very uncharacteristic of Iceland. But such threats have been made. It's very unIcelandic."

Hallsson's expansiveness served only to stimulate the reporters, of course.

Rumors were circulating that a certain Icelander was being held for interrogation on the Keiko threats, and the reporters pursued a line of questions about this man. Then they launched a line of questions about the grudge that the people of Eskifjördur, bitter at having been passed over as hosts for the sea pen, were rumored to hold against Keiko. After a few minutes of this, Diane Hammond stepped in to correct the negative drift. She pointed out that poisoning Keiko's fish would not be such a simple matter, as most of Keiko's diet was now *live* steelhead, and from there she segued smoothly into an appreciation of the athleticism of the steelhead. "Steelhead trout are very fast fish," she concluded. "If Keiko can chase down a steelhead, he can chase down anything. A fifteen-pound steelhead is a very fast fish."

Steelhead are fast fish, indeed, but Keiko's steelhead, as I had learned from his Oregon trainers, were enfeebled by truck transport from the hatchery and by the ozone in Keiko's pool. A couple of weeks ago, Dianne Hammond had admitted to me her doubts about Keiko's ability to catch fish without tank corners against which to pin them. Like any good spokeswoman, she was delivering something less than the entire truth.

"I understand that the trainers didn't really want to come here," I suggested to Nolan Harvey.

"Well, it's Iceland," he said. "A lot of people, especially the trainers, thought it was going to snow, it's going to be blowing wind. They really didn't know anything about the spot. And we do have a few people on our staff who are Irish and who were more than happy to go to Ireland. But now that everybody's been here, and they've seen it, they're in love. They've already fallen in love with this town."

"So you have no regrets?"

"Absolutely not. I love it here. Dianne, my wife, and I were here in July. Neither one of us wanted to go back to Oregon. We had to go back to help prepare for Keiko's departure, but we both love the island. The people here have adopted us very well. We want to become part of the community here."

By two in the morning, most of the reporters had retired for the night. Several of us lingered around the monitor, hoping that www.keiko.org would return to life. The website's live streaming video would permit us to witness Keiko's departure from Oregon and his flight across, yet simultaneously allow us to be on hand to greet him when he arrived—a kind of journalistic omniscience that we were reluctant to give up. I sustained myself on hors d'oeuvres that I had filched as emergency rations from the party on *Herjólfur*. From a pint carton I drank an Icelandic beverage called "G-mjólk." I could not quite place the taste. The main ingredient of G-mjólk is *orka*, whatever that is.

Finally I gave up and headed home to my hotel. The waterfront was deserted. The village streets were empty. A ghostly column of light appeared above the dark summit of the rock called Stóraklif, then another spiked above Heimaklettur. The aurora borealis. In the sagas, I supposed, a bright display of northern lights like this one would have portended the return of Keiko, the hero—the whale was due to arrive in just eight hours—but the more modern explanation is a storm on the sun. I wondered whether that distant storminess—solar flares—were responsible for knocking Keiko's website out of cyberspace.

The pale columns of the aurora borealis were forever shifting. They flared up into banners, spilled downward as curtains of light, reformed as columns, vanished, reappeared in different spots. They marked a kind of celestial tide-rip where the solar wind meets Earth's magnetosphere. The universe is full of these echoes and symmetries; currents stir up phosphorescence high in the firmament, just as down in the oceans of Earth.

Another shaft of northern light lengthened over Midklettur, above the sea pen. I wondered whether Keiko, after twenty years of southern exile, would remember the aurora borealis. A whale spends its life buoyed between immensities: the profound ocean in one direction, the infinite sky in the other. As a calf, respiring, Keiko had commuted rhythmically from stars to depths and back again. Both vastnesses have their local signatures. He must have learned them. If the undersea voices here did not inform Keiko he was home—the warbling of beluga, the popping of shrimp, the birdy *oink oink* of harp seals—then maybe the aurora would tell him.

26

GLOBEMASTER

THE DAY OF KEIKO'S RETURN DAWNED CLEAR, FOR ICELAND, WITH BIG patches of blue sky. Four hundred feet above Keiko's sea pen, sheep were grazing on the steep green summit slopes of Home Rock. A ewe and lamb contoured the edge of the cliff, placidly cropping breakfast a single false step away from certain death. The sea haze had withdrawn, and for the first time I could see the mainland of Iceland. Fifteen miles across the channel rose the green lower slopes and white, lenticular ice field of the glacier Myrdalsjökull.

Heimaey is a small island, with nothing very far from everything else, and the airfield is just a twelve-minute walk from town. The press corps ate hurried breakfasts, emptied the hotels, and rode up in caravans of minibuses to the airstrip. I went up myself on foot. Each step uphill opened up better views of the Myrdalsjökull ice cap on the main island. The weather was almost nice. It was an auspicious day for the whale's arrival.

The two runways of the Heimaey airfield intersected to make a cross. The runway on which Keiko would be landing had been cordoned off by rope. Along the edge of the tarmac, small tumuli of black basalt poked above the tundra grass. Each little summit was crowded with reporters and cameramen and it bristled with tripods and big video cameras. The tallest tumulus, which flew the airfield's wind sock, had drawn a particularly dense aggregation of the press. I joined this group. We scanned the skies like millennialists awaiting the Second Coming. The rippling red-and-white wind sock was the flag of our movement. Phalanxes of telephoto lenses aimed at the point of the expected materialization. From each tumulus, anxious men and women in bright-colored parkas searched the horizon beyond the sea stacks to the northwest, hoping for a glimpse of the speck that would grow into the Globemaster III, the giant cargo plane carrying Keiko. We looked a little crazy, I thought. We looked wishful and deluded, like cargo cultists on some ridgetop in New Guinea.

From the direction of Iceland, two fast-moving dots appeared low in the sky. This proved a false alarm. The dots grew rapidly into a pair of big USAF helicopters from the American base at Keflavík, on the Reykjanes Peninsula of southwestern Iceland. The helicopters came sideslipping in, flattening wide circles of tussock grass, and they landed. The airmen disencoptered in camouflage uniforms, armed with their personal video cameras, and they searched out good camera angles not already taken by the professionals of the press. I was glad to have representatives of the Air Force show up, for I had questions about this runway, which was beginning to seem awfully short. The C-17 is a huge plane and the runway was only 3900 feet long. When I expressed my reservations to the airmen, they assured me that the C-17 Globemaster was designed for short landings. They described the exceptional brakes of the aircraft and explained how the special mounting of the engine helped reverse thrust. The airmen deployed for Keiko.

In the 1950s, U.S. aircraft from the base at Keflavík, with fifty-caliber machine guns, used to strafe Iceland's killer whales for target practice and for fun. Hundreds were killed before the practice was stopped. It was good to see these airmen take up positions with nothing but video cameras in their hands. There is such a thing as progress.

The acting secretary of the U.S. Air Force, F. Whitten Peters, had come out in one of the helicopters. Secretary Peters was dressed like an ace from the First World War, in a brown leather flight jacket with scarf. The bright red scarf was patterned with helicopters and orcas, nicely symbolic of the truce between the Air Force and the whales.

Paul Irwin, president of the Humane Society of the United States, sat at the base of a small tumulus with his back against the tussock grass, watching the sky. The Humane Society had a considerable investment in Keiko, having contributed a million dollars toward construction of his facility in Newport. I strolled down to Irwin's tumulus and settled in beside him. As we waited for this morning's epiphany—the whale's appearance in the sky—Irwin and I discussed the Oregon chapter of Keiko's saga, just concluded. We lamented the feuding that had marred Keiko's time in the United States.

"Our board was anxious to see Keiko get out of Mexico," Irwin told me. "He was going to die there. But in Newport we hoped for something that went beyond Keiko. We hoped that the Newport facility would become an institute for ongoing marine-mammal research. We need to develop a credible pool of expertise on this subject. We live in an age of environmental holocaust. We need to learn to transmigrate populations. It may be necessary to use captive populations to save a species. Everyone has opinions; we need *data*. We need facts about how you can return captive animals to their own environment."

Two things had killed the Humane Society's hopes for the Newport facility, Irwin said. One was the lack of a new orca candidate for rehabilitation, given the determination of the Alliance of Marine Mammal Parks and Aquariums never to provide one. The other was the feud between the Oregon Coast Aquarium and the Free Willy Keiko Foundation. The Humane

Society's dream, now abandoned, had been that Keiko be the archetype for a whole legion of big rehabilitated whales. "What Keiko has become is a symbol," Irwin said. "We're not disappointed, but it's a much different outcome than we envisioned."

"Really?" I said. "It wasn't disappointing?"

Irwin exhaled. " 'Disappointing' is the word," he confessed. "The facility that was built in Newport was a state-of-the-art aquarium. We hoped it would be a beginning."

THE C-17 GLOBEMASTER III APPEARED and circled the island to land from the east. The Globemaster III is a plane so large that on certain tacks it seems not to be moving. It disappeared behind the little volcanic mountain called Háubúr, and when it reappeared it was gigantic. For one hallucinatory moment, as the Globemaster dropped toward the runway with flaps down, it looked larger than the island upon which it was trying to land.

The Globemaster was designed to fly big payloads into short, rough landing strips. Any other plane with Keiko-carrying capacity would have required twice this runway's length. "The C-17 is the only plane in the world that could perform this mission," General Michael Ryan, Air Force chief of staff, had boasted. I found it hard to believe, despite the assurances of General Ryan and his Keflavík helicopter pilots, that the pilot of this Globemaster really imagined he could land here. The angle of attack of a C-17 is alarmingly steep. The plane touched down with explosions of smoke from the tires and swerved sharply left, but maintained control and stopped with some runway to spare.

Lanny Cornell, David Phillips, Jean-Michel Cousteau, and other members of Keiko's innermost circle disembarked from the Globemaster. On the ground they reunited with staff from Keiko's second circle. There were emotional embraces all around. Ann Moss was there, and Katherine Hanly, and Mark Berman. The cargo bay had been so cold that none of the human passengers had slept for more than an hour. Their faces were tired but ecstatic. They walked over in a group to where we in the press had gathered, behind a rope strung up to restrain us.

"Keiko was very relaxed. We're euphoric," Dianne Hammond told us.

A female reporter standing beside me turned to a colleague. "They say he's relaxed," she muttered. "Maybe it's true. How would we know?" Bob Ratliffe of Craig McCaw's Foundation, a multitasker, alternately addressed the gathered reporters and his cell phone. "If he knows whether he's home or not, I can't say," he told a reporter in the flesh, and in the same breath he informed some incorporeal reporter, over the phone, "There's no doubt about it. He's a very emotional and emoting animal. But he's also very moody."

An interviewer from the Discovery Channel was holding a microphone up to David Phillips.

"He vocalized a little at the beginning and at the end," Phillips was saying.

"Does it sound like a happy holler or an anxious holler?" the Discovery Channel wondered.

"It's hard to interpret," Phillips said.

Lanny Cornell, for his part, was not interested in describing Keiko's flight. Dr. Cornell had attended many killer whales on overflights of the North Atlantic, and the details were now old routine for him. Cornell had never shipped a killer whale by Globemaster III, however, nor had he witnessed a midair refueling, and all he wanted to talk about was the amazing precision of that maneuver. The veterinarian, a military buff, had looked up through the cockpit canopy as the grandissimus of the air tanker's fuel hose extended down toward the Globemaster. He could not get over how close together the two huge aircraft had flown. He marveled at the deftness of the pilots. His fascination with giant animals was transferable to behemoth cargo planes, it seemed. If the killer whale is one sort of globemaster, then the C-17 is another.

On touchdown, Dr. Cornell, hearing a pop, had assumed that a chain on Keiko's cradle had broken. Otherwise he had been impressed by the softness of the landing. Bob Ratliffe of the McCaw Foundation and Jean-Michel Cousteau had shared that impression. "I was expecting something a bit rougher," Cousteau said. It all depended upon where you sat. David Phillips, seated directly over the landing gear, had been sharply jolted and for a moment thought he was meeting his Maker.

The rumor began to travel among the reporters that the C-17's landing gear had been broken. Gudlaugur Sigurgeirsson, press officer for the town of Heimaey, arrived from the Globemaster with a damage report. Introducing himself, Sigurgeirsson begged us to save ourselves strain and conserve a lot of Icelandic consonants by simply calling him "Guli." It was true, Guli said, the rumor was correct. "I understand a tire blew," he told us. "I understand an axle went as well."

Keiko had broken the Globemaster.

The C-17's bay door opened. From under its high tail, the Globemaster slowly gave birth to Keiko's cradle. We could not see the whale himself, just the freight car–shaped cradle, inching outward on a motorized gurney. The freight car was draped with a white banner advertising the names and logos of sponsors: UPS, Warner Bros., Icelandair, RealNetworks, Ericsson, Craig O. McCaw Foundation, Kawasaki, Oregon Coast Aquarium, Aqua Lutig, Free Willy Keiko Foundation, www.keiko.org, and more.

A forklift sped onto the runway, as airport fire trucks do in emergencies.

In its steel arms before it, the forklift proferred a box of crushed ice with shovels buried in it. On Keiko's last trip, his flight from Mexico to Oregon, the whale's metabolism had melted all the ice in his cradle, and he had begun to overheat. Here on the Heimaey airfield Keiko's water temperature was fine. The ice was not needed, and the forklift driver relaxed and just stood by. A big UPS flatbed truck with a "Welcome Home, Keiko" sign on the cab drove onto the tarmac and hitched to the container. The truck spouted a puff of diesel, and Keiko was on the move again. The whale left the airfield in a caravan with police cars and other vehicles, flanked on foot by security people in yellow vests. The UPS truck moved so slowly that by jogging now and then, the security people and reporters on foot could keep pace. Keiko's trainers, dressed in their blue-and-yellow splash suits, perched on top of the cradle, making stroking motions. None of the rest of us could see what they were stroking. This container, for all we knew, might have been a decoy or hoax.

American and Icelandic flags waved by the roadside as we entered town. Overnight new *"Velkominn Heim Keikó"* banners had been unfurled high on the façades of buildings, and much of the populace seemed to have turned out. The route was not *lined* with spectators—there were too few Westman Islanders for that—but onlookers had gathered in knots at intersections.

"We're coming up to 'Breakfast Street' here," one journalist said to another, as we reached the intersection with Vestmannabraut.

"Breakfast Street and Fax Street," amended the second journalist.

The journalists did not need to learn the real names of Heimaey's streets. Keiko's fifteen minutes of fame would soon be over, for this chapter of his life, at least, and by evening almost all the journalists assembled here would be gone.

THE WESTMAN ISLANDS HAVE COME to world attention just three times in history. The first was 1963, when the newest member of the group, Surtsey, made its debut, erupting from the sea's surface with a roar of steam and a stratospheric plume of fire, smoke, and ash. The second was 1973, when the volcano Helgafell burned and buried half of Heimaey. The third was September 10, 1998, when the most famous whale in the world arrived home.

On this third occasion, the inhabitants did not seem particularly to crave world attention. Heimaey is a town of fishermen and fish-plant workers, not the sort of community prone to sentimentality about the finned resources of the sea. There was a Norse reserve and skepticism in the men. In the faces of the women I could not detect much welcoming warmth for their gigantic new neighbor. Several spectators complained that you could not even see the whale. The caravan surprised one citizen as he stepped from his house. With a bitter smirk, this man turned on his heel and strode back inside. He wanted no part of this. Most adults in the crowd seemed determined to show by their expressions, or lack of same, that they were not impressed by this foolishness. The children were entirely different. Several juveniles were escorting the caravan on skateboards. One boy ran alongside the UPS truck, flashing the V sign with both hands. A small girl, watching the parade from her father's shoulders, chanted, *"Keiko! Keiko! Keiko! Keiko! Keiko! Keiko! Keiko!"*

A reviewing stand had been erected on the waterfront. Its bleachers looked down on the barge that would transport Keiko out to his cove. The sun was bright but the wind still nippy, and the spectators jamming the bleachers wore wool caps and parkas. The mood was festive. Nearly half the crowd was made up of children waving small Icelandic and American flags. A big green crane on the barge swung landward and lifted Keiko's cradle from the UPS truck. The cradle tilted slightly, and for the first time the public could see inside. There really was a killer whale in there. All the trainers had dismounted but one, and this man rode in the front of the cradle, stroking Keiko's head reassuringly. The cradle swung slowly seaward past the green hull of a big seiner moored along a dock behind.

This seiner was *Gudrun,* the vessel that had captured Keiko twenty years before. By pure coincidence, or by some eerie synchronicity, she had called on the Westman Islands this week. *Gudrun* had been modified, with a second deck and new radars added since she captured the calf that her crew had named Siggi. Of course, Siggi had been modified himself—he was now Keiko and he had added decks of his own, in a figurative way.

Two tugs pushed the barge toward the sea pen in Klettsvík. A small fleet followed: The VIP boats carrying Free Willy Keiko Foundation luminaries and other important people. A herring boat comandeered by some enterprising news team. An orange skiff carrying Jean-Michel Cousteau and the adolescent aquanauts of his documentary film, all dressed in identical jackets. A small ferry that had been designated as the press boat sallied forth with its railings and roofs jammed with journalists and cameras. Directly across from the sea pen, where the 1973 eruption had built a long spit of black cinders, a crowd of locals had gathered to see the whale.

Aboard the press boat, television journalists began their têtes-a-têtes with their cameras. "Those white specks you see atop the cliff are sheep," an American newswoman told the folks back home. "Keiko's closest neighbors will be sheep." She gestured up at the lofty flocks on Heimaklettur behind her. Her cameraman panned up the face of the cliff, following her gesture.

Print journalists sought places apart from the crowd and began earnest cell-phone conversations with editors back home. These talks had the look of soliloquies, for the cell phones were cupped against the wind and nearly invisible. Each reporter seemed to be in lively conversation with himself, like a schizophrenic street person. "I thought we should work in kids' quotes," Brad Cain of the Associated Press was telling his stateside editor. "'Keiko is so good for Iceland!' Just to get a kid quote in." A herring boat packed with spectators cut inside the press boat, obscuring the view. "We can't see anything! This is a tragedy!" cried a female photographer shrilly. Gudlaugur Sigurgeirsson, the press liaison, assured all hands that the boats would form a skirmish line before Keiko was lowered into his pen. Every photographer would get a clear shot.

"Even if Keiko never leaves this bay, he's better off," said Judy Muller of ABC Television, looking earnestly into her camera. "He'll have access to plenty of live fish, and be able to communicate with passing pods of whales."

The ABC cameraman moved his tripod several feet backward, framed Muller again in his viewfinder, then gave her a nod. I was surprised at how much the cameraman seemed to control things; it was a little disappointing, like learning that it is really a sergeant who runs the battalion.

"Even if Keiko never leaves this bay, he's better off," Muller repeated, with small changes in inflection. "He'll have access to plenty of live fish, and be able to communicate with passing pods of whales."

It was uncertain, in fact, that Keiko would be able to communicate with passing whales. Cetologists worried that the Heimaey pen site was a little too well protected. Any vocalizations Keiko made from the confines of this rocky cove would have to deflect around two promontories to reach open water, and of course any calls inward from wild whales would have to clear the same obstacles. David Phillips, among others, had been arguing for a system of hydrophones and speakers that would project Keiko's voice out into the ocean.

Judy Muller began a third reading of the same lines, but a gust of wind sent spray and mist over the rail. The camerman, lightning quick, covered the lens with his hand. When the mist dissipated, he nodded to Muller, and she tried again.

"Even if Keiko never leaves this bay, he's better off. He'll have access to plenty of live fish, and be able to communicate with passing pods of whales."

But would Keiko be better off, really? As those passing whales passed on, their voices receding in the distance, how would Keiko feel? A sense of déjà vu? He had heard orca voices recede once before, on the day of his capture by *Gudrun* at the age of one or two. For all her reiterations of the idea, I was not sure Judy Muller had thought the matter through.

The green crane on Keiko's barge lifted the whale from his container. He rose suspended in the sling, his beak protruding slightly forward and his flukes dangling aft. Keiko's flukes were beautiful, creamy white on the ventral side, with black trim. Through apertures in the hammock, the big, black, obovate paddles of his pectoral fins protruded, outspread to either side. As the crane swung him out over the pen, I was struck by how still he remained. In midair, as the crane began to lower him, he waved his flukes once slightly, then held motionless. His trust in his trainers was extraordinary. It was hard for me to imagine a similar equanimity in a human being. If one of us had been lifted entirely out of his element by a team of sea lions, say, or a gang of muskrats, would he have held so still?

On the question of dolphin captivity, I am myself an abolitionist. I do not believe in any sort of zoo. The captivity of killer whales seems particularly hard to justify. I believe that our descendants will find it unfathomable that we, for our amusement, imprisoned these regal, intelligent, social, free-swimming creatures in small tanks in order to perform for us. Our descendants will be right. And yet inevitably they will have oversimplified the thing. They will have failed to understand that however wrong and twisted, there was something wonderful, miraculous even, in the relationship between these enormous captives and their turnkeys.

Now, in Iceland, as Keiko swung slowly over the superstructure of his sea pen, he had confidence, somehow, that his trainers were looking out for him—that these humans knew what they were doing. His shadow on the water came up to greet him. The shadow paddles of his pectoral fins reached out and touched his real pectoral fins, yet still he held motionless. Even as his flukes and pectoral fins dipped under, he did not move.

"Touchdown, Keiko!" a radio reporter with a German accent sang into his microphone. As the whale and his hammock sank half-under, there came a brief, tentative, low-amplitude swimming motion of his flukes. Keiko ceased abruptly and held still again. His training had kicked in once more. Then suddenly the pumping of flukes resumed, it grew stronger, and the whale, thrashing the surface white and frothy with his tailfin, swam off the sling, and a cheer went up from the boats.

On the sea-pen platform, Keiko's trainers hugged, and officers of the Free Willy Keiko Foundation did the same. There were embraces all around: Katherine Hanly, David Phillips, Cousteau, Ratliffe, Ani Moss.

The whale dived, checking the bottom of the pen, perhaps, then resurfaced and commenced swimming the pen's circumference.

How did this greenish water, murky with planktonic life, seem to Keiko, after years in the pellucid, sterile, ozone-treated water of his Oregon tank? How did it feel it to cruise along a wall of net instead of concrete, a wall permeable to the current and the sounds of the ocean beyond? Would the voices of these nesting cliffs—the *kiti-wake kiti-wake* of the kittiwakes, the *auk!* of the little auk—ring any bells for this whale? Or the cries of the storm petrel, called *stormsvala* here in Iceland, or the black-backed gull, *svartbakur,* or the skua, *skúmur,* or razorbill, *alka,* or fulmar, *fyll,* or Manx shearwater, *skofa*— might one of those have done the trick?

And what about the undersea voices?

The harp seal wanders these waters in summer. In vocalizing under the surface, harp seals are fond of making a simple sound and repeating it once. Two seems to be their favorite number, and their most common call is a plunky *oink oink.* Up close, this sounds dim-witted, but with distance, and with multiplication, the calls blur into a lovely multitudinous whisper. Would this music, the windy murmurous song of the whole harp-seal nation, sound familiar to Keiko?

Humpback whales were hereabouts, having dispersed over their high-latitude summer feeding grounds. Now, in September, as the days grew shorter and the night sky began to fulminate with northern lights, some humpbacks had turned to migrate south again. Humpback whales have huge voices. Lone males, singing, generate as many decibels as a Globemaster III in warming up. Water is a good conductor of sound. If any humpback was singing within a hundred miles, Keiko would hear, and would remember, perhaps.

The narwhal, which inhabits these waters, has the most bizarre voice in the sea. This big arctic dolphin, named *Monodon monoceros,* "One-tooth one-horn," by Linnaeus, is the source of our myth of the unicorn. The males grow sixteen feet long. Add nine feet of tusk, and bull narwhals are as lengthy as bull killer whales. The narwhal's song is as strange as its dentition. Narwhals have such powers of projection that a pod passing your boat can be heard distinctly in the air. If you are underwater, the sound rocks you: First a ratchet sound, like a fishing reel unwinding. Then a noise like the cooing of doves, which plummets suddenly to a deep, croaking roar—scary, like the call of a Micronesian pigeon, if you have ever heard one of those. Then a labored whistling, as if somewhere on the seafloor a humanoid creature, some sort of merman with sleep apnea, were dozing fitfully on his back. Then the fishing reel again, paying out line. Then a groan like a tree creaking. Then the trumpeting of an elephant with a very thin trunk. Then an insistent noise, something like a donkey's braying. Then the fishing reel once more. Then that same elephant with the overpressure in his trunk. Then a guttural, lionlike roar. After that, a moment of quiet, as if the lion were gathering itself, and finally a piercing cacophony of cries, as if the lion had just scattered a flock of gulls.

If Keiko in calfhood had heard a performance like that, he would remember it, surely, would he not?

Or was there something in the embrace of the ocean itself, some quality of salinity, or chemistry, or magnetic field, that told Keiko he had come full circle? If water suffused with ozone—the superoxygen that sterilized his Oregon pool—makes one sort of sensation on the skin of a whale, does the ordinary oxygen of Icelandic water make another? Keiko could not smell, but he could taste. Did his tongue find clues in the very molecules of water?

Or had he been away so long—twenty years now—that all these voices and sensations were fresh?

27

---·---

FIVE HUNDRED KILLER WHALES

AN HOUR AFTER KEIKO'S SPLASHDOWN IN HIS NEW SEA PEN, THE PRESS BOAT came about and we headed back to harbor. Through my binoculars I watched the pen recede behind us. Keiko had finished his initial explorations. He was lolling now at the surface, just off the central platform. One of the trainers, Jennifer Schorr, sat in her blue-and-yellow splash suit on the platform edge, her legs dangling in the water. She did the splashy, two-handed fingerwalk across the surface that was Keiko's signal to approach. When the whale obeyed, Jennifer scratched a three-foot length of his back. Through the big ten-power binoculars, I saw her examine her fingertips with distaste. Keiko had been slathered in a special grease to keep his skin moist during transport, and this was packed under Jennifer's nails. The whale blew, and Jennifer, David Phillips, and the other Keiko people on the platform ducked their faces away from the mist of his spout.

On the press ferry, none of the reporters looked back toward the sea pen. Keiko was already old news.

Attention had shifted ahead to the harbor and the next assignment, and all talk was of flight schedules out of the Westmans. When Gudlaugur Sigurgeirsson stepped forward to announce that this ferry would go to Rekjavík tonight, with room for one hundred journalists, men and women all over the crowded vessel thrust hands high and volunteered. No one wanted to be stuck here. One television reporter, a young Englishwoman, was almost desperately anxious to guarantee herself a place on the ferry. The three-hour ferry voyage to Iceland was not fast enough for her, apparently, for on being promised a spot, she hedged her bets and quietly began asking about plane schedules back to Rekjavík. Keiko had returned home; now what about *her*?

As the press ferry disgorged its passengers on the Heimaey dock, there was a disturbance at the foot of the gangway. Two women had fallen into each other's arms there. They hugged long and hard, cheeks glistening with tears. Television cameramen converged in a circle to film the embrace. The two women were built the same—mother and daughter, from the look of them. They separated to arm's length and beamed at each other through their tears. Hand in hand, they set off down the dock, their joined arms swinging freely. They were careful to avoid looking into the cameras of two

Latin cameramen who backtracked ahead of them, crouching slightly as they filmed in retreat.

The soundman of this Latin team was unemployed in this sequence, so I asked him what the drama was all about.

"The dreams of these people," he explained in halting English. "Willy free."

We spoke in Spanish, and I learned that the younger woman was eighteen, her name was Mariana Savietto, and she was a winner on *Sorpresa,* the most popular television show in Argentina, which airs on Canal 13 in Buenos Aires. Lucky guests on *Surprise* get to realize their dreams, and Mariana's dream had been to witness Keiko's return home. The dream had come true. Walking down the Heimaey dock, swinging arms happily with her mother, Mariana started to skip, forcing the Argentine cameramen to backpedal faster, with occasional desperate glances behind them, so as not to stray backward off the pier.

Back at the press center, the press corps fell to their laptops and commenced knocking out stories. All eight tables were busy with earnest keyboarding. David Phillips and Dianne Hammond dropped in to answer questions. Phillips, I noticed, was sunburned from the reflected sunlight on the sea pen. As the print journalists labored against their deadlines, Keiko appeared on *Sky News.* Almost everyone stopped to look up at the televised whale, huge on the press center's big rear-projection monitor. Someone turned up the volume. "There are more than five hundred killer whales within five kilometers of his sea pen," the commentator was saying. David Phillips and I exchanged wide-eyed glances and we laughed. Television news can be a little too instantaneous. Five hundred killer whales within five kilometers of *anything* would be a visitation more ominous than any biblical plague. Five hundred killer whales would be crazy, inexplicable—unless all the orca tribes of Iceland were massing to bust Keiko out of his pen.

The U.S. ambassador to Iceland, Day Mount, dropped in, looking very Icelandic in a gray sweater-vest and dark jacket. He was blending in nicely with the locals. I asked him whether it had taken political courage for Iceland's prime minister, David Oddsson, to invite the whale to his country.

"Absolutely," the ambassador answered. "It took a lot of political courage." Oddsson had stood up to a number of elements in Icelandic society opposed to the whale, Mount said; it was he who had made it happen. Then Mount added, "With a lot of work from Dave Phillips and friends."

The ambassador and I looked across the room toward Phillips. I was startled by the change in the environmentalist. He seemed suddenly to have hit some sort of wall. Two minutes ago, conversing with journalists, he had looked very fresh; now he was bleary. His mouth had fallen half-open with fatigue and his eyes had closed to slits. His five-year campaign for the whale—the negotiations with Reino Aventura in Mexico, the dickering with Warner Bros. in Hollywood, the struggles to restore the animal's health, the fundraising efforts, the sponsorship deals, the feuds in Oregon, the long months working behind the scenes in London and Dublin and Reykjavík, then last night's sleepless flight in the cold cargo bay of the C-17—had all finally caught up with him. He had been running this last leg on fumes, and the last of those had just run out.

Major Chip Wiggins, the C-17 pilot, filled us in on the flight, and the reporters listened attentively. The press loved Major Wiggins. He was a tall, well-made, boyish, aw-shucks, all-American sort of specimen, a hero pilot straight from the comic books, everyone agreed. Speculation was rife among the reporters that the rough landing of the Globemaster would be bad—disastrous, even—for Major Wiggins's career, and everyone hoped this would not be so.

"The failure proves the capability of this craft to land safely in rough conditions," F. Whitten Peters, the acting secretary of the Air Force, said. This sounded a lot like destroying the village in order to save it, but I thought I understood what Peters meant to say.

The discussion of the broken landing gear seemed to revive David Phillips, who had been sitting directly above the wheel well. He now appeared to relive the jolt. The sleepy slits of his eyes came wide open. *We broke his hundred-eighty-million-dollar plane!*" he muttered. He shook his head in amazement, then subsided into fatigue again.

It was Lanny Cornell's turn to speak.

"A whale . . . ," Dr. Cornell began, then he choked up. For a moment he could not continue. It was astonishing to see the veterinarian's rugged face break up with emotion. It was like watching cracks appear on Hoover Dam. Dr. Cornell quickly regained control of himself and discussed the regime of stamina training and speed training that he and his colleagues planned for Keiko. Then he took questions.

"Could he jump out of the pen?" a reporter asked.

"He could if he wanted to. He doesn't know he can do it."

"How will you wean him from humans?"

Cornell anwered that the plan was to scale back Keiko's interaction with his trainers, but the veterinarian did not himself see dependence upon humans as a big problem. "I think if Keiko had the opportunity to join killer whales, he'd do so in an instant and leave every human companion behind," he said.

A reporter asked about the odds of Keiko's finding his family.

"I think if we tried to find his family, our chances would be almost nil,"

Cornell said. "If *he* tried to find his family, I think his chances would be better."

"Do you know anything about his family?" an Englishman asked. "Did he have brothers and sisters?"

"I have no idea."

"If he does find his family, how would you know that?"

"We won't."

By five o'clock, the press conference had dispersed into knots of reporters, each with an Air Force officer or Keiko official at the nucleus. A drift toward the doorway had begun, when Bob Ratliffe tapped on the microphone for attention. "There's breaking news," he said. When the room quieted, Ratliffe announced that a dolphin had entered Keiko's cove and was vocalizing with the whale.

Linda Moore Dunston, author of a nearly finished Keiko book for middle-schoolers, clapped both hands to her mouth and her eyes filled with tears. Free Willy Keiko Foundation officials hugged and exchanged high fives. Dr. Lanny Cornell struggled again with his emotions.

"A harbor porpoise, almost certainly," Cornell said. "Within twelve hours of arrival, he's already vocalizing with another cetacean. It doesn't get any better than that."

Male killer whale, southeast Iceland

Wild killer whales spy-hopping in the waters off the coast of Iceland
where Keiko was captured

Keiko performs at El Nuevo Reino Aventura

Keiko and his fans in Mexico City

Keiko on the set of
Free Willy with
Jason James Richter

Keiko's Oregon facility under construction

Keiko breaching from his Oregon tank

Keiko in the public viewing window at the Oregon Coast Aquarium

David Phillips poses in front of the plane that would carry Keiko to Iceland

The bay pen in Klettsvík Cove in the Westman Islands, Iceland

Keiko "bows" in his
winter bay pen

Keiko plays with one of his
Boomer Balls in the cove.

Tobba and Keiko during a windy training session

Keiko's boat, *Draupnir*, caught in a storm

High winds in the bay pen

Keiko on a "walk" off the Isle of Surtsey

A blood sample is drawn off the North Rocks in the Westman Islands

Frank Haavik examines Keiko after his accident under the ice

Keiko's ice lacerations

Keiko's healing scars

Colin Baird and Keiko in Norway

Keiko spy-hops

28

SEATABS®

KEIKO LAY AT THE SURFACE OF HIS BAY PEN ON HIS BACK, HIS WHITE BELLY TO the sky, his pectoral fins in the air, outspread. This was his first morning in the pen, and he seemed already at home. A trainer, Peter Noah, drifted alongside him in a black-and-yellow splash suit, scratching the cream-white underside of his flukes. Keiko's eyes were underwater. His beauty dots—the three dark spots on his white chin—were in the air. He flattened his pectoral fins against his sides ecstatically. He seemed to be having a good time.

Peter Noah boosted himself up over the trailing edge of the flukes, and for a time he worked almost entirely out of water, cupped in the shallow white basin formed by the flukes. He raked two-handed, scratching the flukes in vigorous semicircular arcs, pausing now and then to flick Keiko's protective ointment off his fingertips. Keiko rolled slowly on his side, and as his tailfin came vertical in the water, it tipped Noah gently off. As the trainer slid into the water, he never stopped working, continuing to scratch the tailfin as he went overboard. Now, in the water alongside Keiko again, he concentrated on the part presented to him, the whale's caudal peduncle—the tailstock. Then Keiko yawed slowly onto his stomach, and Noah began scratching along the last few feet of his spine. On this black, dorsal side of Keiko, in the area around his dorsal fin and his blowhole, you could see the opaque, whitish waxiness of the moisturizing ointment, patterned by semicircular five-fingered scratchmarks. The semicircles overlapped, like scales, as if Keiko were the biblical sort of leviathan.

After fifteen minutes or so, Peter Noah hauled out, as bulky as a walrus, his mustache dripping. He stood, teeth chattering, on the grating of the seapen platform. I grabbed one of his hands to check its temperature. It was like ice. Keiko's insistence on being scratched barehanded worked a hardship on his keepers. I wondered whether they ever held it against him. When sensation returned to Noah's fingers, he commenced scraping grease from under his nails and flicking it away.

The mood today on the bay pen was subdued and postclimactic. The triumphalism of Keiko's return was over and the quotidian had begun. Keiko's new boundaries, the tawny inner cliffs of the North Rocks, hemmed us in on three sides. At the waterline the cliffs were marked by a narrow, intertidal band of red-brown rockweed. Above that rose hundreds of feet of sheer, wind-smoothed walls, whitened by the guano of guillemots and murres wherever the birds had found a few millimeters of ledge for roosting. The occasional *baaa* of a sheep carried down from the green slopes above the cliff tops.

"Up," then, "Blow," a trainer recited into a tape recorder. She was doing an ethogram—a running account of what Keiko was doing. After a moment, she said, "Down." Keiko had submerged. On occasion she would say, "Not," which meant that she could not see Keiko and was unable to report his behavior.

Lanny Cornell and his wife, Kathy, sat watching the whale. They both wore jackets that read, "SEATABS®, Keiko's Iceland Express, Pacific Research Labs Inc., El Cajon, CA." Seatabs are an invention of Dr. Cornell's. During his employment at Marine World, he had grown impatient with the inefficiency of feeding handfuls of assorted multivitamins to the marine mammals. He thought it would be convenient if he could get it all in one tablet. The crucial ingredient in Seatabs is thiamin. Sea mammals eat fish, and many fish species have an enzyme that destroys thiamin. Dr. Cornell's amazing little pill restores that balance. Keiko is a living advertisement for Seatabs, and great quantities of those pills had accompanied the whale to Iceland.

Cornell craned to look up at the rock walls that protected this alcove. "We couldn't have found a better place if we built it," he said. "When Jeff Foster and Nolan Harvey came here, they knew right away that this was the place. Scotland kind of took itself out of the running. So much paperwork. It would have been years before we could set up there. Ireland welcomed us with open arms, but there were no killer whales off Ireland. I nixed Ireland myself."

"Down," the trainer dictated. After a considerable interval, she added, "Up. Blow. Down." The recitation was like a lullaby. Everyone on the bay pen was tired. Dr. Cornell had not recovered from the cold, sleepless flight in the Globemaster, none of the rest of us had adjusted to the new time zone, and we were all weary from all the press conferences and bustle of yesterday. Everyone seemed ready to talk of something besides Keiko. Dr. Cornell and his wife spoke for a while of a man they knew, a veterinarian injured by a lion. The mauled man had required surgery on his head and had been confined to bed for a year. There are hazards, obviously, in large-animal veterinary practice.

Dr. Cornell, stirring himself, walked to the edge of the platform, where he conferred with Peter Noah as they both studied Keiko. Kathy Cornell watched her husband with his famous patient. Keiko's bent fin seemed to remind her of another case; she told us that Lanny had once treated a bull killer whale with a necrotic dorsal fin. The fin had not responded to treatment, so Lanny had been forced to amputate it.

When Dr. Cornell returned, I asked him about this amputation.

"It was terrible for me," he said. "I hated that we had gotten to the state where I had to do it. He'd injured it to the point where if we didn't do it, it was going to fall off on its own and he would have bled to death."

Judy Muller of ABC Television and her crew arrived in a skiff. She set up at the edge of the platform, facing the camera, with Keiko framed in the background. One of Muller's crewmen held a reflector and experimented with it, bouncing light into her face. "He couldn't echolocate in the echoey walls of his tank," Muller said. "In this natural environment, he'll be able to use his skills at last." The ABC crew did a number of takes, with Muller echoing the same observation, "He couldn't echolocate in the echoey walls of his tank . . . ," again and again. After the last take, Muller joined several of us along the wall of the sea-pen bungalow. *"I can't tell this story in a minute and a half!"* she protested. ABC News had informed Muller that her Keiko story would have to be trimmed. The report of Special Prosecutor Kenneth Starr on the misadventures of President Clinton, just out, and Mark McGwire's ongoing assault on the home-run record, in combination, were squeezing the whale out of the news. The talk turned to Mark McGwire. Someone spoke of his big, ripping swing, and we discussed the muscle-building dietary supplement credited with bulking him up for his run at the record. This captured the interest of Ani Moss of the Free Willy Keiko Foundation.

"What does McGwire take?" she asked.

"Seatabs," said Lanny Cornell.

Jeff Foster went into the water to work with Keiko, but hauled out a short time later. "He doesn't want to play the normal game," Foster reported. "He just cruises around about this much underwater." The trainer pointed to his own knees to indicate how deep. "It's hard to stand on him." Foster gazed back at Keiko, slightly exasperated, I thought, and perhaps even a bit apprehensive. That Keiko no longer wanted to play the normal game, that it was hard to stand on him, seemed auspicious developments to me.

THAT AFTERNOON, UPON RETURNING FROM the bay pen, I set out to climb Eldfell, "Fire Hill," the red-cinder mountain formed by the 1973 eruption of the volcano Helgafell. The summit would provide a semi-aerial view of the bay pen and show Keiko in his new context. I needed a walk, besides.

The climb started a half block from my hotel, at Kirkjuvegur, "Church Street," which once ran through the center of town but now, after Heimaey's devastation by volcano, marks the town's eastern edge. On the near side of

Kirkjuvegur were whitewashed two-storey houses; on the far side a reddish-black, clinkery escarpment of 'a 'a lava about four storeys tall. The city of lava towered over the city of men. The flow seemed to have stopped dutifully at the curb of Kirkjuvegur, as if on a "Don't Walk" signal. The lava had cooled and hardened and come to a permanent halt while waiting for the light to change. Climbing a wooden stairway up the escarpment, I came out on a ridgetop scattered with tombstones honoring the neighborhoods buried beneath. About a dozen of the 415 houses lost to the eruption were commemorated. On one boulder was a marble plaque engraved, "Sixteen meters below this stone is the house of the Kiwanis Club Helgafell." Naming the club "Helgafell" had done nothing to propitiate that volcano. The building had been destroyed by its namesake, anyway.

Volcanic landscapes are prone to peculiar distortions of scale. The great shield volcano Mauna Loa, on Hawaii Island, is the most massive mountain on Earth, yet gives little sense of its size, and from most angles looks like a gently sloping hill. The effect of Eldfell is the opposite. Eldfell is much smaller and nearer than it looks. I budgeted two hours to reach the summit but found myself on top in forty minutes.

"Fire Hill" is not quite dead, for its curving summit ridge is marked by a steaming line of fumaroles. The fumaroles were small and wispy, dissipating instantly in the sea wind, the vents showing less as white plumes of vapor than as dark, wet patches of cinders where the vapor had condensed. The smell of sulfur came and went on the wind. Sitting at the crest of the miniature mountain, I glassed the sea pen below with my binoculars, looking for Keiko. He was a big animal, but most of him stayed submerged, and the distance was too great.

Then I cursed and jumped up. The geothermal warmth of the cinders under me had grown unpleasantly hot on the seat of my pants. I moved to a less active spot.

Iceland is doubly volcanic. The island does not simply sit astride the spreading center of the Mid-Atlantic Ridge; it has also drifted to a position atop the hot spot of the Icelandic thermal plume. Iceland lies on the very crosshairs of the god Vulcan's future intentions for this planet. Some weeks before Keiko's departure from Oregon, I had asked David Phillips whether his foundation had given much thought to the fact that Iceland was a spreading center atop a volcanic hot spot, that Heimaey Island had been the site of a major eruption twenty-five years before, and that back then the bay in which he intended to keep the whale had nearly been sealed off by lava. Phillips gave me a pained look and answered that he and his colleagues had never considered it.

On Eldfell I stood again, for the seat of my pants once more had grown unpleasantly warm. I walked over to the nearest fumarole, dropped to my knees, and sniffed at the vent. My glasses fogged white and my head jerked back as if from ammonia salts. The fumarole smelled as sweaty and foul as a locker room in hell. It stank of the depths of the earth and superheated brimstone and the certainty that someday Heimaey would erupt again.

That would be a fit conclusion to Keiko's saga, I thought.

Another big eruption would force the hands of the whale's keepers. If a new eruption followed the course of the last one, and lava began obstructing the harbor mouth again, then all the release protocols drawn up for Keiko would go out the window. The whale's trainers would have no choice but to entrust him immediately to the sea. Keiko would have to make a run for it, following the decreasing temperature gradient out into the cold Atlantic.

From the bay pen, I swung my binoculars along Keiko's escape route, panning down the harbor strait and out to open water. It would be a fine pyrotechnic ending. The island would rumble. Lava would fountain skyward from rifts, incandescent orange with a jet-engine roar, and the sky would turn smoky red over the volcano. Lava bombs would fall like meteors. A black plume of ash and smoke would rise to heaven and generate its own lightning. The sea would boil where the molten rivers entered it, and the island's inhabitants would flee in fishing boats, as they had in 1973. Keiko's departing spouts would show rosy in the hellish light. It would be Judgment Day, with a twist: The sea, instead of giving up its dead, would take back one of its living.

ANOTHER POSSIBILITY, OF COURSE, WAS that Keiko's saga would end not with a bang, but a whimper. Craig McCaw had promised that if Keiko never proved sea-fit, he would be maintained for the rest of his life in this bay pen, or some other. This alternate scenario, too, was not hard to imagine. As the possibility of release faded, the romance would depart the project. Keiko would become just another captive whale. The media spotlight would move elsewhere. *Free Willy* and its sequels would become oldies, rerun only on obscure cable channels late at night. The trainers who remembered the glory days would be replaced, with attrition, by trainers who did not remember—a kind of skeleton crew hanging out at the sea pen, waiting for an old whale to die.

Craig McCaw was willing to consider this sort of denouement, but for me it was an unacceptable ending. Keiko had to be released. It was not certain that he would survive, but then life is never certain for any of us. There were huge risks and unknowns: Keiko was steadily growing stronger, heavier, more skillful at catching live fish, yet this grown whale, twenty years old, was still infantile in his understanding of the ocean. Until yesterday, when he had flown in from Oregon, his habit had been to gather his Boomer Balls and various rubber duckies about him before tucking in for the night in his tank. Dr. Cornell's Seatabs could correct deficiencies in thiamin, but not deficiencies in experience. No one has figured how to distill that into a pill. Still, Keiko had to be pushed from the nest. We push our own kids out, even when we are full of doubts that they will make it. We have to let them go, because they can never become whole, adult people if we do not. If we can summon the courage to push out our own flesh and blood, then why would we do less, or more, for a whale?

29

COVEN OF EELS

Two mornings after Keiko's return to Iceland, *réttir,* autumn roundup, began on the island of Heimaey. Islanders climbed rope ladders up natural chimneys in the cliffs of the North Rocks and they scattered across the mountainous green moorland on top, collecting the sheep that had grazed there throughout summer. From the platform of Keiko's sea pen, cranning up, I watched the sheep congregate in small, agitated flocks and trot along the cliff's edge, fleeing the shepherds. A force-9 gale was due today in the Westmans, and its advance winds were gusting hard over the summits. I waited for a windblown sheep or human to lose footing, tumble down the steep grass slope, and pitch off the cliff, but somehow it never happened. If sheep gnash their teeth during *réttir,* Icelanders say, then winter will be harsh. If sheep have any apprehension about heights, I thought, then these must be gnashing their teeth hard right now. The coming winter figured to be a brutal one.

We sat in the lee of the dry house for protection against the wind. None of the trainers on duty looked cheery. The warm season is so abbreviated in Iceland. There were nine days left in summer, yet already this autumn roundup, and already gale-force winds.

Jeff Foster knelt at the edge of the water, scratching circles on Keiko's rostrum. "Peter says he thought he might have a sore pec, but no sign of that," Foster said. He stood, scraped Keiko's protective ointment off his fingertips, and flung it away. Today less of the whale was waxy with ointment. All the scratching of his trainers was cleaning him, and a large portion of him forward of the dorsal fin was shiny black again. Cleaning ointment from a killer whale is almost a problem of *acreage,* like chipping paint from a barn. Foster held up a pair of yellow swim fins and showed them to the whale. "See these? Now I can move you around. Now I have the power to move a nine-thousand-pound animal." With that, he set Keiko to the task of practicing the presentation of his flukes, a maneuver necessary in providing blood samples.

Up on the bridge that spanned the pen, Lieutenant Colonel Fred Cianciola, one of the officers of the Globemaster III, stood beside the trainer Jennifer Schorr. Elbows on the rail, the two looked down on the whale.

"I finally did something really important," Cianciola said.

Jennifer raised her thick, dark eyebrows quizzically. Cianciola explained that his daughter was a huge Keiko fan. Until the daughter heard that her father was to fly Keiko to Iceland, she had not been much impressed by his career.

"Flying the president of the United States around didn't count?" Jennifer asked.

"Not at all. That was nothing," Cianciola said

Jennifer laughed. She told Colonel Cianciola what life was like with Keiko, this cetacean who outranked the commander in chief. She described the frustrations of her first weeks as a Keiko trainer. "He wouldn't eat for me. Wouldn't swim across the pool for me. He would do everything except what I told him to do. We always kind of laugh about who is training whom."

Ann Moss had taken refuge in the lee of the sea-pen bungalow. She watched the whale over her collar, turned up against the wind. It was Ann who had set the Willy-Keiko phenomenon in motion, indirectly, with her idea for inserting the tuna sandwich into *Lethal Weapon 2*. Now the Keiko story seemed to be nearing its conclusion. It appeared that life really would imitate art; that the whale soon would escape to the wild. "It took a pod," Anne said. "A pod of normally fractious people all pulling together. There was a synergy necessary to make it happen. And it was an *international* pod. People in Mexico, the United States, Iceland."

ON RETURNING TO TOWN FROM the bay pen, I walked over to the Náttúru-gripasafn, the Aquarium and Museum of Natural History. I was curious about the background sounds Keiko might be hearing in his cove. I hoped the aquarium might have some of those fish that make noise, and I wanted to look at the mounted specimens of the sea creatures that were now Keiko's neighbors.

When I arrived at the Náttúrugripasafn, a Chinese girl of about five years old, an adoptee from the mainland, I supposed, was playing at the door. "Keiko, Keiko, Keiko," she sang to herself. I tried to catch her eye, but she ignored me. "Keiko, Keiko, Keiko, Keiko," she sang.

This month the Náttúrugripasafn was featuring an exhibit on some Atlantic puffin research by two Westman Island high-school boys, David Egilsson and Bjarki Steinn Traustason. Their work had won the Iceland division of the YEER contest, an international high-school science competition. They were headed next for Berlin. Both boys—the tall and willowy Egilsson and the more compact Traustason—were on duty in the museum to explain their project and answer questions. Egilsson told me that their area of study was

Stórhöfdi, "Big Head," the peninsular crater of volcanic tuff at the southern end of the island. The boys had distinguished twelve colonies on Stórhöfdi. They had identified 96,000 established nesting burrows and had estimated the puffin population of this one crater at 250,000 birds. Their charts and graphs were impressive; these boys were the best and brightest of their Vestmannaeyjar generation. I asked the two young naturalists for their opinions on Keiko.

"I think they're blowing it up a little too much," Bjarki Steinn Traustason told me. "Keiko finding his whole family, I find that very . . ." Bjarki searched for the English word but could not find it. He wrinkled his nose and gestured dismissively. "Americans are trying to make him like a person. *One hundred and eighty million kronur!* I would think they could use that for homeless people, or health care. He's really just only one whale. It wasn't really, you know, *bad* in Newport, Oregon."

The director of the Náttúrugripasafn was a large, affable man named Kristján Egilsson. Egilsson told me that his mother-in-law had started the museum in 1964 at the behest of the island's mayor. Egilsson himself had been a plumber when the directorship later fell to him. When I suggested that a background in plumbing must be useful for a director of a provincial aquarium, Egilsson smiled and spread his big hands in agreement. Like the two young puffin investigators whom his museum was hosting, Kristján Egilsson was skeptical about the repatriation of Keiko.

"It's good to have tourists, but this place is so small we can't take too many," he said. "At first I just thought the Americans were sending Keiko to us because he was so sick. They wanted to get rid of him. Many people thought this. Because we had heard so much about his sickness. And another thing also I misliked. They chose two places in Iceland, Eskifjördur and here, and I think it started some kind of fight between these two places. Eskifjördur started to try for him first and they thought they would get him. Then the Keiko Foundation people came over to the Westmans and saw that this was a very good place." Egilsson shook his head slightly. "It seems a little bit strange to us to take an animal who has been kept twenty years and bring him back."

The director gave me a quick tour of his museum.

We paused at the fish exhibit. I was particularly interested in the fishes of Iceland, for these were the creatures Keiko was most likely to meet in his new digs. The fish specimens were all stiffly posed and heavily shellacked. There were several blackened, mummified sharks. There was the huge, flattened disk of a sunfish, as leathery and cracked as an old saddle. In Iceland the sunfish is called *skötuselur,* "seal-ray." The name is apt; this strange, gibbous fish really does look like some disastrous genetic experiment in the recombination of seal and ray. The seal-ray, like the killer whale, is a surface-dweller, one of the species Keiko might encounter on his release. If Keiko passes anywhere near one, he will be unlikely to miss it, as seal-rays grow ten feet across. "Fishermen here often catch them in the net," Egilsson told me. "My father was a fisherman. He often brought them home. Taste good! My mother would put him in milk. Overnight. To get the blood out. In those days there was not so much to eat, like now."

Aside from sunfish, I learned from the museum exhibits, Westman Islanders also eat gannets, puffins, dulse, and other sorts of seaweed. A great delicacy here, as elsewhere in Iceland, is *hákarl,* which is shark buried in sand for months until it putrefies. Not long ago Icelanders filled up on *hvalreki,* those whales that drifted in with the ice. Kristján Egilsson grew up in a subsistence tradition that did not turn up its nose at any sort of seafood. The Westman view of marine resources is short on preciousness and long on pragmatism. It was not so surprising that Egilsson and his fellow islanders should be skeptical about the world's strange preoccupation with a single Icelandic whale.

The twelve tanks in the aquarium room displayed an assortment of Keiko's new neighbors. All of Iceland's market fish swam there: haddock, cod, pollock, ocean perch, halibut, lemon sole. There were starfish, lumpfish, mollusks. There were king crabs in the middle of the interminable king-crab courtship, which requires the male to lift the much smaller female on the forklift of his claws, then carry her about for three months or so, until she finally warms to him. There were bright yellow anemones that Keiko would have found attractive, surely, if whales had color vision. There were *steinbítur,* "stone-biters" as Icelanders call wolf eels. The stone-biters had a tank to themselves. They had visages that looked quarrelsome—cold, savage eyes, huge canine teeth—but in fact they loved contact and lay heaped in a single knotty mass on the bottom. In the wild, wolf eels are given to denning. Here in captivity they had fallen back on the cold-blooded comfort of one another. They slithered slowly forward en masse, insinuating themselves over and under one another, to the front of their tank, pressing against the glass to watch us. Here and there a wolf-eel cheek or chin flattened against the glass. The stone-biters looked like a coven of witches, or, if not the witches themselves, then like ingredients in their stew. Wolf eels live at killer-whale depths, between fifty and five hundred feet. This fanged, haglike face was another that Keiko might meet someday soon.

As I left the Náttúrugripasafn the Chinese girl was still playing out front. She swung upside down from a metal rail there, singing, "Keiko, Keiko, Keiko, Keiko, Keiko, Keiko, Keiko, Keiko, Keiko," in some sort of nonstop prayer or invocation.

* * *

THAT EVENING, FJARAN RESTAURANT, THE fanciest place in the Westmans, filled up with celebrants. Keiko's army divided itself into regiments inside. Those reporters who had not yet escaped the island clustered at one table. The brass of the Craig O. McCaw Foundation and the Free Willy Keiko Foundation gathered at a second table. Keiko's trainers sat at a third, and Jean-Michel Cousteau and his film team occupied a fourth. At a fifth table, Ann Moss hosted a core group of enviros and cetophiles. Among Ann Moss's guests were early friends of Keiko like Nancy Azzam and Katherine Hanly—both consultants to the Free Willy Keiko Foundation since its inception—and David Phillips and Mark Berman of Earth Island Institute. There was an empty chair at this table, and I was invited to join.

The environmentalist table discussed the failure of the C-17's landing gear. "Don't you see, it was part of Keiko's magic," said Ann Moss. "It's the magic that's been working for him every step of the way." Moss believed that Keiko led a charmed life. The magic of Keiko, as she explained it, had gravitated downward, suffusing the landing gear, which in buckling had absorbed the shock, allowing the whale to emerge unscathed.

"Like the crumple zones in a Volvo?" I asked.

"Yes," said Ann Moss.

Raising her wineglass, Nancy Azzam saluted her environmentalist colleagues. "The people at this table are the people who really got all this to happen," she proclaimed. "The trainers *think* they were the ones. They have no idea of the work that went before."

The Craig McCaw table, animated by whatever aperitifs the billionaire was ordering, was the most raucous in the room. Bob Ratliffe, Craig McCaw's right-hand man in Keiko matters, left McCaw's table and made the rounds of the others. Lit up brightly by triumph and by beverage, Ratliffe threw his arm over the shoulders of a pair of environmentalists and leaned in over their table. "This is just a fringe party," he teased the environmentalists. "I represent the guys who really got it done." He alluded to his work as Keiko's point man in Washington, and his trials and tribulations in dealings with the National Marine Fisheries Service. "It's been like three-dimensional chess," he said. "It's the most interesting time I've had in my life."

The environmentalists finished a second round of pre-dinner drinks and loosened up considerably. The table was sanguine about Keiko's release. Several were convinced that this event was imminent.

"You think he's ready?" I asked.

"Of course," said Nancy Azzam. "He *is* a killer whale."

But was he really? I wandered. A killer whale is not just flukes, fins, and a black-and-white paint job; a killer whale is a repertoire. It is not simply flesh and bone, but a tissue of skills and understandings. A whale, like any other organism, is an interaction between its genes and the particular place it was meant to be. Creatures with long juvenile dependency periods, like great apes, owls, humans, and killer whales, are animals with a lot to learn. The calf Keiko had been yanked from school early. The ocean is a big, cruel place, and he had not even begun to learn the ABCs of it. How would he be received by wild pods, as he swam toward them in his good-natured way, a subadult male with a bent dorsal fin, doing his rooster and siren imitations or talking like a bottlenose dolphin? Keiko was a twenty-year-old virgin whose sex life until now had involved only inner tubes and Boomer Balls. He knew nothing of carousel feeding, sharks, winter storms. His great talent was in rolling on his back in a med-pool tank and peeing on command. Keiko had rich experience of human beings, yes, but how would that help him out in the Denmark Strait or the Greenland Sea?

30

TURK-GUDDA

In the center on Heimaey Island, in a rolling green common below town hall, is a statue to Gudrídur Símonardóttir, known also as Tyrkja-Gudda, or "Turk-Gudda." The plaque at the base notes simply: "Born 1598. Taken by the Turks 1627."

The Turkish raid of 1627, the lockjaw epidemic of 1847, and the eruption of 1973 are the three great catastrophes of Westman Island history. The "Turks" in fact were Barbary pirates working out of Morocco and Algeria in the days when North Africa was part of the Ottoman Empire. They were led, oddly enough, by a Dutchman, Jan Janezen, a religious fanatic and convert to Islam who called himself Rais Múrad. The pirates raped, pillaged, and plundered, razing farms and burning churches. They killed 36 islanders, kidnapped 242 men, women, and children, and left Heimaey in ruins. That North African pirates should have gone pillaging so high in the North Atlantic, nearly to the Arctic Circle, was a profound and enduring surprise to the Westman Islanders. The local Norsemen, descendants of Viking raiders like Erik Bloodaxe and Thorarin the Overbearing, got a big dose of their own medicine. Today, almost four centuries later, Westman Island parents still threaten misbehaving children with retaliation by the Turks.

Of the kidnapped Westman Islanders, many quickly renounced Christianity for Islam. Some young women became concubines in Algerian harems, and some young men threw in their lot with their captors and became pirates themselves. Most of the others died as slaves, fair-skinned toilers under the North African sun. Turk-Gudda was one of the few who ever made it home.

Gudda's statue on the town-hall common is of reddish-brown volcanic rock, very rough-hewn. The sculptor seems to have liked the stone pretty much as it was, and scarcely bothered to lay a chisel to it. The Gudda of the statue has no features, as such. From some angles you can see her, a tall woman in shawl or veil; from others she looks no different from any number of volcanic séracs and mini-pinnacles atop the lava flow looming above town.

Stopping by the statue one day, I realized why it drew me: Keiko, too, had been captured by the Turks. His kidnappers were not really Turks, of course, but then neither had been the kidnappers of Turk-Gudda. Where

Gudda spent ten years under the Algerian sun, Keiko spent his ten years under the Mexican sun. Like Gudda, Keiko was eventually ransomed home to Iceland again.

Gudda's story has come down to us like a saga, a narrative entirely of external events. From North Africa she wrote a letter to her husband, Eyjólfur Sólmundarson, in which she may well have revealed details of her Algerian sojourn, as well as her feelings about her captors, but only the beginning of that letter has been preserved. Gudda was ransomed in 1636, made her way back to Copenhagen, met the poet Hallgrímur Pétursson, and, believing her husband dead, took up with the poet and was impregnated by him. The cuckolded Eyjólfur Sólmundarson—betrayed less by his wife than by fate and the Turks—was for the moment alive, but then obligingly died that same year. Turk-Gudda and Hallgrímur Pétursson married and moved to Iceland.

That Turk-Gudda, on her return from captivity, was able to mate successfully with one of her own kind—and an illustrious poet, at that—was encouraging. Whatever had happened to Turk-Gudda in the Algerian desert, it had not precluded a fruitful union. Perhaps Keiko would someday be fruitful, too, making the transition from sex with Boomer Balls and inner tubes to sex with actual female orcas.

There are big problems, of course, with Gudda as a metaphor for helping illuminate Keiko. She was human, he is whale. Her tale is dark in precisely the spot where Keiko's tale, too, needs light—at its very heart, in the matter of her feelings about imprisonment and exile. Yet whenever I stopped by Gudda's statue, I worried the problem over.

It seemed to me that there are three possible explanations for why Gudda's Algerian period should be such a blank. One possibility is the erosion of time. Gudda, on returning, may have bored her neighbors silly with tales of her captivity. She may have sung of Algeria like an uncaged bird, only to have the details lost over the centuries. A second possibility is discretion. Gudda may have chosen silence about her time in Algeria. Several Westman Islanders suggested to me that the very sobriquet "Turk-Gudda" conveys a certain disrespect. For seventeenth-century Icelanders, there was more shame attached to victimhood than we attach today. "Born 1598. Taken by the Turks 1627," her statue says, and nothing more, as if she sailed out of existence when she departed with the Turks. "Survived and returned to Iceland 1636," would have been a charitable postscript, but the plaque is silent on that. If Turk-Gudda hoped to outlive her nickname, she may have decided not to dwell on those days.

A third possibility was that Gudda simply lacked the words. How would she explain to Icelanders a parched, winterless land of olive trees and date palms and camel markets and arabesques? How would she convey an astronomy in which the sun, instead of taking its normal, oblique, Icelandic path across the sky, leaps every morning to the zenith, hangs there all day, then plunges to the horizon each evening?

And how would Keiko, for his part, explain his incarceration with bottlenose dolphins, and the applause of Mexican crowds, and the lovely Karla Corral pouring out her heart to him by poolside? How would he explain movie acting, and the fusillades of camera strobes flashing from aquarium windows each time he swam by, and the millions of Lilliputians who trooped by to see him in his various tanks, and the appalling taste of frozen squid, and the wrestling shows he watched on television, and that crazy woman who flung her jewels at him, and the terminally ill visitors in wheelchairs who rolled to the edge of his slide-out to lay hands on him for absolution? How would he convey, in a believable way, the giant cranes that swung him through the air? How would he explain the midair refueling of a Globemaster III? Even if the whistles and grunts of orca language allowed sufficient range of expression, how would Keiko do justice to a single detail of the past twenty years of his life?

Herman Melville, as epigraph to his epilogue for *Moby Dick*, borrows a line from Job: "And I only am escaped alone to tell thee." His narrator, Ishmael, alone of the *Pequod*'s crew, survives the collision with the white whale. If Keiko succeeded someday in hooking up with a wild pod, he only, alone of all captive orcas, would have escaped to tell. But what could he possibly say?

31

STORMS

THE WESTMAN ISLANDERS LAUGHED AT THE BOATS THE FREE WILLY KEIKO Foundation had brought to the islands, and they laughed at the foundation's two Jet Skis. Keiko's little fleet, they said, was hopelessly inadequate for the conditions here. Keiko's team was annoyed. Jeff Foster, who had picked the Westmans, had seen big weather in his whale-catching days in Iceland; he and Nolan Harvey, in their list of the fourteen arguments against Iceland, had not neglected to mention the thirty- and fifty-foot seas common for long periods; but both felt comfortable with the shelter in the Westmans and both were satisfied that they had chosen good vessels. The boats were sturdy little Stabi-Craft, twenty-one-footers with twin 115-horse Evinrude engines. The Jet Skis were perfectly good Kawasakis. Klettsvík, Keiko's Cove, was less than a mile from the dock in Heimaey harbor, on a narrow channel protected by the four-hundred-foot cliffs of the North Rocks to one side and by the slopes of the volcano Helgafell to the other. How bad could it be, that short commute from town to the bay pen?

It could be just awful.

Between the September of Keiko's arrival and December of that year, a dozen hurricane-force storms blew through the Westmans. Sometimes the storm lasted a day, other times much of the week. On average, one crewmember calculated, there was a hurricane in the Westmans just about every other day.

"It was just so beautiful and calm and pristine," Dane Richards says of the pen site in summer. "The perception at the beginning was that this was a very well-protected bay. We just never knew that hundred-mile-per-hour winds were very common there."

Richards, a stocky Californian in his mid-twenties, a jack of several trades, was a member of Keiko's advance team. He arrived in the Westmans in July of 1998, two months before the whale. By August, he and his colleagues had successfully anchored the pen in Klettsvík Cove and were assembling the medical lift when a sudden storm blew in. The cliffs did not block the eighty-mile-per-hour wind as anticipated; they accelerated it, funneling it down the passage to the harbor, whipping up so much spray that there was a whiteout along the surface. From the overlook across the channel, Richards and his mates could not see the pen in the whiteness of spume. Directly above the pen was a steep chute up East Rock, with a puffin-hunters' hut built into the rock near the top. Above the hut was the gap between Middle Rock and East Rock. This notch was the shortest way out of the funnel of the passage. Richards watched the wind and spray whirl up off the channel, blast past the puffin hut, and whip out through the notch, gaining speed as it went.

"We were sitting there going, Whoa!" Richards says. "We understood a little bit more of what we were dealing with. We saw some of the dynamics. We'd go out and see how the anchors did in that type of situation. We saw some of the changes we'd have to make."

Late in September, when we in the press had departed the Westmans for warmer climes and Keiko had had a couple of weeks to settle into his pen, the hurricane that his staff would call "the Med-Lift Storm" struck the Westmans.

"We knew that they had some wind here, but that was our first big storm," says Jeff Foster. "We lost the med lift in that storm. It was just destroyed. Two-hundred-mile winds. It's like a freight train. On the bay-pen in storms, you're sitting in that little green dry house. When it starts blowing over one hundred twenty miles per hour, the wind forces water up under the windows and sprays in like a squirt gun. We had to put bars in front of the windows. The glass windows bend. You have to pressurize your ears, as if you were diving. It's pretty amazing."

The med lift sat on Fiberglas pontoons that were filled with air to raise the apparatus and emptied to lower it. The surge and the current through the cove battered the pontoons against the metal bars of the pen, cracking them. They could no longer hold air. The crew, unable to raise the lift, were helpless as the pontoons crunched against the bottom with rhythmic *kabooms* that rattled the whole pen with each blow before finally breaking up.

The two halves of the pen had been named the North Pool—the one nearest the cliff—and the South Pool. The pen was designed so that by raising the net between sections, the crew could isolate Keiko in the North Pool, the South Pool, or the Medical Pool. To extract the broken med lift, they isolated the whale in the North Pool, then hitched the med lift to their boats and dragged it out, aided by the lifting power of huge air bags that the islanders used to raise anchors. The air bags were the first of many borrowings from the gear and expertise of the Icelanders, and eventually Keiko's crew would employ the bags to reposition their own bay-pen anchors and to move the component they called the "Big-Ass Chain." For this first emergency use of the bags—the retrieval of the med lift—the islanders watched with morbid curiosity. The locals had argued from the beginning that Keiko could not survive storms in that pen. Now, in the wake of the Med-Lift Storm, they saw the whale's team lower the South Pool net, hitch their boats to something beneath the water, then attach air bags to that sunken object. They watched the slow, funereal procession of the boats from Klettsvík Cove back to the harbor, dragging something ponderous. Much of the town gathered dock-side to witness the sad end of Keiko's saga. Some were mournful, others grimly satisfied at this confirmation of their predictions. They peered into the chop of the departing storm, waiting for Keiko's lifeless hulk to material-ize. What emerged instead was the battered corpse of the med lift.

"We were wondering how Keiko was going to respond," says Jeff Foster. "He'd been twenty years in pools that had never had more than a ripple through them. So we were a little concerned. In the bay pen we had chop, and water going over the top of the rails—pretty rough. But he's out there, and he's playing and arching his back and just loving it. He just loved it."

THE WEATHER OF KEIKO'S FIRST season in the Westmans would prove to be the roughest of his sojourn in the archipelago and the windiest in the mem-ory of the islanders. Vast volumes of water moving across the great expanse and depth of the North Atlantic piled up against the shallows of the Mid-Atlantic Ridge in the one spot—Iceland—where that submarine feature rises above the sea, and huge rollers pounded through the Westmans. The funnel of the harbor mouth at Heimaey seemed to call out to every howling gale of the jet stream, every hurricane tracking up from Cuba on the Gulf Stream. One blustery day, an anemometer mounted on the dry house had just started recording 140 miles per hour when it ripped off the side of the building.

"You're out there in middle of winter, there's only a few hours of light, it's overcast or snowing and blowing a hundred and twenty," says Jeff Foster. "It's so windy out there! I mean, I'm a pretty big guy. I was following another guy about my size, going across the walk, and he was filming. It was eight o'clock in the morning and pitch black out. We were wearing goggles and everything. A huge gust sprays him like a shotgun. I looked at him and he wasn't there. He'd been picked up and thrown about twelve or thirteen feet. People don't understand. It's like standing up in your car at a hundred forty miles per hour, and somebody squirts a fire hose at you, ice-cold water, and throws ice cubes at you."

Foster laughs an unmerry laugh.

"We'd get out there with Keiko and do behaviors. We'd be in one-hundred-twenty-mile winds, and we'd get in the water with him. Until you've seen it like that, you wouldn't believe it. You wouldn't think we'd be stupid enough to get in there, with four-foot breaking seas and spray, swal-lowing water."

Beneath the surface, it was not much better.

"We had to dive to do reattachments and repairs and whatnot," says Dane Richards. "We'd be drilling down there, one diver working, and the other guy just holding onto him. We had a chain on the bottom. You'd hold the chain with one hand and hold the guy who was drilling with the other. You'd be streaming down there like a flag in the wind, and then all of a sudden the current would switch, and you'd be streaming back the other way. Smári would be working on something down there—Smári Hardarson, this Icelandic diver—and I'd have to swim up to lift the chain over his head. There were some crazy, interesting dynamics in that cove."

DANE RICHARDS GOT HIS JOB in the Westman Islands through nepotism in its purest sense, as he is a *nepos,* a nephew, of Dr. Lanny Cornell. When Dane was a boy, his uncle, then vice president and head veterinarian at Sea World, introduced him to Shamu, Namu, Kamu, and other famous killer whales. Dane had his picture taken with those celebrities, and he liked them well enough, but what really impressed him, at ten years old, were the penguins. He was amazed by the penguin capacity for fish and by the rate at which they swallowed them.

In college, Dane worked odd jobs at his uncle's animal hospital and occasionally filled in at Pacific Research Labs, Cornell's little company, shipping Seatabs and other vitamins to various marine parks. He went out on calls with Cornell, treating bulls and horses in the field, and he witnessed the procession of cats, dogs, sheep, goats, and horses that came through the hospital. Once he watched Cornell remove gravel from the paw of a white tiger. He never saw his uncle turn away any creature except for one field mouse. Dane assisted the veterinarian in a number of operations on horses. In one of these, intestinal surgery on a very old animal, the task was to remove swallowed stones. First Dane held a bit in the old horse's mouth to keep it from chewing on the tracheal tube as it went under the anesthetic, then he and his uncle donned gowns and masks. As Cornell removed loops of large intestine, he draped them across his nephew's forearms. Cornell felt for stones in the intestine, removed them—thirteen in all—then sutured up the incisions and returned the intestine, coil after coil, from Dane's arms to the horse. Dane, in the slobbery pre-surgical job of holding the bit in the horse's mouth, had worked ungloved, and for three days afterward he could not get the smell off his hands. "Every time I ate, I would remember," he says. "Oh, that horse again."

This fragrance—a not-so-delicate infusion of old-horse saliva, dental plaque, and blood—is not for everyone, but Dane did not mind it. He liked working with animals, and after three years studying mechanical engineering, he switched to biology and spent even more time in the company of his uncle. His animal-care experience was a qualification for the Iceland job, and so was his skill with tools. Dane's father, Bob Richards, is a plumbing contractor competent at most everything—roofing, framing, drywall, electrical—and he taught his son those arts in remodeling houses. In 1992, Dane, his father, and his brother-in-law built Singing Hills Hospital for Dr. Cornell. It was Cornell who suggested that his nephew try for the Iceland job. "I had boat-handling skills and a background in construction," Dane says. "I had my degree in biology and I'd worked with animals. And Lanny Cornell was my uncle. I would have never had the opportunity if it were not for Lanny."

"You were glad you got the job?" I asked him once.

"Oh yeah. I was just blown away."

Blown away he almost was. In what the team called "transports," Keiko's daily ration of 120 pounds of fish was ferried from town to the bay pen. When winds reached eighty miles per hour, the transporters tried to disembark at the North Pool, where the water was calmest. The trick was to step safely from the pitching boat to the pen's Chemgrate deck, then struggle toward the dry house through gale-force wind carrying sixty pounds of fish in two buckets. The Chemgrate was three feet wide, but in those conditions it seemed a tightrope. The transporter would hook his right arm, with its thirty-pound bucket of fish, over the rail so as not to end up in the water. Videotaping seems to have been a particularly chancy undertaking. In one of the staff's favorite bits of tape, recorded by the trainer Stephen Claussen in winds exceeding one hundred miles per hour, cameraman and camera suddenly go airborne. There is a brief aerial view of the platform, then Claussen is slammed to the deck, and the scene closes with him crawling across the Chemgrate toward the dry house.

In conditions of extreme wind or cold, the team wore orange flotation survival suits. Through their first few storms, they kept their survival suits on even when inside the dry house. If the house should lift off, like Dorothy's homestead departing Kansas, they would not have to spend three minutes donning the suits. Then the weeks passed. No one blew away. The crew developed faith in the hurricane straps that locked the house to the bay-pen platform. Their fear subsided, and they began removing their survival suits as soon as they fought their way inside the door.

The bay-pen evolved as the crew adapted it to the conditions. They added more flotation underneath the dry house and the wet house, as the weight of those structures caused the platform there to sink. They replaced the dry-house windows with safety glass. They tightened up and reconfigured their moorings. The pen was moored by Seaflex, a kind of rubber bungee cord, originally in five-strand sets out to the north and south, and four-strand sets to east and west. This was not enough.

"They started snapping on us," Dane Richards testifies. "They snapped or broke, and we actually moved in a few meters toward the beach. We ended up doubling everything, ten-strand Seaflex north and south, eight-strand east and west. We put more scope on everything. Originally we didn't have enough scope on the anchors. We were dragging anchors all over the place. The surge would sometimes rise and subside more than two meters at two-minute intervals, and when that happened the anchors were just hanging. We ended up going to a five-to-one ratio on scope, and backing up the anchors with chain."

The crew loved the Chemgrate skin of the bay-pen platform. It provided good traction underfoot yet allowed the wind to blow through. The dry house and wet house acted as sails, but in the rest of the structure, thanks to Chemgrate, there was little wind resistance. The bridge was a problem at first. It arched across the middle of the pen, allowing the staff to cross directly from the dry-house side to the wet-house side without walking all the way around the perimeter. It doubled as an observation post during Keiko's four-hour ethograms, providing a high vantage from which the ethogrammer could look deep into the water to see what Keiko was doing. In storms the bridge was unwalkable. Covered with three-quarter-inch plywood, it caught the wind, tried to sail away, was snatched back by its hinges, then tried again, bucking and tossing throughout the storm—a flying bridge in a new sense of that term. "Why don't you put Chemgrate up there?" Lanny Cornell asked on one visit. They put Chemgrate up there, and the flying bridge was tamed.

IN JANUARY OF 1999, THE Free Willy Keiko Foundation closed its headquarters in Newport and moved its operations to Iceland. Beverlee Hughes, the foundation president, Nolan Harvey, its director of animal care, and Dianne Hammond, its external affairs officer, all resigned. Harvey and Hammond did not want to make the move to Iceland—a dramatic change of heart by the couple. On the day of Keiko's repatriation, five months before their resignations, Nolan Harvey had told me that he and his wife, on arriving in the Westmans in July, had fallen in love with the place and had not wanted to return to Oregon. Those summer sentiments had blown away in winter gales.

In March, the Free Willy Keiko Foundation merged with the Jean-Michel Cousteau Institute and became a new entity, Ocean Futures, with Cousteau in charge. On Keiko's website, the old illustration on the home page, a photo of Keiko, was replaced; the new masthead showed Keiko and Cousteau side by side. The story of Keiko, in Ocean Futures brochures and literature, became the story of Keiko and Jean-Michel Cousteau.

Keiko's staff settled into their routines. The shift on duty worked out of the dry house, which was equipped outside with the project's third anemometer—the first two having blown away—and inside with a powerful heater, banks of computers, camera gear, and tape recorders, along with games and a music library to pass any slack time between feedings. The shift ashore slept in the converted youth hostel that Ocean Futures rented in town. The original contracts had called for the staff to work six weeks on and four weeks off. Then it was discovered that foreign nationals are allowed to work only 183 days in Iceland—half the year—without being subject to Icelandic income tax. The contracts were amended to thirty days on, thirty off.

Salaries were good, but the work was hard: Twelve-hour days in cold water, scrubbing algae off nets. Storms. The scant six hours of sunlight in midwinter. When the thirty-day work shifts ended, the crew scattered, often to the tropics, in search of new faces and the sun.

Keiko continued his rehabilitation. There were experiments with diet. The team considered trapping live cod outside the harbor and dumping them into the pen for him, but in the end decided on live salmon. In early March, they cut back on the whale's rations of frozen herring and poured in salmon. Keiko was not wild about live fish. Sometimes he held out for frozen herring, other times he relented and pursued the salmon in a perfunctory way. What he liked about herring was the familiar taste, perhaps—that fish is the staple of Iceland's killer whales, and was his staple, too, in captivity in Oregon—or maybe what he liked was the ease of capture. Frozen fish are a much simpler problem than the darting, dodging kind. In May, as the killer whales were returning to their fishing grounds in the Westmans, the trainers cut back on Keiko's massages and his play sessions. They avoided looking him in the eye. The idea was to moderate his fixation on humans and turn his attention to the natural world outside the pen. "It's a difficult step," the project manager, Robin Friday, told a reporter from *The Oregonian*. "Not so much for him, but for the staff, because of that bond, that emotional thing that we have." Keiko, in fact, did not seem much troubled by this standoffishness of his keepers. Perhaps he knew that it would not last. The tough-love philosophy had always been cyclical. Throughout the history of the project, his trainers had blown hot or cold, played good cop or bad cop, according to fluctuations in theory on what it was he needed.

The first nesting birds arrived. Keiko, with his opportunities for anthropology limited by the new hands-off policy, turned instead to ornithology. He showed considerable interest in all the squabbling and courtship and noise on the cliffs above his pen. When eider ducks or puffins or guillemots landed on the surface of his pen, he would give them friendly bumps from below. Killer whales in the Westmans had been observed eating eider ducks, unplucked, with gusto, but that was not Keiko's style.

The campaign to shift him to live salmon faltered, for he never warmed to those fish. In May, the staff backed off salmon, raised Heiko's frozen herring quota, and dedicated their energies to his aerobic conditioning and to beefing him up. The idea now was to vary his feeding in a way that prepared him for the rhythms of gorging and fasting normal for predators like orcas.

In summer it is commonplace for killer whales to enter the Heimaey harbor strait. In early May, thirteen orcas were spotted off the harbor mouth, but they came no closer, unfortunately. In July, with a crossbow, the team attached a tag to a wild killer whale off the island of Surtsey, and the device recorded thirty hours of data, launching a research program into the habits and the DNA of Keiko's local cousins. Keiko never got within crossbow range of whales himself. Summer ended without any contact between Keiko and wild orcas. The Westman whales departed for wherever it is they migrate in winter—no one knows for sure.

The winds picked up again. As in Keiko's first gale season, storms from the south, southwest, and southeast hit the bay pen particularly hard. Storms from the north were easier, thanks to the protection of the North Rocks. In a north wind, the sea pen was the best place on the island to be. On September 10, 1999—the first anniversary, to the day, of Keiko's return to Iceland—the surges of a storm from the south broke out a forty-foot section of the South Pool's perimeter. It was a nice anniversary present, freedom, but Keiko declined. Instead of swimming through the break, he took shelter in the North Pool. It was a little disappointing, worrisome even, that he should prove such a good whale, so resistant to temptation. The manufacturer of the pen's foam-filled pipe, Familian Industrial Plastics of Washington State, sent out replacement piping and the perimeter was repaired.

The plan for Keiko's second winter in the Westmans was to string a barrier net across the mouth of Klettvík Cove, allowing Keiko to leave the pen for the enclosed cove by Christmas. The net, three hundred yards long, had been manufactured in Holland and modified by net-makers in Iceland. In November, Keiko's crew drilled into the basalt walls at either end of the cove and set anchors for the net. They attempted to drill helicals into the seafloor, anchoring the net along its path across the cove's mouth, but the volcanic gravel of the bottom was too loose to hold the shafts, and the bedrock below was too dense for the drills to penetrate. Then bad weather hit. If Keiko's first winter in the Westmans had been the windiest in the memory of the islanders, then his second was the snowiest. A hundred-year storm struck Heimaey Island, arriving from the north, blasting across the low isthmus separating the North Rocks from the Rock fortress of Stóraklif, and devastating the town. Sheltered by the North Rocks, the shift on duty on the bay pen hardly noticed, but the shift ashore took cover as windows were broken and fish totes scattered all over town. It was not until March that the barrier net was in place, attached to the seafloor by a jury-rigged system that incorporated four ten-ton anchors and the Big-Ass Chain.

"That was how we always referred to it, 'Big-Ass Chain,'" says Dane Richards. "It had chain-links that were about three hundred pounds each." It was a big-ass chain, yet Richards watched the barrier net uneasily in the storm surge. "I'd never seen surges like that. We'd stand out there and watch the buoys on the net—these buoys were a meter long—and you'd see twenty buoys at a time go down. Disappear."

The net held, and on March 3, 2000, two months late, the gate to the bay pen was opened and Keiko swam out into the cove. The new U.S. ambassador to Iceland, Barbara Griffiths, had flown to the Westmans for the occasion. The ambassador and a small crowd watched Keiko swim briefly around the cove, make one deep dive, then return to his pen. Later in the day he made four more excursions and began to seem more comfortable in his expanded home. He now had about fifty football fields worth of cove to roam in.

THE BIOLOGY OF ISLANDS IS peculiar. Colonized by "waifs," they evolve in isolation, and the resulting floras and faunas are usually strange—giant tree ferns, huge flightless birds, gigantic tortoises. Finches will fill most available niches on one island, marsupials on another, lemurs on a third. Island culture is the same—the mysterious statues of Easter Island, the sagas of Iceland, the colossal stone coins of the island of Yap. In the Westman Islands, the Keiko project evolved a culture. A clan system developed. The original clan was the trainers from Oregon. Conditions were harsh, attrition was high, and Jean-Michel Cousteau brought in new trainers from Sea World. The replacements were fresh from teaching killer whales to perform in marine parks, and it seemed to them that Keiko needed better instruction. He should be perfecting his bows and breaches, like Sea World whales. Dogmas clashed.

"Sometimes in Oregon I thought the trainers imagined themselves a priesthood," I once suggested to Dane Richards. "They seemed to feel superior to the rest of us—worthier than people who were involved with the whale in other ways."

"Oh, big time," Richards said. "I got the perception that they thought they were better. The Oregon people viewed themselves as a tight-knit group, a tight-knit family. They had the attitude, This is *our* whale. I was dumbfounded by a lot of their perceptions. The people from Oregon, I'd even hear them say, 'I'm only here to see that they don't screw this whale over.' In their opinion, screwing him over was just letting him go and seeing how he did. They said, 'Oh, I've played with this whale for so many years, there's no way he's ever going to be wild again. He's my friend, and he's so gentle with me.'"

The Sea World trainers had brought a new catechism to the Westman Islands, but Richards was not converted. The mission was to make Keiko independent of humans. It made no sense to him to teach him bows and breaches again. In philosophy Richards found himself in some limbo between the clans.

The duty rotation, thirty days on, thirty off, required that the staff be divided into two separate teams, which became two more clans. There was, in addition, the clan of animal care and the clan of marine operations. Turnover of supervisors was high, as was frustration among the workers for time wasted in bringing new bosses up to speed. Lines of authority were unclear. Jean-Michel Cousteau was nominally in charge, and he drew a $250,000 salary, but he seldom came to Iceland. To some it seemed he flew out to the Westmans only for photo opportunities—Jean-Michel Cousteau and Prime Minister Oddsson on the bay pen, Jean-Michel Cousteau on the Chemgrate in a chorus line of Miss Iceland candidates. Craig McCaw still held the power of the purse, but he was disengaging himself from the project. Lanny Cornell had responsibility for the health of the whale, and he could issue his doctor's orders, but he lived half a world away and made his house calls in Iceland only intermittently. Ocean Futures had a board of directors, but it was not an activist board. The staff wondered sometimes who was in charge.

The conflicted little society of the bay pen had its pariah. Dane Richards, nephew of Lanny Cornell, was regarded as a spy for his uncle. Early on, Charles Vinick, who managed the project in Iceland, made a comment about Dane's communication with the veterinarian, and afterward the trainers tended to fall silent in Dane's company. Richards is a friendly, outgoing man, and this treatment was hard on him.

"If it wasn't for Peter Noah, I would never have had any interaction with Keiko," he says. "The trainers just weren't interested. I'd ask questions, but because I was viewed as a spy, I didn't get answers. I did get into the behavioral stuff with Peter Noah. He was great with me. I'd come up from work on a dive, and he'd say, 'Go play with Keiko. Go interact with him for as long as you can.' If it hadn't been for Peter, no one would have offered. It was always *their* whale, and they didn't want anybody close to him, especially the spy. They didn't want to help me at all."

The uneasiness of the Oregon trainers, Dane believes, had to do with his uncle's reputation in the field. Before Keiko, none of the Oregon contingent, with the exception of Peter Noah and Brian O'Neill, had had much experience with killer whales. They had worked with smaller fry—belugas, sea lions—but not orcas, and oversight by Cornell made them nervous. Among the Sea World trainers, Dane suspects, resentment of his uncle went back to Cornell's days as Sea World vice president. "Lanny has his opinions," Dane concedes. Among some Sea Worlders, Cornell was regarded as a Captain Bligh, and his departure from Sea World had been with bitter feelings all around.

Richards, for the record, denies that he was a spy. "It's not like I was going to Lanny and saying they're mistreating this whale, or anything. Lanny would e-mail me, and I'd e-mail him. I'm his nephew, and we love each other."

Recalling those Iceland days, Richards lets out a long breath.

"I volunteered to go to marine operations, because that got me away from the sentiment that I'm a spy. Sitting out there on the pen with some of these people was just painful. You'd sit out there in silence. It would drive me nuts. I'd rather be driving a boat and getting my hands dirty. I ended up to where I'd eat at Lanterna all the time. I'd go in there and eat by myself. I'd go back and talk with the cooks. 'Thanks for dinner, it was excellent.' They appreciate that. One cook was from Croatia, so he was a kind of a foreigner, too. The cooks set me up with a little seat in the kitchen. I would watch football games with them on TV and talk with them as they cooked."

Westman Islanders regarded Keiko's people as clannish and withdrawn, with several exceptions, Dane Richards prominent among them. Ostracized on the bay pen, Richards fell in with the islanders. At Lanterna, at his special seat in the kitchen, he watched football and ate boscaiola, cevapi, pleskavica, and other Balkan dishes served up by his friend the Croatian cook. He was swept up in the three-day pyromaniacal outdoors bacchanal of Thjódhátíd, the "People's Feast." This festival, held on the first weekend in August, celebrates Iceland's first constitution, theoretically, but it feels distinctly pagan, a throwback to the days of Odin. The green amphitheater of Herjólfsdalur—the fertile interior of an eroded crater at the north end of the island—filled up with tents and barbecues. Herjólfsdalur was once the farm of Herjólfur Bardursson, the first permanent settler in the Westmans. Inside his crater archaeologists have excavated a tenth-century homestead thought to be this pioneer's. Herjólfur Bardursson's descendants party above the site, sleeping little through the seventy-two hours of the festival, basking in the unending glow of the midnight sun, thumbing their noses at the past winter's darkness, building huge bonfires, and giving in to the singing, dancing, eating, heavy drinking, and general licentiousness of their Viking past.

"The community was incredible," says Richards. "The people of the community in the Westman Islands were just amazing. I don't have any regrets, even though I was the spy."

Much of his time on the bay pen he remembers fondly. The construction itself was exciting—an international effort of Canadians, Swedes, and others working on different aspects of the frame and nets. He liked the challenge of building a marine pen larger than any attempted before. Even on the finished pen, he was never completely isolated. There was Peter Noah's mentorship, and the somewhat lunatic and narcissistic companionship of his dive partner, Smári Hardarson.

Hardarson, a commercial diver, was one of the first two Icelanders employed by the project. He worked with Richards and the others on the advance team to install the bay pen, then stayed on to do maintenance. In November 1998, two months after Keiko's arrival, Hardarson won Iceland's bodybuilding championship. "Smári could not put the phone up to the same ear as the hand he was holding it in," one team member recalls. "If the phone was in his right hand he could only reach his left ear, because his biceps were too big." Hardarson was impulsive and supernaturally strong. Sometimes, for quick repair jobs underwater, he would not bother to strap on his air bottle, just tuck it under his huge arm and dive in. Smári could be a bit much, sometimes, but he was neither an Oregon trainer nor a Sea World trainer, and this placed him, like Dane Richards, on the outside.

And Richards had the companionship of the whale. When he was not too weary at the end of his day of maintenance, he would jump in with Keiko. When he and Smári were underwater, drilling to improve the anchorage of the barrier net, the whale would swim by to check on their work. "Ten dives, and you'd go home wiped out," Richards says of this labor. "The drill is putting out one hundred twenty decibels, measured a hundred meters away, and you're *holding* it." Dane would see crabs on the bottom, and the occasional sea-jelly drifting by, but he noticed few fish. Despite all the decibels and vibrations of the drill, he would sometimes feel a presence behind. Turning, startled, he would look into the eye of the killer whale, inches away, as Keiko peered over his shoulder. It seemed to Richards that Keiko resented all this human preoccupation with drilling. "What's this all about?" he was asking, or so it seemed to Richards. "What could be more interesting in this cove than me?"

32

OLAFSDÓTTIR

KEIKO'S KEEPERS PLANNED TO REINTRODUCE HIM GRADUALLY TO THE Norwegian Sea through the summer of 2000, leading him out of his cove for a series of ocean "walks." The walk boat, *Draupnir,* was an orange-hulled Norwegian rescue vessel purchased by Ocean Futures to replace the inadequate little Stabi-Craft that had so amused the islanders. *Draupnir* was equipped with what the team called a "toner," a recall device sounding a tone that Keiko was trained to answer. On the starboard side the boat was customized with a work platform cantilevered over the water to facilitate Keiko's feeding and his instruction at sea. The Westman Islanders liked the look of *Draupnir.* They could think of nothing sarcastic to say about her.

In late spring, as Keiko's training for his walks intensified, his team was shocked to learn of imminent construction in the harbor—a new pier for the Westman fishing fleet. The contractor planned a day of dynamiting and two or three weeks of pile-driving. Dr. Cornell, worried that the noise would damage Keiko's hearing, warned that if the whale's powers of echolocation were compromised, he could not possibly survive in the wild. Ocean Futures scrambled to come up with options. The best solution, they decided, was to advance the schedule for Keiko's ocean walks, taking him out to sea during the blasting in the harbor. They entered into hurried negotiations with local officials and the contractor, paid $80,000 to delay the construction, pushed through the emergency permits required to let the whale out of his cove, and nagged the technician building Keiko's radio tags to rush that job.

At six in the morning of May 25, 2000, Keiko followed *Draupnir* through a gate in the barrier net and swam out of the harbor strait into the open ocean. For the first time since his capture, more than twenty years before, he was physically free in the sea.

For months Keiko's team had been preparing for this moment, pushing him hard in his aerobic conditioning, decreasing his interaction with humans, increasing his reliance on live fish, and teaching him to respond to the tone signal. Before Keiko set out, a spotter plane had scouted the sea ahead. On a reconnaissance flight the day before, the pilot had seen seven orcas and six white-beaked dolphins near the island. In the future, spotter planes and helicopters would search for concentrations like this and direct *Draupnir* and Keiko toward them, but on this first trip the mission was to make sure no orcas were around. One thing at a time, the team figured. They wanted to see how Keiko performed at sea before adding the complication of relatives. The island waters were clear of orcas. Keiko covered 8.7 nautical miles in two and a half hours, in a fifteen-knot wind, through four-foot swells with a two-foot chop on top. Dr. Cornell noted that he was energetic, frisky, and that his respiration never rose above normal. When the hour came for the dynamite in the harbor, he was called to the side of the boat with the toner, and a trainer on the work platform held him alongside for the minute of blasting. Keiko did not seem alarmed. When the explosions were done, *Draupnir* led him back to harbor.

"The dynamiting made us go a little faster than we probably would have liked to, initially," Jeff Foster told me. "But it worked to our advantage. That first time we took him out, we just didn't know what was going to happen. Oh, it was a great moment. We worked so hard for this. To get him out in the wild."

SIX WEEKS LATER, IN EARLY July, I traveled to Iceland to check up on the whale. Keiko's people believed that full release was imminent. His ocean walks were going well. The great moment would almost certainly come that summer, they said, most probably in mid-July. There could be no fixed date. The decision to release him would have to be extemporaneous. If Keiko's trainers judged him fit, and if a suitable pod of killer whales showed up, then he would be on his way. If my luck was good, I would be on hand to see him off.

The "Welcome Home Keiko" banners were long gone from the town of Heimaey when I arrived. The stuffed Keiko toys were nearly extinct in the shop windows. The crush of cameramen, journalists, and whale-lovers of two years ago had evaporated. I seemed to be the only writer left on the story. It was Icelandic summer, and the Westmans were in the middle of the season of continuous light that had amazed Iceland's discoverers, the Irish monks, who came in the skin boats they called *currachs,* who named the place Thule, and who marveled that in July they could see well enough to pick the lice from their shirts at midnight. Above the buff-golden cliffs of Heimaklettur, sheep grazed the green tundra of the summit. It was nesting season for puffins, which swarmed about the cliffs along with kittiwakes and fulmars.

Two weeks before, a 6.5 earthquake had hit the Westmans, causing rock-falls on the cliffs of the North Rocks. Bouncing boulders had taken big divots out of the steep slopes of green turf beneath the cliffs. Some boulders had taken seven or eight bites before smashing to the bottom. The impacts had blasted craters and torn great rents in the tussock grass, throwing aprons of black dirt downslope. You could track individual rocks as you would a bounding animal. Several smaller rocks took surprising detours: four divots downslope, then a right-angle bounce and three divots to the side. A few sizable boulders had hopped entirely across the harbor road. The bombardment must have taken some puffins. Surviving birds stood like uniformed doormen at their burrow entrances, at the brink of dark, ragged holes left by the boulders that had narrowly missed them.

The temblor had struck just as Jeff Foster and Keiko were returning to the harbor from one of these expeditions. A big rockslide from Heimaklettur had slumped into the harbor strait, sending a small tsunami toward the whale. Keiko had been unperturbed, according to Foster. He had simply crossed to the other side of the boat.

There was plenty of room at my old hotel. During the Keikofest of September 1998, all accommodations on Heimaey had been booked months in advance, and the town then had teemed with visitors. Now it was a sleepy little island village again. I asked the clerk what she knew about Keiko's release. It was to be soon, she understood. Indeed, she thought it might have happened already.

Alarmed, I called the Ocean Futures number, but no one answered. I walked down to Keiko headquarters on the waterfront, but the door was locked. Stopping by the converted hostel where Keiko's trainers stayed, I punched random numbers on the keypad of the lock, but hit no winning combination. My heart sank. It would be just my luck to have missed the whale's liberation by a few hours. Even now, perhaps, Keiko was bidding adieu to humanity.

I hurried out over the lava flow to Klettsvík Cove. With my binoculars I glassed the cove waters for the whale, but could not spot him. At the base of the sheer golden cliff of Home Rock was the cavelike overhang called Klettshellie. The still water and gilded reflections of this acoustic chamber seemed an agreeable place for a whale to hang out—a sort of cetacean music room—but Keiko was not there. He was nowhere to the east under the wall of East Rock, either. I glassed the line of buoys that marked the barrier net fencing in the cove. Near midpoint, just inside the buoy line, floated a pair of white fulmars, drawn perhaps to the buoys, as to white decoys. The fulmars were totally preoccupied in preening. They did not act like fulmars under which something big was lurking.

Just as I resigned myself to having missed Keiko's departure, he surfaced near the sea pen. The familiar bent dorsal fin was tagged with a Day-Glo orange ribbon. The ribbon flagged the radio transmitter that would track him after release. Relieved, I watched the whale loaf around for an hour. Once or twice he passed near the fulmars, but they paid him no attention. Apparently his ornithological period was over, and he was no longer nudging seabirds experimentally from below. He seemed to prefer the vicinity of the sea pen, attracted, I supposed, by the company of his trainers and security guards, who stood their watches on the pen platform. I returned my binoculars to their case and headed back to town.

On Vestmannabraut Street, I paused to watch a puffin-hunter unload his catch. From the back of his pickup, the man tossed out heavy strings of the birds until a mound of them—black tuxedos, plump white shirtfronts, Day-Glo orange feet, polychromatic parrotlike beaks—lay on the gray cobbles of the street. This seemed an aesthetic disaster, as awful as any massacre of resplendent quetzals or blue-and-gold macaws. An ecological disaster, it was not. Westman Islanders are managing their puffin population well. There are eight million puffins in the archipelago.

Puffins are caught with *fleyges,* long-handled nets, and any other hunting method is considered unsporting. Only immature birds and nonbreeders are taken. Breeding birds are easy to distinguish, for where nonbreeders circle aimlessly about the cliff, the breeders fly straight in to their burrows. The breeders, as if to resolve any doubt, flag themselves by the curious habit of organizing, in neat rows along their enormous beaks, the fingerling fish they are bringing to their chicks. In the old days, puffins were much more of a staple in Iceland. Their feathers were used to make bedding, their breast meat salted and smoked in great quantities as winter stores. Today consumption of the birds has fallen. They are in no danger of following their giant cousin, the great auk, into extinction.

Still, something endearing in the puffin's plumpness, or in the contrast between its comic, bright-painted harlequin beak and the black-and-white formality of the tuxedo, gave me a pang. These puffins looked like a bunch of clowns assassinated on their way to the opera. I thought about Keiko. What a tricky set of rules it is, the one deciding which animals we adore and which we eat.

Next month, August, the puffin chicks of Heimaey—the pufflings—would be attracted like moths to the lights of town. This happens after fledging every August on the island. Unable to fly yet, but capable of gliding, the pufflings set wings and sail down from the cliffs by the hundreds, crash-landing on the dock and in the town streets. Westman children, allowed to stay up late in the perpetual twilight of August nights, roam the streets with cardboard boxes, collecting pufflings. It is common for a human fledgling to return home with a dozen of its puffin analogues. There is a sleepover, the pufflings spending the night in the child's room. The next morning, the children take their boxes to the shore and toss each puffling as high as possible.

The pufflings glide seaward to splashdown. Pufflings must teach themselves to fly, but they are instinctive swimmers, and they paddle out into the Westman waters, milling about offshore until old enough to master flight.

Keiko and the pufflings would be liberated at about the same time, it occurred to me. They would head offshore together. Before the children toss them high to freedom, the pufflings, like Keiko, have had their interlude with city lights and captivity. All that pufflings need is to be pointed in the right direction. I hoped it would be the same for the whale.

Two female librarians were taking a sun break on the steps of the *bókasafn,* the library. Heimaey's library is a huge place for such a small island, but in a way it figured, as Iceland is the most literate nation on Earth, publishing and consuming more books per capita than any other. The Heimaey *bókasafn,* a manifestation of this voraciousness, sits in an honored place beside the town hall on a rolling green common at the center of town. The younger librarian was a sturdy blond daughter of Vikings. The older was sturdy, too, but brunette and swarthier than most Icelanders. I asked them what Westman Islanders thought of Keiko, now twenty-two months into his residency.

"We were hoping Eskifjördur would take him," said the younger librarian. "We don't care about him." She gestured dismissively. "This is a small community. We had to pay a lot of money for Keiko. The plane that brings him damaged the runway. The pilot does not listen to our advice. We had to put one million kronur to fix it."

"Not more?" asked the older librarian.

"No. I think it was a million."

The younger librarian waved in the direction of the sea pen. "He takes a lot of beautiful space over there," she said. "We used to go there but now we can't. My father-in-law had a boat. We would drive it to Klettsvík for a walk where Keiko is today. It was beautiful on a sunny day. There is a sandy beach. A cave called Klettshellie. Now if you go there, you can't have any noise, because of Keiko. Last time I went, I said, 'Scream children! Scream!' I'm sick of him."

These were not timid librarians. I tried to reason with them; surely they must be moved, I suggested, or impressed just a little bit, by Keiko's walks beside the boat in the ocean. The older librarian smirked at this sentimentality. "He's like a little dog," she replied. "With the boat, it's like a yoke. It's like they have him on a rope. When he goes—*if* he goes—we won't cry like an American."

The general hope in the Westman Islands, according to the two librarians, had been that the whale would become a tourist attraction. This had never happened. Tourists went away disgruntled, for they were not allowed near the whale. There had been no benefit to the community. No Keiko books had reached the library. The librarians had asked the Keiko people for literature, but none had been provided.

"We were angry because he found a herd of whales," said the older librarian. "We thought, *Yes!* He'll be gone. But the whales wouldn't take him. He's like a dog. They won't have him."

The Westman Islands would not be burdened much longer by Keiko, I reminded the women. According to his keepers, he would be released within a couple of weeks.

"We don't believe it," said the younger librarian.

"It was to be July 4," said the older. "America's independence day. But he is still here. I don't think he will ever go."

"He'll die here," said the younger.

Hearing this, the older librarian smiled grimly. "I'm waiting for the day," she said.

Leaving the library, I walked down to the tour agency on Vestmannabraut Street. The librarians had suggested that I drop by that shop to learn the tour-industry opinion of Keiko, and it seemed a good idea. Travel posters of Iceland lined the walls: Icelandic ponies. Snowmobiles on Vatnajökull, the biggest glacier in Europe. Icebergs in the aquamarine glacial lagoon of Jökulsárlón. Puffins here on Heimaey.

On the countertop was a stack of street maps of Heimaey with Keiko on the cover. When the tour agent had seen her two customers out the door, she turned to me. She was a tall, cheerful young woman, as heroically built as any iron maiden from the sagas. She denied any personal or professional bitterness toward the whale. What she felt about Keiko was indifference, she said.

"Last summer, Americans came just to see Keiko, and you can't see him. They came all that way for nothing. And some people living here are not so happy. For a time, you couldn't hunt puffins up there, where Keiko is. It was our place; we had always hunted puffins. But I don't think the Westman Islanders *hate* Keiko." She laughed and mimed a sour face. "Not everyone is like the librarian."

AT THE NÁTTÚRUGRIPASAFN, THE AQUARIUM and Museum of Natural History, I found the director, Kristján Egilsson, in the aquarium room, supervising carpenters in the remodeling of a tank. The wolf eels seemed to be supervising, too, from their tank across the room. The wolf eels—or *steinbítur*, "stone-biters," as the Icelanders call them—were interested, as always, by human activity, and they pressed their nightmare faces to the glass. Egilsson told me that the recent earthquake had slopped water over the top of their tank. Mopping up, the director had studied his stone-biters, and they had seemed unperturbed. A little chop in the water is nothing new to a stone-biter.

We adjourned to Egilsson's office. His north window looked straight up at Stóraklif and the big divots that the earthquake's falling boulders had blasted from the green slopes. Kristján Egilsson, I discovered, was now enthusiastic about the whale. This surprised me, for I remembered the Nordic pessimism of his Keiko opinions two years ago. I reminded Egilsson that on Keiko's arrival, he had worried lest the whale draw too many tourists to the Westmans; that he had faulted Keiko's people for stirring up bad feelings between the Westmans and Eskifjördur, the competing site for the sea pen; and that he, like many Westman Islanders, had been suspicious of American motives in sending such a famously sick whale to Iceland. Egilsson was surprised by this recitation of his old views. He suggested that perhaps I was exaggerating his former opposition.

His opinions had changed, in any case. Tourists had not overwhelmed the Westmans, after all. Keiko had proved remarkably healthy. Egilsson had recently accompanied Keiko researchers on several helicopter reconnaissances around the islands, looking for pods of killer whales. Craig McCaw had volunteered one of his helicopters and a pilot for this work. McCaw's hundred-million-dollar yacht, *Tatoosh,* had *two* helipads and helicopters, so the billionaire had one to spare. For Egilsson, an aquarist and a native of the Westmans, the helicopter flights had been exhilarating. A fisherman's son, he had seen his home waters from a vantage his father had never achieved in decades of tossing about on giant North Atlantic swells. Keiko had brought good marine science to the islands, in Egilsson's opinion. Unknown pods of orca had been discovered. Kristján Egilsson was now a strong advocate of the whale.

The museum's receptionist and cashier—Olafsdóttir, I'll call her—had been invited on no helicopter rides. She was not so easily persuaded that the whale was good for Iceland. A small, neat eighteen-year-old brunette, Olafsdóttir had a porcelain complexion, a stud in one eyebrow, and hair pulled severely back, not a strand out of place.

"It's kind of ridiculous," she said. "The money that went to this! They could feed a whole nation! It's very stupid. He's still not catching his own fish. The live fish they feed him, he just plays with them. It's a game for him. They still make him do tricks! It's not working very well."

I asked if the islanders had any special nickname for Keiko's people. Olafsdóttir shrugged. "Just 'Keiko's People,'" she said. I asked about the Keiko Center, which was supposed to operate in conjunction with this museum. Olafsdóttir pronounced it a failure. "It didn't work. It was stupid. Nobody went." I observed that Westman Island children, in the beginning at least, had been enthusiastic about Keiko, and she nodded agreement. "Kids still like him. From around the age of ten." Among Westman Island adults, she said, there was much more ambivalence, and she reminded me that mixed feelings about the whale, and outright Keikophobia, were not limited to Iceland. "One American told me we should shoot Keiko, stuff him, and put him on display in the museum."

She nodded toward the next gallery. Visible through the open door, behind the glass of museum cases, was a selection of stuffed Icelandic fauna: The sunfish that Icelanders call *skötuselur,* "seal-ray," all leathery and cracked with age. A blackened, mummified shark. An abyssal anglerfish, overinflated by the taxidermist, its needly jaws agape below the tassel of its lure. The biggest specimen at the moment was the Atlantic alligator fish or sea poacher, which Icelanders call *attstrendingur,* "octagon," for its eight-sided shape in cross section. The alligator fish was about six feet long, not a third the length of Keiko, yet it almost filled its case. Keiko would not fit in this museum. They would have to build a whole new wing for him.

Olafsdóttir spoke North American English with scarcely a trace of Icelandic accent. When I complimented her on her ear for English, she confessed that her mother was Canadian. Her father, an Icelander, regularly took the family on vacation to that second homeland. It became apparent, as we talked, that Olafsdóttir's Canadian half pulled hard. Her sense of estrangement in Iceland was sharp. The Saga of Olafsdóttir, so far—the first eighteen years of it—was full of the angst of the changeling. Visiting relatives in Canada, she felt much more at home than she did on her native soil. Her values were Canadian values, she said. I asked how Canadian values differed from Icelandic. "It's too lenient here!" she answered. "The kids! In Canada, you say 'Sir,' and 'Ma'am.' Here, there's nothing like that. No respect for elders. Kids do whatever they want in class. We don't have family names in Iceland. I'm just . . . *dóttir.* My father's daughter. It's more familiar here."

Others might see charm in this familiarity—I myself did—but Olafsdóttir did not. Her brother fit right in, she said. Her brother liked Icelandic humor, Icelandic pastimes. He wanted to stay in Iceland. She herself was getting out as soon as possible.

"They don't know what a prom is!" she cried. "They have so many celebrations and festivals, but they don't have anything special for a prom. *I wanted to have a prom!*"

Olafsdóttir laughed, amused in spite of herself by the sound of her own teenage plaintiveness.

"So you were promless," I summarized.

"Yes. No prom."

Olafsdóttir had started a group called "Alien Gathering," a club for young women who, like herself, felt themselves outsiders. She had invited the young female trainers of Keiko to join. The trainers might have seemed ideal candidates—they certainly were resident aliens of the official sort—but they had never come to meetings. Olafsdóttir understood. The American women were here for only six months of the year; it was easier, simpler, for them to keep to themselves.

At Olafsdóttir's elbow, beside her cash register, was a revolving postcard rack, and among the Icelandic scenes were postcards of Keiko. I lifted out a Keiko card. We studied the portrait of the whale, the founder of the Alien Gathering and I.

"He was caught when he was a calf," she said. "I'm so afraid he'll just be killed. Killed by the other whales. Because he doesn't fit in."

33

WHALE WALKING

Scrambling up a volcanic promontory across the channel from Keiko's Cove, I found a clinkery hillock that offered a good view of the sea pen. The hillock was *'a'a* lava, rough and scoriaceous and sharp. Using my daypack for a seat, I gingerly sat and trained my binoculars on the pen. Keiko was scheduled to depart on an ocean walk at about two o'clock this afternoon. At three o'clock, an hour late, *Draupnir,* the walk boat, left the harbor and sped out toward the cove. The little Norwegian rescue vessel had a high bow and a fat orange pontoon for a gunwale. There was a Raytheon radar atop the white fiberglass cabin, and the staff was flying a killer-whale balloon-flag as its colors—black and white, like the Jolly Roger. Keiko heard *Draupnir* coming and waited at a gate in the net. When a crewman opened up for him, Keiko sank inside the corkline of the enclosure and resurfaced outside. At a good eight knots or so, the boat and whale steamed down the strait for the ocean. Keiko stayed close to the hull, surfacing to blow first on one side, then the other.

My backside still pained me, probably, but I did not feel it now, for I was full of wonder at this spectacle. It was a new thing under the sun, absolutely extraordinary—this tandem of boat and killer whale on the open ocean. Yet it had the look of routine. And it *was* routine! For six weeks now, Keiko had been taking these walks almost daily. I remembered the crazy scheme of the cetologist Kenneth Balcomb, who, back in Keiko's Mexican period, had proposed training the whale to follow his sailboat to Iceland. The idea had drawn nearly universal ridicule. But maybe it was not so crazy. Maybe it would have worked.

Keiko and his escort, upon clearing the strait, headed toward the offshore islets of Bjarnarey and Ellidaey. These two islets rise vertically from the water, fortresslike, molariform, their cliffs swarming with seabirds. The birds were not visible to the naked eye, but my binoculars materialized them—ledge-nesting fulmars and kittiwakes making white veins on the cliffs, with flurries of white motes circling as new squadrons of birds arrived and departed. Above the cliffs, the crowns of both islets are demi-bowls of green tundra. Low in either bowl stands a solitary white summer house for shepherds, and high in either bowl graze the white specks of sheep. Somehow sheep and shepherds got up and down the cliffs, though no plausible route is apparent. The islets are a crazy mix of the maritime and the pastoral. They look fantastic, like sheep ranches reimagined by Salvador Dalí. On the horizon beyond the islets, across the channel on the Icelandic mainland, was the long, white, lenticular curve of the Myrdalsjökull glacier.

None of it seemed real. This was a scene from *The Hunting of the Snark* or *Doctor Dolittle* or *Alice in Wonderland:* a killer whale sallying forth with his human friends into this fairy-tale seascape.

When Keiko blew to starboard, the wind drove the rainbow mist of his spout over *Draupnir*'s wheelhouse. I held my binoculars on the prow, watching for the bright explosions of Keiko's exhalations, then the black glistening arch of his back. If Keiko should choose this moment to make his escape, I would be a witness. I found myself wishing for something like this—a sudden detour to freedom. The eastern horizon beckoned—featureless ocean— and nothing physical restrained him, yet Keiko never strayed from the boat. As he neared the cliffs of Bjarnarey, his image in my binoculars began to deteriorate. I was losing him in a static of surface-skimming seabirds. The foreshortening effect of the field glasses only served to thicken the blizzard of shearwaters and gannets and kittiwakes and fulmars. The sea's surface seemed to be evaporating in a flying mist of wings. Keiko entered the channel between Bjarnarey and Ellidaey, then disappeared behind Bjarnarey's shoulder. He would be gone for two or three hours.

The spectacle had been wonderful yet disheartening. Keiko's fitness was steadily improving, he was taking ever longer trips out to sea, and all that was good. But what self-respecting killer whale would let himself be walked at all? "Like a dog," the Heimaey librarian had said. I had assumed for years that Keiko would make a dash for the wild ocean the moment he got the chance. That is what I would have done. Like all Keiko's human acquaintances, I tried to remake him in my own image. Olafsdóttir, who felt herself such a misfit in Icelandic society, worried that Keiko would be killed by other orcas because he did not fit in. Dianne Robbins, Bonnie Norton, and the other animal empaths were sure that Keiko was empathic, like themselves. Wilderness, for me, has always been the best place to be, and I had no doubt that Keiko felt the same. I was wrong. It turned out that I was not a good model for this whale.

THE NEXT DAY, THURSDAY, I sat again atop the same volcanic hillock, waiting for Keiko to return from that day's walk. Keiko was late. My binoculars magnified the spindrift of seabirds working the icy tide rips around Bjarnarey and Ellidaey. The Myrdalsjökull ice field, on the Icelandic mainland, was tremulous with heat shimmer. A single fishing boat stood under the trembling glacier, making a wide turn out toward the Norwegian Sea.

There is no proper "too late" in Iceland—not in mid-summer, with unending daylight to guide the whale and his crew back to harbor—but Keiko was certainly tardy. It was the thirteenth of July, and mid-July was his estimated time for release. It seemed possible that it had happened: Keiko had gone back to his own kind.

Then at last *Draupnir,* with its distinctive orange hull, appeared between Bjarnarey and Ellidaey. I steadied my binoculars but could see no whale. Keiko's people seemed to be returning alone. Mindful that a swimming whale spends most of the time underwater, I kept my binoculars trained on the boat. When *Draupnir* was about a mile off, I saw Keiko break the surface beside it, blow, and curve back under. I was relieved to see him. Yesterday my wish had been that he swim to freedom; today I was glad to find him still with us. Farewells are difficult, and I was happy this one had been postponed. I had to laugh at my vacillation; I seemed to encapsulate, within myself, all the contradictory feelings of my species on the destiny of this particular whale. Keiko was still frisky, apparently, for he and his escort turned out to sea again. They looped around Bjarnarey and it was another forty minutes before I saw them again.

A flock of fulmars accompanied Keiko into the harbor strait. The birds appeared to be using the whale to scare up baitfish for themselves. One fulmar, trimming its white wings, slanted toward the water ahead of the boat's prow, then abruptly flared and veered. Its target patch of ocean formed a swell. The swell's glassy curve morphed smoothly into the glistening black dome and white cheek-blaze of a killer whale. Keiko broke the surface, and the startled fulmar lifted up and away.

The boat passed under my promontory. A trainer, Jeff Foster from the look of him, stood on the work platform, which was cantilevered out over the water, and he flung a live fish out to the side. In a quick swirl of flukes and a churn of whitewater, Keiko turned back for the fish and reached it before the birds could. Foster threw another fish, and Keiko beat the birds to this one, too. It was an athleticism I had never before witnessed in him. For the first time since I had known him, he was moving like a real killer whale.

"WERE YOU THROWING HIM FISH on the way back?" I asked Foster that evening.

"Yes. We have to get his daily intake into him, and we do that usually on his walks. It's fun to see, because there's been competition between the gulls and Keiko. It started in the bay, and now it's continuing out on the walks. Keiko knows if he isn't quick to get those fish, the gulls are going to come down and get them. Which works to our advantage, because we want him to be real quick to capture fish. He's gotten much, much quicker. In Newport he didn't have the room to maneuver he has out in the wild. In Newport, we'd pop a fish in, and usually Keiko would be stationary, and the fish were confused—they weren't used to the tank—so they were slow-swimming and he'd be able to catch them easily. But he was very slow in doing it. Now we're getting him cod and haddock and pollock. And he's right on top of them."

To Foster I suggested that Keiko's maiden walk six weeks ago must have been an amazing moment for all concerned. I asked whether he had felt any anxiety as the whale left the cove for open water.

"You bet. Because you just don't know. I mean, we're teaching him to be a wild animal, but we also want to maintain some kind of control. There's a fine line there that we're walking. We want to be able to maintain him, but get him used to the surrounding areas, let him figure out where he is. Then possibly come in contact with other orcas. But do it gradually.

"Initially, we wanted to make sure he could travel—forty, fifty, sixty, seventy miles in a day. We wanted to make sure that he could dive to certain depths. We wanted to make sure that he could find fish. We've been able to accomplish those goals. Now, in the next couple of weeks, we'll actually take him out to where we know there are a lot of wild whales. We'll put the boat in neutral and let him listen to their vocalizations and hopefully interact with them. So that will really be his first contact."

There had been an equivocal sort of first contact already, Foster said. Keiko was out with *Draupnir* and a smaller boat, *Heppni,* which the team used for shuttles and to advise other boats to keep away. They had cruised into a patch of ocean occupied by orcas and white-beaked dolphins. The engines of both boats were running, and Foster sensed that in the noise Keiko was unaware of the orcas until his fleet was right on top of them. "We don't know how he responded, it was kind of an awkward situation," Foster said. "There were two or three cows with calves, though there may have been more whales underwater."

Draupnir was about a thousand meters from Keiko when the school of white-beaked dolphins passed. The team dropped hydrophones over the side and recorded the whistles and clicks of these *höfrungur,* as Icelanders call them. "They were vocalizing, and Keiko picked up on that," Foster said. "He took off after them like a rocket. I had the feeling that the white-beaked dolphins echolocated and knew that a large animal was swimming very fast toward them, and they broke and swam away really, really fast. And Keiko went after them. He was gone for quite a while, probably twenty minutes. We couldn't see him, but we had the tracking equipment out there, if we needed it. It was really exciting to me. We thought it was very encouraging."

In the twenty minutes Keiko was gone, the team had no idea what he was doing. They called him back with signal tones, but the range of the recall device was only about four miles, and Foster believes the whale was beyond that. *Draupnir* stayed in the same spot, engines running in neutral, and at the end of his twenty minutes unchaperoned, Keiko found the boat again, by dead reckoning, Foster guesses.

"I was surprised how close he stayed to the boat today," I told Foster.

"In and out of harbor, we want him to stay real close," Foster said. "That way we have control. We want to discourage him from swimming out to other boats. So in the harbor area it's important we control him until we get outside. Once we get outside, we want to encourage him to swim off from the boat. And we'll do that; we'll go three or four miles down the way, put the boat in neutral, and let him explore the coastline, or check out fish, or the birds. He's curious."

When it came time to move on down the coast, or to head back to harbor, the team did not sound the recall device, they simply increased the speed of the boat, and this brought Keiko alongside again.

"We keep him usually on the platform side—the side we work him from. But he likes the slipstream on the port side. For some reason, that's his favorite spot. He'll cross over to starboard, the platform side, to check if we're still there, then go back. We don't want the boat walks to be boring, so we try to break it up as much as we can. We'll go like 2000 rpm for five minutes, which is smokin'. I can't tell you how fast it is in that boat, but it's very fast. When he porpoises out of the water at that speed, nearly his whole body comes out. It's kind of like wind sprints. Then we'll drop back the 1500 rpm, which is still about seven knots, and he'll maintain that speed for fifteen or twenty minutes. Then we'll drop down to 1000 or 1200 rpm. That seems to be the speed where he'll swim out away from the boat more. At the faster speeds he holds close. We vary it, and he kind of moves around the boat."

ON THE MORNING OF THE day I was to leave Heimaey, I walked the island road up through the chaotic landscape of the 1973 lava flow. I had lingered in the Westmans as long as I could, in hopes of seeing Keiko released, but I could not afford to wait any longer. It was a sunny day. I walked in a T-shirt, a rare pleasure in Iceland. At the crest of the lava ridge, I followed a spur road out to a scenic overlook above the harbor strait. A big pay telescope mounted there looked across to Klettsvík Cove and the cliffs above Keiko's pen. I fished in my pocket for change. Icelandic coins are made from some tarnish-resistant alloy, always bright. On this day of full sun, the coins in my palm hurt my eyes—a rare discomfort in Iceland. The one-krona piece shows a chromic cod, the ten-krona piece a silvery school of four capelin. It is currency a killer whale would like. I slid some of my dazzling kronur into the telescope and swiveled it across the bird colonies of the cliffs, then down to the bay pen. The view through my binoculars was better, and that view was free, so I switched back to my own equipment.

Keiko's trainers sat in T-shirts on the sea-pen platform, backs against the corrugated wall of the dry house, soaking up the rays. In the languor of their poses, you could almost read the bitterness of the past winter, when storm waves and gale winds had tossed them about this same platform. Keiko, for his part, was spending a good deal of time swimming underwater on his back, showing the white of his underside.

A tour bus pulled up at the overlook and disgorged a contingent of Japanese, several Europeans, and one American family.

"Where's Keiko?" the American father asked me cheerily. I pointed out the whale, who had just surfaced by the sea pen. With the aid of my binoculars, the man spotted Keiko and called out the coordinates to his three small boys. Then he whistled piercingly. "Jump!" he urged. "Jump, Keiko!"

"Jump, Keiko!" repeated one of the sons. After a second, the boy added, impatiently, "Jump!"

The family was accustomed to the acrobatics of Sea World shows, or they recalled *Free Willy* and that final scene where the whale jumps to freedom. But Keiko was no longer in show business. At this distance he could not have heard the family's entreaties, anyway. He declined to jump.

The tourists were reluctant to spend their kronur on the telescope, so I passed my binoculars around. One German tourist murmured satisfaction at the ten-power magnification and he hogged my field glasses long past the time he should have given them up to the next tourist. I noticed a peculiar thing: No one could see the whale while he was underwater. I would have thought it impossible to miss Keiko when he swam on his back, for his belly patch showed as a white streak, followed by a gap and then the triangular white ventral surface of his flukes—a white exclamation mark. When he swam deep, the whiteness of the exclamation mark dimmed and green-shifted, but you could always follow its progress. From this height, it was not hard to track Keiko when he swam on his stomach, either, yet cries of surprise and delight greeted him each time he surfaced, as if he had materialized from nowhere. In the Pacific I have been with Belauan and Yapese spearfishermen, and in the Caribbean with Miskito turtlers, who can follow events underwater that I miss completely; these tourists were to me as I am to those subsistence hunters. I can only think that the tourists were blinded by assumption: that the ocean is opaque; that nothing is certain there until it breaks the surface.

The tour driver gathered his flock, the bus pulled off, and I was alone again.

Keiko was not doing much. I glassed the cliffs of Heimaklettur above his pen. Seabirds milled about the walls: *stormsvala, rita,* the occasional *svart-bakur,* but mostly *fyll;* which is to say, storm petrels, kittiwakes, the occasional black-backed gull, but mostly fulmars. These were Keiko's neighbors. Theirs was the form of government that Melville called a "riotocracy." Their screaming, squawking, and squabbling was so constant that to the human ear—and the cetacean ear, too, probably—it became a kind of silence.

In his cove below, Keiko was not doing anything noteworthy. He had settled into swimming a circle between his sea pen and a storage raft moored seventy yards away. His pattern never varied. He swam the leg from the pen to the raft on his back, with his belly-blaze to the sky. He passed always under the same corner of the raft. A few yards beyond that corner—always at the same point—he rolled to swim the leg from raft to pen on his stomach. He blew always at the same spot. The sea pen and the raft, it occurred to me, were the two places he might expect to find human beings. I counted ten circles, twelve, and then gave up counting. My optimism of yesterday, when Keiko had moved so athletically in chasing down hand-tossed fish, faded. I was doubtful again, for I knew where I had seen this circling before. It was the ritualized behavior displayed by zoo animals—the big cats, especially—after long confinement. It was the endless, hopeless, obsessive-compulsive pacing that marks zoo psychosis as surely as the unseeing stare of the eyes.

THAT AFTERNOON I LEFT THE Westman Islands for Iceland on the ferry *Herjólfur.* As the ferry left its slip, Keiko and *Draupnir* departed Klettsvík Cove for their daily walk, hurrying to clear the harbor strait ahead of us. The good weather held. A light swell was breaking creamily against the base of Klettsnef Point. Keiko himself broke the surface just off Klettsnef's sheer rock wall. The black back of the whale generated its own creamy patch of surf. Keiko blew, then disappeared around the corner.

Herjólfur caught up with the whale on the seaward side of the North Rocks, about a mile off Home Rock. *Draupnir* had cut its motor and was drifting alongside the whale. The passengers all moved to the port rail to see him. A few days ago, Jeff Foster had told me that Keiko was reined in close to the boat only in the strait, from fear of collisions with harbor traffic. Once the whale reached open water, Foster claimed, the whale romped away from his chaperones. This might have been the general rule, but today it was not so. "With the boat, it's like a yoke," the Heimaey librarian had told me. "It's like they have him on a rope." Today, at least, her account was more accurate. Keiko lolled at the surface right beside the hull. I watched him diminish astern until I was the only passenger still watching, and my binoculars could no longer find him. He never strayed from the boat.

Herjólfur sailed westward down the rugged chain of the Westmans. We raised the Isle of Surtsey. This dark new island was named for Surtur, the pyromaniacal Norse giant who is scheduled to set the world ablaze, come Judgment Day. At its birth in 1963, Surtsey exploded from the sea so violently that a black plume of smoke and ash rose to the stratosphere and generated lightning. Today Surtsey sank meekly astern and was soon gone under the horizon. There was nothing ahead but fulmars shearing the surface, riding the updrafts along the crests of the swells. There were a few kittiwakes, and now and then, low on the water, a ragged file of puffins, wings ablur, skimming homeward to the Westmans with their heavy bumblebee flight. A single skua passed, a big, dark, bandit bird searching for some honest working bird to rob. The great shroud of the sea rolled on as it rolled twenty thousand years ago, before the Westman Islands ever showed above the surface. Somewhere behind us, Keiko loafed beside his boat in the company of trainers who, with their predecessors of various nationalities, had cared for him since calfhood. Ahead, that great shroud of the sea seemed a vast, cold shroud indeed.

34

MILLENNIUM

BY THE END OF THE SUMMER OF 2000, KEIKO HAD SWUM FIVE HUNDRED miles in the course of his walks. Jeff Foster and his team, as promised, had brought him to where the wild whales were, placing him in the vicinity of Icelandic pods nineteen times. In each of these encounters, Keiko was within listening distance, and on five occasions he appeared to be in close contact with the other whales. In late August, when the killer whales of southern Iceland left their summer feeding grounds around the Westmans, Keiko showed no inclination to follow. It was a disappointment. Overwintering in his sea pen that year, in the long, dark nights of Iceland's cold season, Keiko had plenty of time for second thoughts, it seems, for in summer of 2001, when the late-night sun and the wild pods returned, he showed a new eagerness for his own kind. To Keiko's people it seemed that he picked up the thread of his reengagement exactly where he had left off the year before.

In late May, he met the first whales of 2001. The helicopter spotted two orcas, a female and a subadult, not far from the walk boat. Five hundred yards from the whales, the boat shut down its engine. The female and subadult approached, and behind them other whales materialized, members of the pod that the helicopter spotters had missed. Keiko submerged slightly beside the hull as whales passed to either side. Neither he nor the wild whales displayed any behavior that looked aggressive. Keiko seemed cautious but not fearful. When the whales passed on, Keiko moved away from the boat, faced the departing pod, and appeared to be listening to them.

The next day, a helicopter reconnaissance spotted orcas closer inshore to the Westmans. One of the wild whales had a drooping dorsal fin almost identical to Keiko's. As the trainers walked Keiko to the area, *Draupnir*'s hydrophones began to pick up orca vocalizations. At sight of the whales, the team again shut down the engine. As the pod approached, their underwater vocalizations crescendoed. Keiko submerged six feet, faced the whales, and appeared to listen to their voices. He sprinted toward the pod several times, fifty yards, one hundred yards, then fifty again, but slowed each time and retreated to the boat. The pod moved on. Later the same day, as Keiko and his entourage neared a different pod of orcas, one young whale swam to Keiko, and the two appeared to play. The juvenile followed Keiko and the two swam a fast lap around the boat. The younger orca seemed to be drafting off Keiko. There was brief physical contact between Keiko and the juvenile, which neither seemed to avoid. Then the young whale returned to the pod, which swam away. Keiko stayed near the boat.

"Keiko and the whales have connected more in the last two weeks than they did all of last summer," Charles Vinick told *The Oregonian* at the end of the first week in June.

By the end of July, not two months later, Vinick was much less hopeful.

Keiko continued to sally forth to meet wild orcas, then sally back to the boat. On June 30, *The Oregonian* reported that "Keiko, the killer whale who starred in the film 'Free Willy,' may never be freed, his caretakers said Sunday." (*The Oregonian* had a special interest in Keiko, as a former Oregonian himself, and it had kept its Keiko reporter, Katy Muldoon, on the beat.) The Ocean Futures staff told Muldoon that even after more than sixty trips out of his pen, Keiko appeared reluctant to rejoin wild orcas; he appeared to be attached to mankind. Time and money were running out, they said. In August, a salmon farm is to be installed next to his pen. Sea lice proliferate on caged salmon, and the food and feces of the salmon pollute the water. Keiko's health would be at risk. Jeff Foster told Muldoon that Keiko had only a brief time to hook up with a pod, for the wild orcas would be departing the Westmans in about three weeks, when the weather cooled. Foster predicted that Keiko would stay in Klettsvík Cove for the winter and would probably be moved somewhere else in the spring.

This loss of optimism, in the space of just seven weeks, surprised me. It seemed to me that Keiko's behavior—his tentative dashes toward wild pods, his retreats, his hanging about the margins of aggregations, his brief playful interactions—was just the sort of behavior you see in outcaste wolves trying to hook up with a new pack, or solitary lionesses with a new pride. It is a tricky business, attempting to ease into a tight-knit family of top predators with big teeth. Here, I thought, the new myth of *Orcinus orca*—that this big dolphin is not a *killer* whale, but an orca whale, peaceful and cooperative and nice—might be working against Keiko. The Ocean Futures staff spoke as if he had failed a challenge. In fact he may have been doing exactly what he was supposed to do.

On this matter of Keiko's failure, as on so many before, Keiko's people were divided. David Phillips, for one, was not ready to give up on his whale or to abandon the Westman Islands.

"The good news is we have a healthy whale," he told me in October, when the wild whales had left the Westmans, leaving Keiko behind once more. "His blood work is commensurate with wild whales. His weight is fine. Everything is physically fine. He has not yet plateaued. He keeps progressing in terms of his social contacts. The first year of his walks, summer 2000, he was really kind of quixotic in his relations with the other whales. In some instances, they'd go left and he'd go right. They'd almost flee each other. But this past summer, he bolted in the direction of the whales a number of times. There were some pods he seemed more comfortable with. There was a lot of acoustic interaction. Touching. No aggressive behavior. But eventually they'd go off one way and he'd just mill around or maybe go off another way."

Phillips and Lanny Cornell were of the opinion that Keiko was on too short a leash. They felt the whale had become too dependent on the boat, which remained his security blanket and umbilicus to humanity. Keiko was sucking his thumb. They worried about his dependence on the fish that the boat carried. When the helicopter spotted groups of orcas, the walk boat would bait him in that direction by tossing fish overboard. This was sending mixed messages. When bad weather drove the boat back to harbor, the crew would bait him along with them, then feed him in his cove as they waited out the storm. This was an instance of the means defeating the ends.

"So one view is that he wasn't feeling like he absolutely had to make it on his own," Phillips said. "The countervailing view is that his interactions with wild whales were better when he had a full stomach and a lot of energy. At the very end of the summer, we decided to pull the boat out of the equation, leave the scene, and let him be on his own for a longer period of time."

For seven days Keiko was out in the wild with no boat contact. The helicopter tracked him by monitoring the signals of his VHF tag. Sentinels atop the Dalí-esque islets of Bjarnarey and Ellidaey were occasionally able to watch him through binoculars. It was late in the season, the whales were dispersing, and neither the helicopter nor Keiko could find many pods. He had a few meetings with his brethren, and all of those were brief.

"He ended up doing a lot of milling around," Phillips said. "There was some suggestion that he wasn't doing all that well by the end of that time. That perhaps he was really hungry. We never saw him feeding—but feeding is hard to see, of course. If the pod is eating herring, there are a bunch of whales around, thrashing the surface, and a bunch of birds raining down. And what's happening underwater, you can't see."

There were other methods of determining whether Keiko was eating. One was to call him alongside the boat, instruct him to open wide, then run a tube down his gullet to sample stomach contents. Keiko had been trained for this procedure, and he was surprisingly amenable to it; but if the experiment was to learn whether the whale was prospering on his own, it would not do to reel him in and entube him. (The Heisenberg principle works with great whales just as it does with subatomic particles.) Alternatively, the team could have induced him to swallow a small thermometer invented for this purpose. Digestion raises stomach temperature enough in sea mammals to indicate whether or not they have eaten. This method had been used in various seals, among them the biggest seal of all—the elephant seal—but it had not been tried with killer whales.

"After the seven days, they sent the small boat out, and he came into the sound of the engine," Phillips said. "I think he was happy to get fish. I think he pretty willingly followed the boat back into the harbor. So that's where we are. He's continued his progress, but he hasn't glommed onto a pod and swum off into the sunset. So now what do we do? It's been three years over there. The past two years have been years of expensive reintroduction efforts, with helicopters and boats out on the water, and with heavy-duty monitoring operations with satellite tags and VHS tags—the whole deal—at a time when the financial realities are really coming home. Craig McCaw isn't going to be able to continue the level of financial support that he's given. What do we do now?"

PHILLIPS SAT BACK IN HIS chair to consider this question afresh. We were in his office at Earth Island Institute in San Francisco. His desk was a white snowdrift of papers. The glass walls of his cubicle were a poster gallery. *The Free Willy Story: Keiko's Journey Home,* read one poster, illustrated by a portrait of Keiko. "Drain 'Lake' Powell," read another. Several of the posters were in the form of charts: "Marine Mammals of the Western Hemisphere" showed all those big mammals in rows. "Pinnipedia" showed the seals, sea lions, and walruses. "Tuna of the World" showed dogtooth tuna, slender tuna, frigate tuna, blue-fin tuna, yellow-fin tuna, albacore, and bonito.

In the main bookcase, stacked six cans deep and twenty cans across, many of those tuna species in the poster were represented in the flesh. There were tuna cans from all over the world. There was "TúnfiskuR," canned in Thailand for OraFoods of Iceland, and "Rochambeau, Thon au Naturel," which contained albacore, and hundreds of other labels in dozens of languages. The effect was creepy and sad. These cans, from the look of them, represented the monotonous diet of some pathetic, shut-in eccentric. In fact, all this tuna was not for consumption by Phillips; it was evidentiary. As part of his ongoing campaign to reduce the dolphin kill by tuna seiners, Phillips and his International Marine Mammal Project had found themselves the international monitoring agency for dolphin-safe tuna. All the giants of the industry—Heinz, Chicken of the Sea, Bumble Bee—had adopted Phillip's standards, and other canners had little choice but to follow. To get a "dolphin-safe" label you had to come through David Phillips. He had ten monitors around the world, inspecting canneries and looking for fraudulent use of the "dolphin-safe" label.

On a secondary bookshelf, nestled among tuna cans, was a gold medal from the Humane Society. The medal showed, in bas relief, a mustachioed portrait of the nature writer Joseph Wood Krutch. Phillips won the Krutch Award in 1995 for his work on Keiko and on the tuna-dolphin issue. Whether from modesty, or from indifference to awards, or from simple lack of wall space due to tuna cans, Phillips had chosen not to display the medal. It lay flat on the blue velvet lining of its box.

"My view is that we've already succeeded," Phillips said, finally. "We've put this whale back, probably within a few nautical miles of where he was captured. There's some pretty good anecdotal information that he was captured along the south coast, not off the East Fiords. He's in his home waters. We got rid of his papilloma, which some people said would never go away. We built back his muscle tone, where a lot of people thought he was going to be a couch potato. He graduated from the sea pen to the netted-off bay, and from there to swimming around with wild whales. In Mexico, if you had told me that we would get this far, I would have said that would be off-the-charts success."

Phillips's computer screen darkened, going to sleep behind him. He was now leaning farther back in his chair.

"So now what do we do?" he asked again.

His hope, he said, was that some way could be found to keep Keiko in Iceland. One option would be to move him to some little Icelandic bay where the effort could continue in a scaled-back way. "Maybe without a net," Phillips said. "A place where he has some supplemental feeding, but the ability to go and come as he chooses."

"With the possibility that one day he won't come back," I suggested.

"Exactly. But this is one of the big problems now—the success threshold has been placed so high. There were a lot of people who felt that as soon as he was out there, his instincts would take over and he'd be gone. Including Lanny. Lanny's own view, now, is that when they let him go, he *did* swim off boldly into the future—but they went and corralled him and brought him back. They brought him back and reinforced him for not taking the final plunge. That's Lanny's version of history. *Their* version is that Keiko was swimming off in bewilderment and fright."

For the public, and for some in Ocean Futures, success had been defined as release and assimilation into a pod of wild orcas, preferably his own family. Anything short of that was failure. A faction in Ocean Futures was now arguing that the mission should shift: If funds could not be raised to keep the project going, and if Keiko was not releasable, then he should be brought to a captive facility where he would have the companionship of other orcas and be guaranteed room and board for the rest of his life. Phillips had determined to resist this option. It would have repercussions wider than Keiko, he pointed out. The captive industry would seize upon the example of Keiko as proof that captive killer whales are not releasable. The millions spent on the Keiko project would have set the liberation movement back, not advanced it. All the effort would have been for less than nothing. Phillips wanted to hold out for a bay, with no more infrastructure, maybe, than a feeding dock. A place where Keiko's gradual habituation to life in the ocean could continue economically over several years. A little bay. A feeding dock. Two or three people rotating the duty there.

"Much less expensive," I suggested. "No more security guards, no more trainers."

"And no more net," said Phillips. "That would be great, because the net turns out to be a huge mess. You've got to clean it underwater, and you've got to attach it to the ground pilings, and everything can go wrong with current battering it."

I asked if there was anyone on the Ocean Futures board who argued for releasing the whale no matter what. Was there a sink-or-swim faction in the organization?

"Yes. There are a couple of people with that view. They're saying, *'Let him go! Just get out of the way!'* "

35

———•———

REGIME CHANGE

THAT WINTER THE STORMS LINED UP, JOSTLING FOR POSITION, AND THEN howled across the Westman Islands, one after another, through March of 2002. Thorbjörg Kristjandóttir, an Icelandic woman who joined the staff that month, was surprised by the violence of the weather. Kristjandóttir hails from the west coast of Iceland, where the winds are not so fierce. On some days that March, she says, it blew so hard that the team could not go out to the bay pen. On other days, she and her teammates could reach the pen, but the seas were too rough to disembark. "We couldn't get onto the pen, so what we tried to do is take the boat out, just dump food in there, and get the hell out again. So Keiko would have something to eat."

Early in that month of gales, I visited David Phillips in his San Francisco office. It was a sunny day in coastal California. The big windows at the rear of the Earth Island Institute office looked out at the rocky eastern face of Telegraph Hill, where weeds in the crevices were already in bloom. March enters like a lamb in California and it leaves, too, like a lamb. Half a world away, in the Westmans, March had come in like a lion and would leave the same way. Wild orcas would not begin arriving for another two months, and Keiko and his crew were killing time in his cove until that belated spring migration.

There had been big changes at Keiko's foundation, and I had come for an update. Phillips's computer screen was displaying research data when I entered. He filled me in, first, on that—the most recent science and the latest attempts to find Keiko's family. The search for the family was not going well.

"We have DNA samples from twenty or thirty whales in Iceland," David Phillips told me. "They have little darts that take a plug from the whale for DNA analysis. The best we've been able to do is find a pod that's related to another orca in captivity up in Canada. We found *its* family, for what good that is. But not Keiko's family."

It was a sunny day in San Francisco. The big windows of the Earth Island Institute office looked out at the rocky eastern face of Telegraph Hill, where weeds in the crevices were already in bloom. In coastal California, March comes in like a lamb and goes out, too, like a lamb. Half a world away, for Keiko and his crew, in Iceland, March had come in like a lion and would go out the same way. The weather would be icy and gale-beaten for many weeks more. The killer whales of the middle North Atlantic would not begin arriving in the Westman Islands for another two months.

"All the acoustic data has gone to Black Hole, which is what we call Woods Hole," Phillips said. "Nothing comes out again. What was happening acoustically during Keiko's interactions with wild whales? What were Keiko's vocalizations, and what were *their* vocalizations? How do you correlate his vocalizations with his behaviors? Well, we don't have access to that acoustic data. Who's paying for it? *We* paid for it. We had hydrophones in the water, too, just like Woods Hole did, and we took all the data and turned it over to them. Where is the data? It's at Woods Hole. They've got some graduate students who are doing their theses on it. They are going to be the ones to write it up, in, like, *five or ten years.*"

The scientists who were advising the Keiko project—John Ford, Paul Spong, Dave Bains, Kenneth Balcomb, and others—were insisting that Keiko's people were not looking at the most important information, Phillips said.

"The acoustic picture!" he cried. "Paul Spong has observed solitary orca whales that are independent for two or three years, then link up with another pod. They're usually related to that pod, and it's much more likely that they link up with somebody that has a familiar call or dialect. It's incredibly important! But the research got turned over carte blanche to Woods Hole. When we ask what the recordings say, they tell us to ask in five years. So we don't know a lot. The science hasn't reinforced the ability to figure how to manage the project."

Since my last visit to Phillips's office, more stacks of tuna cans had appeared on his shelves. The cans were now spreading across the floor from one corner, Phillips's collection growing as his dolphin-safe monitors sent them in from far corners of the world.

I was studying the disorder of the cans when a raucous, squawking, psittacine chatter passed overhead.

It was impossible to see the birds—they were flying directly above the roof—but I could follow the rude, bickering line of sound they traced across the sky. The parrots of Telegraph Hill are one of the wonders of my native city. They are an odd collection of escapees in all colors and sizes, led on foraging expeditions by the commander of the moment—some big African gray parrot or blue-and-gold macaw—and trailed by a swarm of parakeets. San Francisco folklore has two explanations for this flock. One theory has all the birds escaping simultaneously after the crash of a pet-shop van. The other has them slipping out of cages and open windows individually over time—an Amazon green one year, a few parakeets the next, a red-capped parrot and some cockatiels the year after.

David Phillips did not seem to hear the parrots. He worked every day under Telegraph Hill, and perhaps for him the birds had become white noise. For me the cacophony of cries chasing one another across the sky was electrifying, and the acoustic message was clear: The parrots of Telegraph Hill are proof that a big, intelligent, social animal can escape captivity and prosper on its own.

"Keiko is like a stage," Phillips told me. "All these amazing people enter the stage, and then they act out on the stage, and then, most times, they end up exiting the stage."

Shakespeare's version of this passage is more graceful, I thought, but Phillips made a good point. I had been amazed myself by all the actors crowding the stage of Keiko—too many of them, really.

"Some of them, you might think never would have entered the stage. Somebody like Craig McCaw. What's this billionaire telecommunications guy doing in this whale thing? It's really outside his plane of reality. But he gets on the stage, and stays there, and you don't think he's ever going to exit."

An early hint that Craig McCaw might exit after all had come in October of 2001, in what one financial-page reporter called the "ultimate yard sale." McCaw was selling off his hundred-million-dollar yacht, *Tatoosh*. This dreadnought had a swimming pool and came with a fleet of auxilliary vessels: two helicopters with helipad, a forty-foot speedboat, a sailboat. McCaw was also offering an island he owned off Vancouver and shares in various companies. His spokesman, Bob Ratliffe, explained that McCaw intended to use the cash to buy undervalued telecommunications assets. Other sources suggested that McCaw and his family were simply seeking a lower profile.

The truth was that McCaw's universe was collapsing. XO Communications, the telecommunications network he had founded in 1994, had borrowed billions in the past years but had yet to make any profit. After the close of the capital markets in 2001, the company had begun running short on cash. In December, XO Communications had stopped making interest payments on its debt and had tried to negotiate with creditors to restructure the $7 billion it owed. Investors had filed fourteen class actions against the company and McCaw, alleging that management repeatedly told investors it could survive the difficult environment.

"He was on a roll," Phillips told me. "He was on an unbelievable roll. But now his financial empire has imploded. Completely imploded. The two companies that were his bread and butter—he founded them after he got the buyout from AT&T—were XO Communications and Nextel Communications. XO, where he had five billion dollars of stock, is just days away from declaring bankruptcy, and his share value is zero. So he's lost five billion there. He had seven billion in Nextel. Nextel has dropped from eighty-eight down to four, which meant that his value went from seven billion down to four hundred million. So in those two stocks alone he lost twelve billion dollars."

In January, Phillips had received a call from the falling giant. Phillips had been stunned, first, by the mere sound of McCaw's voice over the apparatus. Craig McCaw—Mr. Wireless, telecommunications guru, visionary who put cellular phones in the hands of millions—never used the things himself. He operated instead through many layers of intermediaries. Phillips was stunned, second, by the substance of the call. McCaw told him that he did not believe the Keiko project would succeed with the crew presently on-board. Management at Ocean Futures was not raising the necessary money, or getting the word out, or getting the job done. McCaw was unhappy with the philosophy and orientation of the trainers from the marine-park industry who ran the project on the ground. "Too risk-averse," he complained of the project's management, as he had complained often before. The observation was ironic, perhaps, given McCaw's present circumstances, but Phillips believed it was a good summary of what had gone wrong.

McCaw asked Phillips, who six years before had relinquished control of Keiko, whether he wanted his whale back again.

Phillips was now rounding up funding. The environmental community, he discovered, was not eager to chip in. Wendy McCaw, the ex-wife of Craig, was willing to contribute $400,000 to see the project through, but she had conditions. She and her Wendy P. McCaw Foundation did not want Jean-Michel Cousteau was involved in any way, and she wanted assurance that the Humane Society of the United States would back the effort. These conditions had been met. Paul Irwin of the Humane Society had committed his organization. Craig McCaw and all his people—Bob Ratliffe, John Scully, and the rest—were gone. Jean-Michel Cousteau, president of Ocean Futures, had resigned. Jeff Foster, the director of operations and research for Ocean Futures, would soon be let go, as would all those trainers who, like Foster himself, had come to the Keiko project from marine parks. The Free Willy Keiko Foundation had returned to life, or would return sometime this afternoon, as the matter had gone out today by unanimous consent and would be accepted by the board. Phillips was once again executive director.

He waved a sheaf of separation documents at me.

"I love some of this language," he said. " 'In consideration of the undertakings of Craig McCaw and the Foundation, set forth herein, Ocean Futures does hereby and for its constituents, representatives, administrators, successors, assigns, and predecessors, release, aquit, and forever discharge Craig McCaw, the Foundation, all persons or entities associated herewith, and all of the owners, stockholders, members, officers, directors, employees, agents, and attorneys, each of them, from any and all actions, causes of actions, obligations, costs, expenses, damages, loss, claims, liabilities, suits, debts, and demands, including attorneys' fees and costs actually incurred, of whatever character, in law or in equity, known or unknown, suspected or unsuspected, from the beginning of time to the date of therein.'"

Phillips's inflection rose, for dramatic effect and lack of air, as he reached the climax of this periodic masterpiece. Catching his breath, he gave me a look and laughed.

"I guess that means he's out," he said.

Phillips was in the process of planning for the upcoming summer season. "We've got to change the orientation," he told me. "We need to hire trainers who are there because they are committed to the cause. And we've got to get the burn rate down."

In the McCaw era, nothing was ever done on the cheap, and the burn rate had been conflagratory. Occasionally Phillips, as a member of the Ocean Futures board, had suggested that the Keiko project make use of programs like MARMAM, in which university graduates serve as interns for three or four months of marine-mammal research, gaining field experience—young scholars willing to go anywhere in exchange for a sleeping bag and a small research stipend—but these suggestions had been waved off. Student volunteers had not been the McCaw style. In the new era that Phillips was inaugurating now, there would be no figurehead like Jean-Michel Cousteau, drawing a quarter-million-dollar salary for token work. The new cadre of trainers, people truly committed to the release of the whale, would be smaller. They would be poorer, as well. "The staff had a very, very sweet gig," Phillips said of the old cadre. "They worked one month on, one month off. They got paid vacations every time they traveled out of Iceland, plus per diem, plus free housing, plus a retirement contribution. The whole package was around a hundred thousand dollars per trainer for six months of work."

Throughout the McCaw years, Phillips often wondered whether the project might not have accomplished more, and done it faster, had it had access to smaller piles of cash. He would now have the opportunity to find out.

The plan taking shape for the coming summer would allow Keiko one last chance to join a Westman Island pod. If this did not happen—if the whale had not thrown in his lot with wild orcas by August of 2002—he would be moved somewhere else. In the brutal winters of the Westmans, the burn rate was horrendous, and the new bare-bones budget could not survive another cold season. Some milder bay in Iceland would have to be found for Keiko.

At the top of the list of alternative sites was the town of Stykkishólmur, the largest village on the Snaefellsnes Peninsula, at the entrance to Hvammsfjördur, in west central Iceland. I knew the Snaefellsnes Peninsula, having driven its shoreline two years before, and my understanding was that the weather there is notoriously bad, but Keiko's people, I presumed, had researched the meteorology. Keiko would quickly feel at home, for the little subpeninsula on which Stykkishólmur stands is shaped eerily like the Island of Heimaey. There is a Helgafell, a "Holy Mountain," in the same spot in both places, and both have an offshore island called Ellidaey. West of Stykkishólmur, at the tip of the Snaefellsnes Peninsula, is the volcano Snaefells, capped by the glacier Snaefellsjókull. It was into this glacial volcano that Jules Verne sent his Professor Hardwigg in *Journey to the Center of the Earth.*

In Stykkishólmur the Keiko project would be a mom-and-pop operation. There was a biological research station in the town, with two resident geneticists. Charles Vinick of Ocean Futures, in first describing the Stykkishólmur option to Phillips, said that the geneticists specialized in minkes—or so Phillips understood. Minke whales! he thought. It was nearly perfect. Mom and Pop would be a pair of cetologists.

"Cool!" he said. "They already work on marine mammals."

"No, no, no," said Vinick. "Minks, not minkes."

The Stykkishólmur pair were not cetologists, then, but they were good people, by all reports. Phillips, probing a bit, got the sense that both were entirely behind the goal of release. The Stykkishólmur harbor would be a place where Keiko could come and go as he chose. There might not even be a net. He could be trained to forage on his own, and if pickings were slim, he could come back for food. There was talk of an underwater device by which he could self-dispense his own herring. He would be free to wander in ever-widening circles out into the Denmark Strait, which divides Iceland from Greenland. Eventually, perhaps, he would resolve his identity crisis, adapt to orca life, and never come back. The human scale of the Stykkishólmur solution, after all the millions spent by McCaw, appealed to Phillips. The geneticists would divide their time between their mink hutches and Keiko's dock. The whale's field staff would be reduced finally to just these two.

THE KEIKO PROJECT WAS LIKE a stage, as Phillips had observed. Craig McCaw, who had once challenged his dyslexia by memorizing long passages of *Macbeth,* had seen Birnam Wood advancing toward him in the form of angry creditors and stockholders. In making his exit, he was joining a long procession.

Jason James Richter, who played Jesse in the Willy movies, did not leave the stage so much as depart the cinema. He had a few roles after the Willy sequels, and still had a fan club with a website, but did not appear to be one of those child actors who make the transition. He joined a rock band.

Richard Donner, producer of *Free Willy,* took leave of whales, ending his orca period. After *Free Willy 3,* he made *Lethal Weapon 4,* and *Made Men,* and *Any Given Sunday,* and *X-Men.*

August Schellenberg, who played Randolph, the wise Haida Indian of the Willy movies, found work in television movies, playing a character named Fierce Crow in *Scattering Dad,* and Young Dog in *Out of Time,* and Antonio in *High Noon,* and Sitting Bull in *Crazy Horse.* He remembered his Willy gigs fondly. The two movies in his career he liked best, he would tell an interviewer, were *Black Robe* and *Free Willy.*

Phyllis Bell, the executive director of the Oregon Coast Aquarium, was placed on involuntary administrative leave by her board of directors on June 24, 2002, and the next week she submitted her resignation. Bell told *The Oregonian* that her departure had nothing to do with her health but refused to say more. "I just resigned for personal reasons. That's all," she said. The board of directors, too, was closemouthed. The community of Newport and the reporters of Oregon were forced to cast about for explanations. They noted that Bell's bitter public fight with the Free Willy Keiko Foundation over care of the whale had not helped her reputation, and that departing employees complained of low morale and Bell's authoritarian management. The aquarium had chronic cash-flow problems. Attendance had fallen off after Keiko's departure. Bell had been three to four months behind in payments to a number of vendors, and the aquarium had been forced to restructure its debt. Bell's conversion of Keiko's tank to a "Passages of the Deep" exhibit, with its two-hundred-foot tube through an artificial microcosm of the ocean, had been a gamble. Passages of the Deep had boosted slipping attendance a bit, but its estimated cost of $6.9 million had ballooned to a reported $8.8 million.

At the end of July the truth came out. The real cost of the conversion had been $11 million. Bell had hidden the excess from her board and had applied for an unauthorized $2 million loan to cover it. Another $1 million bank loan had been booked as a contribution, and aquarium officials found $600,000 in unpaid vendor bills. Bell had even stiffed Keiko himself. From the sale of Keiko merchandise at the aquarium, she owed $200,000 in royalties to Keiko's foundation, which had been paying the whale's rent in Iceland. The aquarium defaulted on $14 million in revenue bonds and defaulted in its debt to the whale. Bell pleaded guilty to a felony forgery charge and was sentenced to community service and eight days in jail.

Jean-Michel Cousteau's two Keiko documentaries, *Born to be Wild* and *Gate to Freedom,* never sold to television. They were not as bad as many Keiko people think, but it was clear that Cousteau did not inherit his father's gift for film.

Prime Minister David Oddsson, Keiko's political godfather in Iceland, announced, after a trip to Japan, that he would support a resumption of whaling. After years of quiet opposition to whaling in Iceland, and after the political bravery of inviting Keiko to his country, Oddsson reversed course. Japan, relentless in its attempts to pack the International Whaling Commission, is imaginative in its inducements to small island nations to come over to the whaling side. With Oddsson's defection, David Phillip's domino theory—his hope that Keiko might tip Iceland away from whaling, and that Iceland might tip Norway, then Russia, and so on—seemed dead in the water.

Dianne Hammond, Keiko's former spokeswoman, moved with her husband, Nolan Harvey, the whale's former head trainer, to Bend, Oregon, where the couple started a business building websites. In the winter of 2001, Hammond picked up an unfinished novel she had begun in 1994, before Keiko took over her life. She could not remember the names of all the characters. When she reintroduced herself to them, they forgave her for having abandoned them and allowed her to set them in motion again. In sixth months she finished, and Doubleday published *Going to Bend*.

Jeff Foster, on separating from the Keiko project, returned to his old line of work. Renouncing Iceland, he set about capturing wild dolphins again, first for the "swim-with" programs on resort islands of the Caribbean, then for Burmese resorts in the Bay of Bengal—places free from the constraints of the Marine Mammal Protection Act. He supervised the capture of wild bottlenose dolphins, then trained them to interact with resort patrons. Where his goal in training Keiko, in theory at least, was dehabituation to humans and eventual release, his goal in the Caribbean and Burma was capture and habituation—the Keiko project in reverse. His new work was more in line with his past experience and natural inclinations.

As OLD HANDS LEFT THE stage, new hands made their entrances. The Icelander Thorbjörg Kristjandóttir, "Tobba" to her friends, signed on just as Ocean Futures was dissolving and the Free Willy Keiko Foundation was returning to life. Kristjandóttir, who had never worked in the captive-whale industry, was the kind of handler the new regime wanted. She was thirty-one, a big, hearty, rosy-cheeked zookeeper who, for convenience in working with the whale, wore her blond hair in pigtails. She had grown up in the country an hour outside Reykjavík, not far from the town of Borgarnes.

"I am born on a farm," Tobba says of her background. "I have all my life been around animals. I have this nature sickness. I just really, really love animals. It was a tough time for me, when I was studying in the university in Reykjavík. Especially in the beginning, I felt I just can't breathe in the city. I just had to go out of Reykjavík every weekend and go home to get this mooshy mooshy thing."

The mooshy mooshy thing was communion with the horses, cows, sheep, dogs, cats, and chickens of the family homestead. Tobba had Icelandic horses of her own, Blakkur, an aging black animal of fine character, and Dryri, a roan. In the endless daylight and good pasture of summer, she put her horses through their paces. A mounted Icelandic schoolgirl, like the horsemen of Genghis Khan, has a string of remounts, and like those Mongol riders she has five gears for her steed: *Fet,* the walk. *Brokk,* the trot. *Stökk,* the gallop. *Skeid,* the pace. *Tölt,* the running walk. This fifth gear, *tölt,* is a fine thing to see, and even finer to feel. The tireless, quick-stepping little Icelandic horse glides along so level and smooth that if the rider closes her eyes she scarcely knows she is moving. Tobba played in the fortresslike barns in which Iceland's farm animals withstand the long siege of the cold season. The round baler has since come to Iceland, but the bales of her youth were square. Inside the fortresses of the barns, with those golden building blocks, she built fortresses of hay.

At university, she majored in animal behavior, got her degree in biology, and went straight to work at the Reykjavík zoo. "That kind of calmed my country girl a little bit," she says. She became head of the zoo's education department. One surprise of Reykjavík for Tobba was the estrangement of the city's children from rural life. There is little suburban sprawl in Iceland—the countryside begins abruptly at Reykjavík's outskirts—yet the children did not know where meat and milk came from. Tobba's guiding concern as an educator was to put them back in touch with their roots.

In 1998, when Keiko first came to Iceland, Tobba had led a zoo excursion to the Westmans to meet the whale. In the alternating cycle of training philosophies for Keiko—hands on, hands off—this was a hands-on period, with the staff playing in the water with the whale. The sessions were like performances, and the zoo delegation went home much impressed. Three years later, when Tobba's application for work on the bay pen was accepted, she took out her photo album, looked through her pictures of that visit, thought, *Oh my God, I'm going to work with this animal!*

In her first training sessions, Tobba wondered how she could ever control a creature so big. She was lucky, she says, in apprenticing with trainers who had been working for years with the whale—men and women who alerted her to Keiko's various strategies for hazing newcomers. Tobba had worked all her life with animals, and she had a degree in animal behavior. She was never one of those novices whom Keiko could simply ignore. As initiations by Keiko went, hers was not particularly rough.

"Of course it takes time for him to know you," she says. "He's very curious, you know, in new faces and new people. He paid a lot of attention at first, looking at me and trying to figure me out. So it came step by step. Of course he tries to push you to the edge. You just have to be focused. You have to think, Okay, I'm new at this. It's like when you're teaching. You can't enter the classroom, say, 'Hello!' and be extremely nice, because kids just eat you up. You have to be tough in the beginning. And then start loosening up.

"He is not very different from horses or dogs. You just have to figure, Okay, he's behaving like this, what is he trying to tell me? All animals are like that. Horses! Horses must see you as the leader. Because as soon as the horse sees you are a weak person, then he gets dominant over you, and you start having all kinds of problems. It is more challenging with the whale, because he's always trying to figure out what he can get away with. I'm always trying to be smarter than Keiko, and he is trying to be smarter than me."

When I proposed to Tobba that whales have inexpressive faces, she reluctantly agreed, but argued that it hardly mattered, as Keiko's body language was eloquent and became easier and easier to read. "Sometimes he's in such a good mood!" she said. "That's when he starts playing with his tongue." To my contention that the eyes of whales are unreadable, she took exception. "If he is very upset, you can see red. There is a redness in the whites of a killer whale's eyes, and when he is upset, he opens his eyes wide."

In May, a Canadian named Colin Baird joined the staff, moving into the role Jeff Foster had vacated. Baird was called "whale lead" or "director of the field team." His record was not spotless—he had worked as a killer-whale trainer at Sealand Victoria—but he had also done field research on wild orcas. On the one hand, Baird knew Tillicum, the homicidal captive orca who first killed at Sealand Victoria. On the other, he was acquainted with the wild orcas of the Southern Resident Population of the Pacific Northwest, which cruise the waters just off the tank where Tillicum had drowned his trainer.

Baird is a short, intense, handsome man. His hair is dark, and he is generally dark skinned, too, for he works outdoors in sunlight reflecting off water, yet out of this general swarthiness stare eyes of a startling pale blue. Around his neck in Iceland, on a lanyard, he always wore a pipe whistle. This badge of office might have come off in the shower, or in bed, but never after his alarm clock woke him in the morning.

"Tillicum was no problem, a real gentle guy, as far as I'm concerned," he says. "But Nootka. Nootka, I didn't get along with very well." Baird believes that the death of Tillicum's trainer, a woman he knew, was unintended. "Nothing malicious," he says. He believes that Tillicum just needed better instruction that trainers are not toys. The young woman slipped into the pool, he says, and Tillicum carried her around underwater. As soon as she went limp, Tillicum and the other orcas pushed her to the surface.

"When you're in the business, you have to talk the talk," Baird says of his time at Sealand, and some of that talk he continues to believe. He is convinced that captive dolphins—killer whales in particular—have been important in changing public consciousness about whales and the health of the seas, yet he began to have philosophical doubts about captivity even as he worked in the industry. In 1994, after Sealand Victoria closed, he became a naturalist on the ferry up the Inside Passage, saw wild cetaceans every day, and realized that these creatures were supposed to be free.

The Southern Resident orcas, which Baird came to know nearly as well as the captives he had fed at Sealand, occupy the waters between Puget Sound and Campbell River on the Strait of Georgia. No population of killer whales suffered more in the era when capture of marine mammals was legal in the United States. Between 1965 and 1975, forty-five members of this small nation of orcas were captured and delivered to marine parks around the world. Thirteen were killed during capture. Of the forty-five captured, only one is still alive: Lolita, now about thirty-eight, the oldest killer whale in captivity. With the ban on capture, the Southern Residents rebounded, and today they number eighty-five in three pods. Colin Baird, like other orca researchers in the field, learned to recognize the different pods by peculiarities in the dorsal fins and markings of individual members. The largest, L Pod, has forty-one whales, with two mature males, five "sprouter" males, and sixteen juveniles. K Pod has twenty members. Its grande dame, designated K7, is thought to be in her early eighties. J Pod has twenty-two members, and its grande dame, J2, is herself an octogenarian. J Pod's only mature male, J1, is estimated to be about fifty-two, twice the age that any male orca has ever achieved in captivity.

"This group where I come from, the Southern Residents of Vancouver Island, are the most studied population in the world," Baird says. "I'm used to knowing that there's so many in this pod, and so many in that one. This whale is two years old, and that one is five. In Iceland it's not like that. There had been a little research in the early nineties in Iceland, but there was a real lack of information."

Colin Baird's job, on arriving in Iceland in May, was to make good on the project's last chance to integrate Keiko with the unlettered pods and unnamed whales that summer in Iceland's waters. The big challenge for Baird and his team was to prepare for the summer fieldwork with a diminished staff—now reduced to nine and dropping—and with a gutted budget.

"We started wondering how are we going to have the walking season this summer," says Tobba Kristjandóttir. "The summer before, they had this huge vessel and the helicopter to walk Keiko. Now there was not enough money for that. How are we going to walk him? How can we do it in a secure way? Are we taking a chance, where we just lose Keiko?"

Walking Keiko securely required that he be fitted with a satellite tag and a VHF radio tag. The first would report his approximate position from outer space, and the second would allow a tracking boat to locate him exactly. Problems arose in the fabrication of a new satellite tag, and it was still unfinished as the spring migration of orcas reached the Westmans. Pods were seen aggregating in their usual feeding grounds off the Isle of Surtsey and around the sea stacks called the Pinnacles, seven miles west of Heimaey. Every day counted, if Keiko was to succeed in this, his last chance to unite with Westman whales, but the walk season was delayed. A mold had to be made of his dorsal fin to fit the transmitter to it. Here Jeff Foster was sorely missed, for it was at this interface of whale and technology that Foster was especially deft. Dr. Cornell was persuaded to fly to Iceland to do the job, eventually, but the tag was not ready until July.

On July 6, the satellite and VHF tags were attached to Keiko's dorsal fin. He left his cove for a short shakedown cruise to test the VHF tracking system and the communications gear on the boats. Everything worked. The next day, Sunday, July 7, Keiko and his fleet headed toward the Pinnacles on his first real walk of the season. The boats were *Daniel*, Keiko's forty-foot walk boat for the past two years, and *Heppni*, a twenty-foot open-decked vessel used for transfers, and a new addition, *Vamos*, a thirty-six-foot sailboat whose owner had sailed in from the Faroes and volunteered his services.

The fleet fanned out to reconnoiter ahead, and a couple of miles short of the Pinnacles, both *Heppni* and *Vamos* encountered orcas. The walk boat, *Daniel*, directed Keiko to the spot, and for four hours the boats drifted in the midst of whales. The aggregation was scattered, here a pod of six, there a pod of eight. Keiko ventured tentatively off in all directions, scouting. He and the whales seemed to keep at least a fifty-meter interval between them.

"That first day, he was not going straight out to the wild whales right away," says Tobba. "He had to get used to them all over again. He didn't back off. He was just out there looking."

The team saw no contact between Keiko and the other orcas on the surface, but they had no way of telling what was happening below. On several occasions they saw Keiko swimming rapidly through a patch of ocean where the fluke "prints" of another whale were appearing on the surface. It seemed to the crew that Keiko, once again, despite nine months of wintering alone in Klettsvík Cove, was picking up the thread of his socialization where he had left off the summer before. *Heppni* transferred most of the team ashore, but the sailboat *Vamos*, with the VHF antennae mounted on her mast, tracked

Keiko through the night—or through the endless twilight that passes for night in Iceland in July—and Colin Baird, Tobba Kristjandóttir, and Michael Parks spent the night in *Daniel*. In the early morning of July 8, Keiko swam away from *Daniel* toward whales. The two remaining boats followed at a distance, observing him from one and two miles away.

"On that second day, this little group of killer whales came up, and this young male approached," Tobba remembers. "He was just face-to-face with Keiko, for quite some time. And then they kind of sank. There was so much checking one another out! Then they came up again, and they were on the surface together for a while. Finally this wild whale went back to his group. We started following them. It is just so great to see all these wild whales, and to see Keiko with them, a little bit like a shy kid."

Keiko spent the next three weeks in the company of whales. In the daytime he was usually observed near large aggregations of killer-whale pods as they fed on shoals of spawning herring. In the evening he and the other whales made long swims to the west and south of the Westman Islands. Keiko and the whales sometimes swam sixty miles in a night, and on one night he logged one hundred miles with them.

"In the nighttime, they travel a lot, but in the day they're just relaxing, feeding, and we don't have to be so much on the move," says Tobba. She went out once on the sailboat, but spent most of her time on *Daniel*. "We just tried to be near the wild whales as much as we could. If he was just wandering away by himself—just off somewhere—that was not something we wanted. Because he learned so much by being with the wild whales. He learns much more than just by being out there alone. When Keiko was comfortable enough, he just swam toward the wild whales. Then we would drift back slowly, and when we were far enough away, we would start the engine and go back home."

There was no way to make an accurate count of the whales in the feeding aggregations. The orcas were underwater most of the time. A pod that surfaced to blow astern, when it surfaced again to port or starboard, might be the same pod or a different one. The team estimated as many as ninety to one hundred whales on some days. They began to recognize different pods from conspicuous markings on certain members, and they bestowed individual names. There was Z-fin, a bull whose dorsal fin curved laterally in a couple of directions. There were Benny and Q. One bull had a bent fin just like Keiko's. They distinguished him from their own whale by his lack of adornment—no yellow satellite and VHF tags on his dorsal. One day Keiko showed up with conspicuous marks of his own, his back raked by the teeth of a killer whale. Many other males had these scratches, inflicted by females most likely, in the opinion of the scientists the team consulted.

In the chaos of the feeding frenzy, with whales blowing and diving all around, it was hard to keep track of Keiko.

"Gannets were diving all over the shop," says Baird. "It was full-on craziness. Herring were floating up to the surface. Stunned by tail slaps, probably. We were picking up herring by hand. And the hydrophones were just going mad. We had to turn it down. All kinds of vocalizations—and the echolocations! The sea was just alive with chatter. We had to turn the thing down all the time. Gannets would see something from fifty feet high and dive like rocket ships. Put your head underwater, and you'd see these bubble-bullets of gannets going down."

"And Keiko didn't look peripheral to you?" I asked.

"Well, there were occasions where he was sort of sitting back and watching. Taking this all in. You only had to turn on the hydrophones to wonder what was going through his head. He must have been thinking, Whaa? The sound of it is incredible. He wasn't as active as the others, sounding and diving and feeding, but he certainly didn't disappear. You'd see him in amongst them."

"No sign of them giving him the brush?"

"No. There were too many unrelated groups out there. He was just another animal in the mix. If there had been just one pod out there feeding, they might have wondered, Who is this other animal? But there were so many groups."

IN THE END, THE WALK boat, *Daniel,* whose engine sound Keiko knew well, was called off the chase for good, leaving the field to the silent sailboat *Vamos.*

"A wreck," Lanny Cornell once told me of this vessel.

The veterinarian's judgments can be harsh, and he had never traveled on *Vamos.* I was curious about the opinions of people who had actually put in time before her mast and the VHF antenna mounted there.

"*Vamos* was a . . . colorful boat?" I asked Colin Baird.

"Ah, it was rustic," he answered. "It certainly could use a woman's touch—let's put it that way. The head was a bucket on the floor in the toilet. He had things tucked in every nook and cranny, under floorboards. If you needed to find anything, he had to get it."

The man who knew the nooks and crannies was the owner and master, a middle-aged fisherman, Adam, who had spent much of his career crabbing in the Bering Sea. "As salty as they come," Baird testified. "He had single-handed the boat from Ireland to the Faroe Islands, and then had single-handed to Iceland."

I suggested to Baird that *Vamos,* after the gold-plated whale-walking of the McCaw era, must have been a letdown—a cluttered little sailboat with a bucket for a head. Baird seemed puzzled by the notion.

"Was she seaworthy?" I asked.

"Seaworthy?" Baird replied. He raised an eyebrow, surprised at how far I had sailed off course. "Oh, she was a great boat. She was a Colin Archer. She was especially good for the seas we were in, with the double-ended hull. She probably was the best vessel for what we were doing, with the least impact on the whales. She was quiet. She wasn't running a big diesel engine, like the walk boats. She was a good viewing platform, and she was good for sailing multiple days."

Colin Archer was a marine architect born in 1832 to Scottish parents in Norway. He built his boats on the "wave-line principle" developed by the British engineer John Scott, who held that a boat's hull should be shaped to meet the peculiarities of both the bow wave and the stern wave. Safety was Colin Archer's guiding principle, and his boats are hard to sink. By the time the shipwright died, at eighty-nine, he had built more than two hundred vessels, fashioning them so soundly and safely that a good number are still afloat. In 1871 he built *Thor,* prototype for the modern pilot boat. In 1893 he built the rescue cutter *RSI Colin Archer,* savior of sixty-seven ships and prototype for every Norwegian rescue cutter built for the next thirty years. Colin Archer built the *Fram,* the polar ship in which the Norwegian explorer and Nobel laureate Fridtjof Nansen sailed for the North Pole, and in which another Norwegian, Roald Amundsen, sailed to the Antarctic for his conquest of the South Pole. Colin Archer built the thirty-six-footer now called *Vamos,* the immortal little sailboat that would shadow the killer whale Keiko as he himself shadowed the orcas of southern Iceland.

"*Vamos* was keeping up?" I asked Baird.

"It was keeping up," he said. "The whales would head out, they'd leave the feeding grounds, for six, eight, ten, twelve hours, and then they would come back. It was staggered. All ninety whales didn't leave and return together. Keiko had certain groups that he was more closely associated with, and he'd go with those. That was the standard procedure: They'd take off at night, do a circle, and come back to the feeding grounds all day long at the Pinnacles. *Vamos* was keeping up. I mean, if the whales were really marching through the night on one of these great, long circles—sometimes it was an eighty-mile circle—and if *Vamos* was beating upwind, then she might have trouble. In that case they'd click on the engine and away they'd go."

The little Colin Archer was a fine symbol for the new approach of the Keiko project. It sailed silent, where the helicopters it replaced had clattered after whales with a great whopping of rotors. It sailed free, where the helicopters had cost thousands of dollars each day. It was built by a contemporary of Herman Melville. It became an honorary orca, circling with the whales and never going ashore. The skipper, who slept about five hours a week, by the estimate of Colin Baird, was happy to help in exchange for food, coffee, fuel, and some expense money.

As a rule, *Vamos* kept her distance from the whales, but occasionally the team tried to move in close to get stills and videotape of Keiko's interaction with his kin. That job done, *Vamos* quickly backed off, but sometimes the vamoose of *Vamos* was not quick enough, and the whale noticed.

"We didn't want him to get too much attention from people on the boat," Baird says. "So the term became *busted*. You got 'busted by Keiko.' If you got busted on *Vamos,* the drill was for everybody to run below and keep quiet. Especially anyone with a camera, because . . ."

Baird looked over his shoulder, as if for eavesdroppers, then continued sotto voce.

". . . because he kind of likes the camera. He likes people and attention. So, anyway, we all crawled below. The skipper of the boat, he was so funny. He'd say, 'I can't believe I'm hiding from a damn killer whale on my own damn boat!' He'd peek up. Finally he'd say, 'Okay, he's gone.' "

One night, two weeks into Keiko's time at sea, *Vamos* beat up the east coast of Heimaey Island into the wind, tracking the whale as he followed a group of orcas northward from the feeding grounds. The boat fell behind as she fought upwind. Fernando Ugarte, a staff member from Mexico, called from *Vamos* and asked if the staff ashore could track the whale from land. Colin Baird and his shorebound colleagues tossed a set of telemetry gear into the truck. The signal was clearly coming from their left—the east coast. They drove eastward, then around the island's rimming road counterclockwise, from headland to headland, holding the antennae to the wind. The *beep beep beep* of Keiko's signal was steady from the left, even as they turned the circle, so that soon the signal was coming from the west—the direction of the North Rocks. Baird was puzzled. The signal, he knew, was prone to bouncing around off the cliffs of the North Rocks; perhaps this reading was some sort of VHF ventriloquism. The *beep beep beep* suggested that Keiko and his whales were in Heimaey Harbor or in the sea outside, beyond the rampart of the North Rocks.

"It seems like it's coming from inside the harbor," he radioed *Vamos*.

"Check the bay pen!" Fernando Ugarte answered from the boat.

Baird and his buddies jumped in the truck and drove to the overlook above the harbor strait. They parked the truck, and Baird was raising the antenna when he saw Keiko spy-hop beside the wet house. Baird let the antenna drop. The gate to the barrier net had been left open. Keiko had swum through the gate into the cove, and then into the bay pen.

"The whales literally went right past his driveway," Baird says. "He just ducked in. He spy-hopped to see who was there on the pen. 'Where is everybody?' For us, it was quite fortuitous. It enabled us to go down and get some 'bloods.' The first thing we did, before we fed him or anything, was try to get a stomach sample, to see if he'd been feeding."

Once before that year, working on *Heppni* at sea, Baird and a colleague had used the stomach tube. On that occasion they had been carrying no fish to feed Keiko as reinforcement; they simply showed him the tube and he obliged, opening wide and allowing them to insinuate the thing. Keiko obliged again on his visit to the sea pen, but the results were inconclusive. The next day, first thing in the morning, Keiko swam out through the gate in the barrier net again. *Daniel* escorted him into the vicinity of orcas, and he left the boat behind. *Daniel* was recalled to harbor, and *Vamos* took over once more. Keiko resumed his life with the whales, and he would never return to the bay pen again.

BOOK FOUR
NORWAY

36

NORWEGIAN SEA

AT THE END OF JULY 2002, A STORM BLEW INTO THE WESTMAN ISLANDS, driving the tracking boat *Vamos* into harbor. On July 29, as the waves steepened, the sailboat's crew had a last glimpse of Keiko, who was in the company of wild whales, then the weather closed in and the boat was forced to shore. When the storm cleared and *Vamos* went out again, Keiko had moved off twenty-five miles, according to his satellite signal. *Vamos* sailed to the spot, but by the time the boat arrived Keiko had moved off another fifty miles. The next time the satellite reported its daily fix on him, he had moved another seventy miles. It was a game of satellite tag that the sailboat was losing badly.

"Have you heard the news about the boy?" David Phillips asked me, smiling broadly, in early August. We had met outside a restaurant on San Francisco Bay. I was uncertain which boy Phillips meant. He had a two-year-old son, Cole, very smart, the life of every party, already some sort of Lothario, a magnet for every passing woman between eight years old and eighty. But he also had a twenty-five-year-old killer whale, Keiko, often called "the boy" by his intimates.

"Basically, he's gone," Phillips said. "He just took off. He is moving east at a fairly good clip. Fifty miles a day. Seventy miles a day. Thirty miles. Forty. East, east, east."

It was Keiko then, not Cole, who had made his getaway.

A reconnaissance plane flew eastward from the Westmans to see if it could spot Keiko before he left Iceland's territorial waters. In the area of his most recent satellite coordinates, the plane, flying a search pattern, saw large numbers of white-beaked dolphins, and big pods of pilot whales, and some humpback whales, but no Keiko or any other orcas. Keiko continued to transmit from both his satellite tags. One, the tag that signaled his geographic position daily, showed steady progress east. The other tag collected dive information—frequency, duration, and depth—sending the data up in bursts to the satellite when Keiko's dorsal fin was above the surface. Keiko was diving often and deeper than ever before, with many dives between 75 and 150 feet, and some between 150 and 230. On August 16, he seems to have been chasing something, for he dived to a depth of between 250 and

330 feet. He had been last seen with wild orcas, and it seemed likely that he had set out in their company, but there was no way to know whether he was still traveling with them.

Keiko had escaped all human monitoring, except for the eye of the satellite and the empathetic radar of animal communicators.

In early August of 2002, reports that Keiko was swimming free in the ocean reached Bonnie Norton and another animal communicator, Mary Getten. The news came through the conventional, non-paranormal media. In slipping away from humanity, the whale had neglected to communicate his adventure telepathically to the two women himself. Both Norton and Getten were surprised by Keiko's decision for the open sea, as he had made it abundantly clear, in many communications with both women, that he loved his handlers and preferred humanity to the wild. On August 8 and 9, Norton and Mary Getten communicated with Keiko as he plied the Norwegian Sea.

"I asked Keiko, 'How are you doing?'" Norton would report. "Keiko said, 'If the people won't come to me, I will go to the people.' Skeptical how he might do that, I asked, 'How would you go to the people if you are in the water?' Keiko replied, 'I haven't completely figured it out yet, but staying at my home isn't working either. If I stay in my pen I receive little or no recognition.'"

Keiko steamed steadily eastward six hundred miles, until he reached the Faroe Islands.

The Faroes are not such a wonderful destination for a whale. A traditional drive fishery in the archipelago takes about a thousand pilot whales a year, and those whales account for 30 percent of the meat consumed by the islanders. Faroes means "Sheep Islands" in Danish, and the name is appropriate, but the islands could as easily have been named for *grindahvalur,* the Faroese word for pilot whale. Ten years before Keiko reached the Faroes, one of Keiko's people, Katherine Hanly, had been forced to flee the islands after filming the red seas of this slaughter. Killer whales are cousins of the pilot whales, yet temperamentally different, not given to the fatal cohesiveness that makes a drive fishery possible; still it seemed unfortunate politically, this beeline for the Faroes.

Charles Vinick and Colin Baird flew to the Faroes with tracking gear. They hoped for a sighting, just a glimpse to see if their whale was in good condition and accompanied by other orcas. The two men went undercover, so as to keep Keiko's course secret and avert a media invasion of the archipelago. Shortly after they reached the islands, *Vamos* arrived in the Faroes with more tracking gear, and the two Keiko teams joined forces. They identified themselves as whale researchers who wanted to see a group of approaching whales, one of which they had radio-tagged. This was not exactly a lie, it was a version of the truth, and it played well in the Faroes, where whale research, in the form of catch data, goes back to 1584, with unbroken documentation since 1709. "The first morning we were fine," says Colin Baird. "No one was on to us. We stopped at a couple of marinas and checked with charter boats. No luck there. Then we went to the coast guard to see if they knew of any vessels of the appropriate size. They said, 'Well, *we* can take you.'"

A Faroese coast-guard ship, it happened, was to leave that evening on patrol. The captain led Keiko's people to their cabins, passed them their bedding, showed them where to stow their gear, and offered suggestions as to where they mount the four antennae of the VHF tracking system. He advised them to be back at the ship by five, sailing time. Keiko's undercover agents were stunned by this hospitality and their own good fortune. In fact it was too good to be true. At four in the afternoon, when Baird and Vinick returned to the ship, the captain informed them that the voyage was off. On coming into harbor, the ship had hit a rock, bending a propeller blade and damaging the rudder. She was headed now to dry-dock. The two agents of Keiko dismounted their antennae and offloaded their gear. Keiko was now passing 180 miles north of the Faroes. The window of opportunity to intercept him was closing fast.

"We went back to the coast guard and asked if they had any other suggestions," says Baird. "They said, 'Oh! We have our other ship that we can bring in and pick you up.' So they sent in this ship, *Brimil,* that was only eighteen months in the water. It was brand-new, built in Denmark, this huge sixty-meter coast-guard ship. Fancy. State of the art. We loaded all our gear on there. 'Here's your cabin, and here's the dining room.' It was just incredible."

Brimil took Vinick and Baird to within sixty miles of Keiko's last daily position. Baird stationed himself, with a satellite phone, in a glassed-in crow's nest above the bridge, waiting for Keiko's daily satellite position to come in. Then their good luck turned bad again. The ship had to stop for a fisheries inspection.

"That was their mission," Baird points out. "We were just along for the ride. Well, the fishing boat they stopped was fishing without a license. A big boat, a one-hundred-twenty-footer, out there fishing without a license. So this took some hours for them to process, and send the skiff back and forth, and confiscate the gear, and have the fishing boat sent back to harbor. So we got delayed. We had got Keiko's position. We knew where he was. We needed to get to that position pretty quick. The sooner we get to Keiko's last known position, the better chance we have of finding his VHF signal, which is how we locate him exactly. The opportunity was slowly passing us by. And then they got a call for a rescue. A boat had run over its own nets, just south of the Faroes, which was one hundred fifteen miles from where we were, in the complete opposite direction. We were so disappointed. We were so close."

Brimil steamed back toward the Faroese capital, Thórshavn, on the island of Strömö. She pulled up alongside the dock, and the crew, without bothering to put out mooring lines, offloaded Keiko's team and their gear, then steamed away south. Baird and his colleagues, bumped now from their second ship, began to think that someone, the gods or the fates or the Faroese, did not want them to see the whale. In the streets of Thórshavn they discovered that their cover was blown. "Oh, you're the ones looking for Keiko?" citizens greeted them wherever they went in the capital. They had been on the noon news in the Faroes. Someone in Iceland had tipped off the Faroese press.

Baird hired a helicopter in Strömö and overflew Keiko's latest satellite position. The North Atlantic was stormy, as usual, and they could not spot Keiko or any other whales. "It's easy to miss a whale in a six-foot sea, with the wind blowing forty or fifty," Baird says. "The problem is, every whitecap that spills over draws your attention. You can't do it." They flew back to Strömö. Keiko passed out of range, leaving the Faroes and continuing on his mission east.

Charles Vinick and his party had flown to the Faroes on their own authority. When David Phillips of the Free Willy Keiko Foundation and Paul Irwin of the Humane Society, who together controlled the Keiko project in its new incarnation, learned that Charles Vinick was in the Faroes, they recalled him. Vinick was the last management holdover from the previous regime, and his new bosses were afraid he would give in to an old habit and try to reel Keiko in. They told Vinick they did not want staff chasing Keiko around in boats, and they instructed him to return to Iceland.

Keiko, as was his custom, swam into controversy. On August 21, 2002, Jeff Foster, the former field director of the Keiko project, along with seven of the whale's former trainers—Brian O'Neill, Stephen Claussen, Jennifer Schorr, Greg Schorr, Jim Horton, Tracy, and Steve Sinelli—wrote a letter to Dr. Robert Martin of the U.S. Marine Mammal Commission:

> It has recently been brought to our attention that Keiko has left the Vestmannaeyjar area and Icelandic waters and has traveled more than 300 miles toward the Faroe Islands, where he is currently somewhere offshore. No other free-ranging killer whales were sighted in the area of the signal. The distance from Vestmannaeyjar and potential solitude of the animal represents a serious concern for the ongoing reintroduction effort and the long-term safety of the animal. In our opinion, the ability to intervene using the "walk" boat and return Keiko to the bay pen enclosure has been critical in the past. In order to ensure the safety and well-being of the animal, we feel it is necessary to closely monitor his behavior and have the ability to intervene if necessary.

The Foster letter expressed concern that Keiko had not demonstrated an ability to forage in the wild. Foster took his worries to the press in Seattle, where he now lived. "SOME CONCERNED THAT KEIKO'S A BIT TOO 'FREE,'" ran a *Seattle Times* headline, over a story by its science reporter Eric Sorenson. "The problem is if he goes out there and can't fend for himself, he's going to gradually starve to death," Foster told Sorenson. "That would be in my opinion very inhumane. I think it's too big a gamble to assume that he's doing well, especially when we don't know." Without that visual observation, it's so difficult to say what's happening with this animal."

Naomi Rose, a marine-mammal scientist with the Humane Society, responded, pointing out that data from the satellite transmitter on Keiko's dorsal fin showed he was traveling long distances and diving routinely to considerable depths—indications that he was feeding. "If he wasn't feeding, then he was doing something very energy-intensive for no reason," she said. Bob Ratliffe, the McCaw lieutenant, told the paper that he, too, was confident that the whale was eating. He suggested that the problem was not with the whale, but with the trainers. "Keiko may have done a better job of pulling away from them than they've done of pulling away from him," Ratliffe said.

"Jeff Foster has been saying we should catch him, stick a tube down his stomach, and see if he's been eating," David Phillips told me. "I'm thinking, *Are you crazy?*"

The Foster letter to the Marine Mammal Commission does indicate a kind of craziness. Jeff Foster thought his concerns were normal, but so does the sweetly deranged, doting mother who shows up at her son's dorm room with mop and bucket and cheerfully announces that she is moving in. The time comes when you have to let them go. Foster and his seven colleagues just did not get it. "We certainly hope that our concerns are unfounded and the progress by Keiko towards reintroduction exceeds expectations and that he thrives independently," the trainers assured the Marine Mammal Commission, but was that a real conviction, heartfelt? I wondered about the wisdom of hiring people from the captive industry to free a whale.

"So Keiko leaves the Faroes," says Phillips. "He keeps going east, east, east, and then it's like, Oh, Shoot, he's going to *Norway*. Tell me he's not going to Norway. It's been almost two months since we've given him any food; the former trainers are on the warpath; they're saying Keiko can't be eating, he must be doing terribly, starving and wandering. Meanwhile, he's getting closer to Norway, and we're thinking he's going to turn left, or he's going to turn right. He's not going to go right to the Norwegian coast. It can't happen. This is Norway, one of the biggest whaling nations on earth."

It seemed that Keiko was on a mission to all the last bastions of whaling:

Iceland, the Faroes, Norway. Where next, Japan? At five o'clock every morning in California, Phillips would rise, tired still from fighting off the insurgency of the eight trainers. Rubbing his eyes, he would get on his computer to call up Keiko's daily satellite position. The whale was one hundred miles away from Norway, then fifty miles, then twenty. He held course for Norway's fiordland, the territory of Norway's Coastal Party, a fringe group whose single legislator was Steinar Bastesen, former chief of Norway's Whalers' Association, the man who, four years before, as Keiko flew to Iceland, had protested, "We don't need another whale up here; we have plenty." It was true. There are plenty of killer whales in Norway. The seas around Tysfjord, in the north of the country, have a large concentration, about six hundred orcas. As Keiko neared this orca population center, a new idea began to circulate among his people: Perhaps Keiko had been a *Norwegian* whale all along. Little is known of the migration patterns of North Atlantic killer whales; no one knows where Iceland's orcas come from, when they arrive in late spring in the Westman Islands, and no one knows where they go, when they depart the Westmans in August. It is known that some of the same orcas sometimes show up in both places. Perhaps Keiko was a *spekkhogger,* or "blubber-cutter," as Norwegians call their killer whales. Perhaps this small spekkhogger, captured on his family's summer vacation to Iceland, was now, at last, heading home.

Keiko's trackers, extending the line of his course, figured he would hit the Norwegian coast in the vicinity of the town of Kristiansund, north of Bergen. When Keiko was twenty miles offshore, Phillips dispatched two staff members to Kristiansund, Colin Baird and Fernando Ugarte. Their job was to report Keiko's condition. Was the boy in the company of other whales? Was he starving? Was he disoriented? Was he fine? Nobody knew. Colin and Fernando kept their mission to themselves. Only a handful of people knew that Keiko had reached Norway, and it was important that his location remain unknown. What they wanted to avoid more than anything was the arrival of the armada of the press.

On the morning of August 30, 2002, Phillips called me at my home. He was weary but excited, having just pulled an all-nighter—one of only two or three since his college days, he said. Keiko was just two miles off Norway. He had been tracked farther than any satellite-tagged killer whale in history. Colin and Fernando, on arriving in Kristiansund, had looked around for a helicopter, without success, then had chartered a boat and had homed in on Keiko's VHF signal.

"At about four in the morning, my time, Colin called me on his cell phone from the boat," Phillips told me. "He said, 'Hey, I see him! We found him!' I'd been up all night. The waiting has been . . ."

Phillips searched for the words.

"The only thing like it has been waiting for Cole to be born. I'm on the phone with Colin when I hear, *'Duck! Get down!'* Keiko had been showing no particular interest in the boat, but then he came straight for it from about four hundred yards away."

LATER COLIN BAIRD FILLED ME in on the events of that morning. He and Fernando Ugarte, on flying into Kristiansund in the evening, had checked into a little guesthouse. Keiko was still some distance from shore. The next morning they set up their VHF antennae on the boat they had hired, *Kompass,* a fifty-five-footer, and waited for the day's satellite fix.

"We were waiting for position, waiting for position. When a satellite fix comes in, well, firstly it will rate the signal, on a scale of one to five. If it's a five, then it's maybe only been picked up by one or two satellites, and the triangulation isn't great, so it's accurate only to within a five-mile radius. As the satellites get better fixes, it will give you lower numbers, finally a position one, which can be accurate down to fifty meters. But even then, there's a slight delay in the information getting to us. So when we arrive to that satellite position, we have to use the VHF. As we left Kristiansund Harbor, we turned on the VHF gear, basically just to test it. Right away there's *beep, beep, beep.*"

For a moment, Baird and Ugarte did not know what to make of that sound. For weeks, working in boats and ships and helicopters, they had been trying to locate the whale, straining to hear a faint beep in the buzz of VHF static. "All we wanted was that *beep, beep, beep,*" says Baird, and now instantaneously here it was, clear and bell-like.

"Keiko was at the surface, obviously, because as soon as we switched on, we heard it. We were like, *'That noise! I remember that noise!'* It was great. Me and Fernando, we stopped a mile, three-quarters of a mile, from Keiko. We were just looking through binoculars at him. He was in this really pretty little area. Bunch of rocky outcroppings. He was just rolling in the kelp with his pecs up. Having what seemed to be a real nice time. Relaxing. Whatever goes through their mind, who knows? But it seemed he was very relaxed. We were watching him, and I'm on the phone. He looks great! We wanted photos to send back to Lanny and Dave—something to prove it's not just *us* saying he looks great, but that this is how he actually looks. He looked fantastic."

A malnourished killer whale develops a condition called "peanut head," Baird told me. *Orcinus orca* has a large fatty deposit that gives shape to the bulbous forehead—the melon—the contours of which the whale alters to change the focus of its echolocation. Because the melon acts as a lens for the beam of outgoing click-trains—a beam crucial to the whale's hunt for food—the melon is not metabolized by a hungry whale when it is burning body fat. The melon keeps its shape, while the body loses girth behind, resulting in a saddle or dip behind the melon—peanut head. Keiko showed no hint of this condition.

"We'd sort of drifted into maybe half a mile from him," Baird went on. "He dove, and then, *pouff,* he blew right beside the boat. All of a sudden, he pops up, and we both just dove. We didn't want to be recognized. We were afraid maybe he'd get stuck following *Kompass.* So both of us just hit the deck. I'm still on the phone with Dave. I said, *'We got busted!'* Dave asks what's going on.

" 'Keiko, he just surfaced beside the boat.'

" 'Well, how's he look?'

" *'I don't know!'* "

At the moment, Colin and Fernando were hiding from Keiko and they were in no position to answer the question. " 'We're going to try to get some pictures. I'll call you back.' "

Baird concedes that it was a bit disquieting that Keiko should swim up to the boat. A fixation on boats would be fatal to reintroduction hopes. It was disappointing, too, that there were no wild whales around. But Keiko's physical condition appeared to be excellent. If anything, he seemed fatter than when he left Iceland. Colin Baird was thrilled.

"It wasn't as if he came up and logged or gaped," Baird told me. "It was real different behavior than we'd seen. He started doing these long circles. He'd swim past, dive, come all the way back from fifty meters behind the boat. He'd just do these passes. So it was really encouraging. I don't think I got busted personally. We tried to keep our faces behind the camera, but we had a mission, we wanted to get some pictures."

On returning to Kristiansund, Baird and Ugarte, anxious to e-mail the Keiko images to North America, took their digital camera to a photo shop and handed the memory card to the technician. "We plugged into the computer, and we were scrolling through these pictures," Baird told me. "First there were pictures of us on the *Kompass* going out, and then some faraway distant shots of the area, and then a bunch of Keiko rolling around in the kelp, in among all these little islands. It was just really great to see. Then the next picture was when Keiko popped up right next to the boat. We had ten really good close-ups of Keiko. In one of them, Keiko is turning and is looking up. The guy in the shop stopped dead on the computer. He turns and looks at us, and he says, 'Does he *know* you?' "

Baird was stunned by the question. "Busted" offshore by Keiko; now busted onshore by this photo-shop technician.

"Fernando sort of looks at me," Baird said. "Then very quickly he points at me, says, 'He put those radio tags on.' So now this guy thinks we're just researching wild killer whales. Fernando saved us. The guy e-mailed the pictures, gave us back the card, and deleted everything from this computer. We thanked him, paid him, and off we went."

IN SAN FRANCISCO, ON THE day of Keiko's arrival in Norway, David Phillips, who had still not slept after his all-nighter, was running on adrenaline and his mood was triumphant. "They're firing away with digital cameras," he told me in summary. "He looks great! *He hasn't lost a pound.* He's in perfect condition. It's obvious that he's eating. He's a wild whale. He looks up at the boat and then he takes off."

Phillips paused to savor that moment. I had watched Keiko for years, as Phillips had, and I knew exactly how that last look must have been: Keiko would have half-rolled, to bring his eye to bear on the gunwale. His rolling would have exposed some of the white of his chin patch, which in killer whales begins just under the eye. He looked along the gunwale for familiar faces, saw none, turned and swam off into his future.

"This week Lanny is going to evaluate the photos for his opinion on Keiko's weight," Phillips went on. "Lanny's so funny. He was always the big optimist, but as the news has got better, he's gotten more pessimistic. I asked Paul Spong what he thought the chances were of finding Keiko in good condition, without any big weight loss. Paul said, 'Ninety-nine to one.' I asked Lanny, and he said, 'Fifty-fifty.' I said, 'Lanny! *Fifty-fifty?*' He said, 'Well, he's gone twelve hundred miles, that's a long, hard trip.' I told Pam this morning, 'Wait till I tell Lanny the good news, he'll say he knew it all the time.' When I called him with the word this morning, he said, 'It's just what I've been saying!'"

The next day, a Saturday, Colin Baird and Fernando Ugarte went out again in *Kompass.* Again Keiko's VHF signal led them to the same pretty area of rocky islets and kelp. This time they were careful to keep their distance. Through field glasses, from a couple of miles off, they watched Keiko for hours. They needed to know whether boat traffic was heavy. Was Keiko following vessels? Were any other cetaceans in the vicinity? A high-speed catamaran ferry went by; Keiko paid it no attention. A few commercial boats were going and coming; Keiko was indifferent. None of the passing watercraft, for their part, seemed to notice Keiko. "He was kind of milling around," Phillips reported to me afterward, summarizing the report from his operatives. "He wasn't doing his twenty-mile forages or his deep diving. We actually saw some boats go by, and he just showed no interest. And we were thinking, This is it! He's done it! The first killer whale successfully reintroduced to the wild. We were ready to declare a victory."

It seemed to me, as Keiko's biographer, that the whale had presented us with the end of his saga. It was simple and understated—that quick look back over his shoulder at the boat. The heroes of Icelandic saga often depart the narrative like this, anticlimactically, without much ceremony, and for Keiko, after all the hoopla of his life with humans, a departure like that seemed perfect. He was going out like Geirmund the Noisy, a character in the *Laxdaela Saga*. Geirmund the Noisy had a sword called "Leg-biter," with a pommel and guard all of walrus ivory, with no silver in it. Geirmund and Leg-biter are dismissed from the tale in just nine words. The Icelandic scribe, taking up a quill plucked from the left wing of a raven or eagle, dipped it in ink of boiled bearberry and unsprouted willow twigs, and wrote simply:

". . . and that is the last we hear of Geirmund."

Exactly! That was how the saga of this Iceland whale should end. Keiko Bent-Fin swims under the boat. He half-rolls to look up one last time. He blows, he dives, he shows us his tailfin, and that is the last we hear of Keiko.

37

THE CREATURE FROM KORSNES FIORD

On Sunday morning, September 1, 2002, a thirty-five-year-old Norwegian, Arild Birger Neshaug, was out fishing in his sixteen-foot skiff when he saw movement in the distance on Korsnes Fiord. Beneath the fiord's big, green, glacier-rounded mountains, something dark and low on the water was making for his boat. With Neshaug was his twelve-year-old daughter, Hanne, his friend, Ivar, and Ivar's son, Marius. The four had put out that morning from the Neshaug cabin on Korsnes Fiord just west of the entrance to Skaalvik Fiord. Now all eyes of the fishermen turned downfiord.

The black thing, some sort of sea creature, very large, was hydroplaning toward them at high speed. The two children, frightened, begged their fathers to run for shore. Arild Neshaug throttled up his little four-horsepower outboard and the skiff puttered off toward land, making six or seven knots. The dark creature porpoising after them was capable of thirty and it quickly closed the gap. The sea erupted directly behind the skiff. In a running spyhop, halfway out of water, breached a whale. The whale smashed back in, raising a mountainous fountain of spray. The four Norwegians were terrified. The animal was half again as long as the boat. The Norwegians reached shore at a spot called Kaldbergsnausta, two miles west of the mouth of Skaalvik Fiord. They beached themselves, frantic, like pilot whales pursued by Faroe Islanders, and they ran up to safety between some boathouses. The whale, having treed the Norwegians, waited, swimming sharky circles in the shallows beyond the stern of the skiff.

A resident of Kaldbergsnausta, a man familiar with killer whales, had watched the chase from his house above the fiord. He walked down to the Neshaug party and identified their pursuer as a *spekkhogger,* a blubber-cutter, a killer whale. Arild Neshaug saw that this *spekkhogger* seemed calm. He and his crew returned cautiously to their boat. They noticed now that two yellow ribbons on the whale's dorsal fin flagged two small boxes—transmitters of some sort. This whale, they supposed, had escaped from somewhere. The boy, Marius, remembered an American film he had seen, *Free Willy,* and he commenced calling the whale by that name. The appellation took. "Willy" seemed to humanize the animal, who now seemed almost friendly. The Neshaug party decided they really should get back to the cabin at Korsnes. The two kids climbed in the skiff, and the men pushed off.

It says something about human intuition, and about the animus of this particular killer whale, that the two Norwegian fathers, shortly after being chased high on the shore by a *spekkhogger*, would voluntarily rejoin that creature *with their offspring*. No sea lion or penguin would have ever risked that. The Norwegians motored back to Korsnes, followed all the way by "Willy." The strange persistence of the animal may be explained, in part, by the presence of young Hanne and Marius in the boat. This particular killer whale had a fatal attraction to children. At Korsnes the whale continued to hang about the dock, and the two fathers started making phone calls in an effort to determine the rightful owner. The press got wind of the visitation. They arrived to take photographs and video of the whale with the children of Korsnes, who were now riding the whale's back. One journalist suggested to the gathering that this was probably Keiko, the famous whale that had departed Iceland some weeks earlier. The whale was not "Willy," he was actually Willy.

THE PREVIOUS NIGHT, SATURDAY, COLIN Baird and Fernando Ugarte had celebrated in Kristiansund. Their two days of observation had gone wonderfully. It was true that Keiko had busted *Kompass* on Friday, swimming wide circles around that boat, but afterward he had shown no further interest in vessels, and no watercraft had approached him. His immigration to Norway remained a secret. "We had a nice bottle of wine," Baird says. "We were sort of patting ourselves on the back. We were just so excited. The biggest thing was satisfying ourselves that he was in good shape. We were hoping he would just continue his journey. We would monitor him by satellite, and hopefully he would continue either up the coast or offshore. The next day, Sunday, we didn't go out on the water. We didn't want him to get used to the boat."

That Sunday morning, early, while Baird and Ugarte slept, an old fisherman motored in from the Norwegian Sea, passing by the pretty little archipelago of rocky islets and kelp where the whale was hanging out. Something about the boat had attracted Keiko. Bestirring himself, he extricated his great pectoral fins from the kelp in which he had been playing, and he followed the fisherman into the fiords. In Korsnes Fiord he had parted company with the old man, only to introduce himself, later in the day, to the Neshaug party in their skiff.

In San Francisco, David Phillips had declared victory—not yet to the public, but to himself. He was trying to decide how to celebrate when he got a call from Norway. "Dave, we're in deep trouble," Colin Baird told him. "We just got a report. Keiko's on television. We're on our way in the boat.

We're probably five hours from where he is. He's deep in a fiord. *And there's kids swimming with him.*"

When Baird and Ugarte arrived at Korsnes, they found a circus. Kids were indeed swimming with the whale. More and more boats were arriving, the crowd was growing, television cameras were rolling. NRK Television, Norway's version of the BBC, was filming what would become the opening sequences of a documentary for *Fakta på Lørdag,* "Facts on Saturday," a Saturday evening program. NRK would call this hour-long episode "*Kampen om Keiko,*" or "Struggle for Keiko," and it would become one of the most popular documentaries ever screened in Norway

A scene from the film's opening:

A chunky boy in a black T-shirt treads water on the dark and glassy fiord. Suddenly the boy is lifted skyward. A black, glistening island rises under him. The boy grins broadly atop Keiko's back. From offscreen come cheers and clapping from an unseen boat. Marianne Korsnes, twelve years old, enters the frame, swimming across the still waters of her namesake fiord to join Keiko and the boy. The camera loves Marianne Korsnes and it zooms in a bit—lovely girl with a figure just beginning to develop, in a one-piece bathing suit, her long blond hair darkened by the water. The scene needs her, for the boy is absolutely fearless. Marianne shows a trace of apprehension, infusing some of the dramatic tension necessary to any good sea-monster story. When Marianne reaches him, Keiko is low on the water—not much of him showing—and he makes an easy landfall. Then he buoys up, bigger and bigger, and Marianne has trouble keeping a grip on the slick curve of his flank. She clambers up as if on a capsized lifeboat. She gets comfortable on top, briefly, and then the whale begins to move sideways under her. "Whoa," she says. Keiko stabilizes, and she lays her cheek on the top of his head.

Afterward, on shore, the NRK reporter interviews Marianne. Her hair is dry now and white-blond again. The reporter asks her in Norwegian if she was afraid. "A little," she says.

The next day, Monday, Keiko left Korsnes Fiord, turned right into a tributary, Skaalvik Fiord, and swam deep into that inlet, to the waterfront of the rural *kommune* of Halsa. Here the crowds thickened. Colin Baird and Fernando Ugarte watched, disconsolate, while years of rehabilitation work and boat-avoidance training was undone. "People were swimming with him," Baird says. "He was surrounded by forty, fifty boats. It was just an absolute catastrophe. It was so depressing." When they urged the Norwegians to stay back, the natives grew indignant. Who were these two North Americans to give them instructions? CNN crews arrived. Press and pilgrims from ever wider circles of Europe and the world reached the fiord. So many spectators thronged one floating dock near Keiko that it began to tip and sink. The anxious owner, fearing a Ganges-ferry sort of disaster—"Five Hundred Whale-watchers Drown in Norway"—removed the ramp so the mob could not get down to his dock. The Halsa Kommune and its seventeen hundred residents were first stunned, then thrilled by the world's attention. They interpreted Keiko's arrival as an endorsement. Of all the thousands of fiords in Norway, Keiko had picked theirs. Halsa entrepreneurs printed up "Choose Halsa—Keiko did!" T-shirts, which sold off as soon as the ink was dry.

"Everywhere Keiko goes, people fall in love with him, but in Norway, no one could have predicted this type of reaction," says David Phillips. "Norway is a whaling country. You can find whale meat in the supermarkets. Polls show heavy support for the government's pro-whaling position. But it turns out that Norwegians are really just a bunch of whale-lovers."

Each of Keiko's next four days in Norway was more frantic than the day preceding. The director of "Struggle for Keiko," the NRK documentary, would later admit that his film required no direction. The story told itself. He needed only set up his tripod above the dock and let the camera roll. An Italian man, a longtime Keiko fan, packed up his Volkswagen bus at the news of Keiko's arrival in Halsa and drove north, day and night, to Norway, where he had an epiphanous moment with Keiko. Two Finnish women drove south for the same sort of joyous encounter. Channelers and animal communicators arrived for telepathic conversations with the whale. He told one of them he wanted to go back to Oregon. A German named Helmut, who had once held the franchise for *Free Willy* merchandise in Germany, showed up. On the Halsa waterfront he presented Colin Baird with a *Free Willy* mug in German. Helmut, before going into the Willy business, had been the owner of Rex, the Wonder Dog, Germany's most famous police dog. After Rex's death, Helmut had made some sort of sentimental connection between that famous canine and this famous cetacean, and this wove itself into the documentary.

IN OREGON THAT WEEK, as the crowds thickened in Norway, Bonnie Norton, the animal communicator, was receiving messages from Keiko that he was sad, depressed, and lonely. On September 4, 2002, even as the multitudes fought for position on the Halsa shore and the dock owner was forced to remove his ramp, two animal communicators Norton trusted, "very accurate" practitioners, in her opinion, made telephonic calls to her. The first communicator said that Keiko had told him he was considering "going on land." The second said the whale was thinking of beaching himself, which is another way of saying the same thing. Norton passed this worrisome consensus on to the Norwegian government. "He feels he has done so much to be with people and now cannot be with them," she wrote. "I believe that if Keiko is taken away from people again, he will not survive."

The odd thing is, of course, that at this moment Keiko was more inundated by people than he had ever been in his life. All three animal communicators seem to have missed the news of Keiko's circumstances in Halsa, or to have discounted it. On the day the communicators received Keiko's complaints about loneliness, two close acquaintances were with him, Colin Baird and Fernando Ugarte, and pilgrims from all over Europe darkened his shores. Dogs were barking at him furiously from docks and piers. Thickets of hands were reaching out, tossing fish, and waving. Much of the time, Keiko was retreating to the lee of a moored boat for refuge from humanity. It was as if the psychic messages were arriving in the United States a week or two late. Some glitch in reception—sunspot interference, perhaps—had delayed the mail, causing it to pile up in empathospace.

ON THE FIFTH DAY OF Keiko's stay in Halsa, a curious thing happened: The authorities of the kommune of Halsa actually listened to the pleas of Colin Baird and Fernando Ugarte. On September 6, 2002, in a town meeting, the local government decreed a fifty-meter exclusion zone around Keiko. No more swimming with Keiko or feeding him. Anyone encroaching on the exclusion zone was subject to a fine.

Outside the town hall, at the conclusion of the meeting, a participant, the veterinarian Ivar Vullum, was approached outside by a Halsa farmworker named Frank Haavik. The veterinarian, Vullum, a lean, kind-faced man with a close-trimmed, graying beard, was the local representative of Norway's Animal Welfare Authority, the lead agency in promulgating the fifty-meter zone. Frank Haavik, the farmworker, was what Norwegians call an *alvøser*, an itinerant husbandman with four or five farmers as clients. An *alvøser* moves on rotation from farm to farm, filling in for each farmer for two or three days, allowing the poor man some time off. Haavik was twenty-nine, sturdy, blond, fresh-faced, amiable. He is more comfortable in English than most residents of Halsa, but in finding his way through English sentences, he regularly resorts to two stall words, "Well," at the beginning and "actually" here and there at strategic places in the middle. His "well," pronounced "waal," sounds much like the *hval,* "whale," of the Old Norse and the Icelandic tongue. He seems to be talking incessantly about cetaceans. He and the veterinarian, Dr. Vullum, lingered outside the meeting hall, discussing the whale.

"Well, actually," says Haavik, "I'd been working together with Ivar in the years before, since I started working in agriculture. So I knew him. We talked together about things and we decided, Yeah we probably should give Colin and Fernando a hand, if they need. And they probably will need. They would need help the most, actually, on Sunday. This was the first weekend after Keiko was in the news, so we knew that this weekend would be a pain in the ass."

Frank thought he might volunteer his boat, a sixteen-footer of the type that Norwegians call *skjaergaardsjeep*, "coastal jeep," in rough translation. He presented himself and his coastal jeep to Baird and Ugarte. "Basically I told them that, Yeah I'd been talking to the local veterinarian, and I decided, if you need a hand, I'm prepared to help you. Then we talked together, Fernando and Colin and Ivar and me, and also Lars Lillebo, who works for the Halsa Kommune. We decided we should make up some kind of the paper— flyers—that we can hand out to people, explaining about Keiko."

That weekend, as expected, the crowds were huge; five thousand people lined the shore of the fiord, trying to get a peek at Keiko. The Halsa Kommune had organized for them, with twenty Keiko docents, wearing Keiko T-shirts, circulating, passing out flyers and advising the crowd why it was important to keep some distance from the whale.

"I went out in my boat and tried to keep people away," says Frank Haavik. "And it was pretty easy, because Keiko was very tired at that point. Something was bothering him. He was probably exhausted by people. There was at times forty boats around there. He stayed in an area around this one boat at the dock, and he didn't go away from there. People always say, 'He loves people, he is so attracted to people.' But he showed a sign there, to me. As soon as he found out, There's nobody coming close to me here, he stayed there by that boat. He stayed for five days. Didn't move."

DAVID PHILLIPS WAS DELIGHTED BY the fifty-meter exclusion zone imposed by the Halsa Kommune, but uncertain how Norway's federal government would respond to Keiko. Norway's whaling industry had petitioned the government to deport the whale. One Norwegian whale researcher had suggested that the charitable thing would be to shoot Keiko. The government, surprised at the sudden spotlight of world attention and feeling the warmth, was saying all the right things—that Keiko was welcome in Norway, that Norway had no intention of letting harm come to him—but this was, after all, Norway, the most obdurate whaling nation on earth.

Phillips flew to Norway. Arriving in Bergen to discuss Keiko with officials of Norway's Directorate of Fisheries, which had responsibility for whaling issues, he expected a hard line. Phillips's Earth Island Institute had directed harsh criticism at Norway for its whaling practices—the Norwegians had set their minke-whale quota at 671 this year—and Phillips anticipated some payback.

When he arrived at the Directorate of Fisheries office in Bergen, there were fifteen reporters outside the door. Phillips was stunned. He had no idea how the press had learned that he was in Norway. "Come in! Come in!" said Ove Midttun, the deputy director, and then he waved all the media inside, too—not to stay throughout the meeting, but to ask questions at the start. Deputy director Midttund, a former judge, is a jovial man with a mane of curly hair. He explained that Norway had a very open policy toward the media. Reporters had access to everything. As the horde of journalists crowded in after him, Phillips was struck, as he would be often again in negotiating in Norway for Keiko, by how different this little democracy was from the big democracy back home.

The conversation with the fisheries people began well. The Fisheries director and his staff joked about the irony of Keiko's journey to Norway, a nation with such a bad reputation with whale-lovers.

"They went on to say that they make this big distinction between whales," Phillips says. "They told me, 'We view minke whales as a resource, but we've always been very kind to the orca whale.' Actually, there are reports that they had big bounties on orcas for many years, until thousands of them were killed. But that's somewhat ancient history."

Before Phillips arrived in Bergen, emissaries from the Fisheries Directorate had toured the fiord at Halsa with Colin Baird and Fernando Ugarte, and the emissaries had met the whale. They had come with some medical concerns about Keiko, which Lanny Cornell, who flew in for the occasion, had assuaged. The Norwegian vet, Ivar Vullum, had been impressed by Cornell's résumé and the two had hit it off. Both were horse-and-cow men, fundamentally, but Cornell had sea mammals under his belt, as well, and Dr. Vullum was grateful for the consultation, for he knew nothing about whale medicine himself. The government by now had researched Phillips and his associates. The Norwegians knew they were not dealing with the Sea Shepherd Society of Paul Watson or some other cell of eco-terrorists. In Bergen, as the meeting with the fisheries director progressed, Phillips found he liked the man more and more. He got a strong sense that Ove Midttund was free to make his decision based on what he thought was the right thing to do.

"I went through my whole song and dance," Phillips says. "I gave them the history of Keiko's rehabilitation in Oregon and Iceland, and how well he'd done in coming all the way across, and how happy our vet was with his condition. They said, 'Well, we have several requirements.' And I thought, *Okay, here we go.* 'Our first condition is he should not be in a pen.' I thought, *What? Don't throw me in the briar patch?* 'Our second condition is that there's not to be any commercialization. We don't want Keiko cruises coming by.' I thought, *Yes? This is our punishment?* 'Our third condition is that we don't want conflicts with our industries. We don't want him to be ripping open salmon nets and eating the fish.' There'd been a report that Keiko had scared all the salmon at a big salmon pen. The salmon supposedly freaked out, and their food consumption went way down that day. I thought, *Okay. That can be arranged.*"

Deputy Director Midttun advised Phillips that if Keiko's foundation took care of all expenses and kept the whale healthy, then Keiko would be left in their charge. Norway would stick by Keiko's people. The government would not go with any outside proposals to recapture the whale, and the foundation would be free to shape Keiko's program as it thought best. Phillips was much relieved. He asked if the foundation would need to get a permit. This area of Norwegian law—the regulations applying to semidomesticated killer whales swimming free in the country's fiords—was sketchy, to say the least. The deputy director turned to his departmental attorney. "Do we need a permit for this?" he asked. The attorney said no. In Norwegian law, by the attorney's assessment, Keiko had essentially the same standing as a goat. If a farmer wants to keep his goat outdoors to graze in Norway, he needs no permit, and neither did Keiko in his fiord.

The dossier of Deputy Director Midttun lay open on the table. Phillips, glancing at the folder, could read, upside down, the letterhead of the Miami Seaquarium. It was his first intimation of who was authoring those outside proposals, what institution wanted to recapture the whale.

"It was pure chance," Phillips told me, of the dossier's revelation. "So I said, 'Well, you know, there are a lot of people out there who are trying . . .' And the fisheries director said, 'Yes, we recognize that there are a lot of sharks in the waters. We have our sharks over here, too.'"

The next day, Phillips left Bergen for Oslo, where he met with heavyweights in the foreign ministry, and then with more officers in the fisheries ministry. He believes that both ministries had been instructed to handle the Keiko issue carefully. At a banquet, his hosts in the foreign ministry told him how unusual it was to have CNN, Sky News, and the rest of the international media so hot on a story in Norway. The kindly suggestion by the Norwegian whale researcher that it would be a favor to Keiko to shoot him, the officials said, had tripled news coverage and caused a worldwide furor. Pleas and suggestions were arriving from all over the globe.

Some came from Oregon, and one of these was from Bonnie Norton. Ten days after Keiko reached Skaalvik Fiord, Norton had sent Norway's minister of fisheries a letter offering help.

"Dear Mr. Ludvigsen," Norton wrote. "I believe I have some valuable information to be considered when planning Keiko's future. I'm an Animal Communicator, and in 1997 I communicated with Keiko at the Oregon Coast Aquarium. To my surprise, he very clearly told me that he wanted to stay at the Aquarium."

Norton recounted an experiment that she and two other professional animal communicators, Mary Getten and Teresa Wagner, had conducted with Keiko in summer of 2001. The three empathic women had agreed all to ask Keiko the same question, without disclosing his answers to one another in advance. "In all three communications," she wrote, "Keiko was very clear about his desire to be with people and his insistence that he would never leave his people." Norton conveyed some of the bewilderment that Keiko had communicated to her and to Mary Getten in the middle of his crossing of the Norwegian Sea in August. She informed the minister that she was willing to come to Norway, if that would help. She hoped to hear from him soon.

On receipt of this letter, Mr. Ludvigsen, the fisheries minister, must have realized that he and his government had entered a new dimension. The Norwegians were not in Kansas anymore.

If surrealpolitik had come to Norway, then plenty of real politics was arriving, too. Iceland was inquiring about getting the whale back. The Oregon Coast Aquarium wanted him back. Mexico, through the agency of its first lady, Mrs. Fox, was working toward a return of the whale. "Everywhere he's ever been now wants him back," says David Phillips, and this included places he had never been, like the state of Florida.

In Oslo, in the dossiers of the officers of the foreign ministry, and everywhere else he went in government, Phillips saw the same file he had seen in Bergen, complete with letters from the U.S. National Marine Fisheries Service and the Miami Seaquarium. "Do you want to see what Miami is trying to do?" one official asked. He pushed the letter across the table.

The Seaquarium, Phillips discovered, had submitted an application to The National Oceanic and Atmospheric Administration for permission to capture Keiko and export him to Miami. Later, lawyers for the Free Willy Keiko Foundation would sue under the Freedom of Information Act for a copy of the application, but were told that it was a draft application, not covered by that law. Things would never again be so simple as they were that day in Oslo, when the Norwegian offical simply handed the letter over. Phillips skimmed the page before handing it back. Among other assertions, the Miami Seaquarium was falsely claiming that the Free Willy Keiko Foundation was about to lose its U.S. National Marine Fisheries Service permits for the Keiko project, as a result of the complaints of Jeff Foster and the seven former trainers.

"Miami Seaquarium is the smallest facility in the United States," Phillips says. "It's the worst facility in the U.S. Keiko's pool in Miami would be within inches of the size of the pool he was in at Reino Aventura—it's that small. Can you imagine *that* full circle? Going from Mexico to Oregon, then all the way out to Iceland and Norway, with wild whales, crossing the ocean—only to come back to the subtropics and a tiny captive pen?"

The Miami Seaquarium enlisted Senator Bob Graham of Florida, who petitioned Norway for permission to recapture the whale. The U.S. National Marine Fisheries Service, in response to the letter from Jeff Foster and the seven former trainers, attempted to intervene. On September 6, 2002, the very day that Halsa Kommune, in its wisdom, established the fifty-meter exclusion zone around Keiko, the U.S. State Department, through the American Embassy in Reykjavík, passed on a note from the National Marine Fisheries Service to the government of Iceland. The NMFS suggested that Iceland, under the reintroduction protocol for Keiko, might be obligated to rescue and recapture the whale in Norway. There was consternation in Iceland. David Phillips was furious. The response from Washington was as wrong-headed as the response in Halsa had been right.

In the end, Phillips and his foundation turned back the bid of Senator Graham and the Seaquarium. Iceland was not required to invade Norway in pursuit of the whale. The U.S. Department of Commerce gave the Seaquarium the bad news: "Based on review of the circumstances of this case, and on communication from the government of Norway, NOAA Fisheries has determined that the application you have submitted is premature at this time. The Norwegian government, which has jurisdiction over Keiko, is not considering allowing the capture of Keiko by the Miami Seaquarium or any other entity."

Deputy Director Ove Midttund and his government had stuck by his vow to leave Keiko's fate in the hands of the people who had brought him this far.

On September 26, back in Skaalvik Fiord, an eight-year-old Norwegian girl, Astrid Morken, arrived in Halsa with her harmonica. Astrid came from the town of Skaun, eighty miles away. She had been obsessed with Keiko for most of her life. When she was four, Astrid had asked for a harmonica—her parents had no idea why. Then one day they came upon their daughter watching *Free Willy* on video and playing the Willy theme song along with the boy, Jesse, the whale's sidekick—a harmonica duet.

Now, on a Halsa dock, Astrid commenced playing the refrain from the movie. After a time, Keiko approached. Astrid was perfectly legal, for she was well outside the fifty-meter exclusion zone when she began playing. It was Keiko who came her way. "It was great," Astrid told a reporter, after playing the refrain for close to three straight hours, delighting—it seemed to some— the whale. The story made news all over the world. Astrid, forced to say good-bye to Keiko, cried most of the eighty miles home to Skaun.

* * *

"THAT'S JUST THE KIND OF thing we don't need," Colin Baird told a journalist the next day. "I'm sorry I can't get all warm and fuzzy about it. This isn't about playing with Keiko, or swimming with him, or playing the harmonica for him. It's about trying to return him to the wild."

Baird is not normally so querulous. His nerves were frayed from the attempt to do his job in an impossible situation. In several scenes in the NRK documentary "Struggle for Keiko," the cameras catch Baird trying to escape their gaze, hunkering behind the screen of a bush, holding earnest cell-phone conversations with Dr. Cornell and David Phillips in the United States. He does not look like a happy man. In these chaotic days, he would admit to me later, he was close to quitting.

Back in the Westman Islands, Keiko's foundation and the Humane Society began closing down the operation there. The Iceland chapter of Keiko's saga appeared to be over. The remaining staff was laid off. Preparations were made to dismantle the bay pen and sell off *Daniel* and *Heppni* and the project's vehicles. Thorbjörg Kristjandóttir was asked to stay on and fly to Norway to reinforce Colin Baird. She agreed, thinking the assignment would be brief. In two or three weeks, everyone assumed, Keiko would be on his way again.

The NRK television cameras record her beatific smile, on first seeing the whale again in Halsa. "His mom is here," she told the cameraman. She had no doubt that Keiko recognized her. "It hadn't been so long," she says. "Two months. And I was the good person, because I arrived at the time we really started feeding him, and I was the one with all the herring."

A fine reunion, yet soon enough Tobba, too, was thinking of quitting.

"When I came, we had this keep-fifty-meters-away law, so people were not swimming with him," she says. "But all this boat traffic! And all the people standing everywhere on shore, shouting. It was just a very frustrating time. Yeah, we thought about quitting, both of us. The phone started ringing early in the morning—the press—and it was ringing till the end of the day. Every time you walked out of the door, there was television cameras. *Just leave us alone!* We wanted to work with Keiko, to get him on the road again, but we cannot. He was just sitting by the boat. We were trying to make him do something, just to wake him up, but if we made him do a breach or a bow, we got, 'Hey, come and see the show! Come on! Come on!' The same thing every time we fed him. Keiko needed to work, but we couldn't do it. I was so pissed."

Colin Baird, escaping Halsa briefly, drove into Kristiansund to get a couple of rolls of film developed. He dropped them off at the same shop where he and Fernando Ugarte had downloaded their digital photos of Keiko's arrival in Norway. The clerk who had done that work was on duty. Two weeks before, as Keiko's secret agents perused the whale's pictures, this clerk had suddenly asked, "Does he *know* you?" Fernando Ugarte, thinking fast, had lied that he and Baird were researchers and this was just some whale they had radio-tagged. Now, as Baird entered the door, haggard from the frustrations of the past days, the clerk recognized him from across the room. In mock anger, the Norwegian pointed an accusatory finger. *"Keiko!"* he said.

Hope faded that Keiko would soon resume his journey. There were no orcas now off the central coast of Norway. Keiko could not simply be let loose to wander the fiords, as there were salmon farms everywhere, and boat traffic was heavy. The circus on the Halsa waterfront was an indication of what the whale could expect wherever he traveled in the fiordland. The team briefly considered walking him high up above the Arctic Circle to Tysfjord, where more than five hundred orcas were concentrated, but the herring fleet was thick up there, and salmon farms, too. The orca biologist at Tysfjord, Tiu Simila, whom Keiko's people called "Queen of Killer Whales," was acquainted with Keiko, and she had consulted on the project, but she was opposed to the plan. Dr. Simila was not eager to see the most famous orca on earth take up residence in Tysfjord, upstaging her research and bringing with him the mobs of the press.

Some new bay or fiord would have to be found for Keiko. Halsa was remote, but what he needed, his team decided, was a spot even remoter, some less traveled corner, here in subarctic Norway, where they could walk the whale and monitor him when he took off by himself, yet control shoreline access and keep away the crowds. Colin Baird scouted the region and found a number of promising places—there are a nearly infinite number of fiords in Norway—but his choices were eliminated, one after another, by potential conflicts with salmon farms and commercial fishing. In the end it came down to two places: a small bay in the island kommune of Tusna, and a cove called Taknes Bay. Baird met with the mayor of Tusna. The old fisherman whose boat Keiko followed into the fiords lived near Tusna, and Baird met this man, too. The old salt was apologetic. He told Baird that if he had known what whale he was dealing with, he would never have led Keiko down the fiord. He would have led him back to sea again.

"A great little bay," Baird says of Tusna. "It's not even a fiord, just a long little finger of a bay. It's not a mile long. But it turned out there was a major conflict there with the herring fishery. The bay is a herring spawning ground."

Taknes Bay, on a fiord east of Halsa, was chosen by the process of elimination. Keiko moved once again with human beings to a new home.

38

BLOOD AND ICE

In February of 2003, Keiko took to wandering. The team at Taknes Bay tracked him by car, driving to fiord overlooks where they could pick up the VHF signal from the transmitter on his dorsal fin. At sixty-three degrees north latitude, February days are short, nights nearly endless. The whale seemed afflicted by some cetacean version of the winter malady that Alaskans call "cabin fever." Soon he was straying beyond the range of automobile pursuit. Keiko's scaled-down team—Colin Baird of Canada, Thorbjörg Kristjandóttir of Iceland, and Frank Haavik of Norway—took to the water, following the whale in their twenty-foot boat, or in Frank's sixteen-footer.

"His range increased over the days, and he was wandering farther at night," says Colin Baird. "Our philosophy was to let him go, and follow as best we could. That became a little more difficult, because he was going beyond fifteen miles, traveling farther than we were able to handle in the little boat for such long periods. So we brought in the big boat, *Kompass*. This time of the year, there was little or no boat traffic in the fiords, and our position was that if he wanted to go somewhere, just to simply let him go."

Kompass is fifty-seven feet long, a former Swedish coast-guard vessel enjoying a second career as an offshore fishing charter. The services of the boat, and of its part-owner and captain, Odd Strøm, were put on call that winter. In their own small boats the team followed Keiko's strolls. On *Kompass* they followed his hikes and his treks.

On Monday, February 17, Keiko departed Taknes Bay on one of his walkabouts. Tobba Kristjandóttir spent a sleepless night tracking him by car and established his approximate position. The next day, February 18, as soon as the team had some daylight, all of them, Tobba, Colin, and Frank, went searching for the whale in Frank's sixteen-footer. Frank's *skjaergaardsjeep* is named *Silver* and it is powered by a Honda four-stroke. *Silver* soon proved too small for Keiko's ambitions that day. When a friend of Frank's volunteered his own larger *skjaergaardsjeep* in mid-morning, they switched to that one. Not far from Kristiansund, the biggest town in that stretch of fiordland, Frank got a phone call from a salmon farm ahead. "They told us, 'Well, we have a whale here, so if you want to pick him up, it would be nice.' Because they didn't like to have him there. He stressed the fish. At that point we were probably only about five minutes behind Keiko. So we went and picked him up."

The team led Keiko back toward Taknes Bay. They did not pipe him along with the toner; they simply chummed him homeward by tossing him an occasional fish. It was a meandering voyage, for little fits of wanderlust kept striking Keiko. "We decided, okay, we'll get *Kompass*," says Frank. "Since he has this behavior. Not *strange* behavior, but he wanted to go his own ways, and check out things." They put in a call to Odd Stroem, the captain, and *Kompass* met them halfway back to Taknes Bay. They jumped onboard, and in the comfort of the larger vessel they shadowed Keiko on his errant and whimsical course.

Keiko decided to poke into Skaalvik Fiord, the fiord where he had gathered his big crowds after his crossing from Iceland in the summer. *Kompass* followed him into the wintry fiord and put in at the shipyard dock, across from the pier which, eight months before, had been so jammed with Keiko-watchers that the owner feared collapse. The ship dock was three hundred yards from the edge of shore ice. The team was not particularly concerned by the ice, for Keiko had been close to ice before. Earlier that winter, he had shown a healthy apprehension for the stuff. Several times this season *Kompass* had been forced to make like a little icebreaker and clear a lead for the whale. Now in Skaalvik Fiord the whale's wanderlust appeared to have subsided for the moment; he was content to hang out in the vicinity of the dock. Tobba, who had not slept for nearly forty-eight hours, went below to nap. Frank and Colin, sleep-deprived themselves, if somewhat less so, took turns going out every ten or fifteen minutes to check the whereabouts of the whale. Frank saw Keiko close beside the hull on one of these occasions. Minutes later, when he checked again, the whale was gone.

"I went out, stood for two, three minutes, and I didn't hear him," Frank told me. "Colin came out, and I said, 'Well, it seems like he is gone again.' So we picked up the tracking gear and we couldn't find any signals. We thought he must have gone fast, since he is already gone out. And at about that time we started to hear noises from the ice. Like a bumping sound."

Frank rapped the table to demonstrate.

"We realized that he was under the ice. So we jumped in the small boat and went over to the edge of the ice. Straightaway I tried to tone him. I tried to tone him once, and he didn't respond to that one. And suddenly he just break through the ice. Big crash. *Kappusssshhkkk!* I didn't see it because it was pitch dark. Actually, there was a little moonlight, but I didn't see him, he was too far. It was stars all over the place. It was like ten degrees below, Celsius. And it was completely calm. So you could hear a needle fall. And he just, *Kappusssshhkkk,* through the ice there. And we heard *Psssshhh!* He was breathing very hard. He had to come up. He needed air."

Colin and Frank knew the ice could be dangerous, trapping Keiko if he ventured too far under it, and they knew the thin ice could be sharp, but neither man was enormously worried as yet.

"When we tone him, he did not want to leave the hole," Frank said. "He was just laying in it. Probably because he knew that at this place he could get air. So we toned him three or four times, and suddenly we could hear him diving. We just was hoping he was going in the right way—toward us. He broke through two times after he dived from the first hole. Dive number two and dive number three, I was pretty sure that he's coming in the right direction, because the sound was getting closer to us. But that was some really tough minutes, there. The second time he broke through, he *screamed.* He made a bad, bad sound. I don't know if that was because of panic or pain. I can't describe it. It's like, if you have heard cats fighting? Some kind of noise like that. So it's a not very nice sound. Especially when you knew it came from either pain or panic. The third time he went through, I actually saw him, because by then the guys on *Kompass* had this huge spotlight aiming at the ice."

In the *Kompass* spotlight, Keiko broke through in nearly vertical breach, then crashed forward onto the ice, which broke under him.

"After he dived the third time, he came out from under the ice—but that was actually the worst thing. Because as soon as he came under my boat, they used the big light on *Kompass* and I could see him coming. That was something I probably will never forget. That was an awful sight. His nose still showed black, but the rest was just blood. I saw just the front of his nose, and you couldn't see the rest of him because he was in a cloud of blood."

Frank believes that Keiko's first icebreaking breach, well inland of the edge of the ice, was not the breach that lacerated him, for the ice there was fairly thick—six inches or so, he estimates. Breaches two and three, in thinner, sharper ice nearer the boat, were the breaches that did the damage, in his opinion. Tobba continued to sleep aboard *Kompass.* The two men were afraid to wake her.

"I actually went out in the boat and over to Keiko," Frank recalled. "I had a light with me and I tried to check him out. I could see the huge scratches. I was afraid he had hurt his eyes, or his blowhole. He could probably live without one eye—without two, actually. Some of them are able to do that. But I just wanted to check out how he looked. I've been working with animals from a lot of years, and I'm used to animals hurting themselves, breaking legs. I felt that I just have to go and see how it looked like. So I went out, and he was actually pretty quiet. He was staying just right behind *Kompass,* and I could have a pretty good look. His eyes was nice. And his blowhole was nice."

And the rest of him was hamburger.

"Well, I had a bad night," said Frank. "It's probably one of the worst nights I ever had. I didn't sleep at all. And that's actually the first night I hadn't done that." Frank laughed at his own powers of somnolence. "I have lost actually family members, and still I could sleep. But the whole situation was so scary! Just think if he died in there! If he drowned under the ice, ah, just to handle the media, that scared the hell out of you. Just think all the people who would blame you."

Just think of the necessity of waking Tobba.

"THEY WOKE ME UP, BECAUSE they were going to move him away from the ice—as far away from the ice as possible," Tobba told me. "So they woke me up and said, 'Well, something happened.'"

"They wouldn't tell you?" I asked her.

She shook her head. "Finally they said, 'Well, Keiko went under the ice.' And I said, *What? Is he still there?*' I went out with the flashlight and looked at him, and I was just, *Oh my God.* It looked bad."

For two days after his injury, Keiko's respiration rate stayed high. A day and a half passed before he ate his first fish. He spent his time logging on the surface, not moving much. On the second day, Sunday, a man in a boat appeared in the distance. The man departed, then returned in his boat with a companion and a video camera. Keiko's curiosity overcame his post-traumatic lethargy, and he dived to investigate, surfacing right beside the strange boat and frightening the two occupants. The shock was not in meeting a killer whale, the men would tell Frank Haavik when he motored up. The shock was how he looked. "Monster!" they had thought.

"He looked awful," Frank conceded to me. "I asked them if they could see this from our side. We have a problem. Keiko needs time to rest. Don't tell this to everyone you meet. Especially the press. Keep it to yourself as long as possible. They had already taken some movies, so I basically told them, 'Well, I would appreciate if you never showed this to anybody. At least for some months. I can't take the tape from you, but just . . . please.' *And they didn't!* I never see it on television! They probably have the film, but they never sold it to TV."

The average American boatmen, I thought, would have scrambled to peddle this windfall. I suggested this likelihood to Frank.

"That's one of the funny things about Norway," Frank said. "People don't think that way."

For fourteen days the team kept Keiko away from Taknes Bay, on the other side of the fiord. They wanted to hide him from the media. Photographs of the slashed-up whale were not what they wanted on the evening news all over the world. The team wanted to sequester Keiko, too, from the

Norwegian citizenry, both for his own equanimity and for the peace of mind of anyone who happened to see him. Frank Haavik was particularly concerned with the effect of the mangled whale on small children. "Our idea was just keep him away and see how much he could heal before somebody from the media showed up," Frank says. "We kept *Kompass* with him. After five, six days, he looked much better. Because most of the red color was gone."

"DID YOU FEEL GUILTY?" I asked Colin Baird, months later.

"Certainly guilt," he answered, "but mostly just concern for the animal. Guilt would have been us walking him into ice. But I'm thinking, What could we have done differently? How's this going to look to everyone else?"

"Any feeling of guilt?" I asked Tobba, separately.

"No, because we are not responsible for what Keiko does. I felt bad, but could we have stopped it? We couldn't. No guilt. I didn't allow myself to think that."

"Did you feel guilty?" I asked Frank, when I had him alone.

"Oh, absolutely," he said.

BY THE TIME THE NEWS of the accident reached David Phillips, cosmetic surgery had been performed on the story, if not on the whale. On the night of the ice, Colin Baird had been so sickened by what he saw that he was forced to go below for a while, but by the next day his recounting of the episode had become much more bloodless and matter-of-fact.

Phillips laughs at this expurgation.

"Tobba says that before she looked at Keiko, she had the advantage of them telling her, it's pretty bad, but it's okay," Phillips told me. "She didn't have that first shock of raw hamburger. It was the same for me, because the story had been spun a little by the time I heard it. Then I saw the pictures! The telling of it was not as dramatic as the pictures. Lanny's reaction when he saw the pictures was pretty comforting, though. Very comforting. He's seen a lot of injured animals. He was certainly less squeamish about the pictures than I was. Lanny just said, 'He'll get over it. He's learned a good lesson.'"

39

TAKNES BAY

Dr. Lanny Cornell lay prone at the end of the small concrete dock at Taknes Bay, contemplating his patient, who lolled just off the concrete. Cornell stretched to reach the whale and scratched him vigorously at the base of the pectoral fin. Keiko, the sensualist, lay on his side, the black paddle of his fin vertical, making a grand, lazy gesture at the sky. If this fin had been a leaf, a botanist would have described the shape as obovate. Dr. Cornell wore running shoes, faded blue jeans, a gray sweatshirt, and a black baseball cap that read "Harley-Davidson." He was big in the legs, solid in the ass, wide in the torso—a large man—yet from where I stood he was entirely contained within the obovate outline of the fin.

Keiko rolled downward slightly to bring an eye to bear on his physician. The whale had known Cornell longer than anyone in his present crop of acquaintances, having first met the vet in Mexico. If Keiko associated Cornell with ten years of diagnostic bloodletting, blowhole swabs, penile exams, urine samples, and other medical indignities, he seemed to have forgiven him for it.

Rolling onto his belly to blow, Keiko exposed his back. I was startled by how much of his dorsal surface was wrinkled and reticulated by scars from the episode of the ice. This was the first time I had seen him since Iceland. He looked like someone who had gone through a windshield. His head remained undamaged only in a narrow zone that began at his eye and ran along his upper lip—in that strip he was still black and sleek. Everything above that was crisscrossed with scars and mottled everywhere with the new charcoal gray skin that was replacing patches scraped off by the ice. The new skin had the waxy look you see in grafts on burn victims. It was a wonder to me that Keiko's eyes had been spared. A number of the cuts led straight to them, stopping just inches away.

It was June of 2003. Four months had passed since the accident, and all the wounds had healed, save one big triangular scab atop Keiko's melon. The scab, yellowish white and rough-textured, looked like a return of the papilloma that had plagued him in Mexico. Gone forever was the perfect black glistening smoothness of the dome of his melon. Before the accident, the curvature of that dome had been so flawless that the sun made but a single

highlight on it. Now there were many highlights glinting from Keiko everywhere. No more leading roles for this whale in movies. Nothing but character-
actor jobs, should he attempt a return to the screen.

Dr. Cornell pushed himself up from the dock and sat back effortlessly on
his heels—a very limber move, for a large man of sixty-six. Keiko's appearance did not trouble the veterinarian. "He looks more like a normal wild
whale now," Cornell said. "And he knows a lot more about ice."

Cornell studied the whale through dark glasses secured by a cord lying
across the nape of his neck. The neck was seamed. Had it been a thinner
neck, Cornell might have looked old, but it was a thick neck, still, and he
simply looked weathered. He had acquired those seams in a lifetime under
the desert sun, first as a young cowboy in his native New Mexico, then as a
horse doctor and whale doctor in San Diego.

Keiko, for his part, had acquired his seams in a single night under Norwegian ice. Keiko, too, looked more weathered than old; yet for the first time
I realized he was no longer young. I attempted a calculation in whale years,
but one adjustment was necessary for the shorter life spans of male killer
whales, then another for the abbreviated lives of cetaceans in captivity, and a
third because Keiko was a special case. (His captivity in Oregon had been
atypically healthy. Indeed, for three years now he had not truly been a captive
at all.) It was too complicated to figure the odds on him, so I gave up. Dr.
Cornell, still sitting back on his heels, announced that the healing would go
faster now that summer was just a week away and the ocean was warming.
Cold water, he said, restricts capillaries in the skin and slows healing in
whales.

Tobba held a brief training session with Keiko. When it was over, she
turned the hose on him in reward. She held the stream in more or less the
same spot, allowing Keiko to maneuver under it so that the water struck him
in the places he liked. The melon seemed a favorite spot. For a good while,
Keiko let the stream patter along the blackness of that dome, then he rolled
to receive the stream on the whiteness of his underside. He seemed to hold
the parabola of water longest at the base of his pectoral fins. I wondered
whether this was some sort of G-spot in all orcas, or whether Keiko was especially sensitive there, having been afflicted so long in that region by the
itch of papilloma.

The hose was just a garden hose. It surprised me that a creature so large
would feel much of anything from this slender arc of water. Keiko was accustomed to the cold currents of the North Atlantic, and the abrasion of the
gravel bottoms against which killer whales love to rub, and the smack of the
surface when all five tons of him fell back from a breach, detonating a white
explosion of spray. How could the feeble jet from this little orange hose,

which did not even have a nozzle, compete with any of that? Keiko's rapture was a measure of the sensitivity of whale skin, or perhaps just testimony that pleasure is best administered by someone else.

Lanny Cornell and Colin Baird, as they watched this ritual, discussed Keiko's wanderlust lately. "Spring fever," said Cornell. "Hormonal stuff in spring. This whale's hormones are always high. They just go from high to higher. This whale is so backed up! He's probably having a white-up every other hour."

"He had a white-up the other day, just using the hose," Baird said.

A white-up, I gathered, was whale-people talk for ejaculation.

Keiko was not supposed to be hanging out in Taknes Bay in springtime. The plan for this season had not been for him to sit twiddling his thumbs inside the fiords, but to be out in the ocean seeking his fortune. In January, Norway's herring migrate inshore, and Norway's killer whales follow them in, and Keiko's people had intended to walk their whale out to meet this double migration, confident that he would pick up where he had left off last year. Each of the past three summers had seen increases in stamina and incremental improvements in his acculturation with wild orcas. Keiko's people saw no reason not to expect more of the same in summer of 2003.

But the herring had not come in. For the first time in the memory of local fishermen, some anomaly of current or temperature held the fish offshore. It was an oceanographic hiccup, one of those hundred-year events that happen every twenty, or forty, or occasionally even every hundred years. A few small schools of herring had ventured into the fiords, but now, in June, the great river of fish remained seventy miles off the coast, and no killer whales had been reported anywhere near. Neptune had played a cruel trick on Keiko and his people. "Wait till next year," had become the team motto.

Dr. Cornell had come to Norway to give the whale a routine physical and to supervise the installation of a new battery in Keiko's satellite tag. David Phillips and I, flying over from San Francisco, had met the veterinarian at Heathrow Airport, where we killed time over good English beer while we waited for our flight to Oslo. Traveling from San Diego with Cornell were his nephew, Dane Richards, who had worked in Iceland with Keiko, and Dane's father, Bob Richards, who was himself an old Keiko hand, having assisted Cornell with the whale during the move from Mexico. Dane, the younger Richards, was going to stay in Norway as the fourth member of Keiko's team.

Dr. Cornell was now in his tenth year as Keiko's veterinarian. He had never expected, after his first consultation on Keiko in Mexico, to see the whale again. It had hardly worked out that way. "The story of my life," he told us. "I only went to Sea World to see if I could breed killer whales. I thought I would be there five years, and I ended up spending fifteen."

Two security officers with a pair of dogs on leashes passed down the concourse. The dogs distracted Cornell. He forgot about us to watch them intently. They were bomb dogs, Dr. Cornell said. He explained the temperamental differences between bomb dogs and drug dogs, and the keys by which you can distinguish them. When the bomb dogs were gone, Dr. Cornell's thoughts turned to his patient. "Keiko is the hero in all this," the veterinarian said. "Sixty days at sea. Here's a whale 'languishing' all the way across the Atlantic Ocean. He was languishing forty or fifty miles a day."

KEIKO'S COVE AT TAKNES BAY was a nearly perfect crescent, protected to the north by the Taknes promontory. The tip of that promontory pointed northeast across the water to the approximate spot where three fiords— Korsnesfjorden, Arasvikfjorden, and Imarsund—came together. Imarsund was the shortest route out of the labyrinth to the sea. Standing at the end of the dock, gazing out into the confluence of fiords, I could see no human habitations, no marks at all of man, just broad waterways through a giant landscape of big glacier-rounded mountains. Here and there bare rock was exposed, but for the most part the big shoulders of the mountains were green with boreal forest nearly to their rounded summits. A few high, shallow cirques held the season's last patches of snow. Turning landward, I could see a single farmhouse and barn on the slope above. Far to the south, near shore, was another barn. Keiko's keepers had found him a spot far from civilization and the madding crowd.

The dock projected from midpoint of the cove's crescent. It aimed toward a small island, Taknesholmen, "Small Island of Taknes," which gave the cove some protection from east winds blowing down the length of Arasvikfjorden in winter. From either end of the island, north and south, ran the corklines of a barrier net which, together with the island itself, now closed off the cove. The white floats were strung close together, nearly touching. Keiko's team had laid the net at the beginning of June, two weeks ago. This net was not part of the master plan—it was a step backward on the road to freedom—but the team felt they had no choice. As the weather had warmed, boat traffic on the fiords had increased, and Keiko had sallied forth to investigate each boat that approached. His crew had no warning of these departures, because Keiko heard the boat long before they could. Where Keiko came loaded with sophisticated killer-whale acoustic gear, his keepers were limited by poor reception on the primitive little conch of the human ear. Once Keiko swam behind the island, his people lost sight of him.

One very foggy day before the installation of the net, Keiko had left the bay, disappearing immediately in the mist. Colin Baird and Frank Haavik, rousing themselves, had set out after him in Frank's *skjaergaardsjeep*. They did not hurry, assuming that in the dense fog there would be no boats around. Tracking Keiko's signal, they realized he was somewhere to the right, which meant close inshore. They turned that way, coasting the shoreline until a boat materialized in the fog. The boat was half out of water, run up on the beach. Keiko materialized, loafing in the shallows near the boat. High on the strand, human figures materialized, three terrified Czech fishermen. The Czechs had dropped their poles when Keiko surfaced in the fog right beside their boat. They had run the prow up on shore, and jumped out. As the *skjaergaardsjeep* appeared in the mist and Baird and Haavik retrieved their whale, the three Czechs started clapping and calling out their thanks. It was a happy ending for all, yet worrisome. Keiko could get into trouble this way, a loose killer whale terrifying the neighborhood.

On sunny days, when boat traffic was thickest, Colin, Tobba, and Frank had been forced to spend hours on their stomachs on the dock, holding Keiko alongside with commands in sign language. The barrier net was the solution, a way to keep boats out and Keiko in. The team wanted both to cut down on the hours spent prone on the dock and to prevent a repeat of the chaotic circus of last summer, when Keiko was at the center of a flotilla of pleasure boats, with yachtsmen tossing fish to him and children swimming over to clamber on his back. One habit the team did not want their killer whale to develop, so close now to release, was promiscuous approach to watercraft.

Keiko was penned again.

Moored inside the corkline was one small fishing boat, *Eldorado,* grandfathered into this cove. The old fisherman who owned the boat had been using this anchorage for years before the Norwegian government promulgated its fifty-meter exclusion zone for Keiko. For a time, the whale had followed *Eldorado* each time it went out, but by last winter Keiko had become desensitized to its engine, and he allowed the boat to depart unescorted.

The steep pasture above the cove descended to a beach of stones and slippery dark-green rockweed. At high-tide line was a cordon of red tape strung to keep Keiko watchers back. Farther south down the shore, a section of fence had fallen, and cows grazed right to the water's edge, nonchalant about the killer whale cruising just offshore. Fortunately Keiko was from a herring-eating tribe. Had he had been one of those Argentine "transient" killer whales that come body-length out of the water to pluck sea lions off the beach, then these cows would have been dinner. The cattle were oblivious to this possibility, with a single exception. When Keiko first arrived, one cow had sprinted uphill and had not been persuaded to come back down since. Her wits were sharper, her instincts less bovine, than the wits and instincts of the rest of the herd.

At the foot of the dock was a small barn in which the team stored its heavier gear and tossed empty cardboard boxes of "Tranvag Deep Frozen Seafood." The empties were stacked everywhere inside. "Herring 20 kg net," most of them read. They represented tons of herring, whole quicksilvery schools flash-frozen. Keiko was still a big eater, clearly. He was putting away ninety pounds a day. Adjacent to the barn, as their command post, the team had installed a portable metal shed, with the brand name Letthus, "light-weight house." A set of binoculars hung by the Letthus window, which looked out on the dock and cove. The desk was cluttered with clipboards, daily logs, coffee cups, and a tall five-hundred-milliliter jar of udder cream. One of the farmers of Taknes, seeing the hands of Keiko's crew, chapped and blighted from constant immersion in cold seawater, had taken pity and had made them a gift of the udder cream. He promised them it was the best thing possible to put on the hands, and this turned out to be true.

THE FREE WILLY KEIKO FOUNDATION had rented a two-storey home on the gravel road that contoured the ridge above Taknes Bay. When Tobba had finished Keiko's water massage, she turned off the hose, and we adjourned uphill to the house. The front windows looked eastward down to Keiko's cove through a roadside fringe of firs and birches. I followed Colin Baird into the office. He paused at one of the computers and scrolled for me through a sequence of photographs he had taken of Keiko with wild whales the summer before. The images showed a lot of gray ocean and not much whale. Quitting the Keiko gallery, Colin moused over to check for hits on Keiko's website. "He's number 5 for search hits in Norway," he announced. "Osama bin Laden is at 25. Britney Spears is at 50. Geez, we beat all these guys."

The back door of the office opened on an outdoors deck that the team was using heavily now that the weather was warming. Sunshine has a strong allure after a long winter following an errant whale at sixty-three degrees north. Now and again, through the firs and birches, the sound of Keiko's blows carried up to the house.

The house had two new wood-burning stoves, upstairs and down. On the living-room wall were two framed proclamations, each with the same color photograph of the cove and its little island, Taknesholmen. One announced that Colin Baird was "*autnevnes med dette til æresborger a Taknes,*" an honorary citizen of Taknes, and the other naturalized Thorbjörg Valdis Kristjansdóttir in the same way. The proclamations were signed by Marie Taknes, Edel Taknes, and Eldbjørg Taknes, among other locals. Taknes, then, was both a place and a clan. It was hard to imagine that Taknes in either of its senses could have been any more welcoming of Keiko and his people.

We short-time visitors to Norway—Lanny Cornell, David Phillips, and I—stayed in a guesthouse near the ferry quai in Halsa, commuting out to

Taknes every morning. Three other visiting firemen joined us at the guesthouse. Two, Richard Farinato and Nick Braden, were officers of the Humane Society of the United States, which was funding the Keiko operation in Norway. The third was Susan Orlean, a writer for *The New Yorker* who had written a Keiko piece for that magazine. Orlean was contemplating a book on the whale. She was still riding the success of her book *The Orchid Thief*, which had been made into a movie. She and her editors at Random House were toying with the idea of calling her Keiko book *The Orca Thief*.

The guesthouse dining room was presided over by a big pinto cat who stationed himself in the window. "That's my Keiko," the proprietess told us. "The colors, black and white." Keiko had become a popular name for cats in Halsa. Lars Lillebø, the public-contact officer on Keiko matters for Halsa Kommune, had named one of his kittens Keiko when the whale arrived. That cat now had kittens of her own, little feline Keikos now populating the dock where the whale Keiko had spent his first two months in Norway.

ALONGSIDE THE DOCK, THE TEAM had built a whale-size pen they called the "box-net," in which to hold Keiko while he was fitted with his new satellite tag. "We can't just tie him up," explained Dr. Cornell, "because he's liable to swim off with the dock and injure himself." Colin and Tobba had begun attempting to train Keiko to enter the box-net, but after his season free on the ocean he was leery of nets and enclosures. The box-net was the analogue of the medical lifts of all Keiko's previous pools and his sea pen in Iceland, confinements into which he had always swum dutifully, but he was no longer such a tractable whale. "He figures there's something up," Cornell said after one morning session. "They're just trying too hard. So I had them do a couple other behaviors, just to make him think it's just a normal day."

One evening, up at the house, Colin laid out the transmitter of the new tag and the "boot" into which it would fit. The boot, in its turn, would be attached by a bolt through a fashionable piercing on Keiko's dorsal fin. The men on the team passed the transmitter around. They popped it idly into the frame of the boot and rubbed the assemblage ruminatively. They popped it out and hefted it. The transmitter and boot would rest on the table briefly, then someone would pick them up to play with them again. Tobba felt no obligation to feel the equipment. David Phillips, who was in management, with no hands-on duties, was able to keep his hands off, as well. Lanny Cornell, for his part, was into heavy petting of the gear. "He did try to rub off his first couple of tags. Not the latest, though," Cornell mused, turning the transmitter over in his big hands. Cornell made an argument for a placement lower on the dorsal fin. He asked Colin Baird who was doing the interpretation of the data from the satellite tag, and he suggested that it would be useful if the team could receive daily interpretation. As he spoke, he kneaded the boot of the transmitter with a vengeance, like a pitcher rubbing up the ball. Dr. Cornell, I knew, was strongly ambivalent about the VHF and satellite tags. The veterinarian himself had never told me so, but David Phillips had confided that Cornell sometimes speculated favorably on what would happen if the tags "fell" off. On Keiko's North Atlantic crossing, when the whale reached the vicinity of the Faroes, Jeff Foster and his group of former Keiko trainers had begun lobbying the U.S. Marine Mammal Commission for close monitoring of their old client, Dr. Cornell had muttered to Phillips that he hoped the batteries would wear out. The tags were not optional—they were a requirement of the NMFS permit for the Keiko project—but they also made an invisible tether, a beacon by which the interventionists could find the whale.

On June 15, the day the tag was to be installed, I drove with David Phillips and Dr. Cornell out to Taknes Bay. Cornell was laconic for most of the trip. The talk turned to Keiko and his reintegration with wild whales. "I think it would be much simpler if he got a girl," Cornell said. "Find out what that thing is for."

As the team prepared to direct Keiko into the box-net, Colin Baird asked those of us not directly involved to keep our distance, so as not to distract the whale.

The team had coaxed Keiko into the box-net, his tail had passed inside the gate, when suddenly the surface water of the little pen churned explosively and he was gone, like some colossal bass flipping from the landing net just before you boat him. He headed full steam toward Taknesholmen, the little island. Colin and Tobba stood forlornly on the dock, watching his departure, then took off after him in the boat. Through my binoculars I watched Tobba scan the cove for him, then spot him finally near the south end of the island. Colin motored in that direction. They got ahead of the whale and Tobba tossed herring to him on the move, eight or nine fish, then Colin shifted to neutral and Keiko came alongside. Both Colin and Tobba moved starboard to scratch him on his back and his dorsal fin, and the boat heeled sharply over with all their weight on that side. I sheathed my binoculars and walked down to the dock.

"We blew it. For this week, anyway. We scared him," Frank Haavik told me when I arrived. "Colin and Toppa went out in the boat to calm him down."

The boat came in. Colin tied up and stepped onto the dock, shaking his head. "He's as netwise as anyone," Colin said. "We had him all the way in. As we were pulling up the gate, he turns around real quick and gets his head in the opening. He took off for the island."

Lanny Cornell predicted that it would be a couple of weeks, maybe even a month, before they succeeded in getting the tag on, for the whale was spooked now. The team would have to start all over again in habituating him to the box-net. Cornell suggested that over the next days, whenever Keiko was in the vicinity of the box-net, the team should raise and lower the gate at random in order to desensitize him to it. Cornell seemed unperturbed by to-day's failure—seemed almost to have expected it.

"He's a smart little bugger," Colin said.

"He knows all about nets," agreed Dr. Cornell.

By evening, Tobba's mood had shifted from worry about today's misfortune to a dreamy affection for her whale. "We went out just to calm him down, because he was really upset, just swimming back and forth, back and forth," she told me. "We were thinking, Oh, this will be a huge setback. Now it will be really tough for us to get this done. So we went out there, and I was very surprised, because he just came straight to the boat. If you tried to put your emotions to him, it was like, Did you see what happened? I almost got trapped!

Keiko did not associate Tobba and Colin with his near trapping, or pretended not to associate them, though these two friends of his had been the agents of the box-net plan. "I was very surprised by how fast he was down to calmness," Tobba said. "Well, it did take him some time to get back to the dock, but not longer than I had expected."

"So he didn't blame you?"

"Noooo," she crooned, softly. "Sweet guy."

Twice a day in Norway, morning and afternoon, we would board *Kompass* and walk Keiko down one of the several fiords that intersect at Taknes. One day we would accompany the whale down Korsnes Fiord as far as Skaalvik Fiord or farther. Another day we might walk him up Imarsund. At the start of each stroll, *Kompass* stood off the north end of the little island, Taknesholmen, two hundred yards from the gate in the barrier net, while Colin Baird ferried us out in one of the skiffs.

On the fifteenth of June, the first walk day since installation of the barrier net, Keiko joined us in the morning at the jetty and swam out to the net alongside the skiff. He generally kept his eye above water to watch us. The eye still looked strangely flat to me. It looked painted on, like one of those eyes of Buddha on the whitewash of a stupa in Nepal. Other people believed they could read emotions there, but I still could not. When we reached the net, Keiko waited just inside its cork line, gaping, as Colin drove the skiff slowly over the line and lifted the outboard's propeller to clear the buoys. The gape was one of Keiko's "behaviors," but in this instance it was unsolicited. Five or six inches of seawater pooled in the pink basin at the back of his tongue. "I'll be back right away, big fellow," Baird said.

After off-loading us on *Kompass,* Baird motored back to lead Keiko through the gate. This was the whale's first gate since leaving Iceland, and Baird realized that he had not given the "Go through gate" sign for more than a year. The gate is represented by fingers interlocked in front of the trainer's chest, and it took Baird an instant to remember. He interlocked his fingers in front of his chest. Keiko saw, but hesitated.

Something about the gate, its newness, its closeness to the islet, seemed to make the whale uneasy. He milled about for several minutes before coming to a decision and going through. He was hesitant even when called to *Kompass* with signals from the toner. Once outside the buoy line of the net, he was frisky. He seemed happy to be free in the open fiord.

"Good *boy!*" Dane Richards shouted as Keiko, having negotiated the gate, surfaced to spy-hop beside *Kompass.* Tobba did the shimmy that was Keiko's cue to do his own version of that dance, a head-wag from side to side. After head-wagging several times, Keiko nodded emphatically, then gaped. Tobba tossed him a couple of herring. We set off with Keiko swimming slightly on his side, the white oval blaze of his eye patch in the air. "Such a beauty!" cried Tobba, fish in hand, as she looked down from the deck.

Once we were out in the fiords, Keiko ventured away for brief explorations, then returned to *Kompass.* He would swim for a while to starboard, then cross under the hull, or behind it, and swim to port. "In Iceland he was so much more focused on the boat," Tobba said. "Now he swims so much more underneath. Or straight ahead." Keiko often swam on his side, just under the surface. He looked big that way, in profile, showing a big swath of his white belly patch. When he swam on his side, you could clearly see the cupping action of his flukes, the tips of his flukes turned in on the downstroke to form the cup. The pumping action of the caudal peduncle—the tailstock—was muscular yet nearly effortless.

When Keiko was swimming underwater in normal posture, with his back to the sky, the flukes scarcely seemed to be moving. This is the view that a sailor on the bowsprit gets of dolphins riding the bow wave. The dolphins, in this dorsal view, seem to glide along without any effort at all. This is partly because some of the dolphins—in particular the alpha animals in the sweet spot—are surfing the pressure wave ahead of the cutwater and in fact are gliding along with no effort at all. It is also because in dorsal view, down the axis of the dolphin's swimming stroke, the pumping motion for the observer is minimized.

From the gliding Keiko I looked up to Tobba. She was watching her whale from the rail, a herring bucket at her feet. Tobba was out of stirrups now, but she was an Icelandic horsewoman. I remembered the *tölt,* the running walk of the Icelandic horse, that gait so smooth and steady that the rider has scarcely any sensation of motion at all. Keiko was swimming beside us full *tölt*.

When he swam with his back to the sky, the field marks of his white eye-patches were not visible, but he had a new blaze, the triangular, yellow-white scab on his melon. It was the only ice laceration from last winter that had not completely healed. It lay halfway between his blowhole and his beak tip and it caught the light. When Keiko was swimming deep, this new mark was all you could see of him, a yellow-white dot pacing the boat.

At intervals, Tobba fed Keiko snacks on the move, tossing thawed herring ahead of him. He accelerated for each herring in the series, and each one seemed simply to vanish at the tip of his beak.

Seagulls trimmed their wings and plunged seaward in attempts to steal the herring. One gull finally succeeded. The fish was too big for it, and the gull lifted off with the tail protruding from its mouth and was immediately mobbed by other gulls.

"Keiko has killed some seagulls," Tobba said. "They are so stupid. They are so focused on the herring. Keiko eats them both."

"Good," said Nick Braden of the Humane Society, with feeling. "Serves them right. Seagulls are like rats."

Everyone on deck was surprised by this outburst. Animosity toward seabirds is not normal in an officer of the Humane Society. Nick is the eighth and last child of the Braden family, the subjects of *Eight is Enough*, by Thomas Braden. The Bradens became the Bradfords in the 1970s television series *Eight is Enough*, and Nick became Nicholas Bradford. Maybe Nick's resentment of food stealers had something to do with being the smallest child at the Braden table.

Now and then *Kompass* stopped to give Keiko a rest. On these occasions the whale would circle the boat, looking to see who was on deck. Tobba would have him do a bow or breach and toss some herring to him. Keiko caught all the fish in the air, unless she made a very bad throw. As he waited, gaping, for the next fish, you could see the pool of clear seawater at the back of his tongue. Keiko's epiglottis, I gathered, was the plug in that pink basin, but when he swallowed the fish he must swallow some water, too.

"How do killer whales get rid of salt?" I asked Lanny Cornell. "They must excrete it somehow."

"Renal lobulation," the veterinarian said. "They have lots of little kidney lobes, which increase the surface area of the kidneys. Very efficient kidneys. They also produce fresh water metabolically. For every molecule of fat you chop, you get a molecule of water. Still, hydration is often a problem. In captive situations, we actually feed whales ice cubes as rewards."

I noticed a gray cloudiness on Keiko's corneas. The conjunctiva, I supposed, was thickened to resist pressure and the current. I asked Cornell if he had ever had a killer-whale patient with cataracts. He answered that a couple of his whales had gone blind in one eye—from floating always with one eye to the sun, he suspected. "They seemed to have no problem with it," he said. I asked whether the killer-whale retina had any cones amid the rods—did orcas have color vision?

"They're not supposed to have it," Cornell said. "But I wonder if they can't see color by echolocation."

It was an amazing idea, I thought. I had never heard the suggestion before. And why not hear color? It seemed possible that different wavelengths of reflected sound might signal different colors to the dolphin ear, just as reflected wavelengths of light signal colors to our eyes. The colors of echolocation would not resemble the spectrum we see, of course. They would be an alternative universe of color, a transliteration, like the arbitrary colors NASA assigns satellite images and the imagery of radio telescopes. Cornell kept thinking about killer whales. He was not tired of his subject.

ONE DAY A NORWEGIAN FAMILY walked down from the road and made a picnic of watching Keiko. They were a grandmother, a grandfather, their daughter, and the daughter's boy and girl. They sat in the green, subarctic, steep-sloping meadow of mixed sedges above the fiord, surrounded by yellow and white spring flowers. This morning they were the only spectators. The grandfather was dressed quaintly, in a suit jacket long out of style. Sipping bottled water, the family gazed down at the dock, watching Tobba as she took Keiko through a training session.

The Norwegian family sat at a respectful distance upslope of the red-tape cordon that kept Keiko watchers back. An explanation for the barrier was posted on placards at intervals along shore. "The Free Willy Keiko project is about reintroducing a captive killer whale back to the wild. This is the first time such a unique project has been undertaken. It is very important that Keiko has as little contact with people as possible. He is very used to people after 22 years in captivity. He therefore has been used to human contact. To help Keiko become wild again, it is important to change his focus away from people and toward the ocean. YOU CAN HELP US. Do not try to get Keiko's attention by calling to him or making noise. It is alright to watch him when he is swimming in the bay or when he is being fed, just be calm and quiet. In that case you are helping us bring Keiko closer to the wild."

The Norwegian family, as requested, watched calmly and quietly while Tobba worked with Keiko. Her training session segued smoothly, casually, into an attempt to habituate him to the box-net. Dropping herring ahead of his beak, Tobba chummed him around the end of the dock and partway into the enclosure. When he was two-thirds in, he would go no farther. The last herring sank untouched. It glinted silvery in the sun as it settled, then turned leaden gray, then was gone. Tobba did not press the issue; she immediately pointed back to the end of the dock. Keiko, turning in a gentle swirl, obeyed gladly, and Tobba fed him his last herring in the indicated spot. She concluded the session by having the whale perform several of the partial breaches that dolphin trainers call "bows." One bow was particularly emphatic. On crashing back, Keiko raised a big tumultuous fountain of spray. It was the sort of splash you might achieve by galloping a team of horses off the end of a pier. The Norwegian family, silent until now, applauded enthusiastically. Tobba, smiling, instructed Keiko to do an encore.

And how, I wondered, was this performance so different from the performances of Keiko's youth at Reino Aventura in Mexico? The crowd was much smaller here; it was Norwegian instead of Mexican; but Keiko was still performing tricks for human beings. The sign below this Norwegian family read, "To help Keiko become wild again, it is important to change his focus away from people and toward the ocean." This was indisputably true, yet the Keiko project had never found a consistent or effective means to that end. From Keiko's first months in Oregon, the Free Willy Keiko Foundation, the Oregon Coast Aquarium, and all Keiko's trainers and public-relations people, had claimed to be following a program to dehabituate the whale to humans, even as Keiko exchanged glances daily with thousands of paying customers through the public-side windows, and came regularly to the staff window to watch television or receive instructions, and worked topside with trainers in daily games and conditioning sessions, and held his papal audiences with the terminally ill, and offered his cool rostrum to the cheeks of quadriplegics who had sensation nowhere else, and catapulted himself up onto his slide-out for tête-a-têtes with "wish list" children obsessed with him, and posed for television cameras.

"Do not try to get Keiko's attention by calling to him or making noise," read this sign in Norway. Sensible advice, but a tad hyprocritical, issued, as it was, by handlers who wore pipe whistles around their necks as a badge of office and who recalled Keiko whenever he strayed with the submarine notes of the toner. A peculiar conceit of this program, and of the trainers who implemented it, was that fleeting encounters with strangers focused Keiko unduly on people, whereas his daily interaction with the trainers did not. This made little sense. Who was more likely to reinforce Keiko's bond with humanity: a child who called out to him from the Taknes shore, or the whale's own Thorbjörg Kristjansdóttir—Tobba—who knew him since his days in Iceland, who fed and trained him daily, who was conversant in the sign language he understood, who wore a pipe whistle around her neck, and who once called herself "his mom"?

The day after the picnic of the Norwegian family, it was Colin Baird's turn to work Keiko from the dock. As man and whale collaborated, Colin suddenly remembered the "stationary tail lob," a move in which the trained whale rolls onto its back and spanks the surface with its flukes. "It occurred to me that I hadn't tried it for a year or so," he told us afterward. He spread his arms wide, palms forward, then clapped his hands together in front of his chest, then extended both arms straight ahead: the signal for the stationary tail lob. Keiko thought, *Oh, I remember that!*—or so it seemed to Colin—and he instantly rolled to execute the move.

But perhaps Colin should not have reminded Keiko of the stationary tail lob. Perhaps the stationary tail lob was one of many anthropogenic routines that should have been allowed to slip quietly out of Keiko's vocabulary.

The trainers were in an impossible dilemma, of course. There was no way to keep Keiko active, conditioned, mentally stimulated, sane, without interacting with him. Condor chicks hatched in captivity are fed by the painted beaks of condor puppets, in an effort to keep them from being imprinted by humans. This is not an option with killer whales. A killer-whale puppet capable of instructing an orca is beyond the reach of animatronic science as we know it today. Indeed, puppetry works poorly even with condors. The birds seem to catch enough accidental glimpses of humans, in the course of growing up, that upon release to the wild they tend to gravitate to rooftops and picnic tables. With a creature as brainy as a killer whale, the charade would be over quickly. "Pay no attention to that man behind the curtain!" is not an admonition that would work with Keiko.

For an animal as hopelessly social as *Orcinus orca,* it would have been cruel, probably even fatal, for trainers not to socialize with him. Many observers of the Keiko saga have understood this; fewer have realized that the converse is also true. For a creature as hopelessly social as *Homo sapiens,* it would have been cruel to forbid fraternization with the whale. Fraternization is integral to the nature of both species, and probably inevitable in the case of Keiko.

IF NORWAY'S FISHERMEN WERE RIGHT, then this year's herring anomaly would not repeat. Next season the fish would move close to the coast, as usual, and pods of killer whales would follow them in. If Lanny Cornell was right, then Keiko would pick up where he'd left off in his rehabilitation. With the arrival of herring next January, or the January after that, Keiko would throw in with his own kind. As he headed out to sea, it would mark an auspicious moment in the history of man and the sea. Instead of taking always from the sea, we would for once have given back.

Keiko's saga had been a tale of enormous absurdity. He was a whale who lived as opulently among humans as any caliph or pasha, in a $7.5 million palace, venerated and fabulized, attended by dozens of retainers, masseurs, masseuses, lawyers, trademark attorneys, tax attorneys, public-relations people, security guards, personal physicians; his very breath bottled for scientific analysis; his every blow monitored; his blood proteins relentlessly analyzed; his every squeak and murmur recorded on tape and sent undulating and spiking across banks of oscilloscopes, his blubber thickness measured by state-of-the-art ultrasound devices. As a model for repatriation of captive whales, he was hopeless. We do not have enough whale-loving billionaires to make his example practical. There would never be another whale like him. For this reason—his uniqueness—nothing that had happened to him ever made much pragmatic sense.

And yet, all that said, there was something enormously compelling in his saga. As a symbol and icon he was potent. His story was an *Odyssey* in which the exiled hero wanders land instead of sea; a Book of Jonah in which the whale emerges from the belly of the man; a *Moby Dick* in which Ahab and the whale, instead of going down together, survive, shake hands, and go their separate ways. On his day of deliverance, as Keiko slipped his last bond—it existed now only in his head—and left his Norwegian fiord to encounter the long, unbroken swells of the open sea, he would have brought full circle his reprise of the Haida tale of Nanasimgit. Nanasimgit's wife was a human abducted by killer whales. Keiko was a killer whale abducted by humans. Both eventually find their way home again.

But the climax of Keiko's saga, the most stirring part, would come when he swam out of his own story. The best passage would be this secret part, the chapter we would never know. Keiko would swim out of the narrative. Just beyond the range of movie cameras, and television, and journalists, and editorial writers, and billionaires, and environmentalists, he would swim clear of absurdity. He would leave sentimentality behind, and symbolism, and strained metaphor, and literary allusion, and Hollywood simplification, and the fantastic, anatomically incorrect poster-paint portraits of himself by his armies of devoted third-graders. He would escape the magical thinking of his channelers, the overprotectiveness of his trainers, and the righteous indignation of his advocates in the animal-rights movement. He would outpace the misapprehensions of our present crop of whale scientists, whose hypotheses on whales await deflation by the next generation of scientists, who will be corrected, in their turn, by the generation after that. Keiko would outdistance every sort of falsehood, as those are all human inventions. He would course onward into bracing cold subpolar waters where everything is true. He would swim into anonymity. He would show us his flukes one last time and be gone.

40

FINIS

"IT WENT VERY FAST," FRANK HAAVIK TOLD ME. "THIS WHOLE THING ABOUT his death started on a Wednesday morning. Me and Tobba went out for a walk with him. We each saw that there was something bothering him. We didn't know what. He went out, starting on a normal walk, and he slowed down. He was going slow."

In Frank's Norwegian English, "slow" becomes "shhlow," with extra drag in it. The pronunciation serves, in Frank's narrative, to decelerate Keiko even more. The whale slowed for Frank and Tobba on Wednesday morning, December 10, 2003, in the middle of Norwegian winter, a month before the migration of killer whales inshore.

"But at the same time, he did some very long dives," Frank went on. "Which made us feel, like, *Huunh?* Is he just curious? Is he just checking out things? Or is something actually bothering him? So we just kept on, going slow. And he was staying behind. Then after probably twenty minutes, he just stopped. We kept on, but he didn't. He just stopped. So we decided to go back to the bay."

Keiko had slowed on walks before, Frank said, so he and Tobba were not particularly alarmed. "We didn't feel like this was something very bad. He had been sick before. And we knew that he had been eating up to this point. Usually when an animal is sick, the first sign of real sickness is when he stop eating. Every animal. But Keiko had been eating up to this point. He was eating on the walk. So we went back. We came in from the north, around noon. We didn't have an opening on the north net, so we had to go around to the south net. *And he stopped at the north net!* Which he has never done before. And he just logged. So we thought, Oh, this is strange! Never done this before. It seems like he doesn't have the energy to swim around."

"Around that little island?" I asked, incredulous.

The island, Taknesholmen, is small, and the name, indeed, means just that. It stood at the midpoint of the net dividing Keiko's cove from the greater Taknes Bay, a nubbin of boulders with a canopy of forest on top, just an islet, really. Ten or twelve good strokes of Keiko's flukes should have propelled him around it to the open south gate. It seemed impossible that he lacked the energy for an insignificant swim like that.

"We just thought, Ah, this is strange. But Keiko, he has done a lot of strange things, so we didn't know. We waited. We didn't want to go back to him on the north side and reinforce him for doing this behavior, so we just stayed and hoped that he would come over. It took fifteen minutes and then he start slowly moving. He came alongside the boat, and we walk him around and into the cove."

Frank and Tobba repaired to the Letthus, where they wrote up Keiko's odd behavior in the daily report. The problem, for the moment, was all theirs, for Colin Baird, the field director, was away in Mexico on vacation, and Dane Richards was up in the house. After an hour's wait, at around two in the afternoon, Tobba went out with a pail of herring to do a session with the whale. Keiko would not feed.

"That's the first sign that he was sick," Frank said. "So we thought, Okay, okay, he's slow, he's probably having some kind of an infection, or something. As he had before! He has been slow before! So we knew that this can be over tomorrow, or maybe it takes a day or two. A killer whale, we knew that if he didn't eat for a week, it wouldn't harm him."

They checked on the whale repeatedly throughout that winter-abbreviated Wednesday, and the whale seemed about the same: moving slowly, but with a respiration rate that was close to normal.

"Then came Thursday, which actually was the first moment we realized that he was probably more sick than we thought. He had became lots more worse during the night. So Thursday, the first thing in the morning, we made a phone call to Lanny and explained his behavior. Lanny said, 'Okay, he probably has an infection. You should probably think about giving him some medicine. Antibiotics.'"

The problem was that medicine was delivered to Keiko inside fish, and Keiko had no appetite. They tried to feed Keiko fish laced with antibiotics, but he refused to eat. Tobba e-mailed David Phillips in San Francisco, telling him that Keiko was listless and off his feed.

"This is not unusual," Phillips reflected, weeks afterward. "There have been times in Iceland, in Norway, in Oregon, where he would not eat for a couple of days. We'd check his blood. His white cell count might be high, so we'd put him on antibiotics. It's not even that unusual for a whale not to eat every day, anyway—although normally Keiko's a pretty big eater. But they're not like hummingbirds. Lanny was saying, 'Well, we should do some more "bloods."'"

That night, upon going home, Phillips told his wife, Pam, that Keiko was not feeling well and he was a bit concerned.

"He changed slowly worse and worse during Thursday," says Frank Haavik. "He got more and more slow. His breathing rate went up. It slowly went up. Usually it's around four, five blows in five minutes, when he's logging. Now we are up to six, seven."

In a human being, this rate, seven breaths in five minutes, would be alarmingly slow; in a killer whale, it is panting.

"We again had some phone calls with Lanny. He basically told us, 'Keep an eye on him.' We kept an eye on him all evening and night. Friday morning, when we came down and had daylight, then we see that it is really bad. His behavior had changed even more. His breathing rate was nine, ten, up to eleven. Which is high—eleven blows per every five minutes. So we called Lanny. Lanny said, Okay, this is probably not good. He's probably having pneumonia."

At five in the morning on Friday, California time, David Phillips was awakened by a call from Norway, and learned that the whale was worse. Before the sun came up in northern California, Phillips had several conversations with Lanny Cornell in the southern part of the state. He asked Cornell whether the situation was life-threatening. Cornell answered that if this was viral pneumonia, it could go very fast. Phillips asked if there was any point in Cornell's flying over. No, the veterinarian said; by the time he got to Norway, the infection would have shown itself to be something Keiko could fight off, or something he could not.

"Lanny was hoping they could get him into the box-net," Phillips told me. "Because he thought that might be an easier place to try to do something—injections or something. But they weren't having any success getting him over to the box-net. He was just logging. Milling. He was moving, but he wasn't moving with purpose, and he wasn't responding to the toner, and he wasn't responding to fish, and he wasn't responding to them."

"He took one fish that Friday morning," Frank Haavik recollects. "Just one. During that day, he was more and more over to one side. And he had this strange, very bad way to breathe, like he would lay on his side and he was blowing bubbles. You get scared when you see this. By noon Friday, I knew that this was going one way. This was just a feeling I got. He's dying."

Dr. Cornell, upon hearing a report of these latest symptoms, grew somber. He advised the team to call David Phillips in California so that they could start thinking about what to say in a press release announcing the whale's death. For the two Scandinavians, Frank Haavik and Tobba, this confirmed their intuitions about the fate of their whale. "It was very tough for Tobba, tougher than for me," Frank said. "It's bad. It's very tough for her. It's tough, too, for Dane."

Dane Richards had handled most of the communication with America for the past two days, conferring regularly on the phone with Dr. Cornell, and in these conversations he had tried to be positive and radiate confidence. Now Dr. Cornell, his uncle, whom he had watched extract gravel from the paw of a white tiger, and whom he had never known to refuse treatment to any animal, save one field mouse, and who, with the young Dane serving as his assistant, had draped the lad with loops of horse intestine as he removed stones from the gut of that old nag, now this same Lanny Cornell told his nephew to call David Phillips and start composing the press release on the circumstances of the whale's death.

"At that point he realized," Frank said. "He went up to the house. Dane didn't want to have too much contact. He just had to have some time for himself."

Frank, pausing in his recollection, looked out at the shadows of clouds moving across the bright surface of the bay below us. He wore a blue sweater that accentuated the Nordic blue of his eyes. Then he resurfaced and resumed his account.

"Keiko took that one fish Friday morning. But later, when we went out to the dock, he just took off. He was not interested to have any kind of human contact. When we went out to the dock, he took off forty or fifty meters. When we went back, he got closer to the dock again. But he stayed in the bay. He had the opportunity to go out. Which is a little bit fascinating. Because why did he choose to be in the bay? He had the opportunity to go all the way out of the bay, but he didn't. I think it's the human factor. He probably felt safe, is my feeling. He knew probably from his earlier life that humans are mostly good things. Humans means many positive things. He knows that, as long as I stay here, there's humans around. This is my personal feelings. But I did a lot of thinking around that—why didn't he go?—because usually, in my experience with animals, as soon as they get really sick, they hide. They like to disappear. But he didn't. He stayed."

Frank paused to recollect.

"One strange part was that he went all the way into the box-net in the middle of Friday."

"On his own, into the box-net?" I asked. This detail surprised me. I remembered the previous summer and all the futile efforts to lure Keiko into the box-net to affix the satellite tag.

"Yes, into the box-net. So we ran out. He needed time to turn in the box-net, and we knew that as long as he is there, he can't disappear. So we can actually get to see a little bit of him before he took off. We saw that he actually had the fish halfway in his mouth. Still! Three or four hours after Tobba gave it to him. I don't know what that meant. But I assume it meant he was not with us, in a way. He was just . . ." Frank exhaled air in a hiss. "I don't know. He was just on his way. He was gone. He just carried the fish. And he had another very strange behavior also in the box-net. Because he went in the box-net and he put his nose in the back corner by the dock, toward land, and he starts swimming. Pushing, pushing. We actually figured out, talking to Lanny about it, that he probably wanted to go on the beach. Which was the reason he was pushing. He was pushing for shore. He was lying on his side, pushing."

Stranding in whales is a mystery that has yet to be solved. No one knows why Keiko was trying to strand himself that winter day.

"In the box-net we went pretty close to him, and he was blowing out a bad smell. Oh, that smell! I can't explain. It was just bad. It's like if you have a bad infection in your throat, it *smells*. That was terrible. We could touch him at that point, but I think that he was gone. An unusual thing is the fish. Which I find very strange. Halfway in his mouth. We tried to open or push it, but he didn't move. He just hold. He didn't do anything. Usually you have a feeling that he actually looks at you. But I didn't get that feeling. I didn't feel that I communicated with him. We tried to do some things with him, but he was still with us enough that he didn't want to have contact. So he backed out of the box-net. After that, we didn't have any contact with him closer than thirty or forty meters. He just went out to the middle of the bay and he was on his side and blowing bubbles."

At half-past three in the afternoon, it started to get dark. Frank called Ivar Vullum, the Halsa veterinarian, and they discussed the possibility of an injection. "But Ivar hadn't done this before with a killer whale," Frank said. "And also the amount of antibiotic, almost a quarter of a liter, you can't do that quick. You need to use time. It was a hopeless situation. In a way that's the good part of it. We know that even if we could give him an injection, it wouldn't help. His destiny was already there."

Bad weather blew in with the night, wind, and driving snow. The team set up the tracking gear, because they could not see the whale. They had a strong signal, so they knew Keiko was still in the bay. Tobba glimpsed him once, at about half-past four. After that, there was no discerning him through the flurries of snow. They could not hear the whale. The sound of his blows was lost in the noise of wind and breaking waves. The battery on the receiver went flat, and they hurried up to the house to charge it. Throughout the charging they checked the signal, which indicated that the whale remained in the bay.

"We decided that we were supposed to go down and find him," Frank told me. "When we had charged the batteries—it takes forty-five minutes—we went down. I walked, and Tobba and Dane were supposed to drive down in the truck. They used a little bit more time than me, so I was down there before them. It had cleared up and stopped snowing. We had a little bit of moonlight. So when I got down to the boathouse, I saw him laying behind the little fishing boat, *Eldorado*. He was a shadow between the boat and shore. I stopped and looked. It was a pretty strange place for him to be. He was actually lying on the bottom. His dorsal was up above the water. There's no movement. The first thing that passed my mind is Tobba. I need to prepare her. So I started walking up. I stopped them and told them he's laying behind *Eldorado*."

41

A PYRAMID OF STONES

KEIKO HAD BEACHED HIMSELF ON A RISING TIDE. FOR HIS CREW THIS WAS fortunate, in a grim way, as it enabled them to get a rope around his tail and tow him to the dock. Two hours after they found him dead, they had succeeded in securing him with ropes dockside and had covered him with a huge tarp. It is a point of pride with the team that they enshrouded their whale so quickly. "There is no picture of Keiko dead in the newspapers," says Frank Haavik. "There are pictures of the tarp. If you study the pictures, you can see that there's something under the tarp. You can't tell what it is." Keiko's people had protected his dignity, for the time being, from the vultures of the press.

The team considered a necropsy, but decided against it. Had Keiko died in the United States, in a facility where the procedure could be performed efficiently and discreetly, a necropsy might have revealed evidence of renal shutdown or some other proximate cause of death. But Keiko had died in the fiords of rural Norway. "Necropsy had real limitations where we were," says David Phillips. "We would have had to do it on the beach, which would have involved cutting the whale, butchering him, in public. No one there had any experience dissecting a whale. We were going to get criticized whatever we did. People criticize us for not making every effort to know exactly, to a gnat's eyelash, why he died. But if we'd butchered him on the beach, people would say, 'My God! This friend, this icon, this incredible animal! And your last pictures of him are his entrails being spread out on the beach?'"

For the Norway team, who had slept little during the two nights of Keiko's illness, there was now no rest at all. Frank Haavik was on the phone all day Friday and Saturday with the Norwegian press, then Saturday night, as the Norwegian inquiries began to diminish, morning arrived in the New World and the American press started to call. Throughout that extended Saturday, Frank, Dane, and Tobba were constantly on the phone. Frank spent Sunday talking with with county authorities and the Norwegian ministries of fisheries and the environment. "Fisheries, they opened up on Sunday for us, which is very unusual," Frank says. "We are a religious country, and Sunday is a peaceful day." Frank's call, and then a David Phillips call from California, interrupted the director of fisheries in the middle of a Christmas party, a grave social error in Norway, where work is always left at the office; and yet the director threw himself into the problem. Frank was amazed at how the phone lines lit up and government came to life that Sunday. It was a measure of the Keiko Effect.

The director of fisheries wanted to tow Keiko out to sea, the standard Norwegian procedure with dead whales. None of Norway's previous whales, of course, had been a movie star. Phillips, who was familiar with Keiko's history with the media, knew that the towboat was likely to be followed by a cavalcade of boats swarming with press photographers, all jostling for position at the rails. At sea it would be necessary to cut Keiko open to release gases, then weigh him down to sink him—otherwise the icon would end simply as a navigation hazard. These were not the final photo opportunities that Phillips wanted for his whale. He asked the Norwegians if Keiko could be buried on land. Keiko, unlike other dead whales, would draw processions of mourners, and burial on land would allow some sort of monument to be built to him. The Norwegians were hesitant, as they had never buried a whale before, but in the end they were persuaded.

Frank contacted a bulldozer operator in Halsa and asked the man if he could work quietly. The operator answered yes. Frank instructed the operator not to move his bulldozer before eleven that night, as Halsa is the sort of rural *kommune* where nothing passes unnoticed.

"We were very lucky," says Frank. "It was very cold and a little bit snowing. We had high tide, because we had to plan for high tide. And we had a little bit of snow on the ground, which made it very slippery. We didn't want to harm him, or have any parts come off." The digging went quickly, because the substrate was mostly sand. The bulldozer dug a big hole and they put Keiko twelve feet deep. The bulldozer, in the way of bulldozers, patterned a large area around the hole with its treadmarks, and when the operator had filled in the hole, he drove randomly around some more, to further disguise Keiko's resting place.

HALSA KOMMUNE HELD A MEMORIAL ceremony for Keiko. On the appointed day in January, three weeks after his death, three hundred and fifty Norwegian children arrived in buses at Keiko's dock at Taknes, where they built him a *steinroeys,* one of the stone monuments with which, since the age of the Vikings, Norwegians have buried their kings. Each child, according to the tradition, added at least one stone to the pyramid. Pilgrims from California and Europe placed their stones on the *steinroeys.* One man came from British Columbia "to pay my respects to the biggest influence in my life." Frank Haavik and Thorbjörg Kristjansdóttir spoke briefly, thanking the *kommune* for all their help during Keiko's stay in Norway. The mayor of

Halsa, Margaret Seter, gave a speech. Keiko had changed the community, the mayor told the crowd. People from Halsa were now proud to say they came from Halsa, she said. Before, "Halsa" rang no bell with any outsider; when asked, Halsans simply said they were from near Kristiansund. Keiko had put Halsa on the map. The mayor believed that the whole Zeitgeist of the *kommune* had been changed by the whale. Before, the Halsa psyche had been very quiet, the citizens happiest when not much was happening; now the mayor detected a new appreciation for *events.*

In Oregon a memorial was held at the Oregon Coast Aquarium, where Keiko had lived for nearly three years. A veterinary chaplain delivered a eulogy. Former keepers offered remembrances. A Keiko photo exhibit was hung on the walls, and a preliminary sketch of a bronze sculpture of the whale was unveiled.

"This is absurd," Steinar Bastesen protested, of the Keiko monument in Halsa, in a Reuters story reported from Oslo. "There is suffering and hunger around the world. There has just been a war in Iraq. There are terror attacks, but people don't get the sympathy that a dead whale gets." Bastesen, the sole representative in Parliament for the Coastal Party, was Norway's top advocate for whaling and had suggested the year before that Keiko be turned into hamburger.

"Don't Free Willy, Fillet Him," suggested Jonathan Nicholas, a columnist for *The Oregonian.* "Waldport insurance man Jerry Grady was disappointed at just how quickly those Norwegians buried poor old Keiko on the beach. An opportunity, thought Grady, had been missed. The passing of the great beast, he says, could have been just the fundraising opportunity the Oregon Coast Aquarium has been looking for. At 9,050 pounds, Grady figures, Keiko would have filled about 40,725 tuna cans. 'If the aquarium canned Keiko and sold him in its gift shop at $10 per can, that would bring '$407,250 to the aquarium.' Oh, yes, and best of all, says Grady, it could have been sold as 'dolphin-free!' "

In Jerry Grady's modest proposal, Jonathan Nicholas seems to have seen humor. There are Bastesens in every land.

A documentary on Norway's public television station, NRK, argued that the conclusion of Keiko's saga demonstrated the impossibility of reintegrating a captive whale with wild orcas. It was like expecting a pet poodle to be welcomed by a pack of wolves, NRK said.

"Killer Whale Keiko Dies of Pneumonia," ran the headline of an Associated Press story filed on December 12, 2003, the date of Keiko's death. The reporter, Doug Mellgren, misspelled Dane Richards as "Dale," and he described Keiko as being thirty-five feet long, an exaggeration of about thirteen feet. (No orca longer than thirty-two feet has ever been recorded.)

"Keiko was released from Iceland in July 2002, but he swam straight for Norway on a 870-mile trek that seemed to be a search for human companionship," Mellgren wrote. This notion—that Keiko left the familiar waters of the Westman Islands and his closest human companions in order to journey across the emptiness of the North Atlantic in search of human companionship—is more than a little peculiar. It suggests that Keiko, on abandoning Iceland, somehow knew where Norway was, and knew that people lived there.

Another Associated Press reporter, covering the Oregon side of the story, picked up Mellgren's error listing Keiko's length at thirty-five feet. The whale was growing in legend. This second AP reporter, interviewing the citizens of Newport, Oregon, found that most believed Keiko should never have been taken from their town.

"That's all he knew," Sherrie Jones said of Keiko's pool at the Oregon Coast Aquarium. "He liked people contact, and they kept pushing him away from them."

"He was an icon," said Carole Needham, interviewed with her husband, Dave, at the Galley Ho bar. "I think the aquarium was doing a good job and he seemed happy."

"Everybody was always looking for Keiko stuff," said Debbi Sell, working her shift as a waitress at Mo's Clam Chowder. "We even had a Keiko Root Beer for a while. The kids loved it."

"He played up to the people," said Vicki Soren of Florence, Oregon, interviewed at "Passages of the Deep," the exhibit that had replaced Keiko's tank at the aquarium. "I personally thought he was better off in the aquarium. He'd been in captivity for so long, this is all he knew."

There were contrary views in Oregon, but this one seemed to be the majority opinion in the state: What better place than Oregon for a killer whale?

In a letter to *The Oregonian,* Al Aboleda of northeast Portland wrote, "Keiko's life was devastated when do-gooders decided to end his happy life entertaining kids and adults alike. He could have remained healthier had he been left to enjoy what he loved best. It was obvious from the start that he did not like to return to the wild, but the do-gooders insisted on pushing him off. Now he is gone, and good for him. Bless his soul (if he had one)."

People magazine, in the "Tributes" section of its December 29, 2003, issue, acknowledged the deaths of Bob Hope, who died that year at 100, Althea Gibson, who made 76, June Carter Cash, 73, Johny Cash, 71, John Ritter, 54, Nina Simone, 70, Fred Rogers, 74, Katharine Hepburn, 96, Gregory Peck, 87, and Keiko, whose age went unspecified. The whale's obituary in *People* quoted David Phillips: "He was a huge friend and an amazing teacher." *Entertainment Weekly* remembered Keiko in its "Legacy" department: "He was a killer whale by nature and an Uberfriendly Hollywood celeb by nurture."

Three days after Keiko's death, Greg Bossart of Harbor Branch Oceanographic Institution, in Florida, was interviewed by the online journal *TC-Palm*. "This was a failed and flawed experiment from the beginning," Bossart said. "As far as I'm concerned, Keiko was never a release candidate. He was caught in the middle of a Hollywood movie."

According to *TCPalm,* Bossart had spent nearly three years studying Keiko's wartlike lesions in Mexico—a very long time to engage in the study of wartlike lesions. What *TCPalm* neglected to report—or what Greg Bossart failed to tell the journal—was that he is an employee of the captive-cetacean industry. Dr. Bossart is the veterinarian for the Miami Seaquarium, which on Keiko's arrival in Norway had petitioned the government for permission to recapture the whale.

"Keiko's death from a quick onset of pneumonia off Norway on Friday proved that freedom is not always a happy ending for every wild animal," Bossart argued.

Keiko's death proved nothing of the sort. Death is seldom a happy ending for any animal, captive or free. Everything dies. No one in the Keiko project ever argued that freedom for Keiko would confer immortality on the whale. And the fact is that nothing shortens the lives of killer whales like captivity. Keiko lived longer than any male killer whale under Dr. Bossart's care at Seaquarium.

"I was one of the few public scientists to say he was nonreleasable," Bossart went on. "I think every little child in America hated me. But we as human beings need to understand what our actions mean for the animal. The fact that Keiko spent all this time not being able to feed himself, that he never integrated back into the whale society and always sought the attention of humans proves this was a flawed experiment. Keiko was caught in the middle of it, and ultimately he died for it."

Keiko did not die from flaws in the experiment. He did not die from freedom. He died—best guess—from pneumonia and the complications of age.

On December 27, in an op-ed piece in *The New York Times*, Clive D. L. Wynne, an associate professor of psychology at the University of Florida, and the author of the forthcoming book *Do Animals Think?*, wrote that the Keiko project was "a story of anthropomorphism gone wild." In reaching this conclusion, Wynne employed a fact-gathering method nearly identical to that of his fellow Floridian, the animal empath Dianne Robbins, whose custom was to go down to her Florida beach to channel Keiko in his Oregon tank. For neither thinker was proximity to the subject animal necessary. "'Willy' Didn't Yearn to Be Free," Wynne titled his piece. Associate Professor Wynne, who never met Keiko and has no expertise on killer whales, conceded that the whale spent the summer of 2002 exploring the North Atlantic, and that he "may even have caught a few wild fish," but the fact that Keiko turned up in Norway performing his old tricks is all Wynne really needed to know. "Despite all the money, time and sincere effort, Keiko did not die in the company of his own species, but up against a pier, seeking human consolation."

Keiko did not die up against a pier. He did not die seeking human consolation. In his last hours, he shied from the touch of his trainers, moving off forty meters from human consolation whenever that consolation presented itself. What Keiko was seeking beside the pier, on that one occasion when he ventured into the box-net, dockside, was not human consolation, in the opinion of people who have actually studied cetaceans. He was seeking to beach himself.

"It is a classic anthropomorphic fallacy to believe that an animal's best interests are whatever a human would desire under similar circumstances," Wynne wrote.

Yes, indeed, but this caution applies equally to Wynne himself. Is it any less anthropomorphically fallacious to presume knowledge of what a whale does *not* desire? The thing Associate Professor Wynne himself desires, obviously—to apply his own method to him—is the safe harbor of tenure at the University of Florida, and the gentle remonstrations and pipe-whistle encouragements of his department head, and the cold, dead herring tossed his way in student evaluations. But there are other people who desire the open ocean. The intuitions of the latter group are no less likely to be true than Wynne's.

"Keiko will be missed by millions of people around the world, especially children, and his remarkable story will be told and retold," Paul and Helen Spong wrote on their website. "Unfortunately, it is already being distorted and misrepresented in many media reports."

The Spongs' own view of *Orcinus orca* is unmediated. Paul Spong has spent his adult life studying killer whales from his house on Hanson Island, on Blackfish Sound, near the northern tip of Vancouver Island. There, at the entrance to Haida territory, Spong has joined—to the extent that any modern Canadian can—the "Ocean People," that metamorphic Haida fraternity in which men adopt the fins of killer whales and killer whales take the shape of men. It was on Hanson Island, thirty years ago, that I first heard the voices of killer whales, caught by the Spongs' hydrophones as the whales entered their cove, then broadcast from speakers in their spruces. In the Spong house, the surface blows and submarine whistles mingled with human conversation at the dinner table. No family on earth is more immersed in the lives of wild killer whales.

"Some of the errors are relatively trivial," the Spongs wrote, of the media distortions. "For example, incorrectly stating that Keiko died ten years earlier than is normal. But others are serious and need correction. The most serious error is the claim by the captive industry that the entire project was a 'failure.' It was not. Rather, it was a resounding success in almost every conceivable way. Keiko died a free orca, in the ocean on his own terms."

THE DAY AFTER THE NORWEGIAN schoolchildren built their stone pyramid to Keiko at Taknes Bay, I sat with David Phillips over coffee at a café in Berkeley, California, the town where we both live. We reminisced about his whale.

"There have been some people who say that if Lanny had been there, or if we'd had a care team more on top of it, we might have saved him," Phillips said. "But, Tobba—there wasn't anybody closer to him, and his moods, and how he was feeling, than Tobba. And Dane had previous experience in Iceland with Keiko. He also had the total tether to Lanny. As soon as they saw anything, they reported it. I don't believe they were missing some sign.

"Jeff Foster has said that if he'd been there, he would have been able to save him. Which is very grating, of course, and demeaning to the people who were there. I don't think having anybody different there would have led to a different outcome. In another setting, we might have been able to do some sort of massive IV injection and have him immobilized. Maybe. But where we were, that would have been impossible."

I proposed to Phillips that everyone, early in the project, had been acutely aware of how Keiko's learning curve intersected with the arc of the killer-whale lifespan. Everyone knew they were working against time. I suggested that things had gone so well—the whale growing steadily bigger, stronger, more adept at feeding, more comfortable with wild whales—that everyone lost track of time.

"It's so true. I think we lost sight. Usually I cover most of the angles. Usually I'm pretty careful to be watching all the balls, but this time I didn't. I've got various second-guesses. I think Keiko was on too short a tether. In Iceland, when Foster and those guys had the helicopters, every time he got too far, they'd reel him in. But it's easy to say that now. There was no road map. There were no benchmarks to evaluate him against. Everyone on the outside was watching it like a hawk, so there was a tendency to be super careful and risk-averse. I don't feel that the trainers were actually *sandbagging* it, but there was an attachment to Keiko, among staff, that worked against us. There was no huge rush to have him totally off on his own.

"The other thing I really second-guess myself about is that we didn't find his family. I think we needed a separate track for that, with a separate staff and a separate agenda and budget."

His personal reaction to Keiko's death was complicated, Phillips told me.

"I definitely feel like I lost a friend. We've been, like, eleven years. I've been with him at every stage, trying to do the right thing for him. I do not regret for a second the time I put in. I think he had an incredible chance to go free. I think he had an incredible life. As Lanny says, everything we did after we put him in that UPS plane in Mexico was gravy in his life. Because he was not going to make it in Mexico. We extended not only the length of his life, but the quality of his life. He was swimming tight circles in a small pool with papilloma all over him, and by the time we finished with him, he was out with the big boys, swimming around with wild whales in the ocean.

"As for the impact of the whole project, I honestly believe that we have fundamentally shifted public attitudes. Attitudes as to whether this sort of rehabilitation and release is possible. Attitudes towards whales in general. We have legions of kids in every place Keiko ever was—in Mexico, in Oregon, in Iceland, in Norway—kids who look at whales differently, kids who look at the issue of captivity differently.

"People say, 'Geez, you spent so much money!' Well, it was *Craig McCaw's money*. If it hadn't been spent, it would have been lost in the dot-com collapse with the rest of his fortune. Gone! If it wasn't spent on Keiko, then it would have been spent on Craig's sailboat, or a sailing race, or something like that. And the fact is, you couldn't have spent the money in a way that produced a more fundamental shift. If you'd put that twenty million dollars into general education about the fate of the world's oceans, and about orcas in captivity—if you'd bought a bunch of ads and made a bunch of school tours with that money—you wouldn't have had a drop in the bucket of the impact we've had. It's hard to think of it this way, but it was a very *efficient* use of resources.

"*And what a ride he had!* If you charted all the times that people said he wasn't going any further! Even Lanny wasn't positive he was going to survive Mexico and make it to Oregon. Then there were the people who said the papilloma would never go away. Then the people who said we would never get him into Iceland. He'll never get out of the sea pen. He'll never swim with wild whales. He'll never feed himself. All these 'nevers' that he overcame on this incredible odyssey."

42

FREEDOM

KEIKO'S TEAM IN NORWAY, FRANK HAAVIK, THORBJÖRG KRISTJANDÓTTIR, and Dane Richards, succeeded a little too well in spiriting the whale to his secret grave. The sudden dematerialization of six tons of whale led to theories that Keiko never died at all. In March of 2005, fifteen months after Keiko's purported demise, David Phillips received an e-mail announcing a resurrection.

"Dear Mr. Phillips," his informant wrote. "My name is Chris Shields. I am or was a big fan of Keiko. I do not believe he is dead. You were tricked by Dr. Cornell who has been doing this for over fifty years without being caught for it. I went to Six Flags Marine World to see Shouka and I saw that Shouka has the same markings as Keiko, the 'paw print,' etc. I was asked to call Shouka to the viewing window by one of her trainers. I called her 'Keiko' and she came to Keiko's name. No other killer whale would have come to Keiko's name."

The e-mail was written all in capital letters, in the style of Western Union or Dr. Lanny Cornell. Dr. Cornell is not above practical jokes, and it crossed my mind, when Phillips copied me this note, that it might be a hoax by the veterinarian.

"I had a very special bond with Keiko," Chris Shields went on. "When I met him for the first and last time before he went to Iceland, I went over to pet Keiko with one of his trainers named Peter. When it was time for me to leave, Keiko did not want me to leave. He followed me very closely. This same situation happened at Marine World with Shouka. That is how I know Shouka is Keiko. I asked Shouka if she was Keiko, and she nodded her head yes. I asked Shouka if Keiko died of pneumonia. She shook her head no. I asked her if Keiko was put in a sling and transported to a French amusement park, under a false name of Shouka and then sold to an aquarium in Ontario, Canada, which was owned by Six Flags, and finally sent to Six Flags Marine World. She nodded her head yes."

The line, *I had a very special bond with Keiko*, could have been a Cornell joke. Every empath and animal communicator who had ever met Keiko, whether in the flesh or out in the empathosphere, felt that she had a very special bond with the whale. Every parent of every Keiko-obsessed child who ever visited the whale's tank was convinced that child had a special bond with Keiko. Cornell had heard the "special bond" refrain as often as anyone. He might have been moved to parody it.

On reaching the end of the long, impassioned missive, I was convinced it was genuine. Cornell could not have created a fiction like Chris Shields. Shields came with a whole cast of supporting characters. He names several witnesses to the fact that Shouka answered to "Keiko": his best friend Chad Helms, Chad's sister, Kayla Helms, Chad's mom, Kelly Mintz, and finally Chris's own mom, Mrs. Elaine Shields. Dr. Cornell had the imagination to invent these people, maybe, but not the time. "My friend Judith Killian and I are setting up fliers to alert the public but so far no luck," Shields confides. "Mr. Phillips, just to let you know, I have e-mailed Governor Schwarzanegger about the situation as of 2:59 P.M. Sunday, March 20, 2005, and I am awaiting his response to the situation."

Could Cornell have invented that voice? I thought not.

Toward the end of his note, Shields contends that Cornell intimidated Keiko's trainers into silence and ordered that an "American black and white milk cow" be buried in the whale's putative grave. The detail of that black-and-white milk cow—the particularity of it—cemented the matter for me. The black-and-white milk cow was beyond the literary capabilities of a veterinarian.

"Again, Keiko is Shouka!!!" Shields insists. "And if we do not act now, Keiko will never be able to be set free!!!! And Six Flags and Dr. Cornell would have won."

But Keiko was dead, all right. On the night of his death, when Frank Haavik saw the whale motionless in the shallows between *Eldorado* and shore, he turned and walked back uphill to prepare his colleagues. He met Dane and Tobba in the truck halfway. Keiko's inner-most circle had been reduced to these three. Dane Richards had known the whale longest, having worked with Keiko's first crews in Iceland. In scuba gear at the bottom of Klettsvík Cove, drilling to repair the bay-pen net, Dane had turned to see Keiko peering over his shoulder and demanding, it seemed to Dane, *What could be more interesting in this cove than me?* Tobba, for her part, was the whale's chief familiar in Norway. Frank Haavik himself was Keiko's most recent acquaintance, yet in Norway he had spent more time with the whale than anyone.

"So we went down, all the way down to the water," Frank says. "Probably three meters away from him. We just stood there and we . . ."

Frank's voice caught and hoarsened. Behind his blond eyelashes, his eyes reddened suddenly, and his eyelids, too. Frank Haavik is a very fair-skinned Norwegian in whom any redness of eyes shows instantly. He collected himself.

"Yeah!" he resumed. "That was tough. Tough time. Tobba cried. We tried to think together. We had a pretty special time there, standing three meters from Keiko, and he was dead. The most famous animal in the world was actually dead. We were the three people who knew him."

Frank gazed out the window. A yacht race had begun in the blue water of the bay below us. The tight cluster of white sails at the start, several minutes ago, was scattering to the north, dispersing like a windblown cloud.

"Actually it was strange. The weather was starting to get a little bit better. We had moonlight. It was very special. It was just sad. It's like if you have had someone of your closest family who has been very sick for a long time—though Keiko, of course, he wasn't sick for a long time. But if you have somebody close to you, which has been sick, it is very sad when they pass away; but also, in a way, it feels like a relief. It's good in one way. And the same feeling I actually had with Keiko. He suffered that day. Friday. A really tough day. The toughest day in his life, I would probably say. For us, it was like, Okay, it's over. We don't have to worry. He is actually resting. He's in peace. Which felt, in a way, good. Because this animal has been in human control for all his life. We agreed, we said to each other, now is the first time we can say he is free."